The Four Hills of Life

STUDIES
IN THE ANTHROPOLOGY OF
NORTH AMERICAN INDIANS

Editors
Raymond J. DeMallie
Douglas R. Parks

The Four Hills of Life

Northern Arapaho Knowledge and Life Movement

Jeffrey D. Anderson

Published by the University of Nebraska Press
Lincoln and London

In cooperation with the American Indian Studies Research
Institute, Indiana University, Bloomington

Library of Congress Cataloging-in-Publication Data
Anderson, Jeffrey D.
The four hills of life: Northern Arapaho knowledge and life movement / Jeffrey D. Anderson.
p.   cm.—(Studies in the anthropology of North American Indians)
Includes bibliographical references and index.
ISBN 0-8032-1057-4 (cloth: alk. paper)
1. Arapaho philosophy.   2. Arapaho Indians—Economic conditions.   3. Arapaho Indians—Politics and government.   4. Wind River Indian Reservation (Wyo.)—Social life and customs.   I. Title.   II. Series.
E99.A7 A53   2001
978.7'63—dc21
00-053686

Contents

Illustrations

Map

Figures

Tables

Contemporary Arapaho Orthography

b   voiced bilabial stop, but unvoiced as [p] finally

c   voiceless prepalatal affricative, but voiced as [j] initially

e   close-mid vowel, long form as /*ee*/

h   aglottal fricative *i* front-close vowel, long form as /*ii*/

k   voiceless velar stop, but voiced as [g] initially

n   alveolar nasal

o   close-mid back vowel, long form as /*oo*/

s   voiceless alveloar fricative, [ş] in Southern dialect

t   voiceless alveolar stop, but voiced as [d] initially

u   close-back vowel, long form as /*uu*/

w   voiced bilabial semivowel, but voiceless finally

x   velar fricative

y   voiced mediopalatal semivowel, but voiceless finally

3   voiceless dental fricative, same as [θ]

'   glottal stop, same as [ʔ]

Preface

The research that has culminated in this book had four consistent aims. I realized at the start that, despite the vast ethnographic literature and substantial linguistic evidence, no systematic, total treatment of the Arapaho sociocultural system had ever been undertaken. Although much of that Arapaho material has been used for ethnological theory construction, from Boas's pivotal comparative study of North American art (1927) to Lowie's work on age societies (1916) to Eggan's work on kinship and seasonal morphology (1937, 1966), and Lévi-Strauss's study of myth (1968), no project had aimed to elaborate Arapaho language, culture, and history as an interconnected whole. I do not profess to have achieved finality in covering all the evidence, but I have begun that project by interrelating hitherto disparate domains of evidence.

Second, during the five and a half years I spent in the Northern Arapaho community on the Wind River Reservation, I listened carefully to what people talked about, "watched on" (a reservation term) at social events, interviewed knowledgeable people, and participated in efforts to reinvigorate culture and language. My first two years were devoted to language study, for which I also had to learn, with little prior linguistic training, the complexities of Algonquian grammar and phonology. What I began to realize was that the rich ethnosemantic content and ethnopoetic play of Arapaho had never been systematically related to art, myth, history, and ritual. Only three major descriptive linguistic studies have been devoted to the Arapaho language. Kroeber's work in the early 1900s on Northern Arapaho and Michelson's on Southern Arapaho offer much to be explored for understanding the connectivity of language and culture. Salzmann's more recent comprehensive treatment follows a descriptive formalistic approach to provide an invaluable overview of grammar and phonology, but it does not explore relations to cultural and pragmatic meanings.

Through the use of these studies, field interviews, and my observation of ways of speaking, I came to appreciate much of the cultural background, fluidity, play, musicality, and contextuality at work in the Arapaho language. Many key terms and accepted glosses throughout the ethnographic and ethnohistorical treatments therefore began to take on more and more meanings as my research moved forward. In this study I try, though not always with complete inclusiveness, to evolve multiple meanings and leave open the conceptual boundaries for connectivity to culture and history as well as among multiple fields within the language.

Most of the research I was part of was initiated by Arapaho groups and organizations, often with the intent to interpret, amend, or add to existing published or unpublished sources and evidence. Almost all of those efforts aimed to collect and publish knowledge for local use in schools and the wider community. The language dictionary sessions involved review of and additions to the first Arapaho dictionary (Salzmann 1983). Other research drew description and narration from a focus on old photographs taken during the early reservation period by the missions and the Wind River Indian Agency. There were also sessions centering on buildings, art forms, stories, landscape, agency records, and ethnographic material itself. By talking about these texts and objects, elders and other knowledgeable people followed personal, linguistic, cultural, and historical connections to many places, times, words, and meanings that then began to draw my thoughts and perceptions into a densely reticulated web of relations. In time, instead of always focusing discussion on a preselected topic, we often let people make connections freely. As a result, I also searched for connections or waited for them to develop. It is upon such connectivity that this book is founded.

Third, I almost immediately recognized at Wind River that the Northern Arapaho age-structured and consensus-based political economy, as described by Loretta Fowler (1982), had given way to stronger family boundaries, political factionalism, and intratribal divisions. "Tribal politics," from which Fowler rightly held that the Northern Arapahos were an exception among Plains tribes, had arrived at Wind River at least by 1988. Certainly, occasional moments of consensual decision making by elders still occur, but those are overshadowed by groups competing for the scarce resources distributed by centralized administrative structures. My own inquiries led me to consider that this process is not necessarily all negative but is an expression of social forms and adaptive strategies that have persisted in Arapaho society over the long duration of contact history.

Fourth, I listened to what Arapaho people talked about and observed the contradictions generated by efforts to negotiate, resist, or appropriate aspects of the white world, the boundaries of which have become increasingly fluid yet dynamic. Through participation in community activities, I became increasingly, though never totally, immersed in, the lived contradictions of modern reservation life and the various strategies employed for family, group, community, afd tribal empowerment. As I moved back and forth between cultural worlds, often several times a day, I also became personally and sharply aware of the social distance between Indian and non-Indian people and places. For me this transcultural commuting defined the "contradictions" ever more sharply. Each and every day of my participation in community programs and activities presented contradictions in and of lived experience and practice, not as abstract theory reflecting on conceptual inconsistencies. Along with lengthy discussions with Arapaho people concerning many issues, I was afforded a more critical understanding of the powerful contradictions in the relationship of Euro-American society to the Northern Arapaho people, both in the present and into the past. It is upon this type of critique that this book draws its "evidence" to identify the contradictions engendered by Euro-American knowledge, life models, and personhood.

Because of a tight academic job market, the low expense of family living in Lander, Wyoming, just off the reservation, and my growing involvement in the Arapaho tribe, I stayed much longer at Wind River than I had planned. For five and a half years, I typically began each morning with my own research or writing, and then drove to St. Stephens and Riverton for my several jobs, all of which allowed time for various research projects along the way. The routine was broken by occasional community activities, ceremonies, gatherings, school programs, and meetings to attend. Other time was given to researching local archives, doing art work, drinking coffee, and driving around to visit. At some point in my research, I ceased deliberately "doing fieldwork" and began to participate, "watch on," and just listen. I soon realized that the presentation of knowledge to researchers has resulted in the strategy of front stage–back stage compartmentalization oriented to the white world in general. Indeed, most of the people I came to know at Wind River assumed that my "research" would follow the pattern of previous researchers, who had come to the reservation for short periods of time to collect data in interviews about past traditions. As time went on, I tried more and more to understand in the present context what I heard and observed rather than to collect data to be taken back home for later analysis. Ironically, over time this mission for understanding also became increasingly elusive. Thus I do not pretend to present a complete "Arapaho perspective," for such an attempt would be disrespectful to the multiplicity of views held by Northern Arapaho people and the complexity of the Arapaho language, culture, and history.

Acknowledgments

In the summer of 1988, I visited the Wind River Indian Reservation for the first time and received official permission from the Arapaho Language and Culture Commission (ALCC) to pursue research on the Northern Arapaho tribe. In the summer of 1989, I returned and stayed until the fall of 1994. Since then I have returned for short visits and have cherished ongoing relationships that I know will last the rest of my life. Throughout my experience I participated in various language reinvigoration initiatives, local research projects, economic development efforts, and postsecondary Native American studies programs. Though not always successful, I tried and continue to try to "give something back" to the Northern Arapaho tribe, which has been so generous to me and has graciously tolerated my social mistakes, cultural awkwardness, speech errors, and personal struggles. The gratitude and respect I owe to the Northern Arapaho people will remain perpetually at the center of my life as we continue to share knowledge.

On many occasions people told me not to let specific things I heard or saw leave the reservation, and I have diligently endeavored to honor those boundaries. Today there is much discussion and some disagreement about where the boundaries should be drawn, but I have tried to apply the judgment I also acquired during my five and a half years at Wind River. Throughout this book I have endeavored not to expose personal information about individuals' or families' lives or relate sacred knowledge as the elders define it. I listened to the advice of elders and others to the best of my ability and have tried to recognize the individual people I learned from. By getting involved in activities and looking on, I learned much more than even I am always consciously aware. For two years off and on (1989–90), I was allowed to assist in the ALCC's dictionary revision project, and during that time I learned from Helen Cedartree and Robert SunRhodes both specific features and the whole beautiful expanse of the Arapaho language. During the same period, I was allowed to attend Arapaho language classes sponsored by the ALCC through Central Wyoming College, taught by Richard and Alonzo Moss. For four years, I also served as director of educational services at the North American Indian Heritage Center and thus participated in many projects in or for the community: for example, the center coordinated cultural education activities for the local schools, organized summer school programs, presented lectures, conducted cultural tours, prepared museum exhibits, carried out historic photography research, gathered oral history accounts, wrote grant proposals, arranged for the publication of educational materials, and assisted with programs for economic development and the revival of traditional art forms. At Central Wyoming College I served for three years as an adjunct instructor in anthropology and Native American studies and for two years also as Native American studies and student activities coordinator, especially for American Indian students and organizations on campus. Throughout my stay I was fortunate in and outside those official roles to participate in many events, such as organizing powwows, working at ceremonies, cooking feasts, picking chokecherries, helping with art fairs, and taking part in local conferences and seminars. I was also involved in artistic production, various fund-rasing activities, grant applications, and so forth.

I cannot specifically thank all the people who had a part in the research for this book, but the following individuals have contributed much to my learning about Arapaho language, history, and the contemporary situation: Robert SunRhodes (deceased), Helen Cedartree, Martha Woodenlegs, Vincent Bell, Anthony Sitting Eagle (deceased), Mark SoldierWolf, Eva C'Hair (deceased), Joe Goggles, Jimmy Blackburn, MaryAnne Whiteman (deceased), Mary Kate Underwood, Arnold Headley (deceased), Cleone Thunder, Bill Thunder (deceased), Ruth Big Lake, Jeanette Bell, Annie Wanstall, Richard Moss, Paul Moss (deceased), Pius Moss (deceased), MaryAnn YellowBear, Lenora Hanway, Elizabeth Brown, Vincent Redman (deceased), Florence Redman, Marie Willow, Annette Bell, Viola Wylie, and the entire Spoonhunter family. To all of these people, my many students, and countless friends: you have my undying respect and gratitude in a good way. Individuals' insights or statements are acknowledged throughout the work by the person's name in parentheses.

The principal grant support for my research came from the Spencer Foundation Dissertation-Year Fellowship and a National Institute for Mental Health Research Service Award. The Phillips Fund of the American Philosophical Society and the Institute for Intercultural Studies awarded small grants in the early stages of my research. For income to support my family from several part-time jobs or grant-funded projects in Wyoming while I did research and wrote my dissertation, I am very grateful to Central Wyoming College and the North American Indian Heritage Center. For occasional income from contracted services, I must also thank St. Stephen's Indian School and Arapahoe School. I thank Colby College for a half-year sabbatical, two summer research grants, and other assistance, which allowed me to finish this book and continue to maintain my relationship with the Northern Arapaho tribe.

A number of colleagues also reviewed my research and writing at various stages, including Raymond Fogelson, Paul Friedrich, Nancy Munn, Raymond DeMallie, John MacAloon, Karen Blu, and Carolyn Anderson. For their guidance and encouragement, they all have my respect and gratitude.

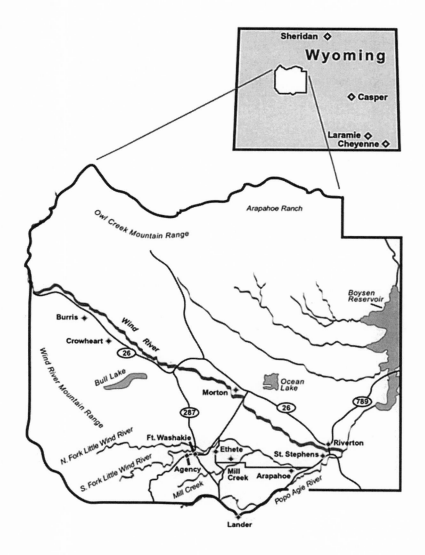

Wind River Reservation (after Fowler 1982)

1
The Northern Arapahos

Cultural, Linguistic, and Historical Background

The Northern Arapahos (*hinono'ei*)[1] are an indigenous people of the central Plains culture area of North America. For establishing when and how the Arapaho peoples entered the Plains west of the Missouri River, there is no direct archaeological evidence or historical documentation. Scott (1907:545) and other early researchers acknowledge this unanswered (and perhaps never-to-be-answered) question of Arapaho origins. Mooney (1896:954) concludes, probably following Clark (1885:39), that the Arapahos were originally an agricultural society inhabiting an area near the Red River in Minnesota and likely entered the Plains in company of the Cheyennes in the eighteenth century. Arapaho groups have long been allied with the Cheyennes and share many cultural affinities with them; but the two languages, although both are members of the Algonquian language family, are quite different. According to Kroeber (1902:4, 1939:81–82) and Michelson (1912), Arapaho is distinctively isolated from other Algonquian languages, suggesting a long separation from the Great Lakes groups and ancient habitation in the Plains area that lasted perhaps as long as a thousand years.

Arapaho stories favor both northern and eastern origins. Various accounts relate that the Arapahos became distinct from the Gros Ventres or even a "lost tribe" as a result of an ill-fated crossing of a frozen river somewhere in the far north (Arnold Headley; Michael Whitehawk's narrative in Crofts 1997:86–87). During the crossing the ice broke, leaving two groups separated by the river; those who were on the ice at the time perished. Consistent with such a history, past and present Arapaho observers note linguistic and religious affinities to the

---

[1] Transcriptions of Arapaho terms in contemporary Northern Arapaho orthography are given in italics. Historical transcriptions of Arapaho terms are given in roman type. Bracketed insertions in quotations are mine unless otherwise noted.

Cree peoples, called "rabbit people" (*nookunneno'*) in Arapaho. In 1900 Cleaver Warden told Kroeber that Cree words were intelligible to Arapaho speakers (Kroeber 1916–20:Notebook 25:6). There is also a deep stratum of Cree connections to Arapaho religion as found in the Rabbit Lodge preceding and in preparation for the Offerings Lodge (Sun Dance) (Helen Cedartree; Robert SunRhodes).

Favoring eastern origins is another version of the ice-crossing story, set on the Missouri River (Michelson 1910, narrated by Jessie Rowlodge, "Horn Hacking on the Missouri"). There are also elements of farming associated with the most ancient and sacred Arapaho religious artifacts. Furthermore, the *beesowuunenno'*, an Arapaho subtribe, is said to have come from the Eastern Woodlands, as reflected in the name's alternative meanings, 'wood lodge' and 'big lodge,' for the dome-shaped, wood or brush-covered dwelling forms typical in that area. As the story goes, the *beesowuunenno'* joined the Arapahos proper, bringing with them the Flat Pipe (*se'eicooo*) and the most sacred traditions of the tribe surrounding it.

It is difficult to uphold a simple theory that a single proto-Arapaho people or tribe split into the three tribes of the Gros Ventres, the Northern Arapahos, and the Southern Arapahos (see Trenholm 1970). It is just as likely that there were a number of dialects, bands, or subtribes that merged into or separated from each other throughout precontact Arapaho history. Moreover, the singular east-to-west trajectory assumes the existence of an Algonquian cultural and linguistic center in the Great Lakes, but there is no direct evidence to connect Arapaho origins with such a center. It is just as likely that there were also north-south cultural and linguistic connections over a long period of time, as suggested by the Cree connections.

Finally, there is evidence to support the possibility that Arapahos were present on the Plains long before contact with non-Indian peoples and the entry of other groups (e.g., the Cheyennes, the Lakotas, the Crows, and the Shoshones) into the area. In 1914 Sherman Sage narrated that his ancestor six generations before had observed Mount Specimen emitting smoke, thus establishing Arapaho presence in the Front Range of the Rocky Mountains by at least 1700 (Toll 1962:21). He also said that the Arapaho people had a historically prior claim to the Black Hills area, explaining why even Lakota leaders recognized the Arapaho presence at councils pertaining to the region (Greene 1941:37).

In sum, the Arapaho people have long been placed in the background of Plains culture and history, though they have a deeper history and a much more significant role in the development of the culture area than either popular or academic treatments usually recognize. The Arapaho people identify themselves as the source of many traditions associated with Plains Indian cultures. It is also known historically that the Arapaho peoples introduced and expanded new traditions, such as the Ghost Dance and Peyote worship. Though not always significant in the available evidence or observed events, the Arapahos have been a strong force in Plains history over what the historian Fernand Braudel calls the *longue durée* (1972:21; cited in Fogelson 1989:137).

Before their intense contact with Euro-American society, which began in the 1850s, Northern Arapaho bands were unified by a ritual complex called the *beyoowu'u*, literally 'all the lodges' (*bey-* 'all' or 'complete' /*-oowu'* 'lodge'/*-u* pluralizer) which consisted of the Offerings Lodge, the women's Buffalo Lodge, and a sequence of men's age-grade societies. The only ceremony of the *beyoowu'u* that has survived to the present among the Northern Arapahos is the Offerings Lodge (*hoseino'oowu'*), commonly referred to as the Sun Dance, which parallels the temporal structure, exchange relations, and knowledge transmission of the age-grade lodges and the women's Buffalo Lodge. All other ceremonies dissolved before or during the early reservation period.

The *beyoowu'u* system was shared with the Southern Arapahos and was similar to that of the related Gros Ventre people. In addition to the lodges there were various other life transition rituals, including childhood ceremonies, funerary practices, specific vows, offerings, and fasts. One of my aims in this book is to show that those rituals and the life transition ceremonies of the *beyoowu'u* expressed and generated movement through a total Arapaho life trajectory system. An understanding of that temporal system will also involve articulating connections to distinctly Arapaho dimensions of knowledge transmission and ways of defining personhood.

Like several other societies with long histories in the Plains area, including the Blackfeet, the Mandans, and the Hidatsas, the Arapahos and the Gros Ventres were characterized by a distinctive age-grade system (Lowie 1916). Contrary to Lowie's conclusions (1916:954), there is thus a rough correlation between age-grade formation and earlier presence or cultural influences in the Plains culture area. Societies known to have entered the Plains later (e.g., the Cheyennes, the Crows, and the Lakotas) had ungraded societies. Lowie is perhaps correct, however, in suggesting that the age-graded tribes were once in close proximity. In all these systems, male age sets moved through the graded sequence by participating in a series of lodge ceremonies, accumulating knowledge, and earning increasing power over and responsibility for junior persons' movement. Beyond the lodges themselves, Plains age-grade systems maintained enduring bonds between bands and camps, organized male activities, and served as the basis for recruitment to political leadership and positions of ritual authority.

The Arapaho system, as Kroeber (1904:153–54) presented it, consisted of a sequence of grades listed here from youngest to oldest.

Kit-Foxes: *nouunenno'* 'kit fox men'
Star Men: *ho3o'uhuunenno'* 'star men'
Clubboard Lodge: *hiice'eexoowu'* 'clubboard lodge'
Spear Lodge: *biitoh'oowu'* (no translation known)
Crazy Lodge: *hohookeenenno'* 'crazy men'
Dog Lodge: *he3owu'oowu'* 'dog lodge'

The junior Kit-Fox and Star grades did not have lodge ceremonies and therefore are not included among the *beyoowu'u*. Age sets formed in those first grades, though, served social functions and continued to pass through successive lodges together.

The two groups of oldest men were also set apart from the younger men's age-grade system, because in them rested the highest level of knowledge and power of all the lodges. Both the Old Men's Lodge (*hinono'oowu'*), and the Water-Sprinkling Old Men (*ciinecei beh'iihoho'*, referred to here as the Seven Old Men), were thus set apart because of the sacred knowledge and power they held. It is not clear from the literature that the Old Men's Lodge was an age grade per se. It is evident, though, that passage through the previous lodges was a prerequisite for transition to the most senior groups. Most sacred of all, the Water-Sprinkling Old Men consisted of seven of the oldest men, who were entrusted with seven sacred bundles used for ceremonial painting in all the lodges and representing their ability to direct all the *beyoowu'u*.

Though most of the attention to Plains ritual has tended to foreground the public domains of male performance and authority, Arapaho women were central in the total system of life transitions and lodges; their roles were not merely complementary to men's roles. Moreover, they were primary agents for many rituals outside the lodges, including childhood ceremonies and marriage, and were focal participants in two women's ritual forms. One was the Buffalo Lodge (*benouhto'oowu'*), which involved young women dancers and paralleled the men's age-grade lodge preparations and performances. The other was the women's quillwork society which centered on the ritualized production of quilled objects (e.g., cradles, robes, and tipi ornaments) that were given as highly valued objects of exchange to kin. Women also organized or facilitated other life transition rituals within family and tipi life, including birth, naming, ear piercing, recognition feasts, and funerals. Women's activities in the Buffalo Lodge, quillwork ceremonies, and other ritual practices ordered their life trajectory around their reproductive power, their life-generative roles in close kin relations, their function in mediating with sacred beings (including buffalo, Whirlwind Woman, and others), and, as Lévi-Strauss (1968:250–51) realizes, their ability to transform "raw" materials into the highest expressions of cultural life.

The *beyoowu'u* system, the quillwork society, and other life transition rituals unified families around cooperative practices, defined gender boundaries and forms of power within them, activated relations of interfamilial exchange, generated age-set solidarity, and sustained intergenerational authority. Pervading all ritual practice was the promotion of what I call *life movement*, that is the aim to generate long life, blessings, and abundance for self, others, family, and the tribe. A related function of the ceremonial complex was to reproduce an age-ranked structure and thus reserve for senior men and women control over the tempo, directionality, and movement of junior age sets and individuals through the socioculturally constituted life trajectory. As individuals and age groups moved through the life transitions and age grades, they were allowed access to ever more sacred knowledge and developed toward genuine personhood and Arapaho identity. Beyond the ritual system itself, the resulting age structure was the basis for political decision-making, economic distribution, social control, and patterns of interaction.

Although unified by shared ritual practices throughout the prereservation era, the Northern Arapaho people were rarely together in one place as a "tribe"; rather they were divided into flexible and mobile bands, camps, and family divisions (see Eggan 1966). Each tipi was formed by marriage and the emerging relations of husband, wife, and their offspring. The camp was made up of several tipis, each one including one of a man's several wives, if he had more than one, their children, and other kin. Political and economic authority centered on men, but the nexus of kin relations centered on women, who "owned" the tipis and tended to reside with their own kin. After marriage, for example, a daughter and son-in-law generally resided matrilocally for several years, with the young man considered a "servant" to his parents-in-law (Eggan 1937). Women related as sisters, daughters, mothers, or grandmothers thus formed the enduring and focal relations of tipi and camp life. This system offered a balance between masculine and feminine domains of activity and social relations.

Several camps formed a band. Each band had its own name, identity, dialect, chief, and corporate economic activity. Before direct contact with Euro-Americans, beginning in the late eighteenth century, there were at least four

distinct northern and four or more southern bands, each set forming a loose
common identity as Northern or Southern Arapahos, though sharing a common
identity as Arapaho that was not based on a centralized or confederated political
system. Within each tribe, then, there were band divisions that persisted and
developed well into the early reservation period. Among the Northern Arapahos,
there were, according to Hilger's informants (1952:188), four bands: the Greasy
Faces, the Long Legs or Antelopes, the Quick-to-Anger, and the Beavers.
Instead of or in addition to the Beavers, elders mention that the fourth or fifth
group at Wind River was the Lump Forehead people. Two other northern camps
often mentioned at Wind River are the Bad Pipes and Ugly Faces (Wyoming
Indian High School 1979:1).

Above the band level, the Northern Arapahos, the Southern Arapahos, and
the Gros Ventres, recognize both "tribal" distinctions and a common identity
based in myth, ritual practice, and history. Apparently there were originally four
or five distinct "subtribes," each with its own dialect. Kroeber classifies them
as (1) *nowoo3ineheino'* 'southern or left-hand people', now the Southern
Arapahos; (2) *hoho 'nooxowuunenno'* 'rock lodge men', the most obscure group
with the most distinctive dialect; (3) *hinono 'eino'* 'wrong root people' or 'our
people'; (4) *beesowuunenno'* 'big lodge' or 'wood lodge men' (*bes-* suggests
'wood', *bees-* connotes 'large'), the group from whom some Northern and
Southern Arapaho families still recognize descent; and (5) *hitouunenno'* 'beggar
men', the Arapaho term for the Gros Ventres (Kroeber 1902:5 ff.). By the time
of contact, the subtribes were distributed north and south from the Gros Ventres
in Montana to the southern bands extending to the Arkansas River in Colorado.

In contrast to the hypothesis upon which all of the origin theories operate
(Trenholm 1970:8–12)—the one that holds that all the present tribes split off
from an original Arapaho prototribe entering the Plains in the north—a more
consistent theory is that the five linguistically related groups were long
composed of bands that mixed and separated into different "tribal" formations
over a long period of time. Eventually, those bands formed the three tribes of
modern times: (1) the Northern Arapahos, now residing on the Wind River
Indian Reservation, Wyoming; (2) the Southern Arapahos of west-central
Oklahoma; and (3) the Gros Ventres at Fort Belknap, Montana. Father de Smet
(1863; cited in Scott 1907:552) notes that the Gros Ventres told him that they
split from the Arapahos around 1700, though they joined again briefly in
1818–23. The Southern and Northern Arapaho bands divided perhaps as early
as the 1820s, though exactly when such a split occurred—and whether it
occurred at all—cannot be documented (Scott 1907:551). It is problematic to
consider the three tribes as bounded social entities with distinct cultures and

constant territories from the eighteenth century to the present. For at least three hundred years they have had ties of kinship, intermarriage, exchange, friendship, and religion that persist as a basis for a shared "Arapaho" identity.

In recent years, the Northern Arapahos have become the religious focus of the three tribes, since they alone have been able to maintain the Offerings Lodge (*hoseino'oowu'*) and other ceremonies surrounding the Flat Pipe (*se'eicooo*), the sacred center and original source of all life and knowledge. Rather than political centralization, throughout the history of contact and reservation life, mythico-ritual practices have been the basis for Arapaho unity and identity, crosscutting social divisions. These practices effected a shared system for ordering movement at all levels. That function was vested in age-structured authority for coordinating social relations and the rhythms of life-cyclical, seasonal, and epochal time.

Territory and Seasonal Changes

As established in the Treaty of 1851 signed near Fort Laramie (Kappler 1904:594–96), the Southern and Northern Arapaho territory, shared with the Southern and Northern Cheyennes, encompassed the eastern Front Range and Plains area of what is now the eastern half of Colorado, the southeastern portion of Wyoming, and part of western Kansas and Nebraska. Prior to the treaties, of course, allied and competing Plains peoples shared many regions. Thus, Arapaho bands ranged over an area even larger than that defined by the federal government in 1851; as Sherman Sage relates, "The Arapahos went from the Bad Lands of North Dakota to the deserts of Arizona, and sometimes penetrated considerable distances into the mountains" (in Toll 1962:29).

The seasonal movements and subsistence of the Northern bands of the Arapahos in particular centered in the Parks region of the Rocky Mountains in what is now east-central Colorado. Seasonal band movements involved dispersal of camps in the fall and congregation in bands and occasionally large tribal camp circles during the summer:

> This oscillation between the band and the camp circle was closely related to the habits of the buffalo, on which the High Plains tribes primarily depended. During the fall and winter the buffalo herds broke up into small groups and scattered widely, seeking shelter and forage. The various tribes did likewise. . . .In the late spring and early summer, as grass became available, the buffalo began to congregate in larger

and larger numbers for the mating season. The tribal bands also began
to assemble, both for communal hunting and for the performance of
tribal and social rituals. [Eggan 1966:54]

Northern Arapaho seasonal and life movement was thus tied homeostatically to
the buffalo, who in mythical time were human persons and a source of both
knowledge and life movement.

Seasonal movements and camp formations were also coordinated with the
two ecozones of mountains and plains. Arapaho culture is more aptly defined
as a Plains-Mountain subsistence, because it was lived as much in the mountain
valleys and parks surrounded by high ridges and peaks as it was along the river
systems of the open plains. Eggan (1966:54) suggests that in midsummer the
camps moved into the mountains, where the valleys and parks formed natural
game surrounds for buffalo and other animals. The camps stayed out of the high
mountain valleys and off the plains in winter, separating into smaller camps in
sheltered areas at the base of the Rocky Mountains or other ranges. Sometimes
different bands camped a few miles apart in a big circle. Game that moved into
the circle could then be easily surrounded and hunted by individuals or small
groups. Fall and spring were the most advantageous times for movement
eastward or northward on to the plains for ceremonies, hunting, and trade. By
1800 the Arapahos were trading as far east as the Missouri River (Fowler
1982:15) and as far southwest as the Mexican settlements.

Sheltered mountainous parks and valleys provided security from enemy war
parties, abundance of resources, and natural game preserves. Paralleling the
winter camp formation, there is some indication that the cultural landscape of
Arapaho parks was homologous with the space of the camp circle, lodges, and
tipis discussed in fuller detail in chapter 4. The entrance to the parks opened
through various passes to the eastern foothills, valleys, and plains. The eastern
entrance to the Grand Lake area, for example, is called *teceno*, "the door." As
Sage and Gunn Griswold related, the parks provided what Arapaho people
called "game bags."

Sometimes they would come on little enclosed parks with so many
buffalo that the bottom of the valley would be dark with them. They
told us of one time when the Indians had gone quite a while without
finding game and then came upon one of these little parks, or as they
called them "game bags." There was no means of egress from the park
except the way by which the Indians entered it, so that the buffalo in
the park were unable to escape. [Toll 1962:33–34]

Patrols of scouts could also easily watch for enemy groups entering through the narrow passes. All Arapaho seasonal movements were guided by movement into and out of the parks and the east-west, or upriver-downriver directionality. The seasonal cycle thus followed a pattern of ascending into and descending out of the mountains of Colorado through passes and along various well-defined trails. That movement on the landscape of ascent and descent is central in many dimensions of Arapaho senses for orders of space and time, including life movement.

Much of the age-structured political and ritual authority for leadership and the functions of age grades involved decisions about and coordination of the movement of camps and bands for seasonal subsistence and, in turn, coordination of ceremonies with the seasonal changes. Human movement had to be synchronized with the sprouting of grass, the falling of leaves, the availability of various berries and roots, the changes in the buffalo's coats, the migration of birds, trading opportunities, incursions of enemy war parties, and the knowledge given through dreams and visions. Age grades also served functions for directing a group's movements in traditional forms of warfare, for defending boundaries against attackers and acquiring forms of value through raids on enemy camps. Age brought increasing knowledge of the landscape, animal behavior, plant growth, and weather conditions. Accordingly, the seasonal cycle was never an automatic repetitious cycle of movements to the same places each season year after year; it required decisions and activities carefully orchestrated to adjust to the unique natural, social, and cultural conditions of each season or year.

Dislocation, Relocation, and Reservation Space

When Euro-American westward migration began to intrude into Arapaho lands and Euro-Americans began to settle there (during the 1840s and the 1850s), leaders of the Northern Arapaho bands maintained the strategy of "distance," what Fogelson refers to as "low-profile invisibility[,] as defensive strategy" (1989:142). That was made possible in large part by Arapaho seclusion in the parks and valleys of the various mountain ranges in their territory. After the Colorado gold rush and the Sand Creek Massacre of 1864, those areas, too, were invaded, so the Northern bands moved out of Colorado into Wyoming, where buffalo herds remained and where non-Indians inhabited only several forts. Throughout the period of the 1850s to the early 1870s, the Northern Arapaho bands remained distant from whites and thus are generally only mentioned as an aside to or as implicated by association with events involving the Lakotas and the Cheyennes in the valorized history of oppression and resistance. Before the 1870s, neither Arapaho tribe either aggressively resisted or generously aided the Euro-American presence. Northern Arapaho bands did accept rations from the forts in Wyoming but did not form strong ties of accommodation and alliance with the U.S. military, as did the Crows and the Eastern Shoshones.

Partly because of their neither friendly nor hostile relation to the United States, the Northern Arapahos did not receive their own reservation by treaty. The Fort Laramie Treaty of 1868 (Kappler 1904:998–1007) suggests that the Northern Arapahos be placed on another tribe's reservation, such as the Cheyenne-Arapaho Reservation in Indian Territory or the Red Cloud Agency with the Oglala Lakotas. There were a number of reasons that Northern band leaders resisted those options. First, there was the problem of retaining a separate identity from the larger, more powerful Lakota nations (Fowler 1982:52). Second, by the early 1870s chiefs and elders had decided that the tribe should find a place in Wyoming, perhaps based on the fact that buffalo herds survived there. Third, Arapaho leaders had observed the disease and hunger in Indian Territory and the oppressive conditions at Red Cloud Agency (58 ff.).

Probably the most powerful reason for Northern Arapaho resistance to settling on those other reservations was a revelation that came to Weasel Bear, the keeper of the most sacred Arapaho object, the Flat Pipe (*se'eicooo*). After the treaties of the 1850s and the removal of the Southern Arapahos to Indian Territory in 1869, Weasel Bear was uncertain where to take the Pipe. As it is told by a Southern Arapaho named Black Horse, the Pipe Keeper then fasted, and in his vision of things to come, he saw a great flood. Weasel Bear concluded, "Of course this incident taught me to stay among the mountains, or close to them, but if I go south or away from high places, there would be a deluge" (Dorsey and Warden 1905:Box 2, "Story about the Flat Pipe."). Throughout all Arapaho mythical time and history, the Pipe and its series of keepers have defined the movement of the people. Where the Pipe goes, the people go. As long as it is cared for and stays in a high place, the Arapahos will survive. Following that guidance, throughout the late 1870s Arapaho leaders sought a reservation in Wyoming.

The Northern Arapaho tribe (*hinono'eiteen*) has resided since 1878 on the Wind River Indian Reservation in Wyoming. Although the lands were originally reserved exclusively for the Eastern Shoshone tribe, the Northern Arapahos were assigned to Wind River for a "temporary stay" while their own reservation, to be located in east-central Wyoming, was being established. In return for the Northern Arapahos' service as scouts at Fort Robinson (Nebraska) from

1876–1878, General George Crook promised them their own reservation, which was to be in the Tongue River area somewhere between present-day Sheridan and Casper (Trenholm 1970:258–62; Fowler 1982:63–66). Nonetheless, in 1878 the Northern bands were ordered to Indian Territory; but one band resisted and remained at Fort Fetterman, and the governor of Wyoming suggested that they be sent to Wind River. However, by the early 1880s, the federal government had become reluctant to create a new reservation, so the Northern Arapaho tribe has resided at Wind River ever since. Through political strategies based on a centralizing religious system and age-structured consensus and solidarity, Northern Arapaho leaders were eventually able to gain joint trust ownership and self-government shared equally with the Eastern Shoshones, a former competitor in the western Plains.

Unlike the Southern Arapahos, the Northern tribe was able to sustain a sizable base of trust lands. Though there were substantial land cessions, the two Wind River tribes were able to retain the major portion of the trust lands through the period of the 1890s to the early 1900s, because there was less Euro-American immigration into central Wyoming than elsewhere in the West, where water and other resources were more abundant. Until well into the twentieth century, when local towns boomed with oil and uranium extraction, the Arapaho communities on the lower half of the Little Wind River had relatively few non-Indians to contend with—a contrast with the deluge of settlers experienced by the Southern tribe in Oklahoma.

In comparison to the Southern Arapahos in Oklahoma, the Northern Arapahos were thus more isolated from non-Arapaho influences for a longer period of time. Until the post-World War II era, the Northern Arapahos could exercise some control over what Euro-American elements were appropriated or kept at bay. For most of the elders at Wind River today, though, World War II marked the opening up of the reservation: all eligible Northern Arapaho men enlisted and served in the war, automobile traffic increased movement on and off the reservation, some tribal members took advantage of the 1950s relocation policy to move permanently or temporarily to urban areas, and the surrounding Wyoming economy boomed with uranium and petroleum extraction. As a result, the post-World War II era brought significant changes.

The uneasy coexistence with the Eastern Shoshone tribe also contributed to Northern Arapaho political and cultural boundary maintenance. From the beginning of the reservation period, Arapaho leaders had to gain a legal foothold and sustain their own cultural identity as separate from that of their neighbors, who tended to have more open and accommodating relations with the non-Indian world. During the pre-World War II era, a solid social dividing line existed between the Arapaho and Shoshone areas of the reservation, but today there is greater social interaction and intermarriage between the two tribes. But though the social boundaries have opened, political boundaries have recently been drawn more distinctly. Throughout the 1980s and the 1990s, the two tribes have moved toward internal self-determination by splitting many once jointly administered programs into separate ones, with each tribe controlling its own. Accordingly, it has been years since the joint Shoshone-Arapaho Business Council has operated as a decision-making body. Shoshone leaders have become frustrated with "carrying" the less affluent and larger Arapaho tribe, and the Arapaho leadership has pursued a policy of "doing it on their own" in order to gain sovereign control over the federal resources long shared half and half with the Eastern Shoshone tribe. Since federal funding is based on tribal population, and the Northern Arapaho tribe is now about twice the size of the Eastern Shoshone tribe, separating the control of formerly joint programs could be expected to bring a greater share of federal funding to the Arapaho side of the reservation. As of 1999, Arapaho tribal leaders had separated all former jointly funded and administered programs, including housing, health care, and social programs. That effort is part of a larger movement to reaffirm the boundaries between Arapaho and Shoshone cultural identity, now perceived as moving toward a mixed "Sho-Rap" identity. With increasing intermarriage, family ties, and pan-Indian traditions cutting across tribal boundaries, especially among those of the younger generations, there is growing concern on the part of the more traditional Arapahos that the political and cultural border must be closed.

Today Northern Arapaho communities are concentrated in the southeastern corner of the Wind River Reservation, the fourth largest in the United States. Most of the vast area is unoccupied by humans, from the dry sage-brush-covered terrain on the eastern plains to the wilderness area of the Wind River Range of the Rocky Mountains on the western border. As in most of Wyoming, there are great uninhabited distances between human places on the Wind River Reservation. Automobile transportation is thus now a universal need and an ongoing concern. Within reservation boundaries today, non-Indians outnumber Indians by about two to one. On the reservation borders, the non-Indian population is concentrated in the towns of Riverton and Lander adjacent to the reservation and is dispersed on the operating ranches and farms throughout the irrigable bottomlands of the Little Wind and the Big Wind rivers. Only a small percentage of the Arapahos and the Shoshones still farm their allotted lands.

Arapaho and Shoshone homes and communities are located along the roads paralleling the main river system running west to east in the southern third of the reservation. Residing primarily in this area are about ten thousand Indians, including about three thousand enrolled Eastern Shoshones, five thousand Northern Arapahos, and others who are either not enrolled or are enrolled in other tribes. Within the area of the reservation occupied by Indian people there are two major Shoshone communities, Fort Washakie and Crowheart, near the Rocky Mountains. Fort Washakie is the only Indian community that has the appearance of what non-Indians would call a "town," since the ground plan and many of the buildings were originally built for non-Indians working at or near the agency headquarters located at "the Fort." The town of Crowheart is located about sixty miles north of the Fort and is the center of more mixed-blood agricultural families. The Crowheart-Fort Washakie distinction has long been a basis for Eastern Shoshone factionalism.

Two main Arapaho districts eventually formed around St. Stephen's Catholic and St. Michael's Episcopal missions. When the Arapahos were brought by military escort to Wind River in 1878, camps settled near the forks of the Little Wind and the Big Wind rivers, about thirty miles east of Fort Washakie. In 1884 Jesuits founded St. Stephen's Catholic Mission near the "Forks People" camp of Chief Black Coal, then the principal tribal leader. Until the 1950s the mission was a social center, peopled daily by students attending the mission school, Arapaho workers employed there, and a number of priests, brothers, and sisters. At present, the only regular traffic through the mission is the coming and going of people picking up mail at the post office, commuting to St. Stephen's Indian School, or working at the mission (the workforce is small and predominantly non-Indian). The large mission farm is gone; the staff is a fraction of what it once was; only a handful of Arapaho students attend the voluntary religious education classes; and the schools, no longer run by the church, became a Bureau of Indian Affairs (BIA) contract school system in the early 1970s. For most Arapaho people, the church provides specific ritual services, including baptisms, funerals, and religious holidays. Like other Arapaho community centers, the mission has become a place people visit only occasionally for specific purposes; it does not occupy the center of social life as it once did for many during what elders recall as the "heyday of the mission."

In 1893 another town, called Arapahoe (*hinono'ei'*), was established about four miles west of St. Stephen's (*heeninouhu'* 'long robes place'), near the fork of the Popo Agie and Little Wind rivers. The town grew up around the subagency established by the federal government to serve the Arapaho tribe, thus saving the Arapahos the long trip to the Fort each week for rations, trade, and government business. Arapahoe was a major social center for nearly fifty years. For a time there was a hotel, a mercantile store, a railroad station, a rodeo grounds, the Arapahoe dance hall, and other non-Indian-constructed buildings, including the first housing development of small one-room homes constructed for "old people." For many years a number of Arapaho camps surrounded the town. When the subagency was closed in the 1940s and trains gave way to automobile travel in Wyoming, the community began to dissolve as a social center. Today only the Arapahoe School, the powwow grounds, dispersed homes, and a small post office remain. People come to Arapahoe only for specific functions. As at St. Stephen's, the school has become the main functional center of the area.

Arapaho people refer to the Arapahoe-St. Stephen's area as Lower Arapaho, which is derived from the Arapaho term *hoowuuniiteen* 'downriver/lower people'. The Arapaho communities to the west, upriver, and toward the mountains became known as Upper Arapaho, including the two communities of Mill Creek (*wosouhone'* 'sock place') and Ethete (*konouutoseii'* 'where they shed their coverings'). As a result of allotment in the early 1900s, Arapaho families and camps were dispersed westward along the Little Wind River and Mill Creek. Ethete is located between the Little Wind River and Mill Creek, a tributary, about fifteen miles west of Arapahoe. As a social center at Ethete from the decade of the teens to the 1950s, St. Michael's Mission also had a mission school, a farm, a store, and ongoing activities forming religious, economic, and social ties to the Arapaho people residing on allotments or in camps nearby. The mission was founded in 1910 as an extension of the Shoshone Episcopal Mission at Fort Washakie. Like St. Stephen's, the mission's influence waned as education began to shift to public schools in the 1950s. Nevertheless, Ethete remains the most centralized Arapaho community, with a grocery store, a gas station, a laundromat, a community hall, the Sun Dance grounds, Wyoming Indian Junior High and High School, the tribal government office, various tribal program offices, and St. Michael's Mission. A few miles southeast of Ethete, Mill Creek now centers on a housing development of the same name and Wyoming Indian Elementary School.

Since the 1970s another center has grown up in the Lower Arapaho district around the Great Plains housing development about three miles north of Arapahoe. There is a community hall, an Indian Health Service clinic, a senior citizens' center, a Head Start program, and other social program offices, though tribal efforts to develop retail businesses have proved unsuccessful there. In the 1990s the tribal government offered greater access to social programs and tribal functions at Great Plains, so that Lower Arapaho tribal members could be spared the time and expense of travel to Ethete or Fort Washakie. In time Ethete and even Great Plains may develop into towns like Fort Washakie, but there are still barriers to economic development and a strong pull to move away from the housing developments, which Arapaho people associate with crime, social density, and interfamilial tensions.

During the 1980s and the 1990s, a series of economic development efforts were undertaken in a tribal building along Wyoming Route 789 in the eastern portion of Lower Arapaho, several miles south of Riverton and north of the isolated Beaver Creek housing development. After several unsuccessful business ventures in the building, it now houses a tribal 7–8–9 bingo operation, a gas station, a fast food restaurant, and a convenience store. Those activities provide employment opportunities and a way to keep some Arapaho money circulating within the tribe rather than flowing out to the non-Indian economy, but they have yet to show significant profits for the tribe. The bingo operation is limited because the state of Wyoming has resisted a compact with the tribe for Level II gambling, and there are no large population centers nearby from which to draw non-Indian money onto the reservation. Contrary to popular stereotypes of Indian gaming riches as the "new buffalo," the Northern Arapaho tribe, like most others in the West, continues to experience extremely high unemployment and marginal economic development. Also inhibiting Indian participation in the local economy, there is still a very strong anti-Indian political force in Wyoming masking bigotry that sees reservations as "privileged" areas subsidized and coddled by the federal government, the nemesis of the West.

Within the tribe, the Upper versus Lower distinction preceded the missions as a division between two districts of loosely associated camps. In 1878 there were two main Arapaho bands, one headed by Chief Black Coal of the Forks People and the other by Chief Sharp Nose of the Long Legs, or Antelope People, located near what is now called Seventeen Mile Crossing, about six miles west of the fork site. Black Coal was the principal chief until his death in 1893 (Trenholm 1970:290), when he was succeeded by Sharp Nose. Into the 1930s, the principal chiefship alternated between the two major bands and the two districts, as did social events and some ceremonies. At one time, as already mentioned and as Fowler recognizes, there were many Arapaho strategies in all aspects of life for balancing resources, power, and leadership representation among the various districts.

From 1878 until about the 1950s, Lower Arapaho was the cultural, social, and religious center of the Northern Arapaho tribe. With allotment in the early 1900s, Arapaho camps spread to the west out of Sharp Nose's area along the Little Wind River, expanding the Upper Arapaho district and including the Lump Forehead people, the Sock people, and several other smaller camps. A number of people in the western area served as interpreters and police officers and held other jobs at Fort Washakie. Chief Friday, a transculturalized Arapaho leader and interpreter, for example, had his own camp near the Fort. Early on, the Upper Arapaho communities were thus generally thought of as more progressive and closer to whites, because of their proximity to the Fort and the non-Indian world.

Beginning in the 1950s, the cultural center of the Northern Arapaho tribe began to shift toward Ethete in the Upper Arapaho district on the western side of the reservation. At that time, some families shifted allegiance to St. Michael's clergy and schools, which they perceived as less harsh and less restrictive than those at St. Stephen's. Though St. Stephen's Mission was more successful in maintaining followers early on, for a short time in the 1940s, one priest pursued an antitraditional policy that generated tension and conflict that lingers in the tribe today. To avoid the antitraditional conditions, with the revival of traditional religion from the 1960s on, ceremonial authority and practices shifted to the Ethete area. For example, tribal leaders established a permanent grounds near Ethete for the annual Sun Dance. Formerly, the ceremony was held on the land of each year's sponsor, whether in Lower or Upper Arapaho.

Somewhat later, tribal political administration also shifted toward the Upper Arapaho side. After the Arapaho subagency closed, all tribal administrative offices also moved to Fort Washakie, more accessible to Ethete. With the government policy of self-determination beginning in the 1970s, tribal administrative offices and programs proliferated, all of which were at first based in Fort Washakie. Through the 1990s, the Northern Arapaho tribal government has moved its own tribal offices to Ethete and has taken separate control of many programs once under joint Shoshone-Arapaho administration. Most of the latter have or soon will have offices in Ethete.

With those shifts, Upper Arapaho communities and families have been able to form greater solidarity and gain a majority of the Business Council seats and other political positions since the 1980s. Wyoming Indian Schools, the largest reservation school district, expanded at Ethete-Mill Creek, and reservation employment and resources are concentrated more in the Upper district. Today the division between the districts is a source of some factional competition. In broad terms, Lower Arapahos express estrangement from resources and political representation, whereas Upper Arapahos, once the more progressive, now see Lower Arapahos as less unified, more mixed, and more distant from tradition.

The Northern Arapaho cultural identity today revolves around the awareness that the tribe has been more successful than Southern Arapahos and the Gros Ventres in retaining their language, beliefs, and traditional ceremonies. As in the Plains sign-language gesture of pointing to the heart for denoting the Northern Arapahos, tribal members today still see themselves as the "mother" tribe or, according to Kroeber, as the "father" tribe (1902:6). Other Plains peoples often point to the Northern Arapaho religion and the Sun Dance, in particular, as "closer to tradition" (Feraca 1998:13). Yet, there is a sense that changes experienced by other tribes are now coming to Wind River. Very early in reservation history, as Ben Friday, Sr. relates, "the old people prophesied just when the white men's ways would begin" (Wyoming Indian High School 1979). He goes on to say that their prediction was for a change over the two generations following that of the young people who lived during the first years of the reservation period, which extended roughly from 1878 to the 1930s and 1940s. In some ways this has come to pass. By rough estimation less than 13 percent of the Northern Arapaho people remain fluent in the native language (see Anderson 1998:54), although the Northern dialect is still stronger than that of either the Gros Ventres or the Southern Arapahos. During a period of cultural revival since the 1970s, the Northern Arapaho Sun Dance has also become a focal point for the cultural identity of members of all three tribes, but there is an ongoing concern for keeping "commercialization" out of it, maintaining a centralized tradition, and avoiding the proliferation of Sun Dances and religious centers found in some other tribes, such as the Lakotas and Eastern Shoshones.

In the historical context, the Northern Arapahos were, until recently, also less factionalized and reorganized by Euro-American political structures than either of the two related tribes (the Southern Arapahos and the Gros Ventres) or other reservation communities in general. As Fowler's extensive ethnohistory (1982) documents, Northern Arapaho cultural continuity and consensus politics throughout the pre- and early reservation period were maintained by an adapted Arapaho age structure that served to limit and balance political and ceremonial authority. As some people say, the tribe used to act "as one." Whereas other tribes became polarized by divisions between war and peace leaders, young and old generations, traditionalists and Christian progressives, and Peyote and non-Peyote groups, the Northern Arapahos averted factionalism in the tribal political system for nearly a century from the time of intensive contact in the 1850s until the post-World War II era. Along with tribal solidarity, the Northern Arapahos also sustained cultural boundaries through strategies of distance toward Euro-American society, and through selective appropriation and compartmentalization of non-Arapaho cultural elements. By the 1970s, however, the Arapaho people experienced a shift to what some today call "white man's ways" (*nih'oo3ouuniisinowo*) in political decision making (Mark Soldierwolf). As in other reservation communities, recent and progressing cultural revitalization and self-determination have sought to unify the tribe around a shared ritual focus and centralized government, while family bonds and factional divisions have endured and even intensified during the same period.

The Big Change

In the historical context, as Loretta Fowler contends, an adapted age structure persisted throughout the early reservation period and served to generate unifying symbols and social practices for tribal solidarity and consensus in formal intermediation with the federal government and the non-Arapaho world: "Rather than being riven with divisive conflicts or immobilized by apathy, the Arapahoes have managed to achieve tribal unity in the face of unsettling change and perpetuate a sense of continuity of political ideals despite a series of devastating crises of authority precipitated by subordination to whites during the past 130 years" (1982:2). In a unique balance rather than a split of authority, ritual and ultimate control remained in the hands of elders, and political leadership was limited to persons in the third stage of life, carefully selected by elders. As Fowler and other Arapaho observers recognize, through an adaptive age structure the Northern Arapahos were able to maintain consensus and solidarity under conditions that generated factionalism in other American Indian reservation communities.

When I went to Wind River in 1988, I observed and heard from many folks that the age-structured order and shared symbols described by Fowler had weakened as unifying forces in Northern Arapaho society. People familiar with her work at Wind River concurred, despite their own different places in the community, that what she wrote was true at one time but no longer applied. Simply put, the political economy of the Wind River Arapaho communities has taken on the factionalism typical on other reservations. The order of consistent political leadership shaped by elders' ritual authority, though still functioning to a degree, has moved toward family-, circle-, and district-based competition for scarce forms of value, including authority, economic resources, and knowledge itself. Though religious life remains very strong and centralized, political decision making and structures have become estranged from the once-unifying political-religious symbols, practices, and ways of speaking.

Before World War II, age hierarchy and interfamilial exchange cut across intratribal divisions and provided a stateless, higher order of "tribal" integration for discrete bands faced with a new form of unity resulting from permanent coresidence, unknown prior to the reservation period. In the past fifty years, the age-structured order has given way to a centralized tribal government based on electoral procedures, bureaucratization, and interest group politics. The new system, which older Arapahos often refer to as "white man's ways," has replaced decision making based solely on age. As a result, the Northern Arapaho political economy is now differentiated by familial and factional divisions that compete for scarce resources distributed through centralized economic and political structures. The consensus maintained by age structure, which Fowler observed as late as 1978, though still operating occasionally, especially in areas of ritual authority, has weakened significantly while factional politics have intensified. Consensus formation now rarely goes beyond family, district, and factional boundaries. In general, the tendency of age structure to extend horizontal relations among families and districts has given way to an incipient state-type political order exercising top-down authority that, though it originated in a Euro-American imposed order, has its own unique local form.

In the Northern Arapaho communities, older people talk much about the "big change" they have witnessed in the last thirty years or so, some tracing it to World War II, others to more recent history. Elders exchange concerns about the younger generations, including the effect of language loss, the introduction of "white man's ways" in political decision making, the commercialization of culture, the factional conflict, the changes in ritual forms, the intrusion of pan-Indian cultural elements, and the problems plaguing youth in all impoverished communities. Fowler observed that the continuity between generations had not been "broken," but it seems that ties between age groups today have become at least attenuated, and even fractured in some domains of social life.

Presently, the Arapaho tribal government has neither the pervasive order of age hierarchy nor the idealized regularity of a reorganized constitutional, bureaucratized system. Although political authority is centralized in the tribal government (the Arapaho Business Council), succession to and the tenure of leadership are subject to unpredictable political events and strategizing. For example, even though a councilman or councilwoman is elected by a majority of the voters in a general election, a small minority can vote in the General Council to remove him or her from office shortly after the election. Thus, in the political process, small well-organized groups can wield a great deal of power. In the conflicts and competition for scarce resources, there are also often no agreed-upon rules of the game, so each new situation, such as a General Council meeting, calls forth novel strategies. As most Arapahos agree, "anything can happen," which makes for a social world that is both intriguing and tragic. Paradoxically, imposed Euro-American state-type, bureaucratic structures have, in the last generation, introduced political instability rather than providing the rational consistency and unity intended by their functions.

Family

Equally significant to the age structure, family relations have also served to maintain Arapaho continuity throughout both steady and critical periods during the reservation period and to sustain many of the most important contemporary dimensions of Arapaho life (see Hunter 1977). Countering Fowler's emphasis, family boundaries and factional interests derived from them should not be hastily defined in negative terms as disruptive to a higher order of integration, for they are enduring forms with a long history of effective adaptation to the disruptions and vicissitudes of reservation life. Namely, while tribal government and religious traditions have centralized, the family has retained or appropriated many other functions. Throughout reservation history, individuals confronted with a crisis, a personal challenge, or a social conflict, have found the first recourse for empowerment within the family and the local group, rather than through the tribe or Euro-American institutions. Although a top-down view of political systems sees factional disorder in such empowerment, the Northern Arapaho people, like other reservation communities, continue to consider family relations the most consistent in life. Though they often face difficult internal problems of their own, families provide more enduring and predictable social relations for solving problems than those provided by non-Indian or tribal institutions. Families are the first resort when a need arises and the last resort when all other options fail.

As in the prereservation period, Arapaho kinship is flexible and therefore much more adaptive to redefinition and restructuring than other types of relations. Superseding consanguineous bonds, kinship ties are constructed by shared residence, common activities, and merged life histories. The ongoing social construction of kinship has more to do with shared social space and time than with inherited substance or property. As such, persons who are not kin in biological terms can be brought closer and thus become part of the family, including adopted children, affines, and distant kin redefined in time as closer. Even kinship terms follow this logic. For instance, if a distant female cousin of one's mother lives nearby and participates in the family, she would likely be called "mother." Conversely, a close relative by blood who remains distant from the family will be distanced in the social construction of relations. In both directions, one's actions over time define kinship status.

Given such flexibility, there is no clearly defined term or uniform structure for the nuclear or extended family. Nonetheless, all nuclear families are tied to others. The boundaries between kin and nonkin are fluid and contextually relative. In Arapaho, one's 'relatives' are referred to as *neito'eino'*, which not only denotes 'kin' but also connotes 'friends' or even members of one's circle or tribe. Similarly, the only term I heard in Arapaho for 'extended family' is *hoowuhneniit*, meaning 'all family' (Helen Cedartree; Robert SunRhodes), which also refers to all of one's relations. In the contemporary context, the English term *family* is used for the extended family. Although there is no precisely replicated structure for extended families, family identity is usually constituted through shared descent from a living or deceased grandparent or grandparents and thus around collateral sibling relationships in each generation. As in the prereservation period, women generally form the core of the extended family (see Hunter 1977) for intrafamilial cooperation, such as shared parenting responsibilities, economic support, ritual participation, and political action.

Nevertheless, sense of common kinship among families extends as far back as four or five generations. Several extended families thus recognize alliance and common identity as part of the same circle. Roughly, such a circle of families shares descent from classificatory brothers or sisters (including parallel cousins or, more so in the present, cross-cousins as well) in the grandparental generation.

Extended families also form the main corporate groups for organizing and holding collective ritual and social events, such as feasts, funerals, giveaways, basketball tournaments, hand games, powwows, and many others. If one's family requests assistance for such events, one "can't say no," without being shunned or even alienated completely. In reservation English, families are said to "own ," "sponsor," or "put on" events that have become part of both family and tribal tradition. In a sense, families are associated not only with places in reservation social space but with "times" as well.

As described in chapter 10, the formerly age-structured and life developmental definitions of personhood and channels for relations between persons have been appropriated to affirm difference rather than to reproduce tribal unity. Families and circles have appropriated traditional forms of cultural expression and social control to define family boundaries. Social events in the community, for example, are differentiated according to family and group. Families define themselves by and come together for the activities they sponsor or participate in, such as sports, powwows, cultural education, bingo, art, music, and so on.

In the past thirty years, families have competed with one another more intensely to gain or maintain ownership of or access to tribal committees, school organizations, culture programs, boards, economic development programs, and political leadership positions. A system of age hierarchy, which once prevented the privileging of family ties in public, tribal contexts, has given way to more powerful kinship bonds in many areas of life. Elders used to select members for important tribal positions in order to avoid family control. Given the reality that family bonds are as strong as ever, if not stronger, an individual or a nuclear family must often put family first, for it defines one's place and purpose in life more than the now somewhat distant "tribe" does. In the past, age-structured relations ordered all social space and time. Today, social relations are patterned more by differentiation based on family placement. Residence, the daily cycle, ways of speaking, cultural expressions, and social interaction now determine bonds within and differences between families more than the age structure does. One's individual life trajectory is today more a matter of family cooperation and access to resources, as well as family-sponsored life transition rituals. Political leadership, economic resources, jobs, inheritance of ritual leadership, and ceremonial participation all depend on the family and its connections to organizations and resources in the tribe or even to the non-Indian world beyond. Accordingly, young people mature today in a highly fractionalized world, in which the most consistent identity is generated from within the family.

In early reservation history, the imposition of Euro-American models of inheritance and classification supplied the materials for a changed but persisting family identity. Assimilation was intended to promote the isolation of nuclear families, but the Arapaho people appropriated the Euro-American structures to sustain extended kin relations. Allotment, for example, continues to identify extended families' places and properties on the reservation. Within Lower and Upper Arapaho are "places" for extended families, generally on or near lands allotted to their ancestors two or three generations ago. Thus, allotment contributed a sedentary and historical relationship between family identity and land. Extended-family members try to live near one another, and if they cannot, they continue to identify themselves otherwise with a family area. Similarly, Euro-American family surnames, created by the government agency in the early 1900s, supply the symbolic association between family and land that was once provided by the founding ancestor who had that name. As one travels through the Arapaho communities, one finds each area associated with a particular family name, identity, history, and tradition. It is in these places that Arapaho people feel at home and activate their social lives in relation to the larger world.

Nonetheless, there have been considerable changes over the past generation in the local sociocultural landscape. When I first arrived in the Northern Arapaho community on the Wind River Reservation in 1988, I found that there was no single social center through which all tribal members moved each day. Whereas once the camps of tents or cabins were oriented to the rivers, today social life and homes are shaped by roads and mobility on them. Much of the daily cycle today is thus spent traveling from one specialized social space to another, then home again in the evening. As elders observe, life has become faster, so that people seem to be on the go all the time and thus less likely to stop and visit one another.

Since the 1960s Arapaho housing has shifted to modern ranch-style homes either concentrated in a housing area or dispersed on homesite leases or individually owned trust lands near or along the various roads. There are four main housing projects, including Mill Creek and Ethete housing in the Upper Arapaho district and Great Plains and Beaver Creek housing in the Lower Arapaho area. Because the housing areas are associated with greater social tension, crime, and other contemporary social problems, most Arapaho families prefer living close to their own extended families, away from the more concentrated housing areas. But for families that have no allotted lands or other housing sites available, the housing areas offer the only option to stay in the community rather than move to the non-Indian towns nearby. When extended families can form clustered homes within the housing areas, they tend to remain there. Like other aspects of Euro-American-imposed social space, the housing projects had no logic in terms of Arapaho family and kinship structure. In recent years, federal agents and tribal housing administrators have finally understood this and have shifted to a policy favoring dispersed home sites.

Family, factional, and district boundaries also now differentiate the social space within social events. At General Council meetings, for example, families sit together and roughly in the same relative position from meeting to meeting. In some social contexts, Lower and Upper Arapahos sit apart from each other. There are similar seating patterns at powwows and other social events. At any social gathering, one first looks for and then sits with one's own family, in one's "place." The order is thus quite different from that of the past, when social space was differentiated by gender and age (Joe Goggles).

Most of the boundaries, along with the tensions and conflicts they generate in tribal politics today, derive from competition over the scarce resources controlled and distributed by centralized administrative structures, either within the tribe or in external bureaucratic organizations. The political economy has become increasingly differentiated by competing claims of ownership over resources ultimately situated within structures ordered by or modeled on Euro-American institutions. When threatened with losses resulting from or advancing toward gains within tribal or non-Indian organizations, one first draws on support from one's family. Claims to such centralized forms of ownership tend to militate against the modes of interfamilial cooperation and exchange predominant in the pre- and early reservation contexts.

One factor that contributes to interfamilial competition is the shift of the reservation economy from an agrarian subsistence base to a wage labor–and money-based system of exchange. From the 1880s, when the first gardens and farms were established on prominent leaders' lands, until the end of what could be called the agrarian period in Arapaho history after the 1940s (Fowler 1982:81–83), subsistence depended on redistribution, exchange, and cooperation between families. Today, money and other resources are redistributed not so much through family heads or leaders as "persons," as through a state-type bureaucratic system of positions (non-persons). At one time redistributive feasts and giveaways did serve to equalize surplus resources across family boundaries. Today, feasts and giveaways symbolize divisions between families but have only a nominal subsistence role. At one time most of the objects exchanged had real use value but also real horizontal exchange value to maintain interfamilial bonds. The present system centralizes value in money, which is less "visible" in the social world. It is thus subject to less traditional scrutiny and economic leveling pressures. Money has become the medium for interfamilial competition and factionalism as groups compete for access to the scarce resources distributed through agencies, offices, committees, and schools. The competition for money, jobs, and other resources has, in turn, intensified the social and cultural stratification among families. Families with greater resources are able to perform "culture" more elaborately, as in giveaways, powwow outfits, and feasts. Privately, some younger adults express regret and even resentment that they cannot afford to participate in or sponsor certain tribal ceremonies.

It is thus important for extended families to maintain a conspicuous cultural presence in the public world in order to generate support and recognition from the wider circle. Simply stated, public cultural expressions about the boundaries between families, circles, and factions now compete with the symbolic forms that unite the tribe. On the surface of things, though, each family- or faction-based cultural expression identifies itself with tribal tradition. Therefore, Arapaho cultural identity has become in part a matter of making distinctions, officialized as tradition, between groups. Certainly there are shared "symbols and meanings," but they have gradually become compartmentalized by families and circles.

Accordingly, an Arapaho person's life today takes place primarily in the small spaces of classrooms, a ranch-style house, offices, stores, and automobiles. The typical day for most Arapahos involves staying at home or traveling to dispersed social spaces for school, college, work, shopping, meetings, health care, or other specialized functions. The dispersed, specialized spaces imposed by Euro-American society have contributed a pace and rhythm of scheduling to the Arapaho world. Large collective social events, though still significant, are rare and seasonal and at most involve only a fraction of the tribe. There are occasional events (e.g., feasts, powwows, basketball games, and ceremonies) that draw wide participation, but generally only a small portion of the Northern Arapaho tribe attends. Attendance at the seasonal General Council meetings for all adult Arapahos rarely exceeds three hundred—less than 10 percent of the tribal members eligible to attend (Statistical List 1988).

Initially in my research I struggled to either find a "place" at the center from which to observe or, instead, to float at a distance from all the smaller social places. As time went on, my experiences became confined more and more to smaller places, though my engagement in larger social activities and my understanding increased as time went on. It is wrongheaded to assume, as I did at the outset, that the bird's-eye view of the detached, outside observer and a hurried gathering of data from dispersed sources is the best way to learn more. No ethnographic observer can achieve a sense of sociocultural totality through a panoramic view or by simply moving quickly from one person or group to another. As I spent more time at Wind River, I gradually realized that each family and group has its own place and perspective but that I would learn nothing without sitting down in such spaces and taking the perspectives available in them.

The specialization of social space-time combined with the accentuation of family boundaries is now a strong centripetal force pulling members inward to smaller social spaces. It is those spaces where personal and cultural continuity now begins and ends. And there Arapaho people find a sense of belonging, which continues to maintain their difference from the "white world" beyond, despite the proliferation of "white men's ways." Concomitantly, non-Indian society continues to keep a real social distance from those Arapaho places.

2
The Approach

Life Movement, Knowledge, and Personhood

The foundation of this book is a cultural analysis of the Northern Arapaho sociocultural system, focusing on and interconnecting three core dimensions, referred to in this work as knowledge, personhood, and life movement. The system was generalized prior to the reservation context, but at present it persists in specific spaces and times of Northern Arapaho life. A second focus of the book is the Euro-American personal relations, knowledge, and life-cyclical model that have been imposed on Northern Arapaho life throughout the reservation period (1878–present). The aim is to understand sociocultural change in terms of (1) the contradictions between the two systems of knowledge, relations, and life trajectory and (2) the contradictions inherent in the Euro-American forms. My third objective is to understand some of the effects of those contradictions and the Arapaho strategies for controlling them.

Fundamental to all these concerns is an understanding of a distinct Arapaho "theory of practice" that embodies the concepts of knowledge, personhood, and life movement. The strategy here follows Munn's sense of symbolic meaning:

> I understand meaning as a cover term for the relational nexus that enters into any given sociocultural form or practice (of whatever order of complexity) and defines that practice. The anthropological analysis of cultural meaning requires explication of cultural forms—a working through or unfolding of these culturally specific definitions and connectivities in order to disclose both the relational nature of the forms and the significance that derives from this relationality. [1986:6–7]

Such an approach fits especially well with Arapaho practice and meaning, which are directed to and generated by relational rather than substantive forms. The Arapaho theory of practice aims to construct coherence, order, and structure anew in ongoing practices rather than to replicate or represent models existing prior to action. Practice is thus both the locus for connectivities within a specific sociocultural system and the generative source of meaning. It is also through practice that linguistic, mythical, ritual, and artistic forms converge in a nexus of multiple meanings and functions.

The explication here therefore eschews the tendency to impose categories and relations among them from a footing entirely in Euro-American language and culture. Though interpretive concepts need to be formulated, they must be built up from understanding founded on indigenous meanings in order to avoid what Hallowell terms "categorical abstractions derived from Western thought" (1960:359). It is necessary, then, to begin any cultural analysis with at least an explication of the relevant indigenous categories in multiple relations, functions, and modes of cultural expression.

One of the difficulties with a phenomenological approach to categories is the tendency to construct a generalized or generic worldview without a position in real space and time. As anthropologists have gradually realized, "the map is not the territory" (Bateson 1972:449). Within the territory, perspectives are relative to positions in space and time. For example, in Northern Arapaho life movement, perspective, meaning, and practice are relative to position in the life trajectory, such that the grand, total view of the cosmos, reified by worldview approaches, was accessible only to those in the most senior age groups.

Younger people learn the appropriate practices before they learn the supporting conscious beliefs. In Arapaho life movement, practice thus precedes meaning. In the early days of life, as elder Arapahos today emphasize, children were taught to do things before they learned the reasons why they should do them. Eurocentric life-cyclical space-time concepts predispose toward approaches that schedule the acquisition of the cultural model of symbols and meanings before action, so that ideally children are taught first why and then how they are to do things. The placement of consciousness and meaning before action is embedded in Euro-American cultural constructions of time that order the person as self-consciousness first and as actor second.

Following Hallowell's approach to Ojibwa ontology, I first define the categories for persons and interpersonal relations that are at the foundation of Arapaho knowledge and life movement (see chapter 3). In the Ojibwa and Arapaho systems, symbolic meaning is generated in practices for initiating, maintaining, or transforming relations among "persons." As a point of departure for understanding cultural connectivities in the Arapaho theory of practice, I define four focal dimensions of interpersonal relations: 'pity' (*hoowouuno-*), 'respect' (*neneetee-*), 'quietness' (*teneiito(o)n/y-*), and 'craziness' (*hohookee-*).

The analysis of those concepts and the relations among them draws together evidence from linguistic usage, ethnosemantics, mythological contexts, kinship structure, ritual, and everyday social practices. Upon that groundwork for understanding Arapaho social relations, the symbolic, practical meanings of life movement and knowledge can then be explicated.

The concepts of knowledge and life movement replace static concepts that presume a synoptic view or an a priori system. In another way, life movement and knowledge are built on the ethnosemantics of Arapaho language, myth, and ritual. They are thus midrange concepts that provide connectivity between an outside view and indigenous meanings and practices. Complementing those advantages, the concepts used here are open to the active role of humans in constituting knowledge and life movement. Human symbolic practices construct and reproduce not only meanings and structures but also the tempo, phasing, and direction of knowledge transmission and movement through the life cycle.

In the Arapaho context, ritual practice based on proper knowledge generates life movement. Furthermore, Arapaho life transition rituals activated and reproduced an age hierarchy in each moment of time throughout the life trajectory. The Arapaho age-grade system was similar to but distinctive from that of the Blackfeet, the Mandans, the Hidatsas, and the Gros Ventres. The sequence of men's ceremonial lodges functioned to mark life transitions, allocate political roles, and maintain an age-ranked system of access to knowledge and ritual agency for life movement itself. Socioculturally constructed age distinctions and knowledge exchange were durable strategies for structuring inter–kin group relations, modes of exchange, political leadership roles, cultural identity, definitions of personhood, and social space-time. It is essential, therefore, not to present age-grade systems as only an isolated, formal structure that existed prior to social practices.

Until now there has been no attempt at a systematic cultural analysis of the Arapaho age-grade system as a total system interconnected with the overall life trajectory. Mooney (1896), Kroeber (1902, 1904, 1907), Hilger (1952), Dorsey (1903), and Dorsey and Warden (1905) offer extensive descriptive material and specific cultural connections but little integrative analysis. Lowie (1916) provides a rich comparative study of graded and nongraded societies in the Plains area but only thin "trait" descriptions of individual systems. Fowler (1982) proceeds from age structure as a given and then confines it in her rich ethnohistorical study to political and ceremonial authority for intermediation with non-Arapaho peoples. None of those studies explicates Arapaho age ranking and life movement as a total sociocultural system.

The inclination of comparative approaches to Plains age-grade systems

(Bernardi 1985; Stewart 1977) is to isolate age structure from the wider sociocultural context and then define internal, formal properties, broad social functions, or cultural traits. Stewart's analysis is concerned with the internal logic by which different types of age-grade structures work to move age sets through and construct relations among different age grades. Cultural content and practices are thus relegated to a residual interest. Bernardi is more interested in the social functions of age-grade systems for the social totality. Both Bernardi and Stewart situate age-grade systems as structures that are prior to consciousness and social practice. Ritual practice is considered to merely reproduce objective structures, social relations, and cultural content. This structural-functionalist approach, initiated by Radcliffe-Brown (1929:21), removes time and real social space from age-grade systems. In doing so it overlooks the exchange relations, ritual agency, and knowledge that are structured by and constitute meaningful social practices. By neutralizing time, such an approach estranges rank from practice. In the Arapaho system, senior persons controlled the tempo and spatial boundaries of knowledge transmission and life transition. Furthermore, it is not just the age set itself and the senior agents for transition that are involved. All age groups and relatives and all variations of "persons," extending into the other-than-human realm, are included in ritual processes for life movement and knowledge transmission.

Bourdieu identifies two key concerns for age structure: (1) age distinctions both unify and differentiate through practices, and, (2) the power to make distinctions and the privilege of doing so are unequally distributed:

> The mythico-ritual categories cut up the age continuum into discontinuous segments, constituted not biologically (like physical signs of aging) but socially, and marked by the symbolism of cosmetics and clothing, decorations, ornaments, and emblems, the tokens which express and underlie the representations of the uses of the body that are legitimately associated with each socially defined age, and also those which are ruled out because they would have the effect of disrupting the system of oppositions between the generations. Social representations of the different ages of life, and of the properties attached by definition to them, express, in their own logic, the power relations between age-classes, helping to reproduce at once the union and the division of those classes by means of temporal divisions tending to produce both continuity and rupture. [Bourdieu 1977:165]

One premise that I adopt here, then, is that the life trajectory and knowledge are socially and culturally constituted, not "given" in universal biological or psychological processes. Another central point is that cultural content defines distinctions in and through practice as much as objective "social structures" do. An age-grade system in particular both unifies and divides the life continuum and thus unifies and ranks age groups. Age is therefore also a system for ongoing unequal distribution of value and power. Each Arapaho life transition ritual or age-grade lodge divides an age set apart from the others while at the same time activating the authority and agency of all senior groups to effect unity among the separate age groups. Such a hierarchy, according to Bourdieu, "serves the interests of those occupying the dominant position in the social structure" (1977:165). What Bourdieu's work has done more than anything else is to relativize the content of "interests" to include not just one field or domain preconfigured by some just-so universal need, utilitarian end, or amorphously defined value orientation. Simply put, interests themselves and the content of "capital" are socioculturally constructed in practice.

In the Arapaho case, it is a difference of power in the form of knowledge for generating or disrupting life movement. Given this, the sense of "interests" must be qualified for the Arapaho context. Advancing age status can be seen at another level as increased "costs " and decreasing age-group or self-interests. Senior status requires, among the Arapahos, greater sacrifice, redistributive obligations, and threats to life movement. What did accumulate was knowledge, respect, and the power to direct others. It is not that elders accumulated material wealth or political influence, but rather, that they gained knowledge and thus the power for life movement itself, that is, control over the ordering of space and movement in time. It was not control of production or material goods but of movement in sociocultural space and time.

In the Arapaho system, movement through life is thus not motivated by biological or psychological forces but is generated by humans through their relation with other-than-human forces or beings. Arapaho life movement occurs through proper ritual practices and interpersonal relationships, or "doing things in a good/correct way," for which elders have the greatest knowledge and exercise ultimate responsibility. As in many North American Indian contexts, the primary aim of Arapaho rituals is to promote the health and long life of individuals, families, and the tribe.

The aim of all ritual practice is to do things in "a good way," to borrow from contemporary reservation English, or, in Arapaho, *nee'eestoonoo* 'I am doing it right or correctly' (*nee'ees-* 'correct'/*-too-* 'do'/ *-noo* first person singular actor). Movement through life requires proper actions, which in turn depend on knowledge. Knowledge allows a person and the collective to "do things in a good/correct way." Appropriate ritual action also requires a sequence of exchanges with kin, persons in the age hierarchy, and other-than-human persons. Exchange was not only between juniors and seniors in the age hierarchy; it involved a wider set of relations with other-than-human persons above or beyond the camp circle. When exchanges are done correctly and the proper relations among persons are activated, long life follows for one's family, band, and tribe.

The movement itself is socioculturally constituted, hence the term *life movement*. The ultimate Arapaho concern is to generate life, to live to old age, enjoy health, and have various blessings. Individuals, though, must make sacrifices, must give of their own life to promote the life movement of others. Doing that takes the form of vows to make ritual offerings or sacrifices in order to effect life movement for family members and the tribe as a whole. Like knowledge, life movement itself is transmitted from generation to generation.

The focal concept of *life movement* is thus a more dynamic term than others, such as *life cycle, human development,* or *socialization,* which tend to remove the life trajectory from ongoing practices. Further, the rhythms and phasing of the life trajectory are constituted by human actors differently in each sociocultural system. Each culture's life trajectory has a different shape.

In discussing life transitions, Van Gennep was one of the first to formulate a simple but necessary distinction: "It is appropriate to distinguish between physical puberty and social puberty, just as we distinguish between physical kinship (consanguinity) and social kinship, between physical maturity and social maturity (majority)" (1960:68). Van Gennep thus advances ritual to an active status in dividing the life cycle into stages. It is not just that rites of passage recognize or express changes generated elsewhere in the sociocultural system; they produce and reproduce the meanings of those changes themselves. Van Gennep and others have failed to put forward, though, what the source is for the shape and the phases of life trajectories reproduced through ritual practices.

Social practices construct the stages of the life cycle and passage through them, but only with the assistance, as Van Gennep (1960) notes, of what he calls "supernatural" forces or beings. Following that insight, life transition (what I call life movement), requires supernatural influence or, borrowing Hallowell's term from the related Ojibwas (1960) "other-than-human persons," including spiritual forms above or on the earth, as well as animals. As in other North American Indian contexts, the boundaries between human persons and other categories are always open to movement, exchange, metamorphosis, and appropriation. In Arapaho mythico-ritual life movement, the boundaries are open enough to allow exchanges of power and knowledge. Only in contexts of contradiction, where categorical boundaries become hardened, as in Euro-American space-time, does such borrowing become at once reflective and deliberate.

Life movement, as used here, is not merely a cognitive model of space and time but a generative source for the organization of interpersonal and intergroup relations. To borrow from Bourdieu, age structure was part of the process of Arapaho "collective rhythms" such that the "temporal forms or the spatial structures structure not only the group's representation of the world but the group itself" (1977:163). For example, each stage, age group, or grade was associated with a particular space and function in the camp, the band, and the tribe. Each was also characterized by a different definition of personhood, type of motion, and ways of speaking.

Life movement is treated here as what Munn calls "temporalization," defined as the process through which actors are not just "in time" but are "constructing it and their own time in the particular kinds of relations between themselves (and their purposes) and the temporal reference points (which are also spatial forms)" (1992:104). As a temporal system, following Bourdieu, life movement is inscribed in "practices defined by the fact that their temporal structure, direction, and rhythm are constitutive of their meaning" (1977:9). Arapaho ritual practice does not just happen in a preordered time and space; it also constitutes movement in time for self, age groups, family, tribe, and the world. Life movement is a chronotype, following the definition offered by Bender and Wellbury, in that "time is not given but fabricated in ongoing process constantly being made and remade at multiple individual, social, and cultural levels" (1991:4). Further, to Hugh-Jones (1979), in all cultures the shape of the life cycle is transposed through practice from other levels of space and time, including mythico-ritual, seasonal, and even daily time. "Life time" is thus synchronized with other forms of time that vary both in form and in the relations among them from one culture to another. Rather than constituting continuity and meaning through history, genealogy, rational scheduling, or some other Euro-American chronotype, Arapaho culture has temporalized primarily through what is referred to here as life movement, which is the locus for activating relations to other levels of time and space.

It is necessary, then, to examine Arapaho life movement as a system with distinctive dimensions for constituting "life time." For instance, for the Arapahos life movement was more protracted and channeled than for other North American Indian cultures in general. Fasting was reserved for men and occasionally women in their thirties and forties, as opposed to younger men in other American Indian societies (Hilger 1952:128–29). Political leadership was restricted to men who were in their fifties and had reached the third stage of life (Fowler 1982). Even today, Arapahos do not consider one an adult until at least age forty. Elders were in control of the life movement of those in all lower stages and younger age societies. Particular types of knowledge were accessible at each stage of life, and that access was controlled through the age hierarchy. The deepest enduring cultural "imprints" did not concentrate only in the early stages of life; rather, one came closer to the center of Arapaho culture with advancing life movement and thus did not acquire the most comprehensive mythico-ritual knowledge or worldview until old age.

Different sociocultural systems privilege different meanings and allow access to them at different stages of life. As is clear from Arapaho assumptions that have some lingering power today, childhood is not seen as the most determinative period in a person's life. In the past century, the imposed Western chronotype for the life cycle has privileged childhood and adolescence as the formative stages for all subsequent development. Similarly, many anthropological approaches to cultural systems assume rather than prove that culture is inscribed in the early stages of life. Within the Arapaho life trajectory, events or experiences of one stage do not necessarily irreversibly configure subsequent life development. Though families ensure that a child's life is straight and healthy, they do not do so because of the assumption that early experiences irreversibly define a child's "self." One can act "crazy" in early life and still become a respected political or ceremonial leader in old age if the proper steps are taken to "straighten out." In traditional Arapaho life movement, equally great and even greater formative things happen very late in life from a Euro-American perspective.

To cite another bias, North American ethnography has, historically, suffered from the tendency to elaborate cultural models built up from the "elder's-eye view." That is especially conspicuous in early American ethnography, from which much of the evidence about Arapaho age grades and women's rituals is drawn. A sleight-of-hand is performed by which the totalized cultural model constructed from only one age group's orientation or from those in possession of the most "knowledge" is generalized as a shared cultural configuration. Arapaho life movement recognizes that different knowledge is relevant for different life stages but not that one is more true or authentic than the others.

Such relativity calls forth the need for a different and temporalized sense of totality in cultural analysis. Another of Van Gennep's contributions was to understand rites of passage not in their particularity "but in their essential significance and their relative positions within ceremonial wholes—that is, their order" (1960:191). Pursuing that understanding, the effort here is to present the Arapaho life transitions as interrelated and as phases of a total ritual system. Plains age-grade systems, for example, have never been considered as part of a total system that also includes childhood rituals and women's ceremonies.

Knowledge is defined dynamically here as that segment of culture that moves through a system of exchange, age-structured relations, definitions of personhood, and interpersonal values. Because of that role in exchange, practice, and personal relations, the term *knowledge* is selected over the broader term *culture*, or correlates such as *shared symbols and meanings*, *worldview*, or *cultural system*. According to Fredrik Barth, "the image of culture as knowledge abstracts it less and points to people's engagement with the world, through action. It alerts us to interchange and to flux" (1995:66). Thus knowledge is more dynamic, temporalized, transitive, open, and variable than is culture in a totalized definition. In Arapaho history, myth, and ritual practice, knowledge is culture that is exchanged, enlivened, and empowered in real time. Arapaho knowledge is never a total or closed system, for beyond what can be known there are always mysterious elements and forces, which persons can appropriate for life movement or suffer as life-negating power. Knowledge is not to be understood, then, as a stock of information, cognitive structure, closed rationality or symbolic system passed on automatically from generation to generation. It is necessary to overcome the dichotomy that the formal, directed exchange of knowledge and the pursuit of more knowledge are unique to literate societies, whereas nonliterate systems are assumed to transmit knowledge automatically, informally, and redundantly across time.

In Arapaho mythology, the acquisition of knowledge initiated the movement of time and the ordering of relations between different types of persons. Knowledge and its uses are thus inextricable from the values of pity, respect, quietness, craziness, and others. All movement in time, on the daily, seasonal, life-cyclical, and cosmic levels, was generated by knowledge. In turn, proper knowledge sustains life movement in time. In the beginning the Arapaho tribe was placed not only in the middle of space but also in the middle of time. As long as things are done appropriately, time in this epoch will continue. Thus, at the mythico-ritual foundation, Arapaho cultural identity is identified with knowledge and synchronized with the movement in time it allows. Proper knowledge for "doing things in a good/correct way" was acquired in mythical time (*heeteeniihi'* 'the time before this age') and maintains the life movement of self and others in the present and into the future.

Knowledge, then, is about appropriate ways of acting, not only in ritual contexts but also in the everyday lived world. For Northern Arapahos, knowledge is in and of practice, that is, in "doing things in a good/correct way," including the transmission of knowledge itself. The preparation stage preceding all ceremonies is perhaps more important than the actual performance. It is then that knowledge is transmitted from older to younger participants. All ceremonies are as much learning situations as performances. If the exchange of knowledge is done appropriately, life movement follows, not just for oneself but also for one's family and tribe. If mistakes are made out of lack of knowledge, then life-negating effects follow for oneself or one's family or tribe.

In the historical context, the relationship between Euro-American society and the Northern Arapaho people has always been a difference between and the negotiation of two systems of knowledge. The dominant society has used its knowledge, as much if not more than physical force, to exploit resources, acquire lands, establish boundaries, and reproduce its position of power over time. Though Western knowledge has idealized itself as rational and empirical, its fundamental contradiction is that it has been consistently contradictory toward and thus continually ignorant of local social and cultural realities. There are two types of contradictions, those internal to Euro-American knowledge and those generated by cultural differences from Arapaho knowledge. While Euro-Americans were imposing knowledge in literate, religious, or bureaucratic forms and practices, the Northern Arapaho people were adopting a set of strategies for redressing those forces. Rather than becoming disempowered, they have applied traditional ways of knowing and have invented new strategies as well to maintain the boundaries between non-Arapaho and Arapaho knowledge.

Contradictions

To provide a deeper understanding of historical changes at Wind River, I examine enduring contradictions in several areas of contact between the Northern Arapahos and Euro-American society. Beginning even before the Northern Arapahos were relocated on the Wind River Reservation in 1878, Euro-American society began to impose its own knowledge, definitions of persons, and associated life-cyclical model. That power has not been confined to nor concentrated in bounded persons, institutions, or local contexts alone but has been diffuse, insidious, imposed from a distance, and generally tacit. At the base of all Euro-American modes of dominance is an assumption of a superior knowledge, which veils historically particular policies behind an assumption of universality, historical acts of power behind "timeless" truth, and time-space organizing devices behind a veil of "objectivity." In reality, Euro-American forms of the person, the life trajectory, and knowledge seek to be rational and coherent, but they carry their own internal contradictions and in practice generate lived contradictions with other modes of knowing, ordering life, and defining persons. Simply put, Euro-American forms propose the illusion of rational self-consistency and empirically based practices but become, for indigenous communities, a hegemony of inconsistency, arbitrariness, and, in Arapaho terms, for non-sense, a type of craziness. Just as the industrial economy promises development but delivers underdevelopment, and as a democratic politic offers liberation but imposes control, Euro-American organizing forms advertise intellectual progress, objectivity, and practical efficiency but, in the lived experience of reservation communities, cultivate contradictions, chaos, and confusion. Within that general contradiction, Euro-American knowledge by and in itself generates power that it cannot know as lived contradictions and cannot resolve.

My aim is to identify those contradictions and some of their real conditions in Northern Arapaho society, past and present. That does not require a reification of the present as a pathological deviation from the past, such as acculturation studies often project (Elkin 1940; Gross 1949). Early acculturation studies posit all of the contradictions in the binary opposition of modern versus traditional culture placing the resistance to assimilation within traditional culture itself. Thus, "problems" are correlated with the dissynchrony between two cultures at different stages in a reified model of development. The real contradictions of reservation life emanate, however, from imposed Euro-American forms that do not term themselves assimilation but may be the most successful in achieving it. The contradictions are inherent to Euro-American society and history, not to indigenous sociocultural systems.

The explication of domination here refines Marxist theories of history in which, "to say that contradiction is a motive force is to say that it implies *real struggle, real confrontations, precisely located within the structure of a complex whole*; it is to say that the locus of confrontation may vary according to the relation of the contradictions in the structure of dominance in any given situation" (Althusser 1969:215–16). To extend that statement, the locus of contradiction may vary with the particular ethnic group or cultural context. Within the totality of Arapaho-Euro-American relations, the persistent contradiction has condensed around knowledge and space-time, including imposed life-cyclical models, personhood, and age-structured space.

Most of the history of Indian-white contact has been written at the superficial level of political events, intermediation, cultural difference, or chronology. Only a few scholars have delved into the deeper, persistent contradictions. Among those, Vine Deloria (1988, 1994) predominates because he writes from a unique, critical perspective that looks beyond the surface of historical flux to define contradictions in the totality of contact over Braudel's *longue durée*. It is also informed by a local understanding of the reality of contradictions in American Indian communities. Paradoxically, the total view is often accessible only to a local, indigenous perspective that has over the long term acquired beliefs and practices to know and respond to contradictions.

Without the local and total view of history, there is a tendency to leave explanation at a manifest level. As Gramsci observed of depthless historicism, "they forget that the thesis which asserts that men become conscious of fundamental conflicts on the terrain of ideologies is not psychological or moralistic in character, but structural and epistemological; and they form the habit of considering politics, and hence history, as the continuous *marche de dupes*, a competition in conjuring and sleight of hand" (1988:215). "Critical" forms of American Indian history stop at the exposure of conspiracy, swindling, scandal, tragedy, and open resistance. The same flat perspective has also been adopted for understanding modern tribal politics.

Of course I do not intend to encompass the contradictions in the totality of Indian-white contact, but rather to consider those that I discerned during my stay at Wind River and throughout my research in the literature. Moreover, it is necessary to move back into the enduring Arapaho practices and meanings, based in myth and history, to understand the deeper ground upon which Euro-American forms have been defined and resisted, often in less public ways. In short, the empowerment and resistance that the Arapaho people activated is not visible in Euro-American-based written history or ethnography.

Such an approach requires a local and critical perspective on accepted concepts. For example, it has never been the real purpose or the real effect of Euro-American institutions to "assimilate" or "acculturate" the Arapaho people, even though that was the manifest intent. Even as American Indian peoples have been encouraged to assimilate to a constructed, idealized model of Euro-American culture, Euro-Americans have distanced Arapaho society from, rather than integrating it into, Euro-American society. Assimilation is always accompanied by a seemingly permanent spatial distance and separation. When that contradiction is revealed, the Euro-American imposed forms can be seen to have operated to estrange rather than to assimilate. For example, the missionaries at St. Stephen's established their own bourgeois-adorned dining and living spaces, often with servants recruited from among the older school children, based on the premise that they should be models of white society for the Arapaho people to learn from. Simultaneously, Northern Arapahos have sought, since the beginning of the reservation period, to compartmentalize Arapaho and non-Indian knowledge, personhood, and life paths. Euro-Americans however, have continually resisted labeling their knowledge and life-cyclical model as "culture" by reifying them as universal, rational, and objective forms.

To achieve totality, it is also necessary to identify contradictions that have persisted from the past into the present. One enduring though often identified tendency of present and past ethnographic research, as well as of much that passes for ethnohistory, is to posit North American Indian cultures "in the past," either as pristine, ahistorical cultures or in historical events of contact left unrelated to the contemporary context. Contemporary communities are often placed in an "Other" space-time, removed from both past and present realities (see Fabian 1983). Critical ethnohistorical studies must draw connections between past and present beneath the surface breaks in eventful political history.

The Arapahos' concern about the "big change" occurring over the last thirty years is, I contend, based on an understanding of these contradictions; it is an expression of their desire to regain ownership of knowledge and the tempo and rhythms of their lives. The issues Arapaho people face today are not comprehensible in generic political terms, such as self-determination or sovereignty. They are also neither comprehensible nor resolvable entirely within the categories, strategies, and relationships imposed by Euro-American knowledge, history, and space-time.

More important, the Northern Arapaho tribe has never been completely disempowered or divested of knowledge with which to counteract the forces of Euro-American society. Northern Arapahos employ strategies every day, as they have in the past, to negotiate contradictions that they know all too well but, for the most part, the Euro-Americans know nothing about. The issues and concerns that real people living in reservation communities talk about and even struggle with on a daily basis are generally distant from an outside perspective. Ethnography of modern reservation communities, combining multiple bodies of evidence and time frames, can begin to dissolve some of that distance. As Beatrice Medicine (1987:165–66) suggests, there is still a tendency in anthropology to ignore the importance of cultural constructs in the contemporary context of reservation communities. Closeness to the context, though, requires neither video-like intrusion into the flow of everyday human life nor divulging the tantalizing scenes, gossip, and intrigue of personal or political struggles. I have tried to avoid all of those here. To come very close is not to tell all.

3
Arapaho Persons and Relations

Personhood

As in other North American Indian cultures, Arapaho knowledge and life movement take place in and through interpersonal relationships extending beyond the human realm. Hallowell's study of Ojibwa personhood recognizes this connection between social relations among persons and the Ojibwa correlate of life movement: "The entire psychological field in which they live and act is not only unified through their conception of the nature and role of 'persons' in their universe, but by sanctioned moral values which guide the relations of 'persons'. It is within this web of social relations that the individual strives for *pīmǎdǎzīwin*" (1960:386). The concept of *pīmǎdǎzīwin* is defined as "life in the fullest sense, life in the sense of longevity, health and freedom from misfortune" (1960:383). What is defined here as life movement and the Arapaho sense of *hiiteeni* examined in chapter 4 bears strong resemblance to that Ojibwa concept. To some extent it is a distinctly North American Indian value, though it is even more distinctive to cultures related as members of the Algonquian language family, including the Arapahos and the Ojibwas.

As a groundwork to understanding Arapaho knowledge and life movement, it is necessary to explicate practices for defining personhood and constituting social relations among persons. Both living and knowing require ongoing practices bounded by culturally constituted forms of personhood and practices for activating and sustaining interpersonal relations. Those same value dimensions define the motives for ritual practice, the affective orientation for exchange, and the unifying substance of the family, the tribe, and humanness.

Like the Ojibwa concepts, the Arapaho definition of personhood is thus relational and extends beyond human persons. One of the most difficult tasks of anthropology is to "translate" cultural concepts into terms that are often embedded in Western definitions of personhood. Hallowell reflects on this issue:

It may be argued, in fact, that a thorough going "objective" approach
to the study of cultures cannot be achieved solely by projecting upon
those cultures categorical abstractions derived from Western thought.
For, in a broad sense, they are a reflection of our cultural subjectivity.
A higher order of objectivity may be sought by adopting a perspective
that includes an analysis of the outlook of the people themselves as a
complementary procedure. It is in a world view perspective, too, that
we can likewise obtain the best insight into how cultures function as
wholes. [1960:359]

In this effort Hallowell shows that Ojibwa categories for persons make
fundamentally different distinctions, extend to a wider scope of beings, and
articulate different relations among categories of persons, animals, and sacred
beings.

In Arapaho and Ojibwa practices, personhood and social relations are
relative to the flux of time and, in particular, to the socioculturally constituted
trajectory of the life cycle. The ontogeny of the person is never entirely
preconfigured by biological or psychological universals, nor by enculturation
that ends in childhood. Rather than an enduring intellectual substance and
container of all moral value, as Mauss traces in the history of the modern
Western category of "person=self=consciousness" (1979:88), Arapaho
personhood categories pervading myth, language, art, ritual, and everyday
practices occur in shifting relations constituted by culturally specific morality,
life trajectory, age structure, kinship ties, modes of exchange, and ways of
knowing. In the historical context, the reservation era has brought the imposition
of Euro-American categories of personhood, carried along with other imposed
forms for the life trajectory and knowledge. Those Western structures have
imported their own internal contradictions as well as points of opposition with
the Arapaho forms and relations that are used in defining persons.

The starting point, then, is an analysis of Arapaho definitions of personhood
for both human and, to borrow Hallowell's term, "other-than-human persons,"
including sacred beings, spirit forms on earth, sacred objects, and animals. From
this foundation I move to an explication of Arapaho relational values for
generating life and knowledge, translated as pity, respect, quietness, and
craziness. Each concept is traced from its mythico-ritual and linguistic contexts
to its place in traditional life movement, and I conclude with observations about
contradictions—both contradictions between the Arapaho and the Euro-
American concepts and practices that relate to defining persons and
contradictions within the Euro-American system. Refracting backward from the

present, changes in personal relations inform the ways that elders and others talk about changes in age structure as well as the wider Arapaho way of life. To some extent, these dimensions have endured to the present, although in narrower spaces and times within a more differentiated and fractionalized social world. The intended end point is to understand the reality and surviving force of these concepts in contemporary Northern Arapaho practices.

Human and Other-than-Human Persons

In Arapaho, the broadest category for a person is *hinenitee*. This stem combines with other forms, including what Kroeber (1916:86) offers as θawaθ-inenitä^n (*3owo3nenitee*) 'real person' or 'human being', contrasting with *ceyotowunenitee* 'false, untrue person or spirit'. The former refers to an 'Indian' of any tribe and literally means 'rising person' or 'upright person', since the *3owo3ii-* form denotes 'rising from a prone position', as in getting up in the morning. In the Arapaho Star Husband myth called "The Porcupine and the Woman Who Climbed to the Sky" (Dorsey and Kroeber 1903:321–40), the woman who marries Moon/porcupine is the first rising person and thus the first Indian. In the alternation of time established in the beginning, real persons occupy the daytime, and untrue persons tend to inhabit the night.

Indian people, then, are "real persons," contrasted with non-Indians or Euro-Americans, who are *nih'oo3ou'u*. In one version of Arapaho cosmogony, after the creator made Indians and whites, he turned to the former and "he called them çawaçnenitän [*3owo3neniteen*], 'rising' people [*-iteen* 'tribe' or 'people'], because after he laid them on the ground at night they got up in the morning" (Dorsey and Kroeber 1903:6). Another explanation offered by Arnold Headley is that human bodies are upright, but other animals have horizontal bodies and that is what makes the difference. Standing upright thus separated human persons from untrue persons and animals. In mythical time, all beings were human persons, but, the stories say, some became different tribes, whites, animals, and other-than-human persons. In the same story in which humans became upright, for example, whites were set apart from *3owo3neniteeno'*, who had the original language, red paint, and their own material culture and knowledge (Dorsey and Kroeber 1903:6). Simultaneous with this original mythic unity of humankind and the subsequent differentiation from other peoples, moral values were set in motion for proper relations among persons. That original unity is also the basis for the ongoing possibility of interpersonal relations with other-than-human persons.

Other-than-human persons living on earth are referred to as tcäyatawunenita[n] (*ceyotowunenitee*) (Kroeber 1907:283). According to Dorsey's study of the Southern Arapaho Offerings Lodge, the false people are supernatural beings, or lesser gods living on earth, against whom humans must protect themselves (1903:41). The term combines *ce(e)yotow/b-* 'false' in the sense of artificial with *(h)inenitee* 'person'. The modifier *ce(e)yotow-* Salzmann (1983:92) lists for *ceeyotobee' nuhu'oo3itoo* 'this story is false' and *ceyotowbeicito* 'false teeth'. Such persons as *ceyotowunenitee* are 'false' because of their ability to appear on earth transformed into human persons, animals, or natural forms.

As in other North American Indian mythological traditions, animals too can metamorphose into human persons or false persons. In the beginning buffalo were human beings. Indeed, metamorphosis is the main action trope of Arapaho and other American Indian oral·literature. In the Arapaho language, the inceptive, 'becoming' verb form is used for metamorphosis, such as *bih'ihiinoo'oot* 'she became a deer' from the Arapaho version of the Deer Woman story (see Kroeber 1916:125–26) (Eva C'Hair and Joe Goggles explained this word to me). Anything in the process of transformation or changing states can be described using the *-oo'oo-* aspectual feature, placed intermediately between the verb stem and the person suffix at the end of the construction. In many stories the metamorphosis is not even indicated. Suddenly, between one passage and a subsequent one, an animal becomes a person or vice versa. It is that unfixed capacity of untrue persons that defines them. They are not defined metaphorically but rather by the capacity for metamorphosis, which is tied to the ability to give or take away life movement from human persons. Humans can appear as animals, animals as humans, and untrue persons as either human or animal. All the boundaries between animal, human, and other-than-human are unpredictable and open to metamorphosis.

In mythical time, the beings above (not said of false persons) and animal persons gave knowledge to human persons. Untrue persons can transform into animals, such as Moon, who appears to the woman in the Star Husband myth as a porcupine. Likewise, some other-than-human persons were once human beings in myth or in a former life. The boundaries between categories of animal, human, the beings above, and untrue persons are thus not fixed. In Arapaho myth, dreams, and everyday experience, beings move in and out of these categories. As they do, human persons experience difficulties or acquire knowledge about the world for future practices. The power for metamorphosis is the generative source of life movement. With knowledge and right practices, relations can be maintained with animals and other-than-human persons so that the negative effects of this transformative power can be avoided and the positive effects appropriated for human life movement.

The category of untrue or false persons includes beings who reside on earth and appear as or act like humans, such as ghosts (*biiteino'*), spirit-shadows (*betee3oono'*), and spirits (*cei3wooono'*). As liminal beings they share certain affinities with both the most powerful beings, listed below, and human persons. A *biitei* is the ghost of a deceased person that lingers around the home or the area where it once lived. Generally ghosts are not harmful, though they can be mischievous. It is only the *3iikonehii* 'skeleton', as a remnant of a deceased person, that can be life threatening. A spirit-shadow (*betee3oo*) is the animating spirit of a sacred or powerful object, which needs to be cared for in order to keep the object active. It is thus the focal point for the need to treat such objects properly based on appropriate knowledge. The *cei3woono'* are manifested as spirit stones that enter people's bodies, make them sick, and must be removed through curing practices.

There are also other beings on earth, such as 'little people' (*heecesiiteihiiho'*), who live in the mountains but occasionally come down to encounter humans. Adults used to tell children that if they slept too late, they would miss seeing the little people who come very early in the morning. Like all other-than-human persons, the little people are morally ambivalent, neither wholly good nor wholly bad. On the dangerous side, they eat humans and steal children. In their life-giving ability, the little people can give knowledge as medicine (*beetee*) to human beings through either fasts or visitations.

For the most powerful category of other-than-human persons, the greatest cautions and respect are required, for such beings have the greatest power to disrupt or generate life for humans. This category of persons or so-called supernatural beings is similar to Hallowell's other-than-human category for Ojibwa, *ätíso'kanak* (1960:365), which includes the sun, the four winds, thunder, and others recognized as animate in grammatical gender and as persons in ethnosemantic terms. Kroeber states that these powerful Arapaho other-than-human persons in the above, the beyond, or the earth were referred to in hierarchical order: "The beings addressed in certain prayers are, in order, first our father, second the sun, third hiiteni [the Four Old Men], fourth hitaxusa[n] or last child, equivalent to hiintcäbiit, 'water-monster or owner of water'), fifth the thunder, sixth the whirlwind, and seventh, the earth" (1907:313). In modern orthography, the principal beings are Our Father *(heisonoonin)*, Sun (*hiisiis*), Moon (*biikousiis* 'night sun'), the Four Old Men (*hiiteeni*), Whirlwind Woman (*neyoooxetusei*), Water Monster (*hiincebiit*), Earth (*biito'oowu'*), Thunderbird (*boh'ooo*), and Morning Star (*nookoox* 'cross'). All are considered "owners" in much the same way that human "keepers" of sacred objects are central in Northern Algonquian traditions. According to Dorsey (1903:41), as already mentioned, the false persons of the earth come last in the hierarchical order.

Each being is associated with a particular life energy, shape of motion, and place in the cosmos. During the beginning time, each being was once earthly and humanlike in form but eventually was placed in its present and permanent place or path of movement. *Heisonoonin* is the father of all persons and the creator, who encompasses all other powers and resides in the above (*hihcebe '*), highest and most distant from humans, where he, unlike the others, does not move. Though in the ethnographic evidence there is some speculation of Christian influence, the term *our father* as a form of address definitely predates the missions, since it is documented by Cooper (1934) for the Northern Algonquian groups, which, as also suggested here, share many affinities with the Arapahos. According to a Cree man who Cooper interviewed, "the Supreme being was addressed as *Notawinan* (Cree: 'Our Father') or as *Nus* (Otchipwe: 'My Father')" (1934:19).

The highest and most distant, "unmoved" or "standing" being was referred to indirectly in prayer as *heisonoonin*. Other beings can either move about or live on the earthly plane. Sun and Moon are brothers who travel separately across the sky in their east-west linear motion and day-night alternation on the road (*bo 'oo*) drawn by the Milky Way. The Four Old Men were once human keepers of the Arapaho Sacred Pipe but now sit on respective buttes at the four directions, where they send breath-life (winds) to humans and protect the earth on its borders. *Hiincebiit* 'Water Monster' lives in rivers and springs where he can drown people crossing those waters. He is thus associated with certain animal-like characteristics and the power to pull humans down. Thunderbird, the warrior being, also protects the periphery of the earth, shoots lightning from his blinking eyes, and battles Water Monster. Along with thunder, he is associated with the eagle, electricity, and rapid movements, as needed by young warriors. Whirlwind Woman's spiraling and occasionally stopping motion created women's quillwork designs and expanded the earth to its present size in mythical time. Earth is at the center, both horizontally and vertically, and is the substance of all life that radiates outward from the tipi, the camp, and the Arapaho people. She thus parallels the motion associated with women in Arapaho life movement.

The order of reference in the prayer from Kroeber moves roughly from above to the four directions, to beings residing on or near the surface, and finally to the center and below. All of these powerful other-than-human persons can be life giving or life negating, depending on the appropriateness of the relations humans establish with them through ritual practices. The Four Old Men bring the breath of life to all living things from their position in the four directions, but *neyoooxetusei* 'Whirlwind Woman' can take that breath away. *Hiincebiit* can ensure long life when he receives offerings or can take that life away by drowning people. Human persons must therefore have the proper knowledge for "doing things in a good/correct way" in relations with other-than-human persons in order to generate life movement. Mistakes (*cee3toot*) made because of inadequate knowledge can lead to illness or other misfortune for oneself or one's family.

What all persons have to varying degrees is a power called *beetee*, translated variously as 'medicine', 'sacredness', or 'great mystery'. Paralleling the life power in other American Indian cultures, and cognate with the Northern Algonquian *manitu*, *beetee* is a power that humans, animals, and other-than-human persons can use to generate or disrupt life movement. The term *beetee* can thus refer to anything powerful or uncanny. Fowler uses the term to refer to the "Great Mystery Above" for the Arapaho supreme being (1982:257). Though *heisonoonin* is most powerful of all and, in a sense, originally owns all *beetee*, that power is not exclusive to the creator. A man or a woman with power is said to be *beeteet*, like the Arapaho chief of the period from about 1840 through 1870 whose name was *beeteet* 'Medicine Man'. The term refers to the type of medicine men of the past who had powers to see into the future, read people's minds, hypnotize people, metamorphose into animals, and perform other "mysterious" feats. In historical time the term has been extended to a Protestant minister (*beteenih'oo3oo* 'holy white man'), Sunday or 'holy day' (*beteeniisi'*), and church (*beteentoono'oowu'* 'holy house').

Beetee, then, is not in and of itself a moral force or a sense of the sacred as inherently holy. The ambivalent power of *beetee* is most evident in the misadventures of the trickster (*nih'oo3oo* 'spider'). He can change into an animal, a woman, or whatever shape he chooses in order to deceive animals, persons, or other beings like himself. In the many stories of his relations with humans, animals, or other-than-human persons, he is greedy, hungry, crazy, overly curious, and impetuous. According to one version of creation (Dorsey and Kroeber 1903:16), *Nih'oo3oo* became Our Father after creation, as in the alternative term (*hihcebe' nih'oo3oo* 'Man-Above' or 'Spider-Above'). In the history of contact with Euro-Americans, his name was extended to 'white person'. Though 'white man' is often translated for the trickster figure in stories, Arapaho elders today dismiss any attribution of "creator" to *nih'oo3oo* in reference to non-Indians. Though the name is shared, the creator, *Hihcebe' Nih'oo3oo*, is not a white man. There was no attribution of highest, divine status to non-Indians. There is more discussion of the accepted trickster connection later in this chapter.

Similarly, sacred objects are animate and relate to humans as persons. The sacred Flat Pipe, Wheel, and Offerings Lodge themselves require the knowledge of careful practices and proper relations accorded any person of higher power or rank. Objects vested with a spirit-shadow (*betee3oo*) have life and thus move around, communicate knowledge, and affect human life. Any ceremonial or medicine object must be cared for in order to keep it alive and maintain proper relations. Such objects can also "listen" to and impart knowledge to human persons. Like older persons in the age structure, they can mediate with powerful other-than-human persons above and serve as sources for life movement.

Rather than occupying clear and distinct categories, other-than-human persons all share similar powers and behaviors, different only in degree and possible for human beings to appropriate. Human benefits or dangers from other-than-human persons depend on knowledge and doing things in a good/correct way, especially proper exchanges and activating interpersonal relationships at the right time in life, the seasonal cycle, and daily practice. There are a number of dimensions for relationships with other-than-human beings that are contingent on practice, not preconfigured by classificatory schema or structures. In return for sacrifice and offerings, other-than-human persons will give blessings such as knowledge, health, long life, and abundance to the pledger's family and the tribe.

Appropriate relations with other-than-human persons at the same time involve multiple relations with human persons based on kinship and age-structured ties. One's relationship to sacred beings is tied inextricably to one's social relations with humans. All of those relations are needed to generate life movement and knowledge. The four values of pity, respect, quietness, and craziness, which all persons to various degrees can possess or enact, shape all relations among persons, both human and other-than-human, in the quest to acquire knowledge and promote life movement. The outcomes of human practices thus rest on knowledge about doing things in a good/correct way, configured and activated by these and other dimensions of interpersonal relationships.

Pity

One dimension of relations between persons that pervades Arapaho myth, prayers, historical speeches, Ghost Dance songs, everyday speech, and contemporary discussions is translated as *pity* in a number of ethnographic accounts (Mooney 1896; Kroeber 1902, 1904, 1907; Dorsey and Kroeber 1903). At the beginning of time, humans had no sympathy or pity for each other and therefore lacked directed motion and knowledge (Kroeber and Dorsey 1903:10). Before knowledge and before pity, there was also no movement in time, including life movement. Humanness and personhood thus originated with and depend on the capacity for expressing pity, which set life in motion and activated relations for the first human knowledge.

It is necessary first to analyze the ethnosemantic content and social relations of pity, beginning with a basic contrast between it and the English connotations of the term. The word *pity* in English carries a semantic load weighted by a depth of sentiment somewhat outside of and exceptional to normal human relations. The English word *pity* was identical to *piety* until about 1600, based on the shared derivation from the Latin *pietas* (OED). In the Christian context, pity is identified as an emotion toward suffering, whether of humans or nonhuman beings. Thus, the crucifix evokes piety/pity as well as images of Mary, as in the Pietà, Our Lady of Pity. In the Christian sense, pity often also carries the connotation of mercy as forgiveness and consolement. In its history the term has come to be confined to emotions internal to the Western soul or self yet generated by external events or conditions. In the modern era it has also taken on some moral sense that the person pitied is of lower status, perhaps poor or indigent.

In the Arapaho context, pity is not just a moral sentiment, piety, or a supererogatory value but a prima facie duty to "give something." It is neither a value toward which one strives as an ideal nor a sentiment alienable and prior to action. It is given in and of an immediate relation that generates actions to follow. One has no choice when a pitiful person or situation presents itself. To pity someone is not just to feel pathos for them, which is where the English term stops, but to give or do something for the person or group in a pitiable state. To say, even in modern reservation English, that one pitied someone else means that one gave something to or did something for that person. By pitying a person, one activates or reactivates one or a number of relations between persons. Pity is not just an extraordinary affective state; it describes an action and a relation.

Even though the value of pity for referring to relationships between human beings and between human beings and other-than-human beings is central in perhaps all Plains religious practice and in many other North American Indian cultures, a generic translation applicable across cultures does not suffice for analysis. It is crucial to place it in uniquely Arapaho practices and social relations, especially in the context of age structure and kinship because the mythical ground, social relations, linguistic meanings, and contextual uses of pity vary from one American Indian culture to another. A comprehensive comparison is outside the range of the present study, but three examples of other North American Indian uses of pity suggest some of the variations and commonalities. DeMallie states that in Lakota religion "prayer was the act of humbling oneself before the wakan beings, making oneself pitiable in order to beseech the spirits to activate the kin relationships that bound them to humanity" (1987:42). As in Arapaho practice, poverty, suffering, fasting, crying, and praying evoke pity, which brings blessings or gifts, affords knowledge, and activates relations between all persons, including animals, other-than-human persons, and sacred objects. A further similarity to the Arapaho case is that other-than-human persons are approached as human persons. But prayer and fasting in the Lakota case are based on the spatial distance of *wakan* as "totally other" yet manifested in animals, objects, and human persons (1987:29).

For Arapaho society, pity must be placed in the context of the specific Arapaho age hierarchy and kin relations. Through the pity of those senior in age and other-than-human persons, including animals and spiritual beings, individuals acquire knowledge and thus life movement. Arapaho other-than-human persons are distant but not "other" as in a separate space, because persons intermediate in the age hierarchy form a continuous set of relations with those who are above. Exchange, initiated by pity, maintains, as in the Lakota case, kinlike relations between human and other-than-human beings, but the Arapaho system was hierarchized as an extension of and on the model of age-structured relations.

Pity also extends beyond power to take in material goods and other sources of value, including knowledge, as offered by Buckley (1982:61) for the Yuroks, a remote Algonquian-speaking people of California. In this context pity (*wa'sok*) from spirit forces is necessary for individuals to acquire "esoteric acumen" through training, spiritual ascendance, and wealth: "The supplication of such individuals undertaking elite training [was a] means of obtaining the 'pity' of spirit-beings, and hence their aid in quests for wealth, power, and advantage of some other sort" (216). The more one is pitied, the more knowledge is acquired for ascent in the Yurok aristocratic system of rank. Here, as in both the Arapaho and the Lakota contexts, pity brings knowledge as "blessings" within and activates hierarchical relations. In the Arapaho case, gaining the pity of other-than-human persons does not necessarily bring an individual or a group status or "wealth" or even an accumulation of knowledge and its power. It is more directed toward life movement than toward wealth and rank. Through Arapaho life movement, as one accumulates knowledge, one moves through the age hierarchy but becomes poorer, less attached to worldly things, and less conspicuous in public expressions of status.

In the Flathead families and communities of Montana, O'Nell identifies the continuity of pity and its adaptiveness to modern reservation conditions. As in the Arapaho case, a pitiful state is associated, in one sense, with isolation and loss of relations. She adds that, "'Pitiful' is a term that is often used to describe individuals who because of misfortune are left with little or no family. It can also carry the connotation that someone is materially poor" (1996:99–100). As O'Nell points out, it is the medium for the sharing of commodities, money, and other resources. In the contemporary context, this sense of pity is one of the most general and enduring values in Arapaho life, but it is even stronger within family relations and carries more meanings than isolation and poverty.

In Arapaho, pity directed toward future life movement is also a way of removing burdens or easing a movement that has been slowed by disease, poverty, isolation, grieving, and other misfortune. In the Arapaho context, blessings and knowledge bring life movement as longevity and health not only for oneself but for others in one's family and tribe as well. Individuals generally vow to fast or sacrifice on behalf of a kinsperson who is sick or experiencing some other life-threatening circumstance. The acquisition of knowledge through pity in the Arapaho case was not just a transition for the individual or a reorganization of the self; it was a matter of creating and maintaining social relations with humans and other-than-human beings, as well as extending blessings outward to others in the family and the tribe.

In the context of the Arapaho language there are two terms related to pity and translated as such: (1) the transitive verb form *hoowouunono'*, as in 'I pity him/her', and (2) the form *heetebinouhuuninoo*, as in 'I am pitiful, or poor' (Salzmann 1983:162). Although not all translated Arapaho texts using the term *pity* or *mercy* can be traced directly to the *hoowouuno-* or *heetebinouhuun-* forms, it is clear that Kroeber (1916), Dorsey and Kroeber (1903), Mooney (1896), and Cleaver Warden, an interpreter for all three, translated those forms exclusively as 'pity' or 'mercy' and 'poor' or 'pitiable', respectively.

Paralleling the associative logic for other Arapaho verb forms, the term for pity also connotes a direction and a shape for movement in space and time. Associations are less articulated by noun metaphors than by comparable shapes of motion in verbal constructions, such as the likeness of life to four hills, life to the movement of the sun through the sky each day, and prayers to the smoke that spirals upward. By reference to motion, the stem form *hoowouuno-* can therefore be reduced even further. The prefix *hoow-* denotes downward or downhill motion, and the *-ouu-*, variant of *-[h]onouu-* refers to climbing. All together, the stem suggests climbing down, or at least a downhill descent. Thus pitying connotes making it easy for someone as in a downward motion, as if descending or coasting down a hill.

Opposite terms constructed on the stem *honouu-* alone take on the meaning of immobility or slowed movement. The term *honouuneiht* 'he/she is difficult' or *honouneenoo'* 'it (inanimate) is difficult' connotes, by virtue of the *honouu-* form, a climb upward or ascent, as in the verb phrase *honouuhunoo* 'I am climbing uphill'. Thus, 'easy' implies a downhill motion and 'difficult' an uphill movement combining strength and impeded movement. Pity thus changes slowed movement into easy movement. This is equally evident when the interpersonal relations associated with 'difficult' are included in the analysis. Kroeber's notes translate *honouuneiht* as "at a fixed place, not easily persuaded, can't hurt it, immovable, hard to receive benefits of right away, [use also of lease-payments when agent is unwilling to pay], [Also used of god, hard to live up to on account of 10 commandments], hard to satisfy" (Kroeber 1916–20:Notebook 6:62, Kroeber's brackets). Persons higher in the age hierarchy and above in the other-than-human realm are difficult, that is, more distant than kin or age peers, and thus less moved by pity. Petitions to them require greater difficulties, offerings, and sacrifice, though blessings acquired from them are also more powerful. A "difficult" being, object, or person, then, is one without pity, that is, without the capacity to be moved by others. Anticipating the discussion to come, it is curious that the term is applied to non-Indians in both the political and the religious context. In passing, it is important to note the association with Euro-American ways of distributing goods. For several decades Arapaho leaders fought the government to gain regular per capita payments from mineral leases on the reservation.

To pity someone is to make it easy for him or her, as in a downhill motion. Throughout prayers and songs related to pity, there are also common references to making one's burden light or one's movement easier. As one becomes poor, alone, or old, one's movement becomes slower and more difficult. In Arapaho stories pitiful persons are slowed or immobilized, thus isolated, such as falling behind the moving camp. A pitiful condition is slowed or impeded movement, whereas to pity is to reengage a relationship with a person and then help the person move again. The easy-difficult alternation is also related to the ascent-descent motion within the four-hills model of life movement elaborated in chapter 4. Life movement is a succession of uphill movements, each followed by downhill motion, of difficult ascent followed by easy descent, with each ascent requiring that a burden be shed.

In Arapaho mythology the creation of the earth, the origin of culture, and the acquisition of ceremonies all occur as a result of fasting, a pitiable state (Dorsey and Kroeber 1903:1–8). By fasting alone, crying, praying, and thinking hard, the seeker acquires knowledge as a gift from above, such as from *heisonoonin* (Our Father) or from any of the other powerful beings. In many stories a gift of knowledge is given because a sacred being or animal takes pity on the faster who is alone and without relatives. Thus, the earth was created out of pity, when the creator saw the Flat Pipe floating alone on the water and crying:

> In the first place there was nothing but water, except the water-fowls; and the Grandfather saw that there was a father [flat pipe] of the Indians floating on the water, on the four sticks (tripod). Knowing that the person that was floating on the water was fasting and weeping and crying, and seeing that he was really fasting for the good, the Grandfather took mercy on him. [1903:1, Dorsey and Kroeber's brackets]

The origin of the earth happened as a result of Grandfather's pity on the Flat Pipe, who appears as a person. In other versions a humanlike person, the first Pipe Keeper, is separate from and floating on the Pipe.

Similarly, in a narrative entitled "The Origin of Culture" (Dorsey and Kroeber 1903:8–13), three men fast, thinking hard, until each hears a voice conveying some cultural knowledge. One learns how to corral buffalo and horses, the second how to manufacture knives and bows and arrows, and the third how to ignite fire with flint. In mythical times pity attracts knowledge from above as a gift, which from then on requires humans to reciprocate. As in other contexts, a pitiful situation also requires "thinking hard," or all persons in a group concentrating on one thing.

In the story called "The Origin of the Ceremonial Lodges," a man is about to kill a buffalo cow near the river:

> "Leave me alone; don't shoot me!" said Buffalo Cow, "I want to tell you something which will be for your benefit and the benefit of your people." So the man laid down his bow and looked at the cow. "I have taken pity on you, although you tried to kill me for beef. There shall be lodges for the different societies among your people in which my whole body can be used for various purposes. They shall be in this order: the Thunder-bird, Lime-Crazy, Dog-Soldiers', Buffalo-

Women's, Old Men's lodge and Sweat Lodge," said the cow.

So the man did not kill the Buffalo Cow, but returned to his tipi at once, broke camp and went to the camp circle. He then told the people about information he had received, as a law for them in the future. [Dorsey and Kroeber 1903:20–21]

Out of pity, Buffalo Cow gives knowledge for the Buffalo Lodge and the men's lodges. As in many other stories, a person who is alone encounters an other-than-human person who takes pity and gives him or her knowledge as a "law," meaning a way for acting appropriately in relations with others. The recipient then returns with the knowledge to the camp circle, where the tribe is able then to move and thrive. What is originally an individual acquisition is shared with others. The capacity to show pity and enact it is a marker of personhood, which all animals, spirits, and humans can have. Pity unifies all persons, but it also differentiates through ongoing exchange.

In mythical time, though, human beings themselves are without pity until they acquire knowledge from other-than-human or animal persons. Several stories begin with an isolated person or family for whom the camp circle "had no pity." Animals (e.g., buffalo) take pity on those humans by offering them knowledge that itself engenders pity, as well as other human laws and sympathies. In a story explaining the origin of the women's Buffalo Lodge, a family has only one pony and thus is left behind the rest of the moving camp. They decide to make their own camp. The husband tells his wife, "You know that if people had some mercy upon us they would have given us assistance, but they simply left us" (Dorsey and Kroeber 1903:42). Later on the man receives a gift of knowledge from Buffalo Cow, which allows him to kill buffalo. Upon finally acquiring meat for his family, the man tells his wife, "We have been pitied by somebody" (1903:45). The family eventually returns to their camp with not only the gift of meat but knowledge of the natural laws:

(In the camp, there were old men and women, but they were ignorant of the natural law which had just been given to the race through this man; in fact the people at that time were ignorant of things and to a certain extent wicked. They were without tribal law and had no feeling of sympathy one toward another, and for that reason, this man who had rescued the people from starvation was left behind with such a heavy burden.) This man gave the old people wisdom and knowledge of the various natural laws. He gave them certain degrees with the right to conduct ceremonial dances. [1903:48]

This story is interesting because it places the origin of knowledge and acting appropriately, that is, doing things in a good/correct way in the same moment pity originates among human beings. Further, the abundance of food for life movement is directly tied to knowledge for properly conducting ceremonies.

Pity is also central in song and prayer. A Sun Dance song recorded by Curtis was performed during the preparation of the buffalo hide prior to the lodge:

Hedawunaneina	O may he take pity on us,
Hishish nisana!	Father Sun, O my Father! [1934:198]

The modern Arapaho orthography and literal translation renders this:

Heetih'owouuneeneino'	May he pity (make it easy for) us
Hiisiis neisonoo	Sun, my father.

In a prayer collected by Cleaver Warden for Dorsey (Dorsey and Warden 1905), the capacity for pity is defined as an attribute of leadership. The prayer was given for a man who was taking the office of chief among the Southern Arapahos. In English, it begins: "Of all ages, men, women, children, those who are needy. Listen carefully. This man is selected who shall take pity on you all." The term given in that text for "those who are needy" is "hatabbe no," which I transcribe as *heetebinou'u* 'they are poor or in a pitiful condition', that is, those to whom one shows pity. The verb phrase construction for '(he) shall take pity on you', Warden gives as "haw ton naw woo nah nay ton neah," which is, in modern script, *hootnowouunoneitonee* (old form of future tense, transitive first person actor, plural second person goal).

As in the prayer above, the selection of leaders by the elders required the ability to take pity on others. Indeed, persons who were in a superior position were expected to show pity toward those who were beneath them in the age structure and to mediate through pity to other-than-human persons above or beyond. Thus, pity flows downward in the age hierarchy. In the role of chief, too, the terms carry an obligation to be generous, to give to others who are poor, as in the Arapaho verb stem for 'giveaway' (*neeceenohoo3/t-*), which incorporates *neecee* 'chief'. As one moves to maturity and old age, one's ability to pity others increases as an obligation "to give something back" to one's family and tribe.

In ongoing everyday relations, pity is activated by an Arapaho ethos that pays close attention to the emotional states of others. In the public domain there is a densely encoded symbolic expression of emotions through kinesic and other extralinguistic signs. In such situations, pity is one mode of decoding another person's behavior, to empathize not only with the person's present condition, but also with the longer hardship she or he experiences. If one sees that another person is poor, without a home, clothing, money, or food, then one pities that person by trying to supply them the things that are needed. Children, especially orphans, are pitiable. Today, it is common for an Arapaho person to pity an infant without a family and then adopt the child. Old people and the disabled are also pitied, as are people in mourning over the death of a family member. Those in grief over a tough or strong situation (*no 'oo3oo'* 'it is tough, hard, or strong') should receive pity. Anyone who is alone and without means of support, provided that the situation is not the result of his or her own actions (e.g., drinking), should be pitied. One can also pity persons by telling them something, giving advice, or imparting knowledge to them.

In social relations, one pities another who is having a difficult time through no fault or impropriety of her or his own. People who act "crazy" or "without sense," when they have the ability to tell the difference, are not "pitiable" as such. Arapahos today often say that when they pity someone, they have "no choice"; that is, the obligation is given prima facie without reflection or moral deliberation. The conditions of pitying depend on the relative closeness of the other person to oneself or one's family. In another sense, pitying transcends kinship, band affiliation, or tribal identity, since it can narrow the distance between two persons or groups or, as in myth, two species. Many of the non-Arapahos absorbed into the tribe were found as children left alone on the prairie and were cared for by Arapahos.

In other ethnographic and ethnohistorical treatments (e.g., Fowler 1982:273 ff.), the Arapaho trait of pity is encompassed by "generosity" and not distinguished from ritual or nonritual exchange obligations. Giving because of the need to reciprocate to others for what they have given is different from giving on the basis of pity. The value placed on generosity toward others should be based on pity, since that implies no expectation of return. Pity is involved in almost all forms of social gift giving or exchange.

Some ongoing exchange relations between individuals or families, whether of goods, knowledge, or even persons, are initiated through an appeal to pity. In the traditional marriage exchanges, now extinct, the young man's family would send an old woman to make a formal request of marriage to the prospective wife's family in order to begin discussion and arrange the marital exchanges:

> One day there came an old woman who went to the tipi of this large family. "Will you please take pity on me? I have come over to offer my boy (young man) as servant, in order that he may marry your daughter. It is my earnest desire that my son get the girl as a wife, and I hope that both of you will grant my wishes," said the old woman, shaking hands with the family. [Dorsey and Kroeber 1903:90]

The same pattern is followed for an exchange initiated between a ceremonial grandson and grandfather, or for any request by a younger to an older person:

> When a young man desired to live to be old, he would go to an old man, especially to one of the seven men of the oldest society, and begin to cry, generally outside of his tent, perhaps at the door, perhaps by the wall of the tent where the old man's bed was. The old man would wait a long time to see if the young man was really in earnest. Then at last he would get up from his bed, and pray for him. [Kroeber 1907:314]

Thus, requests made to senior persons in the age structure for life movement or knowledge often required genuine expressions of pity, such as crying, in order to move the relationship forward.

In both past and present contexts, the practice of crying while praying is a common expression of pity. The term Salzmann (1983:73) records for this is *hoonoonowoo'oot* 'he (she) is crying (while praying, that is, with genuine emotions)'; it is contrasted with *beniiwoohut* 'he/she is crying', used more generally. Crying not only demonstrates one's authenticity; it also gets the attention of those above to 'listen' (*ceh'e3tii-*), whether older or other-than-human persons. Crying shows that one's motives are genuine and thus that one's request, offering, or vow is worth listening to.

In almost all ritual contexts, one makes a vow (*hookooneyoo*) to perform a certain ritual sacrifice or offering, usually out of pity for and in the name of another person, a family member or a kinsperson who is ill or facing misfortune. Such vows were made to participate in the men's age-grade lodges, the women's Buffalo Lodge, the Offerings Lodge , and ceremonies surrounding the Flat Pipe. Similarly, out of pity, women vowed to make robes or other quillwork for relatives facing life-threatening situations. In the ritual process the vow initiates all preparations and activates all necessary relations. A vow based on pity for a close relative must be taken to senior sponsors, who in turn take it to the oldest people able to channel the expression of pity to other-than-human beings. At the same time, a vow based on pity in a dyadic relation activates relations with other kin who will contribute to its completion and with age peers who will join the ceremony. Thus pity for another person motivates a ritual vow, and that in turn radiates outward and upward into other age-structured and kin relations. From a single vow the entire family, camp, tribe, and other-than-human persons become interrelated and focused on one thing. By participating in a ritual, one attempts to receive the pity of an other-than-human person, who will then impart gifts of health, knowledge, and well-being to the petitioner and the person for whom the vow was made, as well as the family, the age set, and the entire tribe.

The pledger for any ceremony or sacrifice thus becomes the focus for pity, activating relations among the one who suffers, his or her kin, those senior in age, and other-than-human persons with the power to effect life movement. One asks to exchange the ritual offering, fasting, or other sacrifice for the relief of suffering of a family member. In some instances one can pity oneself and thus make a vow to overcome one's own suffering. Whether for a particular other or oneself, the vow is brought into the camp circle so that the blessings can extend to all. One should not seek knowledge or blessings only for oneself or one's family, for this could be considered greedy. Rather, one should go forth and extend one's blessings, knowledge, and wealth to others. In the prereservation life trajectory, divestment of earthly belongings in order to be "poor" in old age, for ritual leadership, and in preparation for death was expected. As one moves through life, the burden becomes greater, and one's motion slows as a result of the sacrifices one has made for others.

Much of the "ego psychological" analysis of Plains vision seeking and ritual excludes the value, strong in Arapaho religion, placed on sacrificing and petitioning on behalf of others rather than oneself and on channeling what one acquires as an individual into the collective good. In the traditional Arapaho case, the so-called vision quest had less to do with a personal quest and achieving internal self-organization than with interpersonal relations and collective life movement, though the individual does find life direction through these. It is not so important that vision seeking or vowing the Sun Dance reorder the psyche of the individual participant by giving direction, purpose, and a personal spirit helper as that this personally acquired power be returned to and distributed among kin, as well as to the entire tribe. Like goods, one's acquired knowledge must be "given back" to others. In fact, participating in many ceremonies may shorten one's own life, as a sacrifice one makes to the good of the tribe. In the past some people were reluctant to make a vow or acquire knowledge from other-than-human persons for this reason.

Also, when an individual makes a vow, it is, as people say today, a "heavy load" for the entire family, who must apply resources and hard work not only during the ritual itself but perhaps also for one or a number of years between the time of the vow and its actual completion. The point is not so much that other-than-human persons are so distant that one needs to engage in pitiable actions to get their attention. Rather, it is that one must give in order to receive. The need for a reciprocal relationship with other-than-human persons is an extension of the principles of exchange within the age hierarchy.

The *Nih'oo3oo* stories contain lessons for those who show "no pity" and keep knowledge for themselves. *Nih'oo3oo*, the trickster, shows little pity toward others and feigns pitiful situations from time to time in order to acquire knowledge and power from others. In a story entitled "Nih'ā^{n}çá^n Loses His Eyes," he encounters a man with the ability to throw his eyes up into a tree: "Nih'ā^{n}çá^n went to this man weeping for mercy, and saying, 'I come to you that I may be taught of you how to perform your wonderful trick'" (Dorsey and Kroeber 1903:50–51). *Nih'oo3oo* thus approaches the man as a young person would approach an older man with a request for knowledge or power, that is, crying and "pitiful." In one narrative entitled "Nih'ā^{n}çá^n and the Dancing Ducks," which is still told at Wind River, after some ducks he has killed by trickery are stolen, *Nih'oo3oo* declares, "Hei, whoever is the first person to meet me, is the thief. Let him become blind who stole my meat from me" (1903:59–60). He then encounters a bear who has been blinded by a skunk. The bear asks for his pity, but *Nih'oo3oo* only pretends to help him in order to kill him. Some wolves, the "persons" who actually stole his ducks, steal the bear meat as well. Often, as a result of showing no pity, more seriously, feigning pity or deceiving others with false emotions, *Nih'oo3oo* himself is tricked or punished or experiences some transformation. Of course, since he is immortal, he cannot die or be irreversibly transformed. As a result of his own trickery, some condition of nature or humankind is produced, such as mortality for humans, marriage rules, blindness for moles, or some other natural or cultural phenomenon.

In the historical context, the Ghost Dance was initiated as an effort to gain the pity of other-than-human persons for individual, collective, and cosmic life movement. Mooney's translations of Arapaho Ghost Dance songs often use various inflections of what he renders Awu'năni'ä (*hoowouunonei'i*) (1896: 1014). The term for poor or pitiable Mooney offers as hĕ'tabi'nuhu'ni'na (*heetebinouuninoo* 'I am poor'). For example, this line (in modern orthography):

heetihnoowouuneeneinoo heisonoonin
May you pity me, Our Father. [1896:999]

The theme of pity is pervasive, as in the most often cited Arapaho Ghost Dance
song, which expresses a request for pity from "Our Father":

Father, have pity on me,
Father, have pity on me;
I am crying for thirst,
I am crying for thirst;
All is gone—I have nothing to eat,
All is gone—I have nothing to eat. [1896:977]

Mooney interprets the pathos of this song in Euro-American terms: "This is the
most pathetic of the Ghost-dance songs. It is sung to a plaintive tune, sometimes
with tears rolling down the cheeks of the dancers as the words would bring up
thoughts of their present miserable condition" (1896:977). Certainly the song
does express the historical moment of the harsh conditions in early reservation
life, as those who cite it often emphasize. However, the Arapaho version offered
by Mooney deserves a richer context. The appeal to pity is the way an Arapaho
would normally have to address the distant and unmoving Our Father. The
construction biqăna′kaye′na (*biikonookooyeinoo*) can also mean 'crying-fasting'
as a compound verb form, related to the concept of crying/praying discussed
above. The verb stem for 'being thirsty' (*nookooyei-*) also means 'to fast'. In
another sense, then, the song says 'Pity me Father for I am crying/fasting'. Such
an appeal was not unusual but was consistent with prayers, songs, and appeals
predating and following the emergence of the Ghost Dance. As already
established, such crying is not merely ritual performance; it must be interpreted
in the context of pity, as part of sacrifice and establishing relations and exchange
between persons.

Song number 3 places the relation to whites in this context of exchange and
pity:

hee, teebe tih′owouunonou′u, neniisono′
Yes, at first when I pitied them, my children.
hee, teebe tih′owouunonou′u, neniisono′
Yes, at first when I pitied them, my children.
nih′oo3ou′u
the whites,

nih'oo3ou'u
the whites,
niibinou'u koh'owootino
I gave to them, fruits.
niibinou'u koh'owootino
I gave to them, fruits. [Mooney 1896:961; my transcription and translation]

Another Ghost Dance song defines whites as being "without pity" and thus not deserving of pity in return. Rather, they will in the great change be "put aside" like all misfortune in Arapaho ritual practice and mythical time:

He'yoho'ho! He'yoho'ho!
The yellow-hide, the white-skin (man).
I have now put him aside—
I have now put him aside—
I have no more sympathy [pity] with him.
I have no more sympathy [pity] with him.
He'yoho'ho! He'yoho'ho! [1896:978, Mooney's translation]

The Ghost Dance was thus about overcoming the pitiful conditions of reservation life by an event that would put whites and Indians in their proper relationship to each other. Those without pity would be immobilized and set aside. Those who show humanness as and through pity would regenerate the earth.

Even in political intermediation with Euro-American society, Arapaho leaders often petitioned government officials to have pity, in a sense saying, "Give us what we need, for we are poor." Almost every early speech made to federal officials by Arapaho leaders expresses the impoverished, pitiful conditions (depletion of game, loss of land, and disease) brought on by westward white migration. The Arapaho leaders, like other tribal leaders, were asking the government to be human persons toward them. During a visit to Washington in 1877, Chief Black Coal called upon President Hayes to "pity" the Northern Arapahos by giving them a reservation of their own in return for Arapaho scouts' service to General Crook at Camp Robinson in 1876–78:

Last summer General Crook, Lieutenant Clark, and MacKenzie—we worked together and tried to stop the trouble, and were promised when everything was quiet, and the difficulty settled, we would come to see our Great Father. These two men sitting here—General Crook and

Lieutenant Clark—will remember what we were promised. It was
settled quietly and it is all over and this day I have [come] down to talk
about it. You ought to take pity upon us and give us good land, so that
we can remain upon it and call it our home. If you will give us a good
place to stay where we can farm—we want wagons and farming
implements of all kinds; provisions and annuities of all kinds—all to
be given to us as we want them. [Fowler 1982:65, her brackets]

Thus, pity is historically significant both in particular events and over the long
duration for the Northern Arapahos. Those whites who showed pity and formed
enduring relationships through it (e.g., General Crook) were important to
Arapaho causes. This speech appealed to President Hayes to "take pity" by
giving things that were needed and had been promised, not necessarily just
feeling sorry for the Arapahos and exercising Christian charity, as might be
surmised from a Euro-American point of view. It was a way of asking the
president to treat the Arapahos as humans, as persons. The Arapaho leaders
appealed to American officials in what they considered "human" terms, but it
is apparent that the message was not usually received in that sense. From a
Euro-American perspective, it can be interpreted as "begging from the poor,"
from an "Other" in a deficient state or low status.

The promise and the request for a Northern Arapaho reservation was, of
course, never honored. It is clear that as time went on, the Arapaho leaders
appealed to government officials for pity less and less. The tribe gradually
realized that white officials must be dealt with in white man's terms; thus, they
desired to learn to read and write, and they selected leaders who could deal
aggressively with whites. Fowler (1982:177) asserts that this shift from the Old
to the New Council was marked roughly by the transitional year of 1937. As in
the Ghost Dance songs, the Northern Arapaho people learned that "whites have
no pity." Agents of the government were perceived from early on as "difficult
to move" *(honouuneiht)*.

The Northern Arapaho people in the late nineteenth and early twentieth
centuries also appropriated Christianity in Arapaho terms of relations and
personhood, including pity. In a manuscript from the papers of John Sifton
(1908), an early Jesuit missionary at St. Stephen's (shared with me by Benjamin
Warren, Jr.), Catholic prayers are translated into Arapaho. I spent an afternoon
with several elders transcribing those prayers into modern Arapaho orthography
and discussing their meaning. The line "Forgive us our trespasses" in the "Our
Father," or the Lord's Prayer, is given in the text as "chi aurinanee tahou che
eniittani." In contemporary Arapaho orthography, it would be

cih'oowouunoni tohou ciini'iitooni
Pity us for we have not acted in a good way. [Sifton 1908; my transcription]

The first construction can be analyzed as *cih-* emphatic command, *-(h)oowounon-* 'pity', and *-ni* plural object. The remainder can be broken down as *tohou* 'because', *cii-* negative, meaning 'absence of', *-ni'i-* 'good', *-too-* 'act' or 'do', and *-ni* third person plural, 'we'. Throughout the Sifton manuscripts, the Christian concept of forgiveness is rendered in *hoowouunon-*, 'pity' forms. Forgiveness is a difficult concept to express in Arapaho. Similarly, the concept of "sin" is alien, because the idea of an accumulation of moral residues for past actions contradicts Arapaho life movement. The concept of pity is also not an object of deliberation by the isolated moral agent as an individual actor. It is neither supererogatory, as with the concept of charity in Euro-American ethics, nor obligatory, in the sense of an abstract principle with a metaphysical, social, natural, or moral force over one's choices or actions. Its force derives immediately and concretely from the person who is pitiful and a social relation to him or her. In short, pity implies practice, doing something for somebody.

In the modern context, Euro-American-introduced institutions and political structures have posed challenges to pity, though, like the Flatheads (O'Nell 1996), the Arapaho people have tried to appropriate those new forms and the resources they provide into traditional social relations. Arapaho political leaders must show pity to the aged, the disabled, children, and those in difficulty, while at the same time meeting the demands of fiscal accountability in Euro-American terms of literate knowledge and scheduled time. In Western bureaucratic processes, resources are distributed by proof of entitlement, based in recordkeeping, ongoing surveillance, and fiscal budgets assigned by calendar time. "Eligibility" is therefore a standard removed from the relationship between the agent and the applicant in space and time. In short, centralized aid programs have been appropriated by white man's knowledge, the rationality of bureaucracy that resides in no person and no real relations among persons. Assistance is given to those who can empirically substantiate the conditions of their lives through literate forms of knowledge, all of which are couched in the assumption that those in authority are responsible and those in need are not.

To some extent, that contradiction and the resulting role conflict between Arapaho pity and bureaucratic scrutiny of need have been, in recent times, one source of fiscal problems and political instability in the tribe. A senior citizen who requests a tribal grant for travel money to go to Billings for eye surgery cannot understand why he is turned down, since funds are obviously available for staff salaries and other purposes less tied to immediate need. In traditional ethics the needs of the children and the elderly should precede and supersede all other concerns and conditions. Much of the present support for people in need is based on severing or distancing the relationship between provider and client. Bureaucratic processing of payments removes the aid from identification with tribal leaders and other persons. Today, assistance has become increasingly centralized in tribal, state, and federal institutions, although recently the Northern Arapaho tribe has moved toward taking over many of these programs, partly in an effort to resolve the contradiction.

The introduction of a money-based, rather than a primarily subsistence-based, economy has also had an effect on Arapaho patterns for putting pity into action. Today, most families, whether some members are employed or not, depend on salaries, general assistance, per capitas, and other payments distributed from bureaucratic institutions rather than by persons. Well into the 1940s, many Northern Arapahos were farmers, ranchers, or dependent on an agrarian network of mutual assistance among families—not on redistributed money subsidies—thus continuing prereservation patterns of interfamilial cooperation. During the agricultural period on the reservation (1900 to the 1940s), families cooperated in herding livestock, threshing grain, putting up hay, and gardening. It was more essential during that period than now to maintain extensive relations with other families along the horizontal plane of society. Today money distributed from the top down divides people.

With the introduction of per capitas, government transfer payments, and other bureaucratically administered services, assistance in times of need comes from centers of redistribution based on knowledge and authority that are separate from the persons who administer the programs. Although interfamilial cooperation survives, it is narrower in scope than it was before the money-based economy was introduced. In some cases, assistance for difficult times has become institutionalized; there are standard payments for particular needs. When resources are scarce, however, as in recent years, competition intensifies.

Within family boundaries, pity remains automatic and involuntary as the basis for the most cohesive ties in social life. In times of crisis (e.g., illness, death, confrontation, or threat) family members come together to form a solid center of mutual support. If an uncle requests a ride to the doctor, a sister needs money for bail, or a niece needs gas money to get to school, one has to help out. "You can't say no to family" many Arapahos told me. Whenever one accumulates money or other resources, there is a general feeling in the family that one should use them to help out others. Hoarding money or other wealth when family members need it is considered 'stingy' (*ceniiko'oobeiht* 'he/she is stingy'). For Arapahos today, the obligation to share with and assist family members often supersedes all other considerations. That is one major source of misunderstanding for most non-Indians; they cannot comprehend why someone would take off work or skip a college class to rush to the hospital because a second cousin has been in an accident, to drive an uncle to the dentist, or to travel to Oklahoma for a grandfather's funeral.

In the contemporary context pity is less extensive than it was in previous times when age hierarchy served as the differentiating and unifying structure. However, families still cohere through pity, especially in crisis, and members of communities still rally to the aid of one another when tragedy strikes. Pity is still at the core of Arapaho social relations and survival strategies. But there is an awareness that money and its centralization in formal organizations have somehow made ongoing relations and exchanges based on traditional values, including pity, more difficult to sustain.

Respect

The general Arapaho term for respect is *neeteenebiit* (nominal form, *neetee-* as root) or *bobooteenebiit*, with emphasis. The prefix of the second variant, *boboo-,* connotes cautious or circumspect actions. In other words, one should be careful around respected persons or objects on earth or in the above, especially those with medicine or power (*beetee-*). Like pity, respect is embodied in practice. In the childhood of the elders who are living today, they were taught to be quiet around their elders, not to walk between older people who are talking, and to shake hands upon meeting. One should especially respect one's elders, opposite-sex siblings, opposite-sex parent-in-law, and ceremonial grandfather or grandmother. Other-than-human persons should be even more carefully respected, along with sacred objects, animals, and plants.

The *neeteene-* form is used in the following statement on respect offered by Richard Moss, an Arapaho language teacher:

> *niito' heeteenebeti*
> First respect yourself.

> *heetne'ni'eeteenowot hinenitee*
> Then, you will respect him/her, a person.

> *heetne'neeteenebeihin*
> Then, you will be respected.

As with pity, only those who show respect will receive it from the elders, their family, and their tribe. Showing respect is a measure of one's maturity and eligibility for leadership.

Fowler presents a brief discussion of the Arapaho concept of respect, which has been the ongoing social glue of the consensus and solidarity that are at the center of her work:

In return for proper "respect" and supplication, the cosmic, natural, and social processes operate harmoniously and the individual's life journey is facilitated. For example, one is respectful toward animal life—the permission and goodwill of a sacrificial dog is sought before the animal is killed for a ceremony. One is respectful toward ritual objects—Arapahoes are careful never to cross the path of the Sacred Pipe. And controlled, harmonious relations between Arapahoes, especially during ritual acts, facilitate the supplication process. Violence toward another Arapaho damages one's spiritual state. [1982:258]

Thus, Fowler also recognizes the link between respect and life movement as well as the extension of interpersonal exchanges to animals and other-than-human persons. The tribal consensus and unity she describes was and is, though less extensively now, generated and maintained by intricate webs of respect relations, not merely by shared symbols and meanings in the public sphere. Respect should not be read as just a general value or a symbolic load, for it is always everywhere situated in particular interpersonal relations, enacted and maintained in ritual and in everyday life. No relations, not even kinship, can be taken for granted; they demand continual actions of respect.

A number of other observers have recognized the Arapaho public ethos of respect. It is what Elkin defines as "shame" (1940:246) and Mooney calls an "accommodating disposition" (1896:957). The reserved, quiet disposition in public situations is in fact a generalized expression of respect. In such situations one should show respect because elders are present, along with one's sisters or brothers, mother-in-law or daughter-in-law, or ceremonial grandfather.

Therefore, public situations require a reserved, circumspect behavior not because of a generalized ethos or value orientation but because of an intricate network of dyadic respect relationships. Because one's siblings, elders, Sun Dance grandfather, and other persons requiring respect are invariably present in tribal gatherings, one must be "careful" so as not to appear loud, jocund, or overly expressive. Reserved behavior is thus not generalizable as a Northern

Arapaho "personality type" or "character." Requirements of respect based on kinship ties and age distinctions are interwoven into public, but not all, social situations.

Respect is expressed through mutual distance and deference. In the presence of respected persons, one should not engage in dirty talk, laugh out loud, or joke around. In the context of kinship relations, respect is how Arapahos talk about what has often been called "avoidance" relationships following Radcliffe-Brown's terminology (Eggan 1937:91). In traditional Arapaho kin relations, respect was prescribed between brother and sister (extending to parallel cousins), younger and older siblings, son-in-law and mother-in-law, daughter-in-law and father-in-law, and ceremonial grandson and grandfather. Respect was thus defined by both age and gender distinctions. Between any persons of different age, respect follows the pattern described by Eggan. Within a generation, older siblings were important parent-like figures for younger siblings and thus deserved respect. In general, age hierarchical distinctions of respect were not generated only within the age-grade system itself but rather were and are also inherent to inter- and intragenerational kin relations. The explication of respect, then, provides a yet-to-be-studied connection between age structure and kinship relations. Furthermore, respect activated through dyadic relations, like pity, has been more durable than age structure, ritual practices, or larger sociocultural configurations.

Respect toward the grandparental generation merges closeness and deference. It was and is common for grandparents to play the most intimate and instrumental role in child rearing. Grandparents and grandchildren are said to be "close" like equals (Eggan 1937:53–54). Respect relations also changed with life movement in that childhood allows more openness with others in general, whereas the middle stages of life require more carefully circumscribed relations toward kin and senior age groups. As one becomes an adult, the range and intensity of the respect one shows toward elders takes on more distance and deference.

Each of the so-called four hills of life and shifts in the domestic cycle of family relations brought a different degree and type of respect relations. Children and grandparents could be close, but in adulthood elders had to be shown greater deference. In childhood, brothers and sisters could be somewhat familiar, but as they moved into the second stage of life, young adulthood, it became necessary for brother and sister to avoid each other. That pattern effected a general spatial division between unmarried boys and girls. The gender segregation in the camp placed young men outside the domestic space of the tipi, in space beyond the camp circle; girls continued to live with and "help out" their mothers close to the domestic space. In young adulthood, respect required "helping out" parents and elders in various ways. Upon marriage, matrilocal residence and bride service typically placed a young man as an affine in his wife's camp, where he maintained a respect relationship toward his mother-in-law; obviously, less, because contact was less frequent, the daughter-in-law showed respect to her father-in-law. As time passed, the in-law respect relationship could lessen. In old age, relations of respect between brothers and sisters could also dissolve somewhat. Among older people there was a form of equality and less distance between the genders.

Respect can be defined in opposition to so-called joking relationships, between same-sex siblings, close friends, or brothers- and sisters-in-law (Eggan 1965:50–58). There are many stories about humorous situations in which no one could laugh because a brother or a sister was present. If, for example, something hilarious happened while a man was in the presence of his sisters or his mother-in-law, he had to "hold it in" until he could sneak out of the situation and laugh freely. There is asymmetry between respect and joking, since the latter gives way to the former in any situation. When a person who requires respect enters a joking situation, it becomes, for either both the individual and the group, a respectful situation. *Respect* and *craziness* are the Arapaho terms for relations of "avoidance" and "joking," respectively. Among equals one can talk "crazy" with insults, innuendos, and wild stories. In the company of those one should respect, there is a need to be still and quiet. The respect-joking distinction is therefore a boundary between two socially constructed domains of action.

Respect is also reciprocal in the relationship between ceremonial grandfathers and grandsons constructed through exchanges in the age-grade lodges and the Offerings Lodge (or Sun Dance). To some extent, respect extends as well to other family members of the grandson and grandfather. As with kin-based respect relationships, one should not speak openly and joke in the presence of a grandson or grandfather. Likewise, a grandson should never jump ahead of or enter the personal space of his grandfather without a formal request or invitation. For example, if a grandson is driving on the highway, begins to pass the car ahead, and then notices that it is his grandfather, he should pull back. Out of respect, too, a grandfather and his grandson should not serve on the same council or committee or work together in the same workplace. Similarly, one should not walk in front of respected persons or sacred objects, as Fowler notes above. Respect also extends to all ceremonial leaders in the tribe, such as the present-day Sun Dance leader and the Four Old Men. As these relations suggest, respect is a pervasive source for the ordering of social space and the orchestration of persons' movements in the world. Respected persons, such as grandfathers, and objects, such as the Flat Pipe, thus control the tempo of others' movement. Because they command respect, they regulate time by governing the speed, phases, and duration of social relationships.

Throughout one's life, respect determines the types and degree of personal expression in ways of speaking. Younger people are not free to express themselves or "speak up" to older persons unless the latter ask them to do so. Within age-structured social situations, respect defines who can speak to whom and in what order:

> "What do they remember about this place?", I would ask Tom. Tom would repeat the question to Sage in Arapaho. Sage would generally relay it, in the same tongue, to Griswold. Griswold would ponder a bit with a sort of inscrutable oriental smile, his eyelids drooping, and then answer Sage in a nearly inaudible whisper. Sage would transmit this to Tom, and Tom would translate it to me. Just why Tom didn't ask Griswold directly I don't know, except that the procedure conformed to the Indian's respect for age. The order of rank was Griswold, Sage, Tom and myself. [Toll 1962:8]

In the old Arapaho ways of speaking, any question of knowledge had to be addressed first to the oldest person present, a pattern I observed in contemporary social interaction, especially research. The questioner's inquiry will be translated or reinterpreted to the oldest person. Then all must wait for a response or for the eldest's referral of the question to someone else present. It was also common, as in Sage's role in Toll's account, for a person who was intermediate in age to serve as a line of communication between junior and senior persons.

If respect protocol is violated, elders intervene with social controls to set the younger people straight. Tim McCoy, the famous Hollywood cowboy and adopted Arapaho, explains:

> Age commanded unbelievable respect among the Arapahoes, and I can remember more than one occasion when a younger Arapahoe questioned the older men about some point. The old warriors would listen for a short time and then one, cutting the younger man off in the middle of a sentence, would say, with calm menace, "When we want to know what you think, then, maybeso, we will ask. But until then, *chiatayee* [*ce 'eiteii*], little fat-bellied baby, shut your mouth!" [McCoy 1977:96]

As in this case, older men and women can control younger people through teasing and gossip. To some extent the requirement that young people should listen instead of talking operates today, though with less generalized force. In my own experience, I sensed from the moment I entered the field that the older people saw me as young. During my fieldwork, because I was still young, I did a lot more listening than questioning. Like the fat-bellied baby, I was sometimes shamed, corrected, and even lectured. When older people are speaking during an interview, one should not interrupt, correct, or ridicule. For research contexts, too, one's self-expression and thus one's personhood are defined by age-structured relations in and through life movement.

Dyadic respect relationships require symmetrical reciprocal exchange as well as deference. Older persons are responsible for the life movement of younger people, but the latter must in turn provide for their elders at every available opportunity. As discussed in chapter 4, older people have a responsibility to "give back" their knowledge and its life-giving power to younger people. As one moves into the second stage of life, more and more respect toward others is required. In the third stage of life, adults take on greater, central responsibilities for offerings, exchange, giveaways, and honoring events in order to both pity those in need and show respect to elders and other-than-human persons. It is also at this stage that one can become respected not only by younger persons but also by one's family and elders.

Throughout the life trajectory, one's life movement through achievements and overcoming adversity must be "honored" by one's family and tribe. Such honoring is a public expression of respect. When younger people or family members of any age do something meritorious, their family and tribe must recognize or honor that achievement by public expressions, such as speeches, giveaways, and honor songs, or by talking to that person in lectures or supporting words. Like pity, respect is a motive for ritual action performed through a relationship to another person. It is also the motive for all ritual exchanges. Out of respect for a Sun Dance grandfather, for example, a grandson gives gifts and feeds his mentor. In contemporary life, public honoring through giveaways, funerals, honor songs, basketball tournaments, scholarships, newspaper announcements, and ever-new forms of honoring family members have proliferated. Within the extended family, the motive to honor the achievements of or memorialize a deceased kinsman has become a basis for intrafamilial solidarity and the public expression of identity.

Respect across gender boundaries also requires reciprocity. In the past, much of the quillwork done through the women's quill society was vowed by a sister for her brother, a mother-in-law for her son-in-law, or a father's sister for her brother's son. To reciprocate, a man gave a horse to his mother-in-law or sister. A woman often vowed to make a quilled buffalo robe for her brother to ensure his safety in battle or to overcome illness. A woman also made a tipi and furnishings for her daughter and son-in-law upon their marriage in order to ensure that the relationship would go well. The pattern of matrilocal residence was based on a period of bride service to the wife's family. As one elder told me, "they were like slaves, and some still are."

Formal exchange relationships between sister and brother, between son-in-law and mother-in-law, or between any two people in a dyadic respect relationship could in time reduce the distance or "avoidance" of respect. As Kroeber observed, "A man and his mother-in-law may not speak to each other. If, however, he gives her a horse, he may speak to her and see her" (1902:10). The right to speak to a respected person, who should otherwise be avoided, required a gift, an offering, or a sacrifice. Since classificatory brother and sister terms extend to all parallel cousins, exchange relationships can extend collaterally across camp and band boundaries. In ritual contexts, reciprocity between ceremonial grandfathers and grandsons maintains interaction between them. Gift exchanges thus counterbalance the distance and alienation to which respect relationships are predisposed. In all exchange relations based on respect, reciprocation was obligatory and expedient. Indebtedness or delay is antithetical to respect. In the context of the age-grade lodges and the Offerings Lodge, an elaborate system of exchange existed between ceremonial grandfathers and grandsons. The formalized gift-giving of respect relationships is distinct, though, from the generosity shown to others within one's family. Respect exchanges symbolize the combination of distance and kinship in order to sustain enduring social relationships.

Respect relationships also require feeding the other person. Out of respect for an elder, one must always offer to feed him or her before making a request for knowledge or any other type of assistance. Traditionally, it was common for a woman to cook a puppy for her brother as a sign of respect. Between families of Sun Dance grandfathers and grandsons, exchanges of food as well as goods create and maintain relationships. As in the age-grade system, the ceremonial grandfather-grandson relationship carries exchange obligations throughout life beyond the ceremonies themselves.

Thus, in all life transition rituals, an older person must be fed and receive gifts. The recipient should not have to request such things. Respect relationships require formal gift exchange, implying balanced reciprocity to sustain enduring ties through time. If a woman made a buffalo robe for her brother, the brother had to reciprocate with a horse, for example. Maintaining the kinship between human and other-than-persons through time also required balanced exchanges, offerings in return for blessings.

Respect is part of the Arapaho concern for doing things in a good/correct way (*nee'eestoo-*), based on proper knowledge. Only by showing proper respect toward others who are higher in the age hierarchy and those who are part of the other-than-human realm will one acquire knowledge and live a long life. As an individual moves through life, respect toward him or her increases, since longevity is evidence of knowledge, power, and supernatural blessing. Conversely, acting "crazy" or disrespectful toward others will shorten one's life. Sherman Sage offers an example of past "medicine" practices for controlling young people who showed disrespect:

> There was an old man who wore a small piece of "medicine" tied to his hair on the back of his head. He was sitting down.—He was the old man who had two wives of whom I told you.—Well, a young man who had gone to Carlyle [Carlisle Indian School] and had come back home was sitting nearby. He thought he was smart. He snapped his fingers like this [thumb over index finger] at the thing in this old man's hair. This old man used his "medicine" on that young man, and he got worms in his nose, and died from it. He tried to get the old man to take them out, but the old man wouldn't do it. That was about 10 years ago [1930]. In early years there were many old men that had strong "medicines." Now there isn't one left who has strong "medicine." This old man was the last one who had such power; I mean the man who had the stick tied to his hair. My grandfather was a great medicine man. He used to talk about God. Everybody talked about his powers. Somebody put a rock in a man's forehead one time, and caused him to have a headache. My grandfather took that rock out. The same man was also wronged in his kidneys by having the bones of a turtle placed in them. My grandfather removed these also. Right now there is no one who does anything like that any more. [In Hilger 1952:133, Hilger's brackets throughout]

It is not clear whether all elders had such power or not, but respect toward elders was, for the Arapahos, equivalent to doing things in a good/correct way. If one did not do things properly, supernatural sanctions, disrespect, and deviance toward elders would impede one's life movement by inhibiting succession in the age-grade sequence, access to knowledge, and ascension to leadership.

Kroeber records another related term for respect in sacred ritual contexts, transcribed here as *neneebenou'u* or *neneebeiht* "they are reverences [*sic*], respected when seen or as to touching" (Kroeber 1916–20:Notebook 6:60, Kroeber's brackets). Such avoidance or distance applies to anything "wonderful" or awe-inspiring possessing *beetee* power. Objects, beings, or persons must be shown respect by avoiding direct touching or eye contact. The persons with the most power must not be touched, spoken to, or looked at directly without the mediation of others with more power than oneself. Thus, according to one version, *heisonoonin* was addressed directly only by the most senior and powerful men, the Seven Old Men of the sweat lodge (Hilger 1952:144). Respect in all its forms requires caution in actions and interaction. Conversely, within ritual boundaries the power of life movement can be conveyed through touching and seeing, yet only through the intermediation of elders and intervening other-than-human persons.

The failure to show respect toward elders, animals, sacred objects, and other persons indicates a lack of "common sense" associated with immaturity and "crazy" behavior (*hohookee-*) (see the section titled "Craziness"). The character *Nih'oo3oo* in stories epitomizes disrespectful behavior, since he shows no respect toward humans, animals, or *beetee* 'medicine power'. A person who is apathetic, careless, and unconcerned about doing things in a good/correct way would be called *ciibobooteiht* (*cii-* 'absence of'/-*boboo-* 'respect, care'/-*teih-* a personal characteristic/ -*t* third person singular). Through carelessness, persons risk shortening their own or their family members' lives.

In the past, those who showed this sort of disrespectful behavior were shunned or shamed and thus treated as nonpersons. A person shunned can be referred to as *hiihoowtokohbeih* 'he/she is a nobody' (Martha Woodenlegs), meaning that one is placed outside the lived social world. Shunning implies distance, but it is the opposite of respect. A number of Arapaho stories have the theme of shunning, such as the one about a chief's brother who is shunned and then later brings back knowledge of the Crazy Lodge (Dorsey and Kroeber 1903:23–30). In such stories, those who are shunned often return with some power or knowledge acquired during their exile from the camp.

In the traditional context, the rules of respect required that children be cautious and circumspect toward their elders. If old men were talking in the tent or the cabin, children had to sit quietly and listen, leaving the area only if given permission to do so. If an elder was smoking tobacco of any kind, children likewise had to remain still and quiet. During meals and feasts, elders were fed first, then others in order of age rank. Quietness, discussed in the next section, was thus a positive expression of respect and implied a receptivity to knowledge imparted by others.

Elders today comment that young people do not show enough respect for elders, other people, themselves, and sacred traditions. Of course it is hard to gauge exactly to what extent respect has declined. However, contrasts discussed by elders living today offer evidence of a significant change in social relations over the past twenty to thirty years. The social distance between brothers and sisters, between sons-in-law and mothers-in-law, and between younger people and elders has been greatly diminished. Children, teenagers, and young adults at times seem oblivious to rules of respect in public and even ceremonial contexts. Members of the older generations (age 50 and over) still extend respect appropriately to opposite-sex siblings and parents-in-law, but among younger people such patterns are much weaker. The relationships of respect between siblings of the opposite sex and between son-in-law and daughter-in-law no longer involve the same distance. In most families, brothers and sisters, sons-in-law and mothers-in-law now talk to each other. Respect, like other cultural elements, has become compartmentalized in space and time, removed from the ongoing practices in the lived world.

Among Arapaho children and teenagers, there seems to be some conflation of respect with the formal authority of non-Indian institutions, especially schools. As part of the Euro-American expression of individuality, young people's rebellion against that authority often contradicts efforts by parents or grandparents to teach and inculcate respect. In short, younger people merge Arapaho "tradition" and the authority of parents, police officers, teachers, and elders. Northern Arapaho people offer several solutions to the chaos or craziness pervading the lives of young people. One solution is to teach respect, thus tapping into traditional values. Another is to reconstitute former roles for disciplinarians, in public contexts and within the family. Elders recall that there were once several people in the tribe appointed to discipline children at gatherings and that, within kin relations, it was up to aunts (the father's sisters) and uncles (the mother's brothers) to set their nieces and nephews straight. Also put forth is the need to enforce even stronger school discipline, comparable to that of the early mission boarding schools.

The loss of respect, then, is one pervasive medium through which Arapaho people talk about changes in social relations in the past generation. Today there is a sense of greater tension and conflict between individuals and between families as a result of the loss of respect in social relations. The respect-based consensus that Fowler observed in Arapaho politics has given way to more interpersonal and intergroup stresses.

In the past, respect was an expression of the ordering of social space-time by age and gender. In the contemporary context, respect is still a pervasive and shared value, but because of an altered space-time in the lived world, respect is limited to particular contexts only, especially ritual contexts. At one level, Euro-American models of the life cycle seek to segregate age groups. On another, space constructed by extended family boundaries now predominates over interfamilial relationships, many of which were based on respect. Younger people commonly refer to respect more as a general abstract value than as a set of particular norms for relationships.

Some Arapaho people now see the loss of respect in interpersonal relationships as the source of other social problems and, in particular, the disjuncture between generations. In contemporary Arapaho culture education programs in schools and other contexts, respect is a pervasive theme. Frequently, elders are asked to come to the schools to speak to children about respect. It has become the value around which many Arapaho people explain and attempt to solve current problems, especially among the youth.

Quietness

The concept of respect overlaps with what can best be translated as 'quietness'. In the transmission of knowledge, the recipient must be quiet in order to hear, listen to, and understand the giver. Life movement also directs one toward quietness in old age. The word for 'quiet' in Arapaho is *teneiitoyoo'* ('it is quiet', 'still'). The root verb form is *teneiito(o)n/y-* , which is shortened to *teiito(o)n/y-* in intermediate positions (e.g., *nihteiitoyoo'* 'it was calm or quiet') and other shortened forms such as commands (*teiitooneihii* 'be quiet, or still!'). In discussions of options for life movement, the "good life" is often equated with the "quiet life " (*teiitooniine'etiinit* 'he/she is living a quiet/good life'). Like many Arapaho associations, the term for quiet draws an image from motion, in this case motionlessness. The *teneiito(o)n/y-* form is also extended to stillness and calmness in the environment. In situations requiring respect toward a person, a ritual object, or an other-than-human person, one should not only be silent but also sit or stand still.

In early childhood, as discussed in the context of respect, children were expected to 'listen' (*ceh'e3tii-*) and be quiet in the presence of older people. Hilger observes that "children were not allowed to participate in adult visiting, but they were allowed to sit by and listen" (1952:115). Outside the space of adult discourse, though, children were allowed and encouraged to be expressive. Elders today state that when they were children, their parents and grandparents expected them to learn by listening rather than asking too many questions or deliberately requesting information. Quietness also pertained to learning by watching parents and grandparents do things, that is, sitting still and looking on. Conversely, in traditional enculturation, parents and grandparents were "quiet/silent" toward children as well. Only when they saw that children were ready to learn about something would they tell them. From a younger person's point of view, then, the older generations often appeared quiet or even secretive.

Fowler also identifies the importance of quietness in what she calls "keeping a low profile": "Arapahoe children are taught and adults reminded not to be obtrusive in their dealings with others: they must avoid direct eye contact and loud, disruptive speech. Arapahoes avoid asking too many or too pointed questions" (1982:262). What Fowler observes as "consensus" in Arapaho politics is also connected to "quietness." When elders or ritual leaders come to a decision based on consensus, then the younger people must accept that decision and be quiet without further dissent or discussion. Today, the residual power of consent generated from the age hierarchy is no longer as strong as it once was, but it is still a force in social relations. For example, when religious leaders invoke the Flat Pipe to ensure consensus, open dissent is out of the question. Also, within families, the younger generations must conform to the opinion or decision of grandparents, especially when it comes to voting in General Council or in family decision making.

Of course, as mentioned earlier in the context of generalized respect, Fowler's observation must be qualified so as to apply to "public contexts of meaning," the primary focus of her treatment of Arapaho politics. One must be quiet in public situations out of respect because one's brother (if female), sister (if male), Sun Dance grandfather, or other respected individual is present. In less restricted contexts, especially among age peers, interaction is open, involves joking, and even leads to "crazy" talk.

The quiet life (*teiitooniine'etiit*) is often talked about as the desirable way of living. Those who opt for the quiet life withdraw from public activity, such as political office or committee membership. They retreat to their own home or land, where they can live quietly. In the traditional life trajectory, one moved from the quietude of infancy to rewards for expressiveness in the second and third stages of life and then returned to a quiet life in old age. In old age people withdrew from the public world, as did the Seven Old Men, discussed in detail in chapter 7, who passed their time "sitting still" inside the sweat lodge. Elders would rarely speak up in other public situations either, unless a divisive or inappropriate way of speaking needed to be controlled. In ritual practices, elders generally directed others with gestures or sign language. Today, at a certain point, usually about age eighty or so, elders "retire" to enjoy a quiet life. At that time they hand over their jobs, ceremonial roles, and community involvement to others. Among elders today, many are quiet in the sense that they do not readily talk to people outside their family circle and stay home most of the time, rarely attending public events. Those elders are consequently the most difficult to interview or contact.

In general, respect is expressed through quiet and still behavior, making oneself as inconspicuous or "small" as possible in comparison to another person or group. It is also those who live the quiet, respectful life who will receive knowledge from other people and sacred beings. Those who are outspoken, confrontational, self-serving, boastful, or crazy are less likely to receive knowledge from others; and if they do, they are more likely to make mistakes and suffer for them in turn. People who follow the quiet life choose not to be outspoken in public situations, run for political office, or otherwise be conspicuous in public. They usually express their opinions or concerns to others, who will then make them known in public gatherings. The crazy versus quiet distinction thus offers two options for one's life. As one moves through the life cycle, one travels from the noisy to the quiet, from the unsettled to the settled, and from the crazy to the mature. Those who are quiet draw respect, but craziness attracts shunning and shaming.

Traditionally, quietness was also part of daily time in the lived world. Each day was expected to begin and end in quietness, with a prayer. At night in the camps, all was to be quiet so as not to attract dangerous things. When walking alone, one had to be quiet in order to listen to the animals, birds, and other sounds. Not only white observers but also other Plains Indian peoples have consistently described the quiet nature of Arapaho people. Of course, such observations are somewhat overgeneralized from situations of Arapaho-white contact and intertribal exchange. On the back stage of Arapaho culture, there have always been situations allowing for joking, loudness, and otherwise "crazy" behavior, especially among same-sex age peers and between opposite sex siblings-in-law. Nonetheless, the religiosity so often observed in Arapaho character centers on "quietness." During prayers and some other ritual acts, the people present are supposed to be quiet so that the being addressed can hear the prayers and respond. Upon observing this "reverence," Mooney referred to Arapahos as "devotees and prophets" (1896:775).

Some approaches to the reserved nature of North American Indian public situations have stressed the repressive, negative side. Elkin glossed Arapaho quietness as "shame," thus imposing a psychological concept that is misplaced and carries a sense of repression. Specifically, he attributes quietness to the "psychological disorganization" (1940:246) resulting from an alienating reservation experience. For one thing, quietness mixed with "silence" is the initial reaction to non-Indians, including researchers. For another, quietness can be mislabeled by a Euro-American definition of normalcy, which stresses the rationality and even mental health of an expressive ethic.

Keith Basso's study (1972) of silence in Western Apache culture provides a comparative example. The occurrences of silence that Basso delineates for the Apache case do support his hypothesis: "In Western Apache culture, the absence of verbal communication is associated with social situations in which the status of focal participants is ambiguous" (1972:83). What Basso defines as silence applies to the Western Apache case but contrasts in some ways with Arapaho quietness. In the Arapaho context, ambiguity of role expectations would apply to some but not all situations demanding quietness and respect. There is a difference, then, between silence and quietness. The former is a suppression of words, the latter a positive expression of receptivity to knowledge and a show of deference.

Quietness is thus both an outer and an inner state. For both it is a sense of inner consistency and social harmony, not a repressed ambiguity of feelings. In all ritual practices, quietness applies to the phase of preparation in which all bad feelings and conflicts must be set aside. As the Southern Arapaho Carl Sweezy states, "when there is true hospitality, not very many words are needed" (Bass 1966:15). In particular, several elders explained to me that the practice of eating before talking about things or making requests helps to "quiet people down first." In Arapaho ethnopsychology, hunger and anger are closely related. For example, the term *3ooxonineet* means 'he/she is hungry/mad'—that is, really mad. Hunger and agitation are further related by the form *hees-,* present in both *heesneenoo* 'I am hungry' and *heesnoneenoo* 'I am angry'. The *hees-* form connotes fast movement, as in *heeso'onotii* 'train', literally 'fast wheel'. When Arapahos are eating, it is common to hear things quiet down and see people become still.

One cannot be quiet and still if one's inner state is confused. Hunger, anger, and other states generate noise and bad feelings in social situations. To be drunk, for example, in Arapaho is *nonsih'ebit* 'he/she is drunk', which literally means 'he/she is confused, all jumbled up inside' (Royce Brown). People with aggressive, fast, or chaotic insides are to be shunned and avoided. When people are mixed up on the inside, whether from drinking, hunger, anger, or grief, they will not "listen."

According to elders, open, loud confrontations were rarer in the past and unheard of in the presence of elders or others toward whom one had to show respect. Generalized constraints maintaining silence can often break into verbal conflict. If one cannot, out of respect for others present, openly confront another person with whom one disagrees, another strategy is to withdraw from or "walk out" of the situation, thereby maintaining silence but using it to express disagreement. To "quit" in silence is thus another way to address ambiguity.

It is also necessary to be quiet toward other-than-human persons in appropriate contexts. At night, all should be quiet so as not to challenge or attract false persons roaming about. In ritual practice, the sacred Flat Pipe and other ceremonial objects are often spoken of and treated as persons deserving quietness. In the presence of such objects, all should be quiet both internally and externally, so that the people's prayers can be heard by beings above and so that the people can hear the knowledge offered to them. When prayers are given in the traditional way today, they are generally quiet, even whispered. I recall some non-Indians' response to a long, quiet Arapaho prayer; "We couldn't even hear it." The point is that if one is too loud, the other-than-human persons will not listen. As in all relations of respect, someone above you will listen only when it is quiet. Quietness in such situations also carries a suspension of conflict and "loud" behavior toward other people. I heard several times, "When you go into a ceremony, you should leave all your anger at the door."

When one receives knowledge through ritual supplication (i.e., prayer, sacrifice, dreams, or fasting), one should also be quiet about it to others. I also heard many times, "You shouldn't go around telling everybody what you've learned." In one sense, such behavior is interpreted by Arapaho people as "bragging" or "showing off." In another, it is inappropriate behavior that risks danger. Ceremonial knowledge must be carefully "bundled" in particular contexts, not made openly available to all. Children in particular can be harmed by the power of such knowledge. Accordingly, those people who live a quiet life are often selected to inherit important ritual knowledge or assume ceremonial leadership positions. They can be "trusted" because they are not likely to share knowledge with others who are not properly prepared.

In the third stage of life, political leadership requires a person to be expressive, that is, "not too quiet" in public. The demands of public roles in the third stage of life require good oratorical skills. In public gatherings, most adult Arapahos find it difficult to "speak up." It was necessary for a political leader not only to speak to non-Indians in intermediation but also to speak to the Arapaho camps periodically about what was going on in the tribe and the world. Associated with the chiefs and ritual leaders was the position of 'announcer' (*nooxneihii*) a person who used to ride around the camp on horseback announcing the day's news and upcoming events. Today, the announcer position is still part of the Offerings Lodge (Sun Dance) camp.

Recent Business Councils have been accused, of being "too quiet," since they now sit among the people at General Council meetings rather than sitting in front. Thus, quietness is perceived as a negative trait for political leadership. By the 1930s those who could "speak up" were often chosen as political intermediaries with the federal government and other tribes, such as Nell Scott, who served for many years (1937–68) as an assertive member of the Business Council (Fowler 1982:186). Since the prereservation period, the principal chief or leader has always been selected for oratorical skills.

Conversely, elders are concerned about the loss of quietness accompanying the weakening of respect. In public situations, the reserved atmosphere often gives way to the constant noise and ramblings of children and young people. Elders say that life is now faster and noisier than it once was. The Sun Dance, for example, used to be the quietest time, when you could not even speak loudly. Now many people comment on the noise, cars, and fast pace of people moving about the Sun Dance. In recent years ritual leaders and security personnel have made an effort to enforce quietness in the campgrounds.

Elders today say that it is harder to correct younger people in ritual contexts because there is so much noise and movement surrounding their personal lives. Older Arapahos reflect that when they were children, the Sun Dance grounds were always quiet, both in lack of noise and in stillness. Some wonder whether the prayers in public rituals can still be heard by the creator, since it is so noisy now. In general, older Arapahos see the fast pace of modern life as making it harder and harder to live the quiet life. According to elders, modern technology has made the world too noisy. It is more difficult to set aside animosities to quiet oneself inside as one enters ritual contexts. Interpersonal, interfamilial, and intersectional conflict does occasionally evoke loud confrontations today. Modern life, with its competition and factionalism, is too fast, too loud, and thus crazy, in Arapaho terms.

Many Arapaho people today face a contradiction between Arapaho quietness and the Euro-American emphasis on expressiveness in the matters of defining persons and resolving problems. Arapaho college students often reported to me that they had a hard time conforming to the requirements to speak up in class or share their problems with others in counseling contexts. It has long been an Arapaho strategy to keep family, community, and tribal knowledge and problems out of the public view. Both positive, sacred and negative, enigmatic knowledge must be carefully bounded. For the latter, some say that quietness prevents the Arapaho people from "looking bad" to the outside world, whereas others interpret it as a form of collective denial to address problems. Whenever an issue comes up for tribal discussion, these two opposing forces can be seen at work. For defining persons, the two orientations are in contradiction, especially for young people.

Craziness

In Arapaho ethnopsychology, 'craziness' (*hohookee-*) refers a type of behavior and disposition with a restricted relationship to knowledge and a lack of direction for life movement. Craziness is variously described as "foolish behavior" or "just going into something without a concern for what you're doing" (Mooney 1896:1033; Hilger 1952:79). In answer to my own inquiries, craziness (*hohookee-* or *hoheis*) is defined as "having no sense," "not caring about what you do," "not seeing the consequences of your actions," and "not in your right mind." It is also associated with "not listening to what others tell you," that is, an inability to receive knowledge through the senses from the environment or from other people. In shape, craziness is thus a crooked, itinerant motion, as opposed to the better "straight life" or "walking the straight path" (Hilger 1952:66; Bass 1966:25). Kroeber's notes indicate that there are two contrasting terms to refer to human actions: *xouubee'*, meaning "straight, open, upright, right," and *ceibee'*, conforming to craziness and denoting "crooked, bad, wrong, foolish" (1916–20:Notebook 6:63). Another connotation of craziness is "overdoing things" or "going to extremes," that is, violating the boundaries of respect and caution for ritual and nonritual practices.

Craziness is thus the opposite of pity, respect, and quietness, though it is related to all of them in intricate ways. Namely, craziness is shown by a closed, unpitying sense for the humanness of others, a youthful lack of respect, and loud, fast behavior. If one's senses are closed, so is one's sympathy and respect for others. Craziness implies stingy, acquisitive behavior, the opposite of pity. "Crazy" people are also immature, in that they lack the respect that is shown by quietness and silence. As one moves through the life cycle, one's capacity for pity, respect, and quietness expands as one's craziness dissolves. Crazy people are perceived as not only uncontrolled and undirected in their movements but also loud. Talking without direction is as crazy as walking without direction. Thus, children and immature adults cannot be trusted with knowledge, because they will not be able to keep it within proper boundaries.

Crazy behavior contrasts with respect relations with others. To reiterate, adults should not act crazy toward those who require respect, such as a man's sister, mother-in-law, or ceremonial grandfather or a woman's brother or father-in-law or any old person. As mentioned earlier, one can be crazy in behavior and speech in what Eggan called a joking relationship (1937:56)—the relationship between a brother-in-law and a sister-in-law, or even between a grandmother and a boy or a grandfather and a girl. Cross-gender siblings-in-law can make sexual jokes toward each other and generally tease each other. A grandmother often teased a young boy that she would be his wife someday. Teasing like that is a form of crazy behavior.

Today, a man who cracks jokes all the time can be called *hohookee*. Among male peers the term, translated 'crazy guy', is commonly used as a teasing form, but it should never be used for elders or anyone else toward whom one must show respect. In the contemporary context, "crazy" in English and *hohookee* or *hoheis* in Arapaho are odd-job words serving a number of functions to describe people who are constantly joking around, out of control, or doing strange things. The term *hoheis* is simply a stronger, superlative term for craziness. A woman who roams about may be called *hoheis*. Today it is commonly used as a teasing form for a "crazy woman," although fluent speakers explain that the term can be applied to either men or women. These terms can also be used in criticizing the behavior of others, for example, people who lack diligence and orderliness in life.

In interaction among equals, craziness is a form of what Bateson defines as "play," or actions that do not denote what they "stand for" (1972:180). As teasing, such actions or words stand for meanings other than those based in the realm of respect. In Arapaho, men and women who joke around are called "crazy" by those who are the butt of their jokes or teasing. One should not act crazy in the presence of a respected person, for any level of respect supersedes joking. For example, if one's sister is present, one can not tease one's sister-in-law. Even when a respected person is not actually present, one should not make crazy remarks about him or her.

Craziness is thus associated with youth and immaturity, that is, with not conforming to practices and demeanor appropriate to one's life stage. It is, however, expected of youth and thus not necessarily behavior to be strictly suppressed, except in some situations, such as ceremonies. As Hilger observes, craziness was used as a descriptor of young people by older generations:

> Sometimes children were scolded. Hurting expressions and ones that usually brought conformity, were "You're crazy," and "You're a ghost!" Quoting a Northern informant: "'He's crazy' is the worst expression the Arapaho used. Even today if a stranger comes around here and does something out of the way and the people don't want us to talk to him, they'll say, 'He's crazy!' and that classifies him for

everybody. Everybody ignores him then." According to a Southern informant, "You ghost" or "You cadaver" or "You dead skeleton" were the worst words an Arapaho could be called. The expression, 'You're crazy'," he said, "is very widely used. It originated in this way: There are certain moths that will fly into the flame of a candle and come back again and again and be burnt. This animal is called hāhā'ka [*hohookehe'*], meaning 'crazies'. Now a person who knowingly goes into danger is called hāhā'ka. When we use this expression there must be reasons for doing so. It might be said to a child that is running ahead so fast that it will obviously push over a bucket of water; or to a small child that is running into a hole of mud which it can see with its own two eyes but does not see in its mind. This can be said to any small child to whom one is related but should not be said to a strange one. A man can also say it to an older boy who acts mischievously, but he cannot say it to a girl. [1952:79–80]

This passage is rich with connotations and uses of craziness heretofore unexplored in the Arapaho cultural context. Craziness here also connotes "going too fast," so that one does not have time to sense danger. As described in the context of life movement, a person's motion becomes slower as he or she matures and ends in the quiet disposition of old age.

Craziness is not arrested development, however, but is regarded as a reality of youth and thus of life. Today as in the past, elders often tolerate some crazy behavior and speech by young people, simply because they are "too young" and that is just the way they will be until they settle down or straighten out. Although young people under the age of forty or so are often criticized for crazy behavior, such as "running around all the time," others may explain this away as an expression of their immaturity. Young people are assumed and generally expected to be crazy. When adults act immaturely, then the term can become a basis for criticism and even informal control through gossip.

The passage quoted from Hilger also reveals that Arapaho senses of persons and life stages are often phrased in terms of animal behavior. The term *hohookehe'* for moth combines the stem for "crazy" with a diminutive ending (-*ehe'*), literally 'little crazy'. In behavior, moths display the rapid, undirected, random motion underlying craziness. As noted in chapter 6, the men in the Crazy Lodge were likened to moths, since they danced into fire as part of the ceremony. Thus, the reference to the crazy motion of moths is more than metaphorical; it describes a power or force of motion that is without direction yet necessary for life movement.

In the modern context, the term for craziness is distinguished from insanity, *tonoowuneiht* 'he/she is insane'. Insanity is a sickness that is permanent and over which one has no control, whereas craziness is situational, and to some extent within one's power to stop, at least among adults. Craziness is reversible, whereas insanity is permanent.

In relation to knowledge, craziness is associated with childlike acquisitiveness and having "blocked up senses" such that one cannot see, hear, or feel the danger ahead. Deafness, blindness, and craziness are closely related. Hilger's evidence also draws a connection between the attribute of craziness and the practice of shunning, which meant forcing a person or family to live alone outside the camp circle. As shunning was explained to me, it makes you a "nonperson," someone who is a "nobody." Anyone who behaved improperly could be shunned, including the deaf, the blind, or the crazy. Shunning is still practiced today toward people who act crazy. One usually does not pity people who are crazy, for they bring their craziness on themselves.

Craziness is not univocally bad in a moral sense; it can be a positive source of power when circumscribed within mythical events or ritual practice and thereby channeled for positive life-promoting results. In stories and traditional ceremonies, crazy behavior was a means of appropriating knowledge and power from outside the camp circle. Going to war is crazy in the sense that one goes head-on into a dangerous situation, as emphasized in the Clubboard and Spear lodges. For those age grades, craziness was also unleashed when members exercised their police function in order to shame a person into conformity. Someone who deviated from the controlled camp movement, as in a buffalo hunt, might have his tipi torn down by the Clubboard men or Spears.

Sacrifices and offerings can be infused with temporary craziness in which concern for personal well-being is set aside in acts to defend or benefit others' life movement. Fasting is a type of ritualized crazy behavior, since one goes off alone and withdraws from sustenance. Crazy behavior also follows the death of a relative, as in the former mourning practice of gashing one's arms or legs. Although self-mutilation is no longer practiced, mourners still describe an enduring feeling of inner craziness. One can also become crazy as a result of other extreme situations, such as the desire for revenge or engaging in battle.

In the men's 'Crazy Lodge' (*hohooko'oowu'*), crazy behavior was channeled into life movement within the boundaries of ritual practice and age structure. The *hohookeenenno'* 'Crazy men' used medicines that made them crazy during the ceremony and able to paralyze and then remobilize people and animals. Likewise, crazy other-than-human persons, including Whirlwind Woman and ghosts, could paralyze humans, causing death or breathlessness.

Children were thus warned never to go anywhere alone for fear of encountering an other-than-human person, such as a ghost or a skeleton. Craziness could thus stop the life movement of others, that is, immobilize them permanently or temporarily, but it could also generate life movement.

During the Crazy Lodge, men acted in "contrary ways," such as saying the opposite of what they meant, knocking down tipis, and, as mentioned, walking into fire (Kroeber 1904:192–93). In other words, the lodge epitomized craziness but as confined within the camp circle and the control of elders. Almost all Plains societies (e.g., the Cheyennes and the Lakotas) had some ritualized form of "contraries," but in the Arapaho context the crazy behavior was associated with men in a particular stage of life and only within a ritually circumscribed context. Compared with the Arapaho case, crazy behavior in other Plains societies was more highly individualized. In the age-grade sequence, the crazy behavior in the Crazy Lodge preempts that type of behavior among men in subsequent stages, as fasting preempts hunger, suffering future hardship, and so on. The expression of craziness was a channel for power and knowledge, drawn especially from outside the camp circle. It was necessary for confronting enemies, for outmaneuvering other-than-human persons, for facilitating a life transition, and for marking other transformations in time. In short, craziness is a source of power for movement of various types on different levels.

Conversely, those who continue to exhibit inappropriate crazy behavior should not be entrusted with ritual knowledge and should not be allowed to fill important jobs in the community. If the elders saw one as too crazy, then one would not be selected for positions of political or ritual authority. But in intermediation with the federal government and the non-Arapaho social world in general, having somewhat of a crazy, that is, outspoken, nature has always been seen as desirable.

Craziness, of course, is not an irreversible trait of a person's character, for it can be redressed through ritual or nonritual action. When younger people act in crazy or crooked ways, older people should intervene to "straighten them out," through lecturing or other forms of direction. Referring to an event in 1879, in which an Arapaho man named Waterman murdered another Arapaho named Fast Wolf, who was from a different band, Fowler tells of a speech made by an old man named Cherries to the murderer's family: "The old man convinced Young Chief [Waterman's kinsman] that Waterman should surrender to the whites at the agency and that to do otherwise would be 'foolish' (that is, hohooko, "crazy"). That which is hohooko is contrary to the natural order, spiritually and socially chaotic. Such elders as Cherries were the ultimate judges of what was "out of order" (1982:117). Waterman did turn himself in and thus acted in a good/correct way. One can be temporarily crazy but then engage in an exchange or a sacrifice in order to put that craziness aside.

Another connection evident in Hilger's work is that between craziness and "untrue, or false persons," such as ghosts or skeletons. Calling someone a *3iik* or *3iikonehii* 'ghost-skeleton' is the worst insult in traditional Arapaho and associates craziness with a state of life movement that is out of phase or not straight, for such beings are thought to wander about aimlessly causing mischief. The ghosts of deceased persons are crazy because they are not in the right place for their stage of life movement. The traditional belief is that the deceased person roams for four days, visiting family and friends, before moving on to the world above (Hilger 1952:161). Some, however, roam indefinitely, not going on to the above (*hihcebe'*), to the home where they are supposed to go in the temporal order of life. Thus, like a person who behaves inconsistently with his stage of life, a ghost is crazy because it is out of place. False persons are said to act in crazy ways, since they roam about at night and without homes.

The most powerful other-than-human persons can also act in crazy ways; that was especially the case in mythical times. For example, the crazy behavior of the trickster *Nih'oo3oo* was an expression of the power behind the creation of things in the world. *Nih'oo3oo* is crazy because he is homeless and always wandering around, overly eager for knowledge and power, which he ultimately acquires and misuses; he jumps into dangerous situations without thinking, never listens, and always goes to extremes in his actions and speech. As a trickster, though, *Nih'oo3oo* was able to transform himself and aspects of the world by virtue of his crazy nature. For example, he made moles blind by stealing their eyes.

By the time of the Ghost Dance at least, the concept of craziness was attached to white people, *nih'oo3ou'u*. One Ghost Dance song repeats *nih'oo3ou'u hohookeeni3i'*, 'white people are crazy' (Mooney 1896:972). Elders today explain that non-Indian people are crazy because "they're always looking for something." Traditionally, that was explained by the fact that they do not keep their navel cords and thus wander around all their lives looking for them. As Hilger mentions, the Arapahos associate the navel cord preserved in an amulet bag with having direction in one's life course (1952:23). The loss of one's navel cord will cause one to search aimlessly, perhaps in other people's property, even to the extent of stealing. The association of white people with crazy behavior is also tied to the identification of them with the character *Nih'oo3oo*, who is always snooping around and inquiring impetuously about knowledge. If another character has a certain power or ability, *Nih'oo3oo* wants it right away. As with immature people, an excessive eagerness for knowledge is crazy. In the historical and contemporary contexts, the perception of whites as crazy has contributed to the Arapahos' cautious strategies for intermediation with the federal government and Euro-American society in general. As Fowler submits, Chief Sharp Nose's last words emphasized this: "The white people sometimes they get tricky" (1982:239).

Today, many Arapaho people describe the modern world and the effects of "white man's ways" as crazy, because of the observation that people are just running around too fast to learn traditions, do things right, visit with each other, and thus be Arapaho. Elders comment that people are now used to making things happen quickly by just turning on a switch and thus take too many shortcuts. They are just "going too fast" to form the relations that once maintained direction for life movement and limits on knowledge. As a result, the tempo and direction of collective life are no longer under the same degree of control—a situation that contrasts with the consensual politics described by Fowler. Though people try to get things under control through traditional ways and relations, at times there is a sense at Wind River that politics and leaders, events and relations, are now beyond control, that is, crazy.

Connections and Contradictions

Respect, pity, quietness, and channeled craziness are ways of defining personhood through relations with both human and other-than-human beings. All four values are interconnected with life movement and knowledge in that they define how and at what pace individuals pass through the life trajectory and acquire knowledge. However, personal self-interest in knowledge and life movement must be superseded by other-directed thoughts and actions. Within the age structure extending into the other-than-human realm, pity, respect, quietness, and craziness admit of degrees and are relative to distance and time. Thus, personhood is articulated by and through the space-time of life movement and knowledge. In the Arapaho theory of practice, then, life movement does not emanate from natural processes or from an automatic inculcation or enculturation. It is a process generated by proper relations toward other persons, extended through kinship and age hierarchy and into the realm of other-than-human persons.

Pity, respect, quietness, and craziness are interconnected and overlap in actual practices. Respect subsumes quietness, and both are inseparable from pity. Craziness is opposite to the other three but can be channeled into those other values through ritual action. For purposes of explication, all the values are strands for connectivity among various dimensions of culture and society, including kinship, language, exchange, age structure, myth, and art. Because of such interlinkages, these values resist singular translation and reduction to one function for each of them. For instance, pity overlaps with generosity, love, compassion, and sympathy, but in part eludes and contradicts the prevailing Euro-American ethos surrounding these terms. Pity merges what Western ethics distinguishes as fact and value, voluntary and involuntary, duty and end, self and other, and intention and act. Western assumptions about social morality tend to emphasize the restrictive functions of norms and values. In interpersonal relations, Arapaho forms are not merely controls or boundaries on human practice and consciousness; they are also positive means for the expression of personhood and the generation of life movement for self and others.

Arapaho ways of defining persons and constituting relations thus often come into contradiction in the lived world with Euro-American-imposed forms. In broad terms, modern Western ontology is grounded in the equation of person with self with consciousness, when in fact, as Mauss (1979:89) traces, the relation is a historical and cultural fact. A Western ethos assumes isolation of individual consciousness prior to action and as the locus for the movement in progressive, linear time. This conception of self is thus part of the closed system of knowledge that Euro-Americans have consistently taken for granted as given in their efforts to transform indigenous peoples (see Deloria 1994:192). Within that system the person is defined in an anthropocentric position as a sentient, self-conscious, or ensouled individual in a personal or immediate relation to a universal, such as God, nature, nation-state, land, or market. The Western self stands alone in time, too—though of course ideally equal to all other selves—before massive forms, such as nature in science, God in Protestantism, nation-state in liberal political philosophy, universal categories as in Kantian rationalism, or the market in modern political economy. The self is also defined as a consciousness that endures throughout the life cycle and from one social context or set of relations to another. There is thus irreversibility and separation from social relations in the Euro-American conception of self. By contrast, aspects of self that change and adapt to social situations are generally equated with conformity, superficiality, or inauthenticity. Within that framework, rational life decisions ought to be made independently of social ties and cultural context. Euro-American legal, political, religious, and educational institutions presuppose the moral capacity for choice as a basis of personal freedom and for holding individuals accountable, guilty, or sinful for their actions. The internal contradiction is that once the individuated self is severed from social relations, it is subject to the power of distant, universalized larger authority and finds connections to local human experiences problematic.

Accordingly, Euro-American-imposed institutions seek—but can never achieve—totalized legal-rational authority that eschews relational values, such as Arapaho pity and respect, dependent on local knowledge. At the same time, appeals to such authority must be explicit, assertive, and systematic in the pursuit of individual rights and needs. Forceful persuasion, either oral or literate, becomes a necessary medium for self-expression. For almost all Western psychologies, self-expression is affirmative, liberating, and healing. Expressiveness and individuality, closely linked in Euro-American definitions of personhood, stand in contradiction to Arapaho values.

All elements of the Western self become evident in the ways many non-Indian people present themselves in the reservation context. In the extreme, there is a kind of egoistic imperialism through which the non-Indian individual takes over the situation and places himself or herself at the center of space and time. Supported by their own knowledge and sense of time, many non-Indian persons go about trying to construct the meaning and agenda of the situation through self-action before they have even established any relations with the others who are present. Consistently, non-Indian encounters, whether in tourism or research, tend to equate Arapaho quietness with uncertainty, ambiguity, or even repression. Going beyond the Euro-American psychological premium placed on self-expression, quietness is not a repressive force but a positive way of activating relations with others and the context. The contradictions were apparent in many encounters that I observed, such as tourism, which I took part in for several years. Non-Indian visitors often expressed to me that Arapaho people do not "want to talk to them," do not "seem to pay attention to them," or do not "show appreciation of their actions." From the other side, Arapaho people have the sense that such visitors expect them to drop everything else in their lives and attend to them every moment.

From an outside perspective, self-expression is defined as empowerment, whereas silence is identified as repression or censorship. Accepting this Euro-American influence, many people in the tribe, especially younger generations, experience a sense of repression and have a stronger will to express themselves openly. Within traditional definitions, unrestricted expressiveness is negative, since it generates tension and conflict between individuals or between groups.

In general, there has been a trend toward increasing expressiveness in some public Arapaho contexts, both within the tribe and toward Euro-American authority. However, that is not identical to the self-actualizing non-Indian discourse. In most instances public expressiveness engages family and community interests in opposition to those of other groups. In public contexts for openly expressing interests, Arapaho people do not walk in alone, either literally or figuratively. When non-Indians encountered Arapaho group expression through a spokesperson, they tended to regard it and react to it as a disruptive action outside of and challenging the formal structures.

Pity also competes with Euro-American ways of defining individual rights and entitlement to resources and care, which require the individual to prove by documentation or persuasion that he or she is morally and legally deserving. In many ways the relation of persons to resources is defined by fixed sums, as in budgets, food orders, waiting lists, and future plans. Tribal leaders and workers often experience role conflict between bureaucratic demands for accountability and the pity they try to activate for persons in need. An immediate situation of need may be incompatible with the availability of money. Some leaders find that they fail no matter what they do. If they allocate funds to those who need them, there is a budget shortfall somewhere else. Non-Indian agencies and agents then categorize them as irresponsible and withhold future funding. If they stick to budgetary policies, they appear to be stingy and without pity, thus falling short of Arapaho expectations of leaders.

Modes of respect can also clash with Euro-American structures. Within Arapaho relations, age is still a very strong source of respect, whereas in Euro-American terms status and prestige are more closely tied to position within formal structures. In most cases such positions are based on credentials of educational attainment and work history. Although there is respect and need for such positions in modern tribal government, there is also an abiding suspicion of such expertise when the person who possesses it cannot form relations with other people in lived experience. Too much professionalism in defining self can engender a sense that one is disconnected or floating. What non-Indians enact as impartiality, Arapaho people can often perceive as being nobody nowhere, floating about without connectedness to the local context.

With regard to age and respect, Euro-American society offers an obvious and enigmatic contradiction. As many have noted, institutions, communities, families, and individuals aim to promote health and longevity, but they segregate and disengage older people. Life is regarded as a finite substance that can be measured according to how much is left. Institutions and popular culture thus identify youth with more life, whereas Arapaho values continue to associate old age with "more life," as more knowledge, respect, and personhood. Younger Arapahos are thus caught in the contradiction between traditional values and the bombardment of Euro-American images that define old people as of the past or out of sync with the modern moment. In short, young people receive conflicting messages: respect elders but see them as part of the past and not the present or the future.

The contradictions are therefore not just between Arapaho and Euro-American definitions of personhood, for externally imposed meanings and practices import their own internal contradictions. For Arapaho people, as for all tribes, the federal government has continually promised freedom through the assimilation to individuated selfhood, yet it has at the same time imposed massive formal structures to control every aspect of people's lives in reservation communities. Joining the white world promises freedom and growth but often delivers racism and bourgeois conformism, even greater strictures and pressures than those of reservation life. Education and upward social mobility promise greater freedom and self-realization, but for many young Arapaho people, they bring only a greater sense of confusion and being controlled.

Secondly, institutions inculcate a Euro-American value of "objectivity" as rationality to be exercised by the individuated self. Many times I heard non-Indians express the feeling that Arapaho students, officials, or educators could not be "objective," that is, could not detach themselves from a social, cultural, and subjective relation to other persons. From the other side, non-Indians appear to Arapaho people as floating and crazy because they are without real relations with others. The contradiction is that behind Euro-American objectivity there are self-interests that account for abrupt and enduring inconsistencies in the policies and institutions imposed on reservations. Ironically, the free-thinking self, making decisions according to rational, objective standards intended to promote consistency across time, acts in each moment to advance political or economic interests in ways that are erratic and irrational to an outside observer. That is a fact, though, that the prevailing Euro-American ideology has rarely comprehended or acknowledged over the long duration of culture contact. The contradictions thus elude non-Indians and persevere from past into present and future.

Thirdly, there is still a chasm between Arapaho and non-Indian persons at Wind River. Euro-American institutions promise equality and inclusion while continuing to invalidate Arapaho personhood in everyday social relations on and off the reservation. Even within some reservation schools, non-Indian and Arapaho (or Indian) social worlds remain segregated. Non-Indians define Arapaho people as persons and selves within narrow, formal contact situations, but in general they continue to regard them as nonpersons outside those contexts. Repelled by the threat of invalidated personhood, Arapaho people keep their distance.

In contemporary Wind River life, references to pity, respect, quietness, and craziness, along with related terms, all recur in discussions of the changes the Northern Arapaho tribe is experiencing. On one level, there is much concern about the loss or weakening of those values; on another level, people continue to practice them in uniquely Arapaho ways that set the community apart from the surrounding non-Indian world. Indeed, in my own experience, they are the most enduring Arapaho elements at the center of personal, family, and tribal identity, even though many people feel that their role in everyday social relations and tribal political processes is slipping away. They survive to shape, define, and assist in understanding the tempo and direction of life movement and historical change, but they strain to resolve the contradictions with and within Euro-American modes of personhood.

4
The Space and Time of Life Movement

Shaping Time

A space-time approach to the explication of life movement and its connections to the wider sociocultural system can draw in multiple strands and levels of meaning. From a broad overview of ethnographic sources, it is clear that orders of space and time in many cultures seek some degree of homology and transposability among different levels, including that of the life trajectory (see Hugh-Jones 1979:233 ff.). This pattern is evident in many North American Indian cultures, but it has been elaborated only for a few, such as Tewas (Ortiz 1969), the Ojibwas (Hallowell 1955), the Navajos (Gill 1982), the Lakotas (Walker 1980), and the Hopis (Whorf 1956). In those contexts, self-similar forms of space and time also tend to recur across different domains of cultural expression, such as myth, language, art, architecture, and social structure.

The core proposition of my approach is that human groups borrow orders of space and time from one field to bring sense to others, including the life trajectory. As in most sociocultural systems, Northern Arapaho forms of space and time are similar in structure and transposable in practice at different levels. Along the spatial dimension, the body, the tipi, ceremonial lodges, the camp circle, and the cosmos share a common directionality and orientation. On the temporal side, ritual process, the seasons, the life cycle, and epochal time of the earth are all ordered by the same space-time. Further, the same shapes and motions pervade different domains of cultural expression and practice, such as myth, ritual, art, language, and personal relations. Homologous forms also order both space and time dimensions, thus the use of the term *space-time* to recognize that interrelationship (Munn 1986:3–13).

For present purposes, the life trajectory is explicated by connections to other levels of space and time, as well as multiple domains of cultural expression. Van Gennep (1960) recognized that as a total system, rites of passage configure the unique direction, shape, and phasing of life stages. Each rite must be understood as a part of a whole temporal order, then, which varies from one culture to another. The life cycle can be plotted as a spatial form that represents time: "Thus it would be possible to draw a diagram for each people in which the peaks of a zigzag line would represent recognized stages and the valleys the intervening periods. The apexes would sometimes be sharp peaks and sometimes flattened lines of varying lengths" (Van Gennep 1960:194). Although recognizing variation, Van Gennep imposes a Western, geometric order of space and time. Such use of Euro-American abstract, neatly drawn, Cartesian geometry in analyses of space and time only reifies fixed, a priori structures. What Van Gennep and other "structural" researchers fail to recognize is that the shaping of space and time in practice continually borrows from other levels and domains of meaning within a sociocultural system. Therefore, it is necessary to identify the precise spatial and temporal forms distinctive to each sociocultural system, rather than reifying an objective structure detached from the agency of real actors, intentions, and practices.

As set forth in chapter 2, Arapaho life movement is a transposable and homologous "sort of time," that is, a temporalization or chronotype, in that it is synchronized to the shape, tempo, rhythms, and phasing of cosmic, seasonal, and daily time. This transposability is not just an abstract cosmology reified in collective consciousness but rather is generated and reproduced through practice (Hugh-Jones 1979:235–36). Practices do not just happen in it, represent it, or conform to it; they actually construct the order as durational time moves forward from past into future. In the Arapaho context, the order was reproduced in and through age-structured relations, ritual exchange, and modes of knowledge transmission. For Arapaho practice, it is in and through doing things in a good/correct way that both the order and movement through it are generated. Much of Arapaho ritual practice thus places significance on preparation as much as if not more than, on public symbols and meanings performed. There is as much meaning in the process as in the product of artistic forms, ceremonial lodges, public ritual, body adornments, and other cultural configurations.

Arapaho life movement is at once both linear and circular movement shaped by the chronotype of the 'four hills or buttes' *yeneini3i' 3o3outei'i* (Eva C'Hair) or *yeneini3i' ho3outei'i* (Kroeber 1907:314–15). References to the four stages are scattered throughout Kroeber (1907), Dorsey and Warden (1905), Hilger (1952), and Fowler (1982), but the conceptual model has never been fully elaborated. Starkloff defines the stages as "infancy and childhood, youth, middle life, and old age" (1974:75–76). In a similar way, Fowler (1982:7–8) identifies four age groupings: (1) childhood, (2) young person, (3) younger generation, and (4) elders. In a footnote she refers to their transposability: "The 'four directions' of the universe and the perceived course of the sun from daybreak to dark and season to season parallel the 'four hills' of life and the course of the individual from birth to death. As the sun is 'reborn' each day and the earth renews itself, so human life is constantly renewed" (306 n). How this system relates to the historical continuity of age structure is, however, set aside in her work. The four-hills model also entails more than can be encompassed by "renewal," a term I would replace with life movement, as defined above. In short, there was greater spatiotemporal complexity to Arapaho life movement than earlier works have presented.

Transposed to seasonal time, the sequence, both linear and cyclical, is (1) spring, (2) summer, (3) fall, and (4) winter. In ritual practice the associated order of cardinal directions is (1) east, (2) south, (3) west, and (4) north. The fifth point after four movements in prayer or ritual is a return to the center, often followed by gestures to above and below. East relates to spring and childhood, south to summer and youth, west to fall and adulthood, and north to winter and old age. Each is also associated with a different color: east is yellow, south red, west black, and north white (Crispin 1935).

The four-hills model is further transposable to the cosmological movement of what Kroeber translates as "the four generations" (1904:205). After the earth and humans were created, *Nih'oo3oo* returned to the center to place the Arapaho people in the middle of the earth: "Since then there have been three lives (generations); this is the fourth. At the end of the fourth, if the Arapaho have all died, there will be another flood. But if any of them live, it will be well with the world. Everything depends on them" (Dorsey and Kroeber 1903:16). It is interesting to note, given the space-time connection, that not only are the Arapahos placed in the middle of space; they are also placed by this epochal progression in the "middle of time," a phrase borrowed from Gill (1982:19). As on all other levels, life movement is thus dependent on knowledge and appropriate practices.

Mark Soldierwolf explained to me that each of the four generations or eras is associated with a type of bird. This last generation begins with the bluebird, brought back to life in the story entitled "Blue-Bird, Buffalo-Woman, and Elk-Woman" (Dorsey and Kroeber 1903:388 ff.). Before this were the ages of the blackbird, the yellowbird, and the red bird. In each generation, which Kroeber notes is said to be one hundred years, White Owl sits in the middle of the time circle and watches the other generations of birds pass by. The center is the most sacred and powerful place because it is the final place and is unmoving in time and space.

It is the same in life movement; the elders sit in the middle, watching the passage of younger people through the life trajectory. For instance, in the camp circle, the sweat lodge for the oldest men was placed in the center. White Owl and old people are both associated with winter. Old age is the winter of life and White Owl the winter bird (Dorsey and Kroeber 1903:231). Owls are also associated with death: "It is said that the owls are bad people, for they carry off many sick people, i.e., influence the people to die" (246). In another version, Chief Left Hand of the Southern Arapahos states that "sometimes the dead turn into owls" (Hilger 1952:161). In the daily cycle, owls are associated with night, the end of the day (Dorsey and Kroeber 1903:231), and in cosmic time with the division or the endings of epochs.

As in other Plains Indian cultures, the counting of age by winters expresses that the person has overcome periods of suffering and hardship. Years and the ages of persons were counted by "winters" as days were counted by "sleeps." In the Arapaho language, the word for year is identical to that for winter (*cec*). Mothers counted the ages of children with marks on hide scrapers showing the number of winters since the children were born. When a child was about eighteen years old, he or she continued the count. Even today, some Arapaho elders comment on how the winter has affected their age mates. One can say that someone has "made it through another winter" or that "winter has been hard on him." Winter is thus associated with old age, the north, and the division of time.

The four-stage cycle is also followed in all ceremonial movements. Everything must be presented first to the east, then clockwise to each of the other directions, returning at the end to the center. In one description of the naming ceremony, supplied in chapter 5, the four positions are linked directly to the four stages of life, such that presenting the child to each of the directions in succession expresses completion through the four stages and thus the desire for long life. The movement toward each direction in ritual movement is a prayer to each of the Four Old Men, each of whom sits on one of the four hills, ridges, or buttes. Similarly, spatial directionality is homologous with the four-stage temporal movement of epochs, seasons, and the path of the sun each day. The tipi faces east, along with the opening to the camp circle and the opening for the sun to enter the world each day. All entrances in space and beginnings in time are associated with the rising sun *niicihbisiseet* ('where it emerges, walking or slowly moving'). In myth many origin events of the distant past (*heeteeniihi'*) occurred in the east. The east-west axis thus crosscuts the four-directional circular movement. The sun road begins in the east and ends in the west. The place of prominence for those of age seniority is in the west, the direction of the setting sun (*niitne'iseet* 'where he sets' or *hihcowoonou'u'* 'where he passes'). It is also said that the afterlife is somewhere in the west (Mooney 1896:983). It is a thus place of stopping and the "quietness" of dusk.

After death the soul travels westward to the afterlife. In the tipi or any other dwelling or lodge, west is the position of prominence. In the tipi it was the place where the head of the household sat and where sacred objects were placed. If an older person entered a tipi, he or she would sit there. In the Offerings Lodge, the Flat Pipe and the sacred wheel are placed on the west side. The west is also where the highest-ranking dancers stay throughout the ceremony. Within the camp circle, the large tipi of the Keeper of the Flat Pipe was also on the western side (Mooney 1896:960).

Kroeber refers to the "four hills" in prayer as well as in artistic symbolism. An old man offered this line in a prayer that a young man requested: "Four ridges [*hee yeini3i' ho3outei'i*] may you pass over, young man, said the sprinkling (?) old men" (1907:314–15). Almost all prayers ask other-than-human persons to listen and take pity in order to give long life, which is often phrased in terms of the four-hills shape, as well as in other terms, such as the four directions, the path of the sun, and traveling along a path. The precise meaning of *yeneini3i' 3o3outei'i* or *ho3outei'i,* the Arapaho animate term for the four stages of life and the four periods of epochal time, is flat-topped hills or buttes, with divides or ridges between them. As Kroeber illustrates, the four-hills figure also pervades Arapaho artistic forms. Drawing on his classic study of symbolic design, he shows the four hills of life represented on one rawhide bag as four trapezoid-shaped forms (1902:130–32):

Figure 4.1. The four hills or buttes of life.

Certainly the four-hills model is not unique to Arapaho culture; it operates in other North American Indian cultural contexts and thus lends itself to future comparative study. Alexander (1953:174 ff.) cites the presence of this model in other Plains Indian cultures, specifically the Omahas and the Lakotas. He also extends the four-hills model to other rites and practices outside the Plains:

Among the most affecting and significant of North American customs
are the rituals which mark the four prime moments of an individual's
years—the infant's reception into Life, the youth's solitary Vigil and
quest of Vision, the man or woman's Self-Proof and recognition, often
accompanied by a new naming, and finally the old man's ritual
Memory and Passing, or for any man his Last Singing. [1953:174]

The same model is evident in Walker's material on the Lakotas, in which Tyon
identifies four stages of life, "babyhood, childhood, adulthood, and old age,"
that are likewise homologous with the four seasons and epochs (Walker
1975:215). There is also evidence of the four-stage life trajectory in Ojibwa,
Navajo, Ponca, Beaver, and other North American Indian cultural systems. It is
not enough, however, to understand each system using generic spatiotemporal
categories and distinctions, such as "circularity" and "fourness." Each system,
though grossly homologous with others, divides space and time in a unique way.

Distinctive in the Arapaho context are the shape, the tempo, and the rhythm
of life movement, as well as the associations of each stage with personhood,
knowing, and kin- and age-structured relations. In one way Arapaho life
movement was relatively protracted, not only in comparison to the Euro-
American model but also relative to other North American Indian societies. For
example, whereas Alexander considers the vision fast to be a transition to the
second hill, in the Arapaho case it seems that medicine was reserved for the
transition to the third stage. At least in terms of acquiring knowledge and
religious authority, Arapaho life movement was more drawn out and precisely
age structured than in most other Plains contexts. The life movement of
individuals was also channeled and governed by age hierarchy more than it was
in ungraded Plains systems.

In the prereservation context, the conceptual order of the entire Arapaho life
cycle was a complex temporalization with a constitutive phasing, tempo, and
directionality, as well as distinctive and cumulative knowledge, practices, and
symbolic forms (e.g., colors and animals) for different stages. Different age
groups and each gender were grounded in different spatial domains, expressed
in life transition rituals. Overall, the life trajectory was not just an objective
social structure through which individuals or age groups moved. The movement
itself, the construction of spaces, and the phasing and tempo of movement were
all dependent on relationships between different levels of the age hierarchy and
between humans and other-than-human persons. For time to move and life to
change, proper knowledge is thus required for doing things in a good way and
maintaining good relationships. So Arapaho space and time are not just four-

dimensional; they invoke fifth, sixth, and -nth dimensions of practices and meanings, including knowledge and the values explicated in chapter 3.

The Four Old Men

Dimensions of Arapaho life movement are also identified, borrowing Hallowell's concept discussed in chapter 3, with other-than-human persons, who are continuous with and an extension of the age hierarchy into cosmic space and time. Life movement is not only controlled and channeled by age hierarchy among humans but also requires the participation of other-than-human persons. In Arapaho space-time, other-than-human persons have specific places in the cosmos; they also follow distinctive and overlapping shapes of motion. It is therefore necessary to understand the relational position and dynamic movements of such beings, rather than just to isolate them in terms of inherent qualities or traits. The four-hills chronotype itself is identified with the Four Old Men, who are responsible for the succession of stages in time and directions in space. In mythico-ritual contexts, together they represent the totality of life movement.

In discussing the Sacred Wheel (*hotii*), a sacred object second only to the Flat Pipe, Dorsey recognizes the relationship of the four-stage model to the Four Old Men and the concept of "hitanni" (*hi(i)teeni*) , which Kroeber translates as 'life principle' and Dorsey equates with the Four Old Men:

> The Four-Old-Men may also be called the gods of the four world quarters, and to them the Sun Dance priest often makes supplication that they may live to a great age. The Four-Old-Men are also spoken of as the Thunderbird, having power to watch the inhabitants, and in their keeping is the direction of the winds of the earth. They therefore represent the living element of all people. If the wind blows from the north, it is said to come from the Old-Man-of-the-North, who controls the wind of that end or quarter of the world. . . . The Four-Old-Men, are considered as ever-present, ever-watching sentinels, always alert to guard the people from harm and injury. The same word, hítanni, is also applied to certain markings used in the Old-Woman's [quill society] lodge, the meaning of which is given variously as the four elements of life, the four courses, the four divides. Thus it is said that when one traveling the trail of life gets over the fourth divide he has reached the winter of old age. [1903:14]

The Four Old Men are not just symbolic of but *are* the "four hills of life" and life movement in total. In space they sit on the boundary, sending life to the center and repelling life-threatening forces from outside. Each of the Four Old Men resides at one of the four directions, which are not necessarily precise cardinal directions but are oriented by the direction of the rising and setting sun. Each is associated with a season and one of the four stages of life. The four each reside on a butte at one of the four cardinal directions, where they send wind, the breath of life, defining the changes of seasons (Crispin 1935).

They are the former keepers of the Arapaho Flat Pipe (*se'eicooo*), as well. As an extension of the age hierarchy and the Pipe Keeper's role, they define the movement of the people in time and do not wander away from their watchful position as sentinels. They embody the principles of discarding life threats beyond the periphery and behind in time, placing life-giving power in the center and modulating the movement of all beings in time. In short, they define boundaries in space and in time. In repelling life-threatening forces from the outside and sending life-giving power from the periphery to the center, the Four Old Men are the apotheosis of the linear outward-inward directionality of Arapaho space and time in ritual practice. Harmful elements are "discarded" beyond the boundaries and positive elements drawn to the center. In total, they are associated with the dual directionality underlying the four-phase chronotype of pushing outward and drawing inward between the center and the periphery.

Ascent and Descent

Suggested in the discussion and graphic representation of the four hills and the functions of the Four Old Men above is alternation between ascending and descending as a fundamental duality in Arapaho space-time. The four-hills linear movement is an alternation between ascent and descent, as in the rising and setting of the sun, which guided the daily cycle of prayer. Starkloff notes that the four-stages-of-life model is widespread among American Indian cultures but that the Arapaho "Four Buttes" version is distinctive:

> The picture of the butte makes the imagery more striking: man approaches four high, flat-topped, natural hills in order—infancy and childhood, youth, middle life, and old age—while the other world waits beyond the final descent. A butte has steep rocky sides and is never easy to ascend; once scaled, it affords a stretch of flat space for walking, and a panorama of the world. Descent is again arduous, but

one knows that one must go down, and begin the next climb.
[1974:75–76]

To recall the connection of life movement to pity elaborated in chapter 3, ascent, as suffering, followed by an easy time is replicated in each life stage. One rises to the top of each hill, has an easy walk along the top for a while, and then descends into the next stage. Temporal movement in the four-hills model involves ascent to the position, remaining stable for a time, then descending from that stage. It is also a transformation of the duality of discarding and bundling, such that through life one must "discard" the burden of the previous stage while keeping its life-giving force before entering the next. Life history and collective oral history also focus on episodes of hardship and overcoming them. The ability of a person to overcome life-threatening experiences is proof of her or his life-promoting power, which can be distributed to others and channeled into long life for them. Thus, war stories were and are commonly told in ritual contexts as a symbolic expression of overcoming hardship.

The ascent-descent model also expresses the seasonal movement of the people into and out of the mountains, as stated in chapter 1. In the Arapaho seasonal cycle, small dispersed bands ascended into the mountains in late spring and summer to hunt buffalo and descended in winter to camps in the foothills of various ranges. As in the design from Kroeber (fig. 4.1), the spaces between the hills are said to be "lakes," which suggest camping places, for moving camps either with the seasons or as one travels. According to Dorsey's evidence, it is possible that the two alternating axes of day-night and summer-winter formed the four directions associated with the Four Old Men:

Another priest states more definitely that the Four-Old-Men are Summer, Winter, Day, and Night, who though they travel in single file, yet are considered as occupying the four cardinal points. Thus, according to direction and the Arapaho color scheme, Day and Summer are the Southeast and Southwest, respectively, and are black in color, while Winter and Night are the Northwest and Northeast, respectively, and are red in color. [Dorsey 1903:14]

The alternation of day and night, summer and winter is also associated here with the alternation of red and black, the two basic colors in Arapaho color symbolism for all dual alternations.

In Arapaho mythology, the alternation of day and night is, as Lévi-Strauss (1968:223–25) discovered through a structural analysis of the Arapaho Star

Husband myth, the irreducible opposition from which all other alternations evolved. As discussed elsewhere, the alternation between day and night, established by the creation and the separation of the sun and the moon, initiated time, the ordering of space, and the origin of the Arapaho (*hinono 'ei*) people. In the Star Husband versions, the origin of cultural knowledge from above also co-originated with the alternation of day and night. To make a further connection, Arapaho ritual practices, prayers, songs, and dances concentrate on the transition between day and night, that is, dusk and dawn. There are many specific distinctions in the Arapaho language for phases of the sun's rising and falling. In Arapaho space-time, the day-night alternation as dawn : dusk defines the east-west trajectory across the sky.

Within the four-stage model, then, there is a two-phase alternation that is equally operative and perhaps more fundamental in Arapaho practices. It is also at the connection between linear and circular movement. The two-phase alternation represented by a line bisecting a circle is, I suggest, distinctly Arapaho. Dorsey establishes the duality and the circle divided into red and black halves for the Sun Dance, at all levels including the lodge itself, the buffalo skull pattern, and body paint forms (see Dorsey 1903:60–61). On the Northern Arapaho flag (fig. 4.2), created in the 1950s, for example, there is a circle represented, bisected into red on one side and black on the other. Similarly, in a set of designs referring to the creation myth, Kroeber (1907:plate 64) illustrates a similar circle with four dots bisected by a line:

Figure 4.2. (left) Arapaho flag design; (right) line bisecting circle.

The two-phase–two-color alternation also applies to movement on other levels of time and space. All good things that are on the inside or that radiate outward from the center, as from a heart, a tipi, a ceremonial lodge, a camp circle, the earth, or the sun, can be associated with redness. The face of an infant is painted red. The earth, personhood, Indianness, hearts, and old people are all red. By contrast, black is associated with motion from outside and good things brought into the center. Warriors returning from victory were painted black, as is the outside edge of the Sacred Wheel. The west is also black for the setting sun, the afterlife, and the source of storms associated with Thunderbird.

To summarize, it is possible to diagram the binary alternation at different levels:

red : black

day : night

sun : moon

rising sun : setting sun

ascending : descending

center : periphery

entering from outside : radiating from a center point

The four-phase circular-four-hills shape is thus generated by a transposable duality. In and of life movement, such alternation generates the directionality and placement of individuals and groups in life transitions, age-grade ceremonies, and women's ritual practices. Four-phase and two-phase forms are merged in the Arapaho graphic representation of the Four Old Men and life movement (*hiiteeni*).

Hiiteeni

The Four Old Men and the circular, the linear, and the ascending-descending motions of the four hills come together in the design and concept of *hiiteeni*, a geometric form used in Arapaho artistic symbolism. There are various ethnosemantic senses of the Arapaho term that Kroeber renders hiiteni, which encompasses what I refer to as life movement. In the Dorsey-Warden manuscripts (Dorsey and Warden 1905:Box 2, "Tipi door"), the term is given as "hetanne" or "hitanne" and is said to refer to the four hills of life, the Four Old Men, and the Old Men's Lodge, which is penultimate in the men's age-grade system.

What Kroeber transcribes as "hiiteni" eludes a singular definition:

The writer is unable to give the exact meaning of the word hiiteni, mentioned above. This symbol is said to signify life, abundance, food, prosperity, temporal blessings, desire or hope for food, prayer for abundance, or the things wished for. . . . It may be best described as a symbol of happy life, or, since in Arapaho symbolism the representation of an object or condition usually implies a desire for such object or condition, a symbol of the desire for happy life. Briefly, it may be called a life-symbol. [1902:40]

Kroeber glosses the *hiiteeni* symbol as 'life principle' for reference purposes throughout his work. Shown in many variations in figure 4.3, the life symbol can be represented as a square, a rectangle, a diamond (rhombus) shape, a trapezoid, or the four corners of a rectangular border (Kroeber 1902:138,144)

Figure 4.3. Arapaho life symbol variations: square, rectangle, trapezoid, rhomboid, and corner shapes (Kroeber 1902:42–43,48–49,105–8,112–18, plates 29, 31).

Outside of ritual contexts, the meaning of each design of course depends on the artist's intent, as Kroeber emphasizes, since a rhomboid, a rectangular form, or a square shape can also refer to a camp circle, a campsite, the center of something, a ceremonial wheel, an eye, stops (in a course), a valley, the earth, the ends of the earth, a lake, mountains, the body, scum, a box, a willow leaf, a wormhole, an anthill, rocks, or a track. The unusual diamond shape is also cited in connection with a person, the body, the center, a lake, a navel, and a star (Kroeber 1902:138–43, plates 26–31). What is curious about this design is its prevalence both in the highly ritualized, conventional media of quillwork and body painting and in the individualized, more variable "everyday" art of beadwork and painting.

Kroeber remarks that *hiiteeni* is one of the few "abstract" symbols in Arapaho artistic design, since it does not iconically represent a natural object, an animal, or an other-than-human person. Dorsey and Warden's evidence (1905:Box 2, File 7 1/2), however, identifies the design and the term with the Four Old Men themselves. One interesting characteristic of the rhomboid-shaped life symbol is that it often occurs in pairs or sets of four, as in the four-hills-of-life shape. The association of the square form with the tribe or the camp circle is obvious, given that a square in traditional symbolism represents a circle. The conspicuous homology among these forms is with things that approximate a rhomboid shape (including mountains, the body, a track, or rocks) or a circle (a camp circle, the earth, a lake, a wormhole, a willow leaf, a wheel, or an eye).

Linguistic evidence also correlates *hiiteeni* with multiple but interrelated meanings, including *hiiteen* 'tribe' or 'village'. In one discussion I had with Richard Moss, this is the closest correlation we could establish. The term *hiiteen* derives from a root form *-(h)itee-* 'person' or 'people', as in the word *hinenitee* 'person', central to the discussion in chapter 3. Mary Ann Yellowbear suggested to me that the term might be related to *heteen* or *hiteen*, which is a word used in closing supplications and prayers to invoke "the well-being of all present." It is also connected to the term 'heart' (*betee*) and is perhaps a first person plural inclusive possessive form, meaning 'our heart' (*hi-* first/second person plural inclusive/*-(e/i)tee-* 'heart'/ *-n* pluralizer for possession). Indeed the rhomboid shape identified by Kroeber with the life symbol is also suggestive of the heart figure elsewhere in Arapaho symbolism. The common ground of the two interpretations above rests on the affinity between the *-itee-* form and *betee*, the former defining 'person' or 'people' and the latter 'heart'. Persons have hearts as the center of their being, as tipis have fires. Fire is also associated with a root referring to heart, as *sitee*, or what Dorsey and Warden (1905:Box 1:25) offer as "wood-heart," a shortened version of *besitee*. In general, the *hiiteeni* symbol and term refer to heart, person, fire, and people.

The *hiiteeni* symbol also overlaps with the *Neyoooxetusei* (Whirlwind Woman) design ritually sewn in women's quillworking on tipi pendants, robes, and cradle board covers. Like *hiiteeni*, Whirlwind Woman is associated with the motion of radiating from a central point. These circular forms are variously associated with tipis, the sun, and *hiiteeni*, interlinked through the movement from the center outward of warmth, good feelings, blessings, or good things. From the center or the heart, all good things must be extended outward, such as rays from the sun, heat from the fire at the center of a tipi, the radiance of warmth from the heart of the people, and the extension outward of the life principle itself. Whirlwind Woman is thus the complement of the Four Old Men's movement of life from the periphery to the center. As will be discussed in subsequent chapters, the radiance of Whirlwind Woman is predominantly a

women's motion, whereas movement from outside to inside is chiefly male.
Both are necessary for life movement.

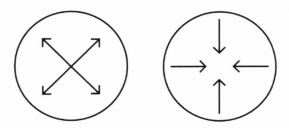

Figure 4.4. (left) Radiative motion of Whirlwind Woman; (right) inward-directed motion
of the Four Old Men.

It was Whirlwind Woman who simultaneously created quillwork designs, the
current extent of the world, and the four-hills-of-life movement. In mythical
time she expanded the earth to its current boundaries by spiraling around but
stopping at the four directions to create the four divides. She is linked with a
spiraling round quillwork design and, homologously, with spreading the earth
outward to its current extent after Turtle the earth-diver brought up a piece of
earth from beneath the deluge in the beginning:

> Whirlwind-woman was several times mentioned as having brought the
> earth to its present size by spinning around it, while it was still small
> after having been made from the mud brought by the turtle from the
> bottom of the primeval water. Her circular course, and her stops to rest
> are represented in decorative symbolism. She is also said to have been
> the originator of quill-embroidery, at which she worked as she circled
> the earth, and of the decorative designs painted on rawhide bags.
> [Dorsey and Kroeber 1903:97–98n]

Within the designs, the stops or divides denote *hiiteeni*, the life principle, or the
four hills of life (Dorsey 1903:14).
     In the quillwork pattern, the four hills are further represented by an
alternation of colors: red-black-white-black-yellow-black-white-black-red. This
four-color pattern, according to Kroeber, is considered the most sacred of all;

it can be transposed from circular to linear shapes. The Whirlwind design merges three types of motion: the four-phase linear motion, circularity, and the movement outward from center to periphery.

Figure 4.5. Arapaho sacred design (Kroeber 1902:65).

The role of the women's quillwork society in maintaining the spiraling, quadrachromatic shape of Whirlwind Woman was not merely a complement to the roles of men in producing other forms used in the age-grade lodges and the Offerings Lodge. Women reproduced the artistic forms of life movement most visible in the lived world of tipi space and covers for the body (i.e., robes and cradle boards), no less ritualized than the ceremonial lodge, the sweat lodge, or the camp circle. Quillwork practices empowered tipis, cradles, and robes with life movement and sacredness. As Lévi-Strauss realized, the circular and linear quill designs were the highest expression of culture (1968:250–51).

When placed in the context of *hiiteeni*, the succession of four hills or stages interconnects multiple modes of shaping time, including linear motion, ascent and descent, the spiraling outward motion from a center point, and the stopping and starting rhythm. *Hiiteeni* is not so much an abstract form as what Sapir would refer to as a "rhythmic configuration" at the base of sociocultural homology: "It is not claimed that the tendency toward rhythmic expression is their only determinant, but it is certainly a powerful underlying factor in the development of all social parallelisms and symmetries"(1949:344). In general, the homology of space and time forms cannot be defined as a simple internalization and objectification of structures that exist elsewhere. Nor can the forms be drawn as if they were unidimensional. It is the rich multiplicity of forms underlying art and language that can shape social formations (the reverse of Van Gennep's suggestion)—in this case the life trajectory and age distinctions. As Sapir pointed out, artistic form can be approached as a generative source for homologous, transposable forms that are found elsewhere in the sociocultural system. Such rhythmic configurations are not just realized in material objects themselves; they are generated out of human productive practice, which always already transcends utilitarian purposes to serve multiple functions. Therefore, instead of mapping or charting the space and time of sociocultural systems using our own geometry, it is necessary to identify the forms used indigenously to generate structures in multiple domains and levels of experience. *Hiiteeni* is one such form.

To summarize at this point, multiple dimensions come together in life movement: the four hills, the four directions, the four colors, ascent and descent, movement inward and outward between the center and the periphery, and spiraling. Life movement is present in art forms, the motions of other-than-human persons, ritual processes, color symbolism, and the ethnopoetics of language. The distinctive, particular phasing and tempo of the life trajectory are reproduced through social practices in which objective structures and conscious orderings come together.

Contact with Euro-Americans and relocation on the reservation transformed Arapaho space-time and disrupted the order. When the four-direction or four-stage model is expressed today, it is generally only in isolated ritual contexts. In other words, rather than functioning as a system that structures all space-time in the lived world, the four-stage model is now itself confined to ritual space-time. Nonetheless, despite the loss of much of the mythico-ritual elaboration and transposability throughout all levels of space and time, the motion shape of the four-phase model does still survive in ritual practices.

Life Stages and Learning

Beyond the chronotype of life movement, the four stages of life are also synchronized with access to knowledge through age-structured relations. Specifically, the Arapaho four hills of life are associated with four distinct ways of knowing and learning. The Northern Arapaho elder Pius Moss defined the four stages of life to me in these terms. Each of the four stages was associated with its own mode of learning or knowledge: (1) childhood was "the age of listening," (2) youth was "the age of doing," (3) adulthood was "the age of giving it back," and (4) old age was "the age of sacred learning."

Parents and grandparents expected children to learn by listening and observing rather than through verbal inquisitiveness or deliberate instruction. As in many other North American Indian cultures, children were discouraged from asking questions or otherwise expressing themselves in mixed generational interaction. Children were taught to 'listen' (*ceh'e3tii-*) when older people told to stories, delivered lectures, or spoke to them in other settings. This emphasis extended into and expanded in subsequent stages of life.

Storytelling was one of the only deliberate, controlled modes of instruction for children. Almost all adult Arapahos today have childhood memories of grandparents telling stories to them. In the age hierarchy, only elders could tell these stories. In the seasonal cycle, storytelling was confined to the winter camp and, in quotidian time, to the night:

> The tribal traditions were related from the first snowfall until the grass began to grow. . . . All other things were told all the year around. The stories that have come down to us by tradition—those told by our old people to younger ones of each generation—are sacred. They are almost like the Bible. They are never told in the summer, but only in winter. Only old people relate them. And you can't go to sleep while they are being told; you must stay awake. [Hilger 1952:78]

When the parents in a family wanted an elder to tell stories, they would formally invite that person and then, before the storytelling began, would provide a meal for the storyteller. Some stories required as many as four complete nights to tell, and some storytellers narrated all night long. The majority of the stories collected by Dorsey and Kroeber (1903), Salzmann (1980), and others were stories told to children. For the most part, children's stories revolve around some type of improper or crazy behavior and the dire consequences that follow. Stories thus reinforced expected and appropriate practices for acquiring knowledge and maintaining relations with others.

Storytelling and listening as a mode of knowledge transmission took place throughout the life trajectory. Childhood listening was preparation for subsequent forms of knowledge transmission in adulthood. During the storytelling sessions, children were supposed to be quiet, sit up, and listen attentively throughout the evening. To show that they were awake, every once in a while they were supposed to say *hiii*, which sounds like the Arapaho word for snow. Storytelling served both to transmit knowledge and to train the listener in how to do things in a good/correct way.

The same pattern endured throughout the life trajectory in all contexts of storytelling. Traditional narratives for adult groups had various degrees of ritual boundaries surrounding them. Among those, the Arapaho origin myth was the most sacred. It could be told only by the Pipe Keeper and only in a highly controlled and enclosed ritual context. The telling of the story was itself a ritual act, in that it had to be done within narrow parameters of correctness. The caution emanates from the sacred Flat Pipe, which is at the center of the myth. As Carter explains, the narrative carries all information relating to the history of the Pipe, its proper uses, and ritual objects accompanying it:

One who wishes to receive this information must make a suitable present to the keeper and abstain from food and water for the 3 days and 3 nights period during which he is receiving the information. He may rest during the day and receives the information only at night. [1938:78]

The entire narrative took three or four nights to tell. As in other storytelling contexts, the storyteller and the recipient engaged in an exchange relationship. The petitioner must give a gift to the storyteller, such as a horse, considered the highest and most appropriate gift. Consistent with the Arapaho theory of practice, the story must be told verbatim or at least within the acceptable boundaries, lest some misfortune befall the teller or his or her family. The audience for the origin myth was probably quite small. The Pipe Keeper would not tell the story often, and only to an individual or a small group of people of the appropriate age and experience. Thus, the cosmology presented in the story was known by only a very small number of people. Any models of "shared" culture must always be constructed with reference to how widely it was shared and what types of persons were allowed access to it.

Other stories were less structured but were similar in their social context to that of the origin myth. One group of stories is called *heeteenoo3itoono*, relating to events "before" this time (*heetee-* 'before'/ *-oo3itoo* 'story'). These are different from *koo3einoo3itoono*, which are old or ancient narratives of events that took place in mythical time. *Heeteenoo3itoono* are legends of a time long ago but after mythical time. Like the origin myth, they could be told only at night and sometimes took four nights to tell. It is clear from what elders told me that the stories all seemed to fit together in a series. Some of the stories collected by Dorsey and Kroeber, for instance, seem to include several smaller stories within them, or at least segments that could have been told separately.

Another type of story is the life historical narrative told at various life transitions. Commonly, when an elder or even a person of a younger generation is asked to speak in a public situation (e.g., powwows, school functions, etc.), life historical episodes and achievements are narrated to illustrate how others should live their lives. The narrator's own life experiences are extended to the person or persons at the center of the ritual. Stories thus offer direction and power for life movement. Traditionally, at ear piercing ceremonies, naming, and some other life transitions, warriors of the past and veterans today relate a war story to illustrate their bravery and sacrifice for the tribe. The storyteller's own strength to endure a life-threatening situation is conferred to the child or other person for whom life movement is sought. Similarly, in other contexts people will discuss other difficult times and how they overcame them. Each tragedy or difficult time is overcome and "discarded," though it is remembered in life historical accounts. Difficult times can include such tragedies as the loss of a family member, serious illness, conflict with others, a clash with white authorities, or a personal problem. In the Arapaho context, the narrated word has "power" in that storytelling can bring health and long life to both the listeners and their kin affected by the crisis.

Another traditional child-rearing practice related to the importance of "listening" was 'lecturing' (*bebiisibetiit*), which often focused instruction to young people in the "age of doing" on how to conduct oneself in a good/correct way. Parents, grandparents, and even older siblings would give lectures.

> Children were trained by being talked to as soon as they were old enough to be talked to. I talked to them anytime during the day or night, whenever I had the opportunity. Sometimes in the evening all would be around in the tipi and I'd start to talk to the children. Instructions were given to children at any time of the year or at any time of the day or night. There were no regularly assigned persons who instructed children. It was up to the parents to instruct their children. Sometimes parents called in an old man of the tribe who had made a success of his own life. The mother would cook a meal of meat and bread, call him in to her tipi, feed him and ask him to tell the boy his experiences; to tell him how he might be good, etc. . . . Parents might also call in an old woman to talk to the girl. . . . The child was guided and talked to up to the time he was married. He was not talked to anymore after that. [Sherman Sage in Hilger 1952:76]

Lecturing and advice to children are distinct from storytelling (*honoo3itootowoo*). As Sage explains, lecturing took place anytime, but storytelling was regarded as specific to season and time of day. During the first two stages of life, lecturing ranged from brief, informal corrections to formal situations similar to storytelling.

Both lecturing and storytelling involved the association of 'listening' (*ceh'e3tii-*) with 'respect' for an older person (*neeteene-*). As pointed out in chapter 3, to respect someone is to 'sit quietly' (*teiitoon3i'oku-*) in that person's presence. Elders today report that they had to sit quietly and listen even when older people were talking among themselves, unless they were given permission to leave. In childhood the capacity for listening was a sign of developing personhood and future life direction, that is, a loss of youthful craziness.

As one became an adult, it was also common, in difficult life situations, to ask an older person for advice for oneself or a family member, perhaps in a formalized manner. The younger person would ask the old man or woman to come to his or her house. Such an invitation carried an obligation to feed the older person, as it would have in any other context. Many people told me, "You have to feed old people whenever they come to your house." After the meal, the younger person would explain to the elder exactly what he or she wanted to know or talk about. At that point it was common for the elder to say that he or she "would have to think about it," thus suspending advice—sometimes until it was clear in the elder's mind. If no response was forthcoming, that likely reflected an unwillingness to pass on the requested knowledge.

Lectures and advice were also offered as components of important life transition rituals, such as birth, naming, and marriage. Like storytelling, lecturing in life transition contexts carried practical moral advice about the stage or relationship the listener was passing into. Like stories, lectures aimed to straighten out the lives of young people. As Kroeber suggests, this portion of a speech by a father to his son who was about to marry was intended to give direction:

> My son, it pleases me much where you found a woman. My son, disregard it . . . even if the others say what you do not like to listen to. Where you are a servant [to affines], you must not mind it. Try hard, my son, not to become, discouraged too quickly. Do not be bashful, but be kind. Do good where you are united. Whatever your father-in-law orders you to do, my son, or your mother-in-law, or your brother- in-law, do that for them. Do not go away without the consent of your wife. Do not roam about without purpose [i.e., don't be "crazy"] . . . Be pleasant to persons who come to your tent, my son. . . . Do not scold your wife. Always treat her well and pity her. Those who try to be good are treated well and are pitied. Do your best and do not become tired. And now look at your tent, your pipe, your food, and your friends. [Kroeber 1907:315–16]

Pervading many lectures or forms of advice are the values of personhood and good relations outlined in chapter 3. All types of narration thus function to make children and young people into human persons.

Closely related to lecturing are two other practices. The first one is speech-making, which occurs at almost every public gathering today, including powwows, memorial feasts, giveaways, school programs, and so forth. Speech-making may be thought of as a collective form of lecturing that combines oral history, life history, and storytelling. A speech, like a lecture, usually explains and emphasizes the significance or context of an event, as well as the forms of personhood and Arapaho identity involved.

The centrality of older persons' advice and speeches to younger people continued throughout life movement. For example, elders were often responsible for "setting someone straight," a speech form that is similar to lecturing. Older people were and are called in to "advise" the parties involved in a dispute, a disagreement, or a misunderstanding. An elder might be accompanied by a group of family supporters when he or she "goes to talk to" the individual or individuals at the center of the problem. Similarly, older people step in to tell the tribe what their consensus should be on political issues. In traditional interfamilial kinship relations, an older person from one family generally went to the other family to offer compensation, resolve a conflict, initiate an exchange, or arrange cooperation. Lecturing, advising, or "talking to" others are strategies for problem solving still used by Arapaho families today. In recent times it has been extended to classroom contexts, graduations, and other learning situations.

Returning to the first stage of life, parents and grandparents often celebrated a child's acquisition of abilities associated with becoming a person and thus began early in the child's life to honor and show respect. According to Hilger (1952:40–43), honoring a child's first tooth marked the ability to chew; first-walk feasts recognized movement outside the tipi, thus becoming an upright person (*3owo3nenitee*); and first-kill feasts celebrated the ability to provide for others. The recognition given to a child during the first stage of life for valued abilities showing that he or she was able to "do things" anticipated the second stage of life. In the first stage of life, rarely did parents or grandparents instruct children deliberately by sitting them down to explain or show them how to do things. Explanations and demonstrations were added to continued lecturing in the second stage of life. Parents and grandparents also carefully observed a child's development in everyday life for signs that he or she was moving in the right direction at the right tempo and thus ready for the subsequent stage of learning.

Described by Fowler as the "younger generation," the second stage is referred to here as "the age of doing" (Pius Moss). By doing things and "looking on," young people were expected to take on the daily chores of camp life. At the same time, emerging respect relationships between brothers and sisters segregated male and female activities and social spaces. From that point on, instruction and knowledge transmission were gender specific. In the second stage youths were allowed more freedom to ask questions and more was explained to them; parents and grandparents offered more intensive instruction through lecturing. Like the age-grade lodges and the women's ceremonies, the second stage stressed service, endurance and productivity. According to one of Hilger's informants, whereas childhood involved mimicking adult behavior in play, later on children engaged in productive activities themselves: "Boys from 8 to 10 years old were taught how to shoot arrows, how to aim at buffalo, how to ride horseback and how to care for horses. When a little older they went out to hunt with the older men, especially with fathers or grandfathers. They learned from them how to hunt" (Hilger 1952:78). By the age of eight to ten, then, boys began to receive instruction from senior men; girls were taught primarily by women. The "age of doing" coincided with the separation of male and female domains of activity.

Brother-sister respect and the segregation of male and female social space were associated also with an effort by the senior generations to keep the sexes apart during young adulthood. As many older women told me, their grandmother, mothers, and aunts always kept a close eye on them. Young women remained close to the tipi and to their "mothers," that is, close to their mother and their mother's sisters. The chores of young women included fetching water from the river in the morning, collecting firewood, cooking, sewing, and other activities associated with tipi social space. Young men were drawn into peer groups outside the tipi and engaged in activities on the periphery of the camp circle, such as hunting, caring for horses, and service to senior age grades. Both genders were "servants" to other people in a sense, a pattern that extended and expanded throughout the second and third stages.

The second stage of life culminated in marriage, which involved a reciprocal exchange of goods between the wife's and the husband's kin. Marriage was followed by matrilocal residence and often bride service to the wife's family; that custom required a young man to act as a servant of sorts to his wife's family. The sense of "doing" continued well after marriage, lasting until one finally became somewhat independent of one's parents or parents-in-law. True adulthood was not achieved until a man and woman became the center of a camp or family group. Therefore, "adulthood," if it can be defined as such, did not begin until one was at least in one's thirties or forties.

The third stage of life is called the "age when you give it back," that is, the time to begin to return goods, knowledge, and other forms of value to others rather than being primarily a recipient. For example, one emerged at this stage into true adulthood as "provider" of material goods for others, both children and older people. The scope of one's life and personhood moved from the family to the camp and the tribe. Crazy behavior was unacceptable at this stage; people were expected to settle down and behave respectfully. Elders did not recognize younger-generation people as adults until about age forty, although, as many people have told me, this varied widely. People became adults at younger or older ages depending on the way they lived their lives. At the third stage men and women not only participated in rituals but began to acquire the necessary knowledge for directing them and for passing on the knowledge to others. Traditionally, only men in this age group were allowed to seek visions and acquire personal medicine. Both women and men could also begin to "learn" more formally about ceremonial knowledge through dyadic apprentice relationships with elders.

During this stage it was also more important to take part in various activities visible in public space, including speeches, political leadership, ritual agency, and economic redistribution. Fowler (1982:103) observed that this particular stage was the one reserved for political leadership roles requiring public-speaking duties. In addition, making sacrifices for others and engaging in exchange relationships were at the center of one's religious and social life. Both men and women became organizers and actors for the life movement of others.

The fourth stage of life (*beesnenitee* 'big person') is defined as the elder stage in modern vernacular. Elders were the ritual authorities in all sacred knowledge and embodied the consensus and unity of the tribe (Fowler 1982). Their space was in the center of the camp. In Arapaho conceptions, achieving longevity is symbolic of having lived in a good/correct way and therefore receiving blessings from above. In turn, those who live a long life have the power to give life movement to others. Elders generally withdrew from direct modes of expression in all areas of public life. However, they continued to play an active role in child rearing, sometimes even adopting children to raise or raising their own grandchildren. Like the seasons, the stages of the life cycle unfold in a circle. Children and elders were seen as "close" to each other. In kin relationships (Eggan 1937:53), grandparents and grandchildren were "close," almost as close as equals. The significance of that relationship is that much learning and ongoing interaction occurred between children and grandparents. Beyond childhood, one could remain very close to specific grandparents, who had helped in child-rearing, while learning to maintain respect and distance toward other elders defined as grandparents outside one's core of family members.

In sum, the life cycle was modulated with respect to the transmission of knowledge. Elders ultimately controlled the process. They made certain that forms of knowledge were conveyed only at certain times in the life trajectory and in appropriate contexts. Only when prerequisite knowledge had been acquired and people acted in appropriate ways would the senior generations pass on knowledge to children or young adults. That principle held for both the age-grade ceremonial system and the socialization process outside the ceremonial complex. Elders today often recall that their parents or grandparents waited until what they believed was the "right time" to explain things to them. For young people this often resulted in impatience and bewilderment. One woman told me that she had asked her mother a number of times to show her how to make moccasins, but each time her mother had said she did not know how. After the young woman had asked around on and off for years, looking for someone else to teach her, her mother walked in one day and said, "I am going to teach you how to make moccasins." Until that time her mother did not believe she was genuinely ready to learn.

Senior age groups also synchronized knowledge, practice, and time, such as the time of day, the tempo of interaction, and the seasonal cycle. For example, elders' knowledge focused on an acute awareness of changes in the natural environment, and thus the elders could sense when collective ceremonies, camp movements, and subsistence activities should be organized and held. Both communal and life transitional ceremonies occurred only at certain times of the year. Moving camp had to be timed correctly with changes in the environment. It is interesting that camp movements, like life movement, were ultimately governed by the movement of the Sacred Pipe. The Pipe Keeper, through the reading of signs in nature and discussion with the elders and chiefs, decided when and in what direction his camp would move. It is not known exactly how other camps, which did not have the Pipe residing in them, made such decisions, since the Pipe was kept in one among several bands (Dorsey and Warden 1905:Box 2, Folder 2).

Contradictions

Different ways that Western and non-Western cultures order time and "life time," in particular, are so ingrained in ordinary experience that the construction of a "metalanguage" (Munn 1992:116) to conceptualize different systems is perhaps one of the most difficult tasks of translation and cultural analysis. In many cases, the orders of space and time in other cultures are reduced by analysts to static, closed geometry. For example, time in so-called ahistorical societies has often been represented by the shape of a circle or assumed to constitute merely alternation (Leach 1961) or a cycle (Geertz 1973), all patterns that presume a time that is unmoving, flat, and closed to duration. First of all, Arapaho life movement is not, in practice, mere repetition, renewal, and ahistorical stasis. Second, life movement is open to durational time, as a set of strategies for giving shape and continuity to past, present, and future. The Arapaho four-stage–four-direction order synthesizes linear and circular motion within the same space-time. Arapaho life movement does not conform to the chronotype of Euro-American history, but it does embody linear, irreversible time. There are other trajectories of linear time than Euro-American historicity.

That realization can extend to an understanding of the contradictions between Arapaho and Euro-American space-time that is able to reveal central and powerful, yet heretofore underexplored, dimensions of intercultural relations and colonization. Power involves the control of time as well as space, and Euro-American power has been extended largely through its mastery of time. Domination, assimilation, and expropriation have always imposed Euro-American knowledge and space-time and, in particular, a model of the life cycle. Life movement and age structure, once pervading all levels of the Arapaho lived world, have become, in the reservation period, a compartmentalized domain within an imposed space-time generated by Euro-American knowledge. Therefore, Euro-American temporalities include not only clock time, as has perhaps been overstudied, but also other, less visible orders of time.

As Vine Deloria recognizes, the contradictions between two systems of time and space are at the source of other contradictions:

> Not only did their geographic confinement work to destroy the sacred calendars of tribes, but the effort to perpetuate traditional life within the confines of the reservation was vulnerable to overtures by the federal government, seeking to make the people abandon old ways and adopt new practices which were carefully orchestrated by a new sense of time—a measured time which had little to do with cosmic realities. It is debatable which factor was most important in the destruction of tribal ceremonial life: the prohibition of performances of traditional rituals by the government, or the introduction of white man's system of keeping time. [1985:18]

The estrangement of indigenous North American peoples from their traditional space thus alienated them from the rhythms and tempos of traditional time.

Because of the intrinsic interrelationship of space and time, the exile of Indian peoples from traditional territories removed them from seasonal cycles, daily cycles, life trajectories, and even mythic time. As a result of displacement, the homology among different levels and the shared dimensionality with space were more difficult to maintain. For some connections it was impossible.

Wherever Euro-American society has expanded its power, it has aimed to universalize its own chronotypes and modes of temporalization for the daily schedule, the annual cycle, the life trajectory, cultural evolution, and world development. Assimilation, conquest, and forced removal have been accompanied by a mission to transform spaces as well, such as in the home, the schools, the workplace, and modern organizations. The interconnected power over space and time is what Giddens calls "time-space organizing devices" or "zoning of time-space" (1987:160). Included are time tabling, clock time, commodification of time, surveillance, cubicling, and functional specialization of spaces and times. Simply put, the ideal type assigns one function to each specialized space and each slot of time, whether in the meeting, the office, the day, the project, the organization, the year, the life cycle, a race of people, or even the events of history and future social development. Instead of being active participants in interpersonal time and space, persons are defined by their places and times in this system. In turn, much Euro-American knowledge is idealized as rational-practical knowledge for the ordering of space and time. The burden is then placed on the individuated ego, extracted from social and cultural conditions, to discover or construct continuity.

For constructing the life trajectory in practice, the Euro-American post-Enlightenment model also transposes from other modes of temporalization, in particular borrowing the chronotype of the "schedule," what Weber recognized as the rationally ordered life sequence, and "history" as a linear, progressive, and developing process. Euro-American models often construct the life cycle as a developing, irreversible process in which a past or early stage of development is ever real in the present personality or mental content of the individual person. The life cycle is thus valorized as the unfolding development of the individual through biographical time, which shares the temporality of history writ large (see Weintraub 1975:841 ff.). Within this "life-time-as-history" model is the assumption that previous events succeed each other but retain the past, situating the individual ego as actor and knower in the locus of space and time.

In North American Indian cultures, the shape of the life cycle is generally not constructed by such irreversibility and individuation. Time is shaped through vows and other experiences to overcome and reverse suffering in and of relationships with others. Such reversals are not accomplished through advanced self-realization by an isolated individual consciousness. Even experiences of self, such as visions and dreams, must be placed and structured in the context of relationships with others. That is exactly the central importance of life movement, age structure, and the controlled transmission of knowledge in Arapaho culture. In the present, however, Euro-American society has imposed its own tempo and rhythms, thus attempting, though not succeeding in total, to reconstruct the Arapaho lived world. In Arapaho prereservation age structure, one's life movement was not in one's own power to control. Rather, it depended on one's relations with human and other-than-human persons.

The once totalized Arapaho system of space, time, and knowledge has itself become compartmentalized in contemporary culture. Moreover, the reproduction of age structure from a transposable four-stage motion and shape has been juxtaposed with a Euro-American life-cyclical model, a set of new life transition ritual emphases, and greater control of life movement by individual families. Elders are therefore no longer a unified age group with sole power over mediation with other-than-human persons to effect the life movement of others. However, the Arapaho people have continually sought to claim ownership of the life trajectory as it has changed.

Conclusion

Arapaho life movement was a synchronizing of knowledge and personhood with a temporal order, itself generated through social practices and relations. Knowledge acquired prematurely could be life threatening to oneself and others. Knowledge had to be channeled, exchanged, and embodied within the boundaries of ritual practice shaped by the four-hills model. The four-phase chronotype of life movement, then, was more than a social or cognitive structure for defining meaning or directing action. It both was inherent in and was a product of artistic production, ways of talking, ritual practice, ways of knowing, stories, personal relations, and other activities. Through social practices Arapaho people maintained the tempo, shape, and direction for life movement and knowledge exchange.

In the movement through different ways of knowing, persons acquired the "practices" before they learned the shared meanings of those practices. Children performed ritual and nonritual activities before they were instructed in their symbolic content or value orientation. Doing and then knowing things "at the right time" governed all temporal movements. For example, as in the progression of ceremonies, the life trajectory was guided by the need for "preparation." One did not just have a ceremony or acquire knowledge at a moment in time. Rather, the preparation phase of all activities had importance equal to that of the actual event. People worked and prepared for a year or several years to participate in a ceremony before they experienced the highly symbolic load of the ceremony itself, the end result. Likewise, each stage of learning anticipated and prepared individuals and age groups for the successive stages. In the life cycle and in ritual preparation, practice preceded the acquisition of a priori conceptual forms and symbolic content. Throughout all practice, the definition of appropriate behavior and parameters of knowledge were relative to time and place on different levels. We are not talking about a process determined by the universal clock of biology or psychology. Each culture actively controls access to knowledge at different stages and thus modulates the temporal order of experiences for those who pass through the life trajectory. For transmitting knowledge the sociocultural clock is a chronotype transposed from other levels of time in a culture. However, in practice the process of synchronizing the transmission of knowledge with time is never totally mechanical and repetitive; it happens in a time that people must continually shape, phase, and regulate.

In general, it is necessary to overcome the tendency to see nonliterate cultural systems as having been reproduced automatically through informal processes of socialization, enculturation, or inculcation. Knowledge is subject to differential access according to age, gender, kin group, or class in all sociocultural systems. In Arapaho life movement, much of culture was bounded and exchanged as knowledge controlled within age-structured relations. The cultural model was not injected in its totality into children, nor into anyone else prior to the fourth stage of life. Only a few of the oldest people—whether Arapahos or other Indians—possessed, at any given time, knowledge of the total cosmological order. Out of that fact has also arisen one of the greatest barriers to understanding the so-called worldviews of North American Indian cultures.

5
Childhood

Introduction

Anthropological orientations to ritual tend to privilege observation and interpretation of public, collective practices or profoundly life-changing transitions. Studies of religion and ritual have often ignored or understated the functions of practices that take place in what are labeled profane or domestic spaces and times. As such, the rituals for children, women, and other persons within the sphere of close kin have been relegated to a secondary symbolic significance and minimal political, economic, and religious functions. In Arapaho life movement, rituals that took place in the tipi for birth, early childhood achievements, women's quillwork, and death must be placed, along with age-grade ceremonies, into a total temporal system. Drawing on Hilger's excellent description (1952) of Arapaho child life, Kroeber's classic work (1902, 1904, 1907), and Dorsey and Warden's manuscripts (1905), it is possible to examine all Arapaho prereservation life transition rituals and age grades as a total process for constituting life, knowledge, and personhood. Included are the rituals for birth, the cradle, naming, ear piercing, the women's Buffalo Lodge, the men's age-grade sequence, the women's quillwork society, and death.

In every Arapaho ritual practice, all age groups participated to some extent, particularly those groups senior to the focal individual or group. Parents and the grandparental generation were present for all childhood rituals. Ultimately, the elders' knowledge and mediation with other-than-human persons were necessary to facilitate both ritual practice and the life movement it effects. The elders also played the most instrumental role by observing and determining who was and was not ready to pass on to another life stage. By carefully watching and mentally recording younger people's life experiences, behavior, and characteristics, the elders governed the tempo and direction of an individual's or an age set's life movement. To play all those roles, older people had to be present to witness, recognize, and honor individual or group achievements or changes.

Childhood life transition rituals often, though not exclusively, took place in the tipi or in other spaces enclosed from the public world, the domain of tribal ceremonies in the *beyoowu'u* lodges. In these smaller contexts, women were the primary organizers and agents for life transition rituals. The agency of women in these smaller spaces and shorter times, though, should not be relegated to a secondary or complementary function compared to the more public roles of men and women in the age-grade lodges, the Offerings Lodge, and the women's Buffalo Lodge.

The power associated with early life transitions is evident in the degree of respectful and circumspect practices surrounding them, especially birth. As Hilger relates (1952:14), women were reluctant to speak about birth, since such talk could produce pregnancy. In many respects birth was part of an enclosed domain of speech and practice comparable to other carefully circumscribed practices for life movement, such as death, sacred ceremonies, and medicine. Like death, birth took place in the enclosed space of close kin rather than in the public field of ceremonies or lodges. In the life trajectory the person moved outward, as for men, or extended generative power outward, as for women, from within the tipi to the camp circle and beyond, and then returned to enclosed space at the end of life.

Birth

At the mythical co-origination of humanness, knowledge, and the alternation of time, the ability of women to menstruate, conceive, and give birth was the first and strongest power for all life movement. Therefore, the interrelationship of blood, life movement, and knowledge is at the center of Arapaho ritual power and practice, as expressed in the Offerings Lodge (Dorsey 1903:177–78). In the Arapaho Star Husband myth (Dorsey and Kroeber 1903:321–51), called "The Porcupine and the Woman Who Climbed to the Sky," a human woman marries Moon, then has the first child, called Little Star, who becomes a messenger from the above and is placed in the above as Morning Star, following the paths of Sun and Moon each day. After Moon kills the woman in her attempted escape to her people's camp below on earth, the child escapes to bring all knowledge of culture, including the Offerings Lodge, to the human, Arapaho, people. The power of women to reproduce and its association with blood, through birth and menstruation, then, is the first and most powerful Arapaho medicine (*beetee*).

Given its great power, birth was carefully circumscribed by appropriate practices. An Arapaho person was born in his or her mother's tipi (Hilger 1952:14). Well into the reservation period (during the 1930s) there were several women in the tribe recognized as "midwives" (*neeseineee3i'*) to assist (1952:16). For a difficult birth, a medicine man would be called in, but otherwise birth was a feminine ritual practice. The midwives assisted by preparing medicinal tea for the mother, positioning her correctly in a vertical, crouching position, catching the baby, and cutting the umbilical cord. One midwife wrapped the afterbirth carefully and tightly in a buckskin bag, then either buried it or hung it in a tree (1952:18). The Arapaho women I talked to said that the bag was buried only when there were no trees nearby (Anita Portwood). As Hilger's informants relate, nothing from the birth was ever burned. All life-giving things within or once within a woman were not to be exposed to extreme heat, at least until after the birth. When a woman disposed of the bag containing the afterbirth, she prayed to other-than-human persons above the ground, in the water, and beneath the ground to insure the long life of the child. The disposal of the bag, then, is an example of "discarding" an object or leaving it behind at a distance, as in the concepts derived from the *hosei*-stem, examined in detail in chapter 11. As in the association of blood, flesh, and cloth hung on trees as offerings in other contexts, it was left behind in a place where it could not be disturbed. Hanging "discarded" or offered objects in trees was common, such as the cloth offerings hung on the center pole of the Offerings Lodge or left in trees for other-than-human persons when traveling. An example is offerings left to *hiincebiit* (Owner of Waters) when crossing rivers or passing springs. Although some objects were discarded, others had to be bundled and kept close to the person, such as the navel bag containing the remainder of the child's navel.

Women were also told that they should be quiet when giving birth: "There is no sense in making so much noise. A woman should have it quiet when a baby is being born" (Hilger 1952:19). Even today young Arapaho women are told not to yell "like white women do." Birth and the preparation for it required the quietness (*teiitoneihii-*) discussed in chapter 3, as did many other ritual contexts governed by the need to do things in a correct/good way. Not only was it necessary to be quiet on the outside, but also, as from the desired effect of tea she was given, the mother becomes "quiet on the inside." In parallel with the quietness required at night, all noises that might attract life-negating forces or beings had to be eliminated from the birth environment. In a similar manner, talking about birth could cause women to become pregnant, so one had to be quiet about birth in everyday speaking.

Conversely, birth itself carries powerful medicine that can negate the life or power of other things and persons. As in some other North American Indian contexts, the power of blood resulting from birth or menstruation is life-giving within a woman but has neutralizing power on all other medicines and ceremonial objects. In other words, women's blood has the power to "immobilize" when not kept separate or within boundaries. All things associated with women's reproductive ability had to be kept separate from medicines, lest the medicines lose their power (Hilger 1952:15). All medicine bags were removed from the tipi where a birth was taking place, based on the belief that they would lose their power if they came in contact with the afterbirth or lochia.

The same power negatively affected uninitiated persons. This follows the general restriction that infants and young people must be kept apart from all powerful medicine, including birth itself. The first two stages of life were carefully separated from all medicine or *beetee*. Access to the most powerful medicine was restricted to the third and fourth stages of life. Such knowledge is considered inappropriate to youth, since it can, if used improperly, immobilize the life movement of children or young people. For example, they were always kept a safe distance from the sacred Flat Pipe and not allowed in or near the sweat lodge. To maintain the boundaries, the life-giving power of very powerful objects or processes had to be mediated by the agency of elders and adult ritual actors with appropriate knowledge.

Furthermore, those persons who do come in contact with something powerful can carry that power on or in their bodies, until that power is neutralized. Negative or positive power can be intentionally or unintentionally transmitted through touch, eye contact, walking in another's path, or other forms of contact. Respecting that power, those who assisted in the birth had to avoid sick persons, lest they worsen the illness of those who were vulnerable. Afterward, all persons who had touched or been in close proximity to birth—and all medicine bags that had been in the area—had to be fumigated through smudging or purified in the sweat lodge in order to remove the power they carried out of the tipi (Hilger 1952:15). Shortly after giving birth, the mother herself was likewise purified by smudging. A medicine man or woman prepared the hot coals and placed the sweet-smelling glands from a beaver, which were probably not "testes" as Hilger states, but the musk or scent glands commonly used for incense. Heat and sweet smells have the power to neutralize the residues of birth and thus to purify a person's body.

Any objects or substances kept close to children must be univocally life-giving, such as the navel amulet bag or the cradle. Shortly after birth the infant was bathed in cool water and then covered with red "war paint" (Hilger

1952:24). Pregnancy and birth were strongly associated with coolness and water. For example, a pregnant woman was warned to avoid getting too close to a fire or a stove (1952:14). Before conception, heat and smudging could have a contraceptive effect, and at times they were employed intentionally for that purpose (1952:9). Pregnant women were also advised to bathe in the river often in order to bring about an easy birth; as the woman faced downstream, the flow of the water would ease the flow of the newborn out of the womb. In other contexts as well, heat was associated with infertility and the immobilization of life movement. As one moves from youth to old age, one moves from cold to increasing warmth. Thus, heat is most strongly associated with old age, as in the sweat lodge of the Seven Old Men. In the proximity of birth or youth, heat has a life-negating power, but for older persons it is reenlivening.

The red paint put on the child was a mixture of ocher and buffalo fat, which had other ceremonial uses and also served as an everyday treatment for various skin problems. Symbolically, redness denotes blood, earth, human life, and above all else, the shared substance of being an Arapaho and an Indian (*3owo3nenitee*) person. In short, paint not only carries a sacredness but also has a direct protective, curing capacity. Painting as a marker of Arapaho identity, age, and rank is used in virtually every ritual context.

Following birth, the navel cord was cut and wrapped so that it could be encased in an amulet bag, usually in the shape of a reptile such as a lizard or a horned toad (Kroeber 1902:54–56; Hilger 1952:22–23). During childhood the mother kept the navel bag for the child. When one became an adult with one's own home, one kept and wore the bag close to one's body throughout life. The main power of the bag was to promote longevity and give a 'straight' (*xouubee'*), noncrazy direction to life. Like all childhood ritual objects and practices, the navel bag gave shape and direction to a person's life movement. Its loss was thought to cause a person to wander around or steal property from others in the search for it (Hilger 1952:23). The navel bag also symbolized a child's first cutting of flesh and therefore the first act to effect life movement through a flesh offering. Upon death, the navel cord was buried with the deceased, for it continued to keep the person's path straight in the afterlife.

The birth and all subsequent rituals required carefully bundling or bounding some elements within close proximity to a child, while discarding others beyond the boundaries of the tipi or the camp. Like all ritual practice, birth had power both for life movement and for immobilizing not only the mother but also others who came in contact with it. Similarly, all practices surrounding birth aimed to generate the right movement in time and to put powerful, respected objects in the right places. Some elements were kept, and others were discarded. Some were kept cool, whereas others were exposed to heat. As a result, the Arapaho people could move their own and their children's lives in the proper direction. Birth and infancy took place in the tipi, the internal social space centering on women's power to generate life. As a child grew older, his or her space expanded into the camp, then beyond the camp circle, and in old age back to the center of the camp circle. Life thus progressed from closure to opening and then returned to closure again.

Cradles

Continuing the process, the cradle was a way of bundling the infant's body and person. It thus provided the first home, vitalized the child's physical and mental abilities as a person, and protected him or her from negative forces. Each cradle design was particular to a single child and embodied the desire for long life and maturity (Hilger 1952:35). The cradle was involved in relations of exchange based on respect, as were various objects in the age-grade system, the Offerings Lodge, the women's lodges, and other ritual contexts. The exchange for cradles, as for tipis and buffalo robes made and given by women, was part of an ongoing intrakin exchange, whereas exchanges in the *beyoowu'u* ritual system constructed or activated both intra- and interfamilial kinship relations.

Shortly following birth, the child was ceremonially placed in a cradle, usually made by an aunt (the father's sister) with several other women assisting, as part of her exchange relationship of respect with her brother. A child's father's sister was classified as "aunt" (*nehei* 'my aunt'), as distinct from the child's mother's sister, who was referred to as "mother" (*neinoo* 'my mother') (Hilger 1952:35). In kin relationships, one's father's sister was more distant than one's mother's sisters, since the former was due respect by one's father. As part of this relation, aunts and uncles (mother's brothers) were instrumental in serving as ritual agents and disciplinarians for keeping a child's life straight. The cradle thus participated in the lifelong formal reciprocity between brother and sister, carried over into ritual responsibilities toward each other's children. The gift of the cradle had to be reciprocated by the child's father, for example with a gift of a horse. It is noteworthy as an aside that almost all ritualized quillwork productions involved gifts between brothers and sisters or through other relations across the gender boundaries characterized by respect.

The production of the cradle was under the control and guidance of the old women who owned the seven sacred quillworking bundles. It was thus itself part of ritualized preparation and artistic production within the women's quillwork society, which also produced buffalo robes and tipi furnishings, both of which likewise cover or contain the body. The cradle was finished before the child was born. The styles of design and color were therefore not gender specific. To make a cradle for her brother's child, a woman had to prepare gifts and food for the old women who were invited to offer instruction. Cradle making was thus a ritual practice involving apprenticeship within a exclusively women's age hierarchy. As elaborated in chapter 8, the aim of the practice was to ensure near replication of procedures and designs for the specific style of cradle chosen (as opposed to less restricted art forms, which were left to individual creativity), while configuring the designs uniquely for each cradle. As Kroeber realized, and as the descriptive evidence about cradles indicates, ritually controlled artistic production was much more uniform in design and symbolic content than other items produced outside of those channels (Kroeber 1902:150). What Kroeber fails to elaborate, though, is how each quilled object was bounded by ritualized art practices but at the same time unique and linked to an individual person.

After the child was born, the maker of the cradle gave it to the child's father, who was often her brother. The mother then brought the child to a tipi prepared by the cradle maker. After the child was given to the maker (aunt) and placed in the cradle, the hood of the cradle was incensed. The maker then prayed for the child's health and long life. Specifically, she presented the child to each of the four directions and thus to the Four Old Men, beginning in the east and ending in the north, a pattern followed in all ritual practices, including the naming ceremony described in the following section. The baby was then returned to the mother according to Hilger's account (1952:37), or to the father, according to Kroeber (1902:16). As for all childhood rituals, a feast then followed for all in attendance.

When a child outgrew the cradle, it was ceremonially dismantled (Hilger 1952:37-38). No cradle was ever used for more than one child. An older woman performed the ritual, in which the frame was destroyed; the quillwork cover was kept throughout the child's life. Again, the ritual included both discarding and preserving elements. This dual practice was also followed for most ceremonial objects made for the men's age societies, the women's lodge, and the Sun Dance.

On one level, different designs on the cradle cover represented different parts of the child's body and desired capacities to be acquired in subsequent stages of life movement (Kroeber 1902:66; Dorsey and Warden 1905:Box 1:84; Hilger 1952:29–38). On one cradle described by Kroeber, the round, whirlwind design at the top represented the child's head or skull. Black quills around the head symbolized hair, the thongs on the side ribs, and the thongs at the bottom legs. As Kroeber states, "red represents blood; black the hair (of youth and middle age); white (the hair of old age)" (1902:67). In short, the cradle symbolized the body at four stages of life. As in all sacred art, ritual preparation, prayers, and sacrifices, life movement is the desired end, and is embodied in the *hiiteeni* symbolism for the Four Old Men and the four stages of life pervading cradle designs.

The museum catalogue of the Field Museum of Natural History describes a cradle rich in various levels and forms of life movement symbolism:

> This cradle, both in form and decoration, is typical of the Northern Arapaho. The disk over the head symbolizes the sun, also the crown of the child's head, and its intelligence. The red and yellow sectors of the disk, meeting at right angles, form a cross, symbolizing the Morning Star or a woman. The white sectors represent the four corners of the earth; the yellow, the light of the sun; the red, its heat; and the black, night. The rattles at the top of the cradle symbolize the hearing of the child. The loops at the ends of these and other pendants symbolize the sun. The band of quillwork around the opening represents the hair of the child; the four pendants attached to it, the four corners of the world; four old men, important in mythology, and the four periods of life. The cross-bars of the band represent the years which is hoped the child will live. The color symbolism is the same as in the disk. The long strips around the lower part of the cradle symbolize the child's ribs; the long pendant with bells, its energy and movements. [Quoted in Hilger 1952:33]

A cradle design thus invoked the four directions, *hiiteeni* (the life principle), the day : night alternation, the counting of years, aspects of the child's body and person, and links to other-than-human persons, including the Four Old Men, Whirlwind Woman, and Sun.

One intriguing association is that between the designs and forms of cradle decoration and those of the tipi. Women quillworkers made both, and, according to Kroeber's material, the cradle was identified with the tipi itself: "These ornaments represent parts of the tent. When the child grows up, it will inhabit its own tent as now it inhabits the cradle. Therefore, the symbolism serves to express a wish that the child reaches the age of manhood or womanhood" (Kroeber 1902:66). Both the tipi and the cradle were "homes" illustrating life movement at different levels of time, including the path of the sun, the seasons, and the epochal ages of the earth. Following that connection, both the cradle and the tipi were expressions of individual identity merged with the most sacred symbols of Arapahoness. In the symbolism of the circular disk, both cradle and tipi ornaments represented the completion of life movement through the four stages or the four directions.

As in the associations with birth above and in Lévi-Strauss's analysis (1968) of the Star Husband myth variations, the daily sun : moon : : day : night cycle is at the mythical foundation of all time passage and, incidentally, the acquisition of cultural knowledge. Therefore, the association of day-night time passage with the acquisition of intelligence, here identified with the sun, is quite appropriate and logical for a cradle. All knowledge originally came from Sun and Moon, to whom human wives were married in the Arapaho version of the Star Husband myth. The alternation of time and of knowledge itself originates in life movement, as in mythical, seasonal, and daily time.

Describing the same cradle for which tipi symbolism was offered, Kroeber's informant offers more interpretation:

> The round ornament at the top of this cradle, besides denoting the head of the child, represents also a tent-ornament, which indeed it also resembles. The tent-ornament signifies that the child, when it has grown up, will have a tent. Above the round ornament are pendants having small hoofs and quill-wrapped loops at their ends. These represent pendants or rattles above the door of the tent. Still higher up than these on the cradle, are two quill-wound strips lying parallel to each other. These represent man and woman, since a man and a woman own a tent together. On the ornament representing hair are several pairs of pendants having loops on their ends. These loops represent the holes in the bottom of the tent through which tent-pegs pass. The whole cradle, owing to its shape and the fact of its being stretched on a framework of sticks, resembles a tent-door, and therefore represents it. [Kroeber 1902:67–68]

The homology associating the tipi, the cradle, and the child's body is not just a matter of metaphor or of constructed similarity; rather, it simultaneously transposes multiple levels of space and time. On one level, both tipi and cradle are constructed of a frame homologous with the body: the tipi poles or the wooden cradle frame are the skeletal structure covered by encultured skin, the quilled covers. In many contexts the tipi is spoken of as a human body, with a backbone, ribs, and ears. On another plane, both embody the cosmos, the extent of the Arapaho world, including Sun, the Four Old Men, and the Whirlwind

Woman. Similarly, the cradle and the tipi both represent multiple temporal cycles, including daily, life-cyclical, seasonal, and mythical-time cycles. It is by virtue of this spatial and temporal transposability of domains that the tipi and the cradle contain "power" and thus were objects of a practice circumscribed by ritual production and exchange. Cradles and tipis are empowered with "blessings" or prayers, that is, "desires for things to happen in a certain way," specifically in the case of the cradle, the wish for long life and health for an infant.

The homology of cradle and tipi is also comprehensible in the child's movement during the first stage of life, as a transition from the containment of the cradle to the space of the tipi. This movement outward from the center extends, for males, into activities in the space beyond the camp circle and, for women, into the ability to radiate life outward from the tipi and the camp. Life begins contained in the cradle, moves to the space of the tipi and then to the camp circle and the world beyond, and in the end returns to enclosure and centeredness in old age.

From the beginning of life, then, Arapaho ritual practice involved constituting personhood, activating exchange relations based on respect, ceremonial replication and animation of objects though art, interconnecting levels of space-time, maintaining boundaries through bundling and discarding elements, and orientation to subsequent, future life movement. To repeat, the production and care of objects for life movement were important as—and perhaps more important than—the publicly visible symbols and the meanings they conveyed. As with the cradle, it was the controlled and channeled making and disposition of the objects, as a transmission of knowledge from elders to young people, that generated power for life movement. It was the knowledge to reproduce the objects that was passed on and not simply the inherent symbolic power contained in them. Objects with enduring power or medicine not only represented persons but also had to be kept and cared for as persons.

Naming

Usually during the first year of life, though sometimes later, a child received a name in a ceremony attended by all the old people in the camp (Hilger 1952:60–64). Parents generally asked an older relative ahead of time to give a name to their child. The naming ceremony took place in the child's home. After praying, the namer usually related a story about where the name originated and, if it was an old name, how it was handed down. The primary aim of the ceremony was to promote long life through the name by activating the child's relations to the elders and the camp and by presenting the child to the Four Old Men residing at the periphery of the earth. Moving to the east, the south, the west, and the north, the namer would repeat the child's new name at each station. When the circuit was completed, the namer, sitting directly to the south or left of the doorway as one enters, passed the child clockwise around the tipi, completing the familiar circuit of east, south, west, and north. Following the universal Arapaho pattern, the child was presented first to the Four Old Men and then to the elders of the camp in the same manner. The pattern also followed the clockwise direction for entering or moving about inside a tipi, though guests moved in a counterclockwise direction (Bass 1966:13–14). The child would repeat the clockwise circuit of tipi movement hundreds of times throughout his or her life. Each person then greeted the child by his new name after the command, "Come here!" (*neheic*). Following the naming there was usually a feast prepared by the child's female relatives (Wyoming Indian High School 1979: "Story," Gabriel Warren).

The names given originated mainly from war experiences, but fasts, special occasions, unusual occurrences, or dream experiences could also be sources. Traditional Arapaho names followed their own grammatical subsystem and composed a distinctive semantic field. Personal name morphology abbreviates Arapaho forms used in other contexts and inverts the order of corresponding glosses used in everyday English speech. For example, the name Howling Bird is rendered *nii'ehii niitou*, literally 'bird howl'. 'The bird howls' in everyday speech is *nii'ehii niiniitoubeiht*. Names relating to war often described a particular act or image in a warrior's personal experience, such as Strikes First (*niitowo'tou*), Kills First (*seiyeneh'ei*), or Kills at Night (*biiko nehe'*). The names relating to war were not used exclusively for males but were also given to girls. Names were thus not specific to gender, except those including the designation of woman, girl, boy, or man. Even some names not ostensibly linked to war originated in such experiences, such as Sage's Arapaho name *Nookhoos* from his uncle's experience killing an enemy in sagebrush (Hilger 1952:64). Also especially common are Arapaho names referring to expressive actions, such as Singing Woman (*hisei niibei*) or Howling Above (*cebe' niitou*). Another remarkable feature is that traditionally, naming employed only the four basic Arapaho colors of black, red, white, and yellow, associated with the four stages of life. There is no old Arapaho name in evidence using green or blue, for example.

The name itself carried the power to ensure health and long life. Inherited names were especially good and powerful names if the previous bearer had lived to an old age. A young person could take a name from an older person, or an elder could give his or her name to a junior kinsperson or even an adult. If the elder from whom a name was taken felt that the person deserved that name, he or she would address the person using that name. If not, the elder ignored it. If the name was acknowledged, the older person would then take a new name or receive one from a yet older person or one who had passed on. Some elders today state that they have no Indian name, because someone else received or took it.

Throughout one's life it was common to change one's name several times. Overcoming "tough" or "pitiful" times was the general reason for name changing. Names were changed after going through a serious illness, fasting, or some other life-threatening or transformative experience (Hilger 1952:61). Also, a person whose life was going in a crazy direction could "straighten up" with a new name. Sage's nephew, for instance, took his name and then found direction in life (1952:63). Like amulet bags, names could keep one's life on a "straight path." In the context of Arapaho rituals, discarding (*hosei-*) an old name places the hardship in the past, almost as though one throws away or sacrifices the difficulty to the passage of time. That does not mean that the difficulty was forgotten or "repressed," but rather that the suffering itself was left behind. Name changing played a dual function in the exchange of life movement. On the one hand, shedding a name signified "discarding" a pitiful or difficult experience. On the other hand, the discarded name itself carried the power to overcome that hardship and promote long life and could thus be given or picked up for the benefit of someone else in the family or tribe. An individual would thereby overcome a life-threatening situation and then "give back" the life-promoting element it carried. A name, like other life-giving elements, was thus channeled through exchange, interlinking past, present, and future. As people relate today, one's life and history then become connected to the name receiver or giver.

A man or a woman who experienced battle or, in reservation times, served in the military would, upon returning, take a new name and shed the old one for another person to pick up. At a public gathering, the name leaver would step forward, tell the gathering what his new name was to be, relate a war story, and then discard the old name, usually symbolizing the action by shedding a cloth or blanket from his back onto the floor. If someone wanted the old name, he or she would pick up the blanket or cloth, thus taking the name. The receiver was generally a younger relative. Occasionally, the name was not taken in which case, older relatives would pick up the blanket or cloth and keep the name in the family's store of names to be saved for future use. Each family could therefore have a pool of names collected in this way or from deceased members to be drawn upon for future naming.

The process of naming and discarding names thus follows the same pattern of ascending and descending through life as if traversing hills. The difficulty of ascent, the burden or heavy load, is shed, and the ease of descent follows. In turn, the burden released becomes a source and lightness of life-giving power to be shared with others. Therefore, an original name, given to ensure long life, must be changed after a life-threatening experience. Once an individual has endured a life-threatening experience and changed names, the accumulated life-giving power of the original name must be given back to others. This follows the general principle that one must return individually acquired power for life movement to kin and the tribe. To keep a powerful name would be "stingy." Once a person's difficulty was suffered and then discarded, it could be passed on to someone else, whose life was then eased by it. The old name, when picked up by someone else, carried the power to overcome such difficulties, hence the use of names from war.

In everyday life one's name was rarely spoken, since forms of address were generally in vocative kinship terms. Out of respect for one's relationship, it was unthinkable to address an elder or one's parent or other relative by name. Names were generally used only for third-person references to a person who was not present. Out of respect for former owners, names also belonged within family relations, as knowledge/power passed by inheritance. The same now applies to English names, which are kept within families and handed down generation after generation.

Naming is one among several childhood rituals still performed and recently reinvigorated in Northern Arapaho culture. An addition to the naming ceremony is a public giveaway to acknowledge the new name. Not all naming ceremonies are followed by a giveaway, but some families feel an obligation to sponsor one. Some families state that one or several of their children do not have names because they have not been able to sponsor a feast and a giveaway. Others simply pass on names less ceremoniously within the family, not feeling the need to involve the rest of the community. As in the past, sometimes elders just name children or adults in public situations in order to recognize or honor them. As the child approaches, the elder might ask if he or she has a name. If not, the old person then gives one. In the contemporary context, the naming process ranges, then, from a more casual, private event to a more public, formal practice.

In comparison to Euro-American naming, Arapaho practices emphasized neither patrilineal descent by surname nor, through a personal name, a unique and enduring self as a point of reference. Rather, they were part of a different temporalization of life movement and relations across generations that interconnected past, present, and future. On one hand, the Anglo-American lifelong surname and personal name constitute a public self as an irreversible life history. On the other, by way of contradiction, they are part of Euro-American literate knowledge, providing a means for bureaucratic control and surveillance. Therefore, one of the first acts of assimilation on reservations, including Wind River, was to impose Euro-American names. However, some family naming practices have been extended to modern names. More on these changes and the Arapaho appropriation of Euro-American naming is offered in chapter 10.

Ear Piercing

Ear piercing was another important childhood ritual for life movement, which the Arapahos shared with other Plains tribes, such as the Cheyennes and the Lakotas. Ear piercing took place either in a private gathering in the tipi or at a public event, such as the Sun Dance (Kroeber 1907:365; Hilger 1952:24 ff.). As in all childhood ceremonies and Arapaho ritual practices, the objective of ear piercing was to promote life movement. When parents wanted their child's ears pierced, they first collected food for a feast and accumulated gifts for a giveaway, such as blankets, robes, and perhaps even a horse. Then the mother asked someone she respected to do the piercing. It seems clear that women organized most of the childhood rituals for their sons, daughters, and nephews. However, Old Man Sage related to Hilger that an old woman pierced a girl's ears, whereas men pierced boys. It was especially auspicious to have a visiting non-Arapaho person with warrior experience pierce a child's ears. To recognize the assistance, the parents cooked for and gave gifts to the person who pierced the child's ears. When the piercing was finished, the parents also held a public giveaway to honor their son or daughter.

During the ceremony the warrior or old woman related a war story from his or her own life experiences, thus drawing a connection between the piercing of an enemy in the narrative and the piercing of the child's ears. As in naming, ear piercing effected continuity between a past pitiful event endured, the present situation, and future life movement. In contrast to the Euro-American chronotype that gives direction to the present through events in an individual's life history, Arapaho practices activated a relation of exchange between two persons or groups in order to redirect the past difficulties of one person toward the future life movement of another or others.

After finishing the story, the piercer prayed and then performed the actual piercing, using a sewing awl, a porcupine quill, or some other sharp instrument. It was considered a good sign if the child cried a lot, for that indicated that suffering had been endured and thus that the child would grow to adulthood. As in other contexts, ritually bounded expressions of suffering through the piercing or cutting of flesh sympathetically preempted future suffering not only for the ritual actor but for others as well. Those who could express suffering in ritual would live quiet lives in future stages. To express a pitiful condition in the present thus reduced the likelihood of future pitiful conditions. Against a quiet background, the outward expression of pain and suffering through crying figures elsewhere in ritual, as a means of getting older or other-than-human persons to pity one and listen to one's requests or prayers. Piercing also marked the child's transition to loudness and expressiveness in social life, as did the ritual for marking the acquisition of speech. Supporting this connection, Straus (1976) suggests for the Cheyennes, ear piercing symbolizes "opening" up the ears so that the child can listen. Ear piercing as "opening up the ears" to listen is consistent with the child's relationship to knowledge in the first stage of life. It is equally consistent with the emphasis on listening in child rearing and other contexts of Arapaho culture.

At the same time, though the quiet life was considered desirable in adulthood, highly vocal, expressive children were viewed as healthier than quiet, more passive children. In short, craziness (*hohookee-*) is not only tolerable in childhood but considered necessary and even desirable. Parallel to mourning practices and other contexts of ritual "suffering," crying out to show one's suffering draws the attention of other-than-human persons above, so that they will "listen" to one's prayers. In mythology, too, crying and the cutting of flesh are common mediating actions between animals and humans, as in the sacrifice of buffalo-people to human beings and between humans and the above, as in the origin myth in which Flat Pipe's crying draws the attention of the creator.

Counting Age

Throughout childhood and into young adulthood, the mother also took responsibility for counting her child's age by 'snows' (*cecno'*). Each winter she marked a stick or her hide scraper with a slash or incision on the end of a row for each child (Hilger 1952:87–88). In the Arapaho language, the word for winter and age derive from the same root, *cec-*. Counting "snows" thus coordinated all people's ages with the seasons. Women also kept count of the hides they had scraped, the tipis they had made, and other products related to women's transformative role in art and life movement. Mothers' achievements and children's ages were thus intertwined.

It is interesting that counting should be so closely related to hides and elk-horn hide scrapers. Hide scraping and preparation were among the most difficult tasks for women, as anyone knows who has tried them. The connection also relates to the mediating role of women with buffalo, as established in mythical time and renewed through the women's Buffalo Lodge. In that mediating, transformative process, hide scraping, hide preparing, and quilling were the core practices for transforming raw material into cultured objects.

The pattern of counting is homologous with the Plains pattern of "counting" years by winters and events. Hilger and others mention that Arapaho people had winter counts, for example, similar to the recording of events by other Plains cultures, but actual hides are rare (1952:86). The buffalo hides quilled and designed by women involved counting as well, in that the value of the robe and the degree of sacrifice were relative to the type and the number of lines quilled (Dorsey and Warden 1905:Box 1:27–38). For men, the count was often a matter of feats performed in war.

The association of marks or slashes with winters, war exploits, hides scraped, hides quilled, and other achievements is patterned by the relationship of overcoming hardship and sacrifice in order to achieve and extend life movement. Counting, like the four-hills model and the circuit to the four directions, is at once a way of measuring, recognizing, and generating life movement. To make it through another winter is to endure hardship, thus demonstrating endurance and life movement. As discussed in chapter 3, life movement is a cumulative process of enduring greater and more numerous difficult times.

Illustrating another perspective on counting, quilled cradle designs, for example, often repeated elements according to a fixed numbering system regarded as powerful or beautiful, such as ten and one hundred, to express the desire for many years of life (Hilger 1952:36). Though there is no specific reference to the effect, the sense of *beetee* as power may be incorporated linguistically and artistically into the numbers ten (*beteetox*), and one hundred (*beteetosoo'*). At any rate, counts from the past brought life movement to the present and also projected from present into the future the desire and perhaps even the power for long life and multiplicity of blessings. Counting and numbering, then, interconnected dimensions of personhood (pity, respect, quietness, and craziness), different levels of time (event, season, and oral history), and various social relations (e.g., mother-child, aunt-brother's child) into the continuity of life movement.

Similarly, the marking of age for children was part of the process by which parents and grandparents continually observed and remained tied to the maturation and personal qualities of children. Later, their accumulated knowledge could be used to instruct, lecture, and guide the person when he or she had become a young adult. Such lessons from elders could "refresh the memories" of the young person as well, thus helping to organize life historical perspectives. Hilger recorded the following about Old Bear:

> Well, this blind old man recorded events mentally. . . . Supposing a man wanted to know his age, or that of his wife or son, Old Bear would say, "You sit down here near me. Well, you were a child at such and such a time, because such and such a thing happened then. Do you remember that?" The one making the inquiry would then recall the event, and thereby a certain year. "Well, the following spring, or year, this happened." It might be another event, and the person would refresh his memory on that event. That old man would keep on telling events that happened each year for 60 years past. [1952:86]

Elders served as repositories of life history and tribal history, and their memories served to direct the future life movement of individuals, families, or the tribe. In this process self-knowledge is vested not within one's own stored memory, self-consciousness, or unconscious but rather is given to individuals by others who have come before oneself in time and now are elders.

Other Childhood Rituals

Elders also witnessed and recognized other achievements in childhood. Hilger describes several ritual feast occasions to honor a child's acquisition of human capacities, including the first-tooth, first-walk, and first-word feasts sponsored by parents to acknowledge that their child had acquired those qualities of personhood. A first-tooth feast was also often a marker for the time to pierce a child's ears (Hilger 1952:40). Within the space of tipi life, all such feasts were ways families and older people showed their respect for a child's life movement and achievements. Such recognition recurred as life progressed; among other things, it included a feast for a boy's first kill in hunting. Children also learned that life movement was relational and not just individual. In particular, they came to understand through these feasts that all things must go to the old people first. As Sage learned, the first buffalo he killed had to be given to an old man in order to show respect and pity (1952:172). Anticipating later life responsibilities, children and youths learned that "giving back" what one acquires is not merely obligatory but is inherent to the experience of life movement.

Childhood rituals, except for special events such as ear piercing, which occurred at the Offerings Lodge, took place in the tipi but anticipated and recognized a child's movement and activity outside in the world of camp life, such as the first-walk and first-kill feasts. At each successive childhood transition, another older person from outside the family of parents and children served as an agent for or a witness of life movement. The same pattern applies to storytelling and lecturing. However, unlike subsequent adulthood transitions, childhood rites were organized mainly by women and sponsored by parents. Like the age-grade ceremonies in adulthood, though, childhood rites activated family exchanges with elders, nonkin, and extended kin. Names, stories, foods, and ritual objects were thus all exchanged in order to generate life movement.

The relationship between children and other-than-human persons and even those senior in the age hierarchy had to be mediated by the parental generation. Elders were always called in to witness and channel life movement, for it was they who represented the collective order and ultimately gave movement and direction to life. Other kin, such as aunts and uncles, also acted to facilitate life transitions. Childhood rites thus involved kin and age-structured relations extending beyond the boundaries of the domestic space of the tipi.

In childhood the individual was almost completely dependent on others to promote his or her life movement. Parents, elder siblings, aunts and uncles, and grandparents kept the child away from potentially life-negating elements and activated relations among themselves for ritual practices to ensure the life movement of children. People in the parental and grandparental generations also engaged their roles as persons to give back to children the life-giving power and knowledge they had acquired through their own difficulties, sufferings, and achievements. Childhood ceremonies further marked the transition from the closed, protected space of the cradle and the tipi into the public space of the camp. For this purpose, they honored and respected a child's transitions toward self-movement, speaking, listening, and other abilities associated with personhood and anticipating subsequent life stages. Each life stage contained the elements of the next, and ritual practices both recognized and constituted those elements.

6
The Men's Age-Grade System

The Age Grades and Knowledge Exchange

Before the reservation period, Arapaho rank and tribal unity were generated through a unique age-grade system for shaping the life movement of men in the second, third, and fourth stages of life. Each set of age peers passed successively through a series of ceremonial lodges marking transitions between the grades which did not correspond to the three stages. In the process each age set accumulated knowledge and ascended into political and ritual leadership roles. Although other Plains groups had military societies, only the Blackfoot, the Mandans, the Hidatsas, the Gros Ventres, and the Arapahos had what Lowie describes as a "graded" system of societies (Lowie 1916). As one point in a larger comparison, Lowie (1916:973–74) recognized the distinctive aspects of the Arapaho and the closely related Gros Ventre systems. For one thing, in Arapaho–Gros Ventre age grading, men who vowed to participate "purchased" the lodge, to borrow Lowie's term for now, from "grandfathers," older men three grades above who themselves had already passed through the lodge and currently "owned" it. In other Plains systems, the "purchase" was from "fathers" two grades above. In the Arapaho system an age set enlisted the assistance of elder brothers two grades above, grandfathers at least three grades senior, and even older men from the most senior age grades. The significant point about this is that the age-grade system was not just a structural succession or knowledge transfer from one age set to another. It was much more than that.

Whereas Lowie's concept of purchase, implying transfer of an exclusive, alienable possession, is perhaps true of other systems (the Mandan-Hidatsa and the Blackfoot age-grade systems focused on the transfer of "medicine bundles" embodying the knowledge of each successive lodge), the situation is more complex in the Arapaho case, at least to the extent that more than a "quantity of knowledge" was transferred. Other areas of Arapaho knowledge transmission could be termed purchase, however, such as the transfer of curative medicines from one person to another, which was confined to a dyadic exchange relationship (Hilger 1952:136). Another distinctive feature of the age-grade lodges was that the system of exchange was also more extended beyond the age grades than it was for other Plains Indians, since many features of the intermediate men's lodges also applied to the Buffalo Lodge and the Offerings Lodge.

In Arapaho *beyoowu'u* rituals, knowledge was a central object of exchange, but it was not considered a commodity that could be transferred between two individuals or two age sets isolated in social time and space. Beyond the knowledge itself, power for life movement was passed from or through one group to another. Ritual exchanges also generated enduring and extensive social relationships beyond those between initiates and initiands, which apparently lasted throughout life. Whereas childhood rituals centered around kinship, the age-grade system extended relations beyond the tipi and the immediate family. In the extinct Arapaho men's age-grade ceremonies and women's Buffalo Lodge, as well as in the extant Offerings Lodge, knowledge participates in an intricate hierarchy of exchange, involving not just ceremonial grandfathers and grandsons but also families; the wider camp circle; the oldest men, who direct the lodges; and other-than-human persons. In short, Lowie's analysis focuses too narrowly on exchange between ceremonial grandfathers and grandsons, that is, on the age sets passing out of and into a grade.

To prepare for and participate in ritual, a wide web of vertical and horizontal relations was activated through exchange. Each lodge was set in motion by an individual's pity for and subsequent vow on behalf of a close family member or kinsperson who had been ill or had suffered other misfortune. Soon after a pledger made the first vow for a lodge, his age-grade brothers had to follow with similar pledges to participate. Once those pledges were made known, the participants' families began accumulating goods for the ritual exchanges involved. During the time between a vow and the performance, a family had to honor its son, father, or brother by making a sacrifice through their work and material goods. Preparation was a crucial phase for activating relations and knowledge to ensure the correctness of ritual practice itself. The initial intent of the "exchange" was thus not for the individual pledger, nor the age set itself, nor the relation between the grandsons and grandfathers alone. Along the horizontal axis of intra- and interfamilial relations, pledges relied on kin and the camp circle for goods to be given to their grandfathers. Along the vertical axis, exchanges activated relations along an age-graded continuum from the junior to the most senior groups. In the traditional age-grade ceremonies and the contemporary Sun Dance, individuals or a group of men who had vowed approached men whom they wanted to be their elder brothers. The pledgers then formally asked older men to become ceremonial grandfathers for the ritual.

The selection of elder brothers was an extension of seniority relations between younger and older siblings. Arapaho kinship terminology distinguishes between elder and younger brother, as well as between older and younger sister. Age hierarchy thus applies to relations within a generation as well as those between them. Within a generation, senior siblings deserved greater respect and served a directive role in life movement. In all exchange relationships for young adults, elder brothers were often the principal representatives of one's interests to others. Ceremonial elder brothers, like consanguineal brothers, acted as mediators for interfamilial and inter-age-grade exchanges. Oftentimes, in the family, the elder brother was—and still is today—like a parent, looking after the younger siblings. As older people say today, "Your elder brother was more like a parent than your mother or father."

The elder brothers and the grandfathers were referred to using the same respective kinship terms as in nonritualized contexts. Both had to be shown respect comparable to but even greater than that due to the respective kin outside the age-grade system. As Eggan observes:

> Ceremonial "grandfathers," however, have to be much more highly respected; among the Arapaho, in particular, there are various restrictions on behavior. It is not permissible to gamble with them, pass in front of them, or take any liberties with them under pain of supernatural sanction. "This 'grandfather' business is dangerous," say the Arapaho. [1937:54]

The grandfathers helped make regalia for the young men and at the same time instructed the initiates on replicating ritual paraphernalia, procedures in the lodge, body painting, dances, and songs (Kroeber 1904:160). In the preparation phase, the grandfathers approached an even older man, also called grandfather, to ask him to direct the ceremony. Ultimately, the Seven Old Men had authority over all the lodges. In making the request, the junior grandfathers had to offer a gift to the senior grandfather, usually something of significant value, such as a horse. Also, on each day of the ceremony, the senior grandfather received food from the junior grandfathers. As in other situations, the oldest ritual agent had to be "fed" by the junior participants who received knowledge. On the final day of the ceremony, the grandsons and their families gave gifts to the junior grandfathers, who had given gifts to and provided food for the senior grandfathers throughout the ceremony.

Lowie's description of age-grade exchange as "purchase," then, is too narrow (1916:973). Although he does recognize the complex and "collective" nature of Arapaho exchange, his treatment cannot resolve the question of whether knowledge is an alienable or an inalienable possession: "A man certainly possesses as a negotiable commodity all the ceremonial knowledge he has ever acquired and which he has never sold; the only question is whether his property rights are indefeasible or terminate with receipt of compensation" (1916:974). In other words, Lowie cannot establish from the evidence on Arapaho age-grade ceremonies whether upon "selling" his knowledge, the individual gives up property rights to dispense the same knowledge again, even though, at a phenomenological level, he continues to possess and even accumulate knowledge as he moves through other grades.

Knowledge transfer also extended beyond the relationship between grandson and grandfather. By participating as grandfathers, men acquired knowledge to perform a ritual from the senior grandfather, whose knowledge was governed by and came from other-than-human persons above. It was thus not only the incoming age set that gained knowledge, for a channel of knowledge through all age groups senior in the hierarchy was activated by the lodge preparation and performance. Only in youth (i.e., childhood and the second stage of life) was it possible to be only a recipient of knowledge. Conversely, by old age, one primarily gave knowledge or served as an intermediary with the other-than-human realm.

As Stewart (1977:328) realizes, the exchanges of goods in the Arapaho–Gros Ventre system were more symmetrical than the transfer of knowledge in other Plains age-grade systems. In no clear sense did grandfathers, or any other group, stand in an asymmetrical "profit" position for passing on their knowledge. In fact, the greatest material expense was likely on the junior grandfathers, who received only a return gift at the end of the ceremony:

It is said that until this time the grandfathers have received nothing from them [grandsons]. They themselves, however, have given considerable property to the old men in charge of the lodge. The grandfathers' wives have also supplied the dancers with food. There is no definite regulation for the amount of payment that is made to the grandfathers. [Kroeber 1904:168]

As mentioned in chapter 4, the greatest burden of generosity was placed on men and their families in the third stage of life, the age of "giving it back."

What Lowie's question and my analysis of it illustrate are the unique and complex dimensions of prereservation Arapaho age structure. Goods, offerings, and sacrifices moved up the age hierarchy extending into the other-than-human realm, while life movement and knowledge flowed downward. Along the ground, goods, offerings, and sacrifices flowed from family and camp into the center, while gifts, life movement, and other blessings radiated outward from the lodge. In all exchanges involving knowledge and life movement, the individual or age set did not act on his, her, or their own behalf. As one moved from childhood into the second and third stages of life, the scope of relations activated for life movement and knowledge expanded horizontally and vertically, along with responsibilities for maintaining them. Accordingly, ritual actors all acted on behalf of others, not themselves. Dancers acted for the persons for whom they made their vows. Families acted for their members in the lodge. The junior grandfathers acted for their grandsons in exchanges with senior grandfathers, who mediated with other-than-human persons. In the process as a whole, no one accumulated value, because everyone was required to pass it on to others through time.

The Age Grades and the Total Life System

The consistent problem in perspectives of Arapaho and other Plains age-grade systems, as illustrated by Lowie, Stewart, and Bernardi, is the tendency to isolate them from relations to other dimensions of the life process. The logic of Arapaho age-grade lodges must be placed within the total life trajectory and ceremonial complex. For example, the "logic" of practices in childhood rites continued into the age-grade sequence, the women's Buffalo Lodge and the Offerings Lodge.

All previous approaches have also been comparative in scope. For example, Bernardi offers a functional comparison of age systems around the world, except for the Arapaho case, for which he says the information is too "limited" (1985:121), though he neither cites nor shows any familiarity with the rich material from Kroeber, Dorsey, Dorsey and Warden, and Hilger. Like Stewart, he begins by treating the age-grade system in formal isolation and thus restricts the scope to a narrow range of functions. Despite the use of what he calls an "ethnemic" criterion for constructing age-class models, that is, relating each system to other elements of its sociocultural context, his analysis of the similar Gros Ventre system leads to the conclusion that it served primarily a "choreographic" function (Bernardi 1985:38–40), that is, for "regulation of dances and songs," including the "purchase" or transfer. What is left is a simple assertion that the age-grade ceremonies were a system for maintaining their own cultural content. As a result he identifies only a minimal (if any) structuring role beyond the ceremonies themselves; he does not correlate the age-grade system with other life transition rituals as part of a total system. As in Lowie's, Stewart's, and even Kroeber's original study, political, economic, and other social functions are set aside.

In fact, Arapaho age grades and groupings performed many functions outside of the ceremonies themselves. Mooney (1896:986–89), for example, cites a number of police, military, and political functions of the intermediate men's age societies. Other evidence suggests that the junior men's societies also played various roles in the camp circle. The functions of the senior men's groups, which were not really age grades, were not exclusively ceremonial or "choreographic," either. Specifically, the senior grades were especially important in selecting leaders, maintaining social order, and regulating the movement of the tribe, the camp, and the band.

Dorsey and Warden describe the roles of the lodge leaders and the men's societies in the movement of the camp. When a camp was preparing to move, the men assembled in their companies, each in its own place. Upon arriving at a new camp, the leaders of the societies directed the formation. At night the society leaders invited their members to feasts in their tipis (Dorsey and Warden 1905, Box A-1, Folder 1:98–99). All of the societies were under the direction of the oldest men, who ultimately guided the movement of the camp and defined its agenda in time. Examined from the perspective of sociocultural space-time, each age group had its own place, type of movement, and degree of control over the movement of others.

On this level, all of the lodges can be understood as functioning, along with kinship, to order social space and time. When the lodges are examined in the context of the entire life trajectory, it can be seen that each age grade or group was channeled into a distinctive social space and tempo or quality of motion. Age distinctions thus functioned to order time and space as movement. Each age grade had a distinct motion, place, and mode of personhood, emphasized in but carried over from the performance of the lodges into everyday life.

It is clear, too, from Dorsey's monograph on the Southern Arapaho Sun Dance (1903), that the age societies assisted in the preparation for and performance of the Offerings Lodge. The age set of the lodge maker who pledged to sponsor the lodge assisted their brother. All of the societies of younger men assisted in the construction of the lodge (1903:77). Dorsey also mentions that the societies organized respective drum groups, alternating to provide songs for the lodge. The age societies also played roles in lodges other than their own; for example, they served as elder brothers and grandfathers for younger societies. It is quite clear that the societies did constitute age sets that cooperated in activities outside of the performance of their own lodges.

Another connection ignored in approaches to age structure are functions correlated with kinship. Even Fowler's ethnohistorical treatment (1982) of Arapaho age structure in the context of political continuity ignores the relationship between age structure and kinship. On a gross level, kinship and age structure were "complementary" to the extent that the latter maintained relations that cut across the divisions between families, camps, and bands. More specifically, age-grade relations were an extension of Arapaho kinship through the creation of horizontal peer relations within an age set and vertical relations among different age groups, paralleling same-sex sibling relations and grandparental roles, respectively. Eggan's analysis (1937:90) of Cheyenne-Arapaho kinship provides the understanding that age grading is a variant of a "generational" system found throughout Plains kinship systems: "In warfare, as well as in hunting, the cooperation of brothers was essential to survival, and I have argued elsewhere (1937:93 ff.) that extensions of this relationship to distant cousins, as well as friends and companions in warrior societies, was intelligible on this basis" (Eggan 1966:58). For men the fraternal bond was the social glue of a generation or an age set; for women the sororal bond also served a unifying function. The age-grade system, following Fowler's analysis (1982), also countered the tendency toward intergenerational disjunctures, a recurring source of social structural stress in ungraded Plains societies with similar kinship systems. The complementary functions were thus in two directions, extending generational solidarity horizontally and intergenerational continuity vertically.

With respect to the former, it is clear that male and female age sets formed before formal entry into the grades or lodges. Childhood age groups for boys and girls were named and recognized. Though the available evidence is somewhat sketchy, it seems that there was one set of terms for girls, another set for boys, and possibly as many as eight terms for different stages of childhood alone (Mark Soldierwolf). Elkin relates:

> Testifying to the pervading character of social stratification along age-lines was the fact that even children were members of well-defined age-groupings. From the time they left their mother's care to play in groups, they were "Blackbirds." At about age ten, they became "Wild Rose Bushes," "thorny," given to fighting and teasing. At puberty when they began to prepare themselves for the activities of manhood, they became "Calves." Although these groupings were not formalized

to the degree of the men's societies, boys were referred to by the name
of their particular group, and excluded older and younger boys from
their activities. [1940:213–14]

Interestingly enough, each childhood age grouping was associated with one of
the basic Arapaho colors except white, the color of old age. Black for
Blackbirds was followed by red for Wild Rose Bushes and then yellow,
associated with buffalo calves. Each stage was also associated with a particular
type of behavior or aspect of personhood. Though more details are needed, it is
clear that age-set formation preceded the formalized age-grade ceremonies.

As they moved into the second stage of life and continued to form age peer
relations, boys and girls were gradually segregated as an extension of brother-
sister avoidance. Among sisters and cousins, girls formed age peer groups close
to the center of the camp; boys were pushed out to space outside the tipi and
beyond the camp circle, where they formed peer groups engaging in games,
hunting, horse care, and incipient war parties. During the same period, boys and
girls formed dyadic same-sex "chum" partnerships, which were usually the
closest and most enduring relationships in their lives (Hilger 1952:110).

After this stage, upon marriage, young men usually moved to their wives'
camps either initially or eventually, and functioned as "servants" to their
parents-in-law. Having been propelled out of his childhood tipi by sister
avoidance, the husband continued to be distant from the women at the core by
virtue of mother-in-law avoidance. The age grades thus created horizontal
"brother" relations among men that endured despite their movement in social
space with changes in the family cycle.

Vertically, the age-grade system, like other ceremonies in the *beyoowu'u*
system, created a web of grandfather-grandson relations that are considered
even today to be stronger than those based on descent. The system also
generated intergroup exchanges and relationships between the families of senior
and junior men, who shared the same mutual respect. Within the camp and the
tribe, the grandfather-grandson relation formed and sustained durable linkages
that countered the tendency for rank and peer solidarity to generate too much
distance and thus disjuncture between generations.

Kit-Foxes and Stars

Young men who entered the first formal grade were called Kit-Foxes
(*nouunenno'* [*nouu-* 'fox'/*-enno'* 'men']). Hilger's evidence suggests that this

group was called Blackbirds among the Northern Arapahos, but throughout the literature and in responses to my own inquiries, Kit-Fox appears uniformly. It is not clear from any sources how men entered this grade or moved on into the Star society that followed. Mooney (1896:986–87) states that this grade was for young men age seventeen to twenty-five, but Hilger (1952:118–19) offers a younger age of twelve to sixteen. As young men moved into the second stage of life, they became more 'useful' (*heniixoneiht* 'he or she is useful, helpful, or mature'), but their ties to the internal space of the tipi and camp became looser.

The Kit-Foxes did not have a ceremonial lodge structure but performed a dance on the open prairie outside the camp circle. Unlike the members of subsequent lodges, Kit-Foxes did not have ritualized paraphernalia to make and wear (Kroeber 1904:181). They did choose elder brothers from among the Clubboard men two grades senior, who would assist them throughout all the lodges. Though Kroeber maintains that neither Kit-Foxes nor Stars had grandfathers, Jessie Rowlodge, one of Hilger's Southern informants, states that the Kit-Foxes did choose grandfathers from the Spear Lodge three grades senior to them (in Hilger 1952:121). It is not clear whether each young man had the same grandfather throughout the age-grade sequence, as is the case with Sun Dance grandfathers today.

The next grade, for young men in their late teens or early twenties, was the Stars (*ho3o'ohuuho'* [*ho3o'*- 'star'/-*huuho'* agents or persons]). Like the Kit-Foxes, the Stars had no ceremonial lodge; there is some evidence that they continued to have elder brothers and grandfathers, from the Spears and Crazy Men, respectively, if the same system followed as that for the Kit-Foxes. According to Kroeber, they had more paraphernalia for dancing, such as lances and rattles, than the Kit-Foxes had. Stars likewise performed a dance on the open prairie. None of the Arapaho sacred medicines were used by either the Kit-Foxes or the Stars. During other ceremonies, the Stars assisted as servants in the senior lodges and the Offerings Lodge. As mentioned earlier, the second stage of life demanded servitude and "doing things" in various contexts.

In accord with that expectation, both the Foxes and the Stars performed many services, but their grades lacked the formal knowledge transmission of subsequent lodges. In Van Gennep's terms, the two grades combined as a stage of "separation" from the social space of the camp circle. Similarly, it is clear that Kit-Foxes and Stars were unmarried men, who had not yet begun to serve in-laws and older generations. They were therefore situated between their family of orientation and their family of procreation, that is, separated from their own families by gender segregation and not yet incorporated into their wives' camps through marriage. Anticipating bride service, the young men at this stage functioned as servants for the other lodges, learning to do things for senior groups.

The Clubboard Lodge

The Clubboard (or Tomahawk) Lodge (*hiice'eexo'owu'* [*hii-* an actor prefix to incorporated noun forms/ *-ce'eex-,* a war club or spike/ *-(o)owu'* 'lodge']) (Kroeber 1904:182–88) is the first grade in the sequence requiring vows, a ceremonial lodge, and active roles on the part of grandfathers. Men who entered this grade were in their late teens to early twenties. As in the Offerings Lodge and the Spear, Crazy, and Dog societies that followed, each man made a vow to participate on behalf of a sick relative or to overcome some other misfortune. Once one man pledged the lodge, then all his brothers in an age set had to follow. If a member were unable to participate, then a substitute could take his place. In so many ways, the age-grade brothers had to follow the grade leader and act in unison, not only in ceremonies but in social roles as well.

The elder brothers, themselves Crazy Men, then met to select the ranks of the different dancers who pledged. It seems that the man who first vowed for the lodge became the highest-ranking dancer. Outside of the lodge itself, he also served as the leader of the age set for various functions of the grade, policing camp movements, sitting in tribal councils, or assisting in other ceremonies. The transition from Stars to the Clubboard Lodge thus brought a shift to specialized roles and from unranked equality to formally ranked membership within the age set.

Following the ranking process, the pledgers and their elder brothers then went out to find ceremonial grandfathers, drawn from the Dog Lodge or higher, to help make their regalia. Older men were reluctant to serve this role and had to be caught by the group. When the sponsor of the dance handed a man a pipe, though, he had to agree to serve as grandfather. Subsequently, each Clubboard man enlisted a reluctant grandfather of the same rank to make the appropriate regalia and paint him accordingly. Then all the grandfathers found a man older than them to be the director of the lodge activities. At this point, if the system of age-grade relations followed the pattern established for the Kit-Foxes and the Stars, such a man had to be one of the Old Men or the Seven Water-Sprinkling Old Men. The junior grandfather presented a gift to the older man upon making his request. After the old man entered the tipi, the group prayed and all smoked. The women relatives of the young men then took food to the grandfathers' tipis in order to "feed" them, as was done before all actions performed by elders.

In this and all the other lodges, there was a three-day period of preparation before the lodge itself. During that time the grandfathers either passed on the regalia that they had used or made the items that were needed. But the grandfathers themselves had to be instructed by the older man in how to paint the dancers. To reciprocate, each grandfather had to give a present afterward to the old man who had instructed him.

Again, it is clear that Lowie's portrayal of the "purchase" of knowledge is oversimplified. In any transfer of knowledge in the lodges, the younger had to make payment to the older person. At the same time, it was always necessary to "feed" older persons upon making a request for knowledge. On each of the three days of preparation, the grandfathers fed the dancers. The old man assisting each grandfather received food from both grandsons' and grandfathers' families (Kroeber 1904:162).

The paint design for the *hiice'eexoowu'* was called 'they who go after women' (*woniseinehii3i'*), an expression of marriageability and the courting behavior of young men at this age. (Kroeber 1904:183). Clubboard men were not allowed to wash their paint, lest it rain during the three days of dancing. Further, as in the Spear and the women's Buffalo Lodge, cockleburs were used, signifying the "desire to marry." In these three lodges, sage, sweetgrass, and dog root from the set of seven lodge medicines were also used (Dorsey 1903:66–68).

The young men in the Clubboard Lodge were ranked by elder brothers in three degrees. One dancer held the first degree and three the second; the rest were the "rank and file" (Kroeber 1904:183). The first- and second-degree dancers carried the flat clubboards or "swords." Referring to the ranked Clubboard men in general, Mooney states that "in an attack on the enemy, it was the duty of these leaders to dash ahead and strike the enemy with these clubs, then ride back again and take their places in the front of the charge" (1896:987). The motion of rapid charging or racing outward and then returning is replicated in many actions in the lodge, as well. The regalia itself carried an obligation governing the movement or immobility of warriors in battle. In other words, the objects made the young men act in certain ways both in the lodge and in functions outside it.

The lowest-ranking dancers all carried sticks shaped like horse heads on one end and pointed on the other. Contrasting with the charge of the high-ranking members, "in desperate encounters, they were expected to plant these sticks in the ground in line in front of the body of warriors and to fight beside them to the death unless a retreat should be ordered by the chief in command" (Mooney 1896:988). Such immobility in the face of attack was carried on and intensified in the succeeding Spear and Dog societies. At this point in the sequence, the movement of men began to be determined by age-set brothers and leaders, to the extent of sacrificing themselves in battle for others, a value that becomes increasingly important in subsequent lodges.

As in the other intermediate grades of the Spears, the Crazies, and the Dogs, a lodge was constructed for the ceremony, a simple dance enclosure with a low fence-like circular enclosure (Pete Lone Bear in Hilger 1952:122). The walls, constructed of poles with tent skins hanging on them, as Kroeber says, were low enough for people to look in (1904:162). Unlike the Offerings Lodge, the enclosure did not have a rafter structure or a center pole. As for all lodges, the enclosure's entrance opened toward the rising sun. On the east, outside the entrance, was a screen where the pledger of the lodge sat with his companions (1904:163). The grandfathers sat on the west side of the lodge, the place of prominence. Crosscutting the rank order, dancers were divided into two groups: the "short men," who sat on the south side, and the "stout men," on the north. Elder brothers sat with their younger brothers. The dancer of highest degree sat closest to the entrance, on either the north or the south side depending on whether he was a stout or a short man. The two sides competed against each other in races and other contests throughout the three days of the lodge. Each morning the men danced and then raced. Racing enacted the motion of leaving and returning to the camp circle as in the raiding, hunting, and scouting associated with young men in the lodge. It was also part of the dual opposition—and the competitive power it generates for life movement—that pervades many Arapaho ritual contexts. Jessie Rowlodge, a Southern Arapaho, told Hilger that the men also competed in singing songs and telling war stories (Hilger 1952:120).

The symbolic movements in the Clubboard Lodge dance itself emphasized warfare and endurance. On the first evening the old man in charge gave the dancers *he3ewoonoxu'* 'dog root', in order to prevent fatigue during the ceremony (Kroeber 1904:183). Dog root was used for strength in all lodges of the *beyoowu'u*, except by the Seven Old Men in the sweat lodge. According to Kroeber the symbolism of the dance referred to buffalo: "The sticks are said to represent buffalo as well as weapons" (1904:188). With the same color dualism for gender in the woman's Buffalo Lodge, the Clubboard Lodge sticks were either white or yellow, representing buffalo bulls and cows, respectively. Those two lodges thus shared association with the tie between buffalo, gender, and life movement. Both also contained symbolism linking gender, marriage, and buffalo.

After the first dance on the evening of the first day, the young men danced on their own (Kroeber 1904:183). They danced at sunrise, then raced to a point outside the lodge and back. The last to return were playfully punished. After the first evening of dancing by the pledger's group and the grandfathers, it seems, as in the other intermediate lodges, that the young men were free to do what they wanted. There was thus more control, containment, and instruction during the preparation phase and the first evening than for the Kit-Foxes and the Stars but much less deliberate instruction and slowed movement than in the senior grades. In social space the Clubboard grade marks the movement of men into the camp circle under the greater control of senior men. The gender symbolism and the spatial configuration thus coincide with the return of the men, through eventual marriage and matrilocal residence, to the camps. In this grade men are still released for powerful movement outside of the lodge and camp circle, as related to war or hunting, but reincorporated, using Van Gennep's terms, within the camp circle.

On the third morning, after dancing and racing, the Clubboard Lodge ended, as the men went to their own tipis. The young men then gave presents to their grandfathers. At the close of the lodge, as in all intermediate men's lodges, the families of the young men sponsored giveaways (Kroeber 1904:168). It is not clear who received the gifts, although Kroeber states that a young man might give a horse to his grandfather's wife. On one level, this pattern is an extension of childhood rites, in which a family sponsored feasts and giveaways to show respect for a young person's transition or accomplishment.

The Spear Lodge

The fourth men's age-grade and the second ceremonial lodge in the sequence was called *biitoh'oowu'* and the men in it *biitohiinenno'*. The precise translation of that term is not known to researchers or current speakers. The Dorsey-Warden manuscripts translate the name of this grade as "Thunder Bird Lodge, and Earthly Lodge" (Dorsey and Warden 1905:Box 2, Folder 5:3). In support of their translation, the word for 'earth' *biito'oowu'* is similar, but Kroeber doubts the connection (1904:154). The name adopted here, "Spear Lodge," is the one offered by Mooney (1896:988) as the name for the grade, though it was also called Staff Lodge for the staffs with curved ends used in the ceremony. Both of these accepted terms refer to the regalia carried in the lodge rather than the literal meaning of the Arapaho name itself.

Men who entered this grade were from their middle twenties to their thirties, although Warden states that men in this grade were over forty (Dorsey and Warden 1905:Box 2, Folder 8). As for all grades, different estimates are given in the literature, and it is evident that counted age was not a criterion for membership. Mooney says that the lodge came originally from the Cheyennes; he also identifies the military-police function of men in this lodge, stating that they:

> performed police duty in camp, when traveling, and on the hunt, and were expected to see that the orders of the chief were obeyed by the tribe. For instance, if any person violated the tribal code or failed to attend a general dance or council, a party of Bitahi'nëna [*biitohiinenno '*] was sent to kill his dogs, destroy his tipi, or in extreme cases to shoot his pony. On hunting expeditions it was their business to keep the party together and see that no one killed a buffalo until the proper ceremonies had been performed and the order was given by the chief. They were regarded as representatives of the law and were never resisted in performing their duty or inflicting punishments. In war they were desperate warriors, equaling or surpassing even the Hichää'quthi. [1896:988].

Spears constrained the camp circle from the outside in, thus turning their war prowess inward to control the movement of the camp. Unlike the other lodges, they could use physical force against tribal members who went beyond the limits of proper behavior, or doing things in a good/correct way, referred to by Mooney as the "law." As in many stateless societies without permanent police and formal authority, some core activities in both subsistence and ritual required the use of force to maintain control at particular crucial moments, such as during buffalo hunting and the *beyoowu'u* lodges.

As in the other intermediate lodges, one member pledged on behalf of a sick relative or to overcome some personal difficulty, and then his age set followed. The roles of grandfathers, the old man, and others followed the same preparation stage as in the Clubboard Lodge. The lodge itself, the preparation phase, and the sequence of events during the ceremony were also similar in form, but there were different regalia and symbolic expressions through movement. One unique aspect of pledges to this lodge is described in the Dorsey and Warden evidence:

> A man just recently passed the Clubboard Lodge can pledge for the above lodge and yet be under the required age; that is on behalf of a sick relative. If it should be vowed without specification, it is on account of evil trespasses on the person or family. The latter is secret

therefore, the tribe takes hold of the matter and push it through, thus cleansing the whole camp, (eradicating the approaching epidemic diseases) and in the end replenish it with fruitful resources. Also a man in the Clubboard who is desirous of becoming a great warrior among his fellowmen, pledges for this lodge when he goes out on a war expedition with comrades. [Dorsey and Warden 1905:Box 2, Folder 8:20–21]

Adding to the transition the grade effected, the Spear Lodge pledge became more intensely engaged in promoting the life movement of others and the tribe as a whole. Completion of a vow could heal a sick relative, discard disease from the camp, promote success in war, and increase the sustenance of the tribe. One significant point in this passage is that pity could supersede age criteria or appropriate intervals between grades when conditions merited it. Following the pattern of the other lodges, the elder brothers were from the Dog Lodge, two grades above, and the grandfathers from the Old Men's Lodge, three above.

Again, the elder brothers arranged for the location and selected the men for the different degrees of rank within the lodge (Kroeber 1904:159). In the Spear Lodge there were six degrees in all, more than in any other lodge, including five special degrees and the rank and file. At this stage rank among age peers and in the public world was more central to personhood than either before or after in the age sequence. Two dancers were selected for each of the second, third, and fourth degrees, and there were four dancers in the fifth degree. The fourth-degree dancers were not society members but younger men who served as attendants. The remaining dancers filled out the rank and file. The intention may have been to shame the men of the lower degrees by placing boys ahead of them in honor and order. As in the other lodges, only one man occupied the highest rank.

In the Spear and subsequent lodges, the highest-degree dancer, unlike the charging Clubboard counterpart, danced following after the other dancers. From this point on in life, highest rank and leadership in general required ever slower movements and a pattern of following others. According to Kroeber: "He is selected as the bravest man in the company. He is supposed to be slow to anger or to move, but, when aroused, to be exceedingly fierce. . . . He oversees the dancers. He makes them assemble early. If they are tardy in coming, he goes to them and strikes them with his club" (1904:169–70). Toward his age mates, the highest Spear Man recapitulated the physical force of control that all Spears exerted in their military-police functions in the camp circle. He had to take on the demeanor of leadership anticipating chiefship, too, in that he was unmoved by external conditions yet ever ready to use the force retained from the previous grade. Anticipating later life, he had to be still and quiet except when provoked to defend others.

Although there were various dimensions of meaning to the paraphernalia produced for this lodge, the main connection was to Thunder or Thunderbird, consistent with the name that Warden gives to the lodge (Kroeber 1904:188; Dorsey and Warden 1905:Box 2, Folder 5:3). As Kroeber states, "The dormant, fierce temperament of the dancer of the highest degree is supposed to be similar to that of thunder. The carving on his club represents the thunder-bird and lightning" (1904:168–69). The lower-degree dancers also carried lances shaped liked thunderbolts. Like the lower-degree Clubboard men, in battle a lower-ranked Spear stuck his lance in the ground and would not move until an age mate plucked it from the ground to release him.

The Spear society thus enacted the motion and character of the Thunderbird (*nii'ehii bo'oo* 'eagle thunder'), an other-than-human person who stands at the boundaries of the earth protecting it from external enemies and sending rain, thunder, lightning, and rainbows from the west (Mooney 1896:968; Kroeber 1907:317). The thunder sounds from the beating of his wings, the lightning shoots out from his eyes, and the rainbow is his fishing line for *hiincebiit* (Water Monster).

In comparison with other lodges, the color black was more conspicuous in the body paint and the paraphernalia for the Spear Lodge. Black was associated with good feelings, especially in victorious returns of war parties, the actions most accentuated in this grade. Successful war parties rode back into camp covered with black charcoal. In designs, the opposition between sunlight and thunderclouds, yellow and black respectively, recurred in all the ranks of dancers, according to the Dorsey-Warden (1905) descriptions drawn from observations among the Southern Arapahos.

Overall, the Spear dance emphasized endurance, as did the Clubboard society, sudden reactions to external threats without retreating, and returning victory and other blessings from outside to the people. As in their police and military roles, the Spear men were placed on the boundary of the camp circle, where they defended the camp and defined its movement from the outside. The younger grades moved out first in battle and camp movements, whereas the senior grades were slower to move. Warlike quick movements extended outward among the Clubboard men but were turned back inward through the Spear men's police function. Together, the Spear and Clubboard lodges affirmed the value of control over self-movement, the power to strike and immobilize enemies, and force to control Arapahos themselves who went beyond the boundaries of acceptable behavior. In all those functions, like the other younger age grades, the Spears remained servants to the senior men who made the decisions about camp movements, the timing of events, and spatial arrangements.

The Crazy Lodge

The next grade an age set passed into was the Crazy Lodge (*hohooko 'oowu '*). The men who entered this lodge were around thirty to forty years old and were called *hohookeenenno'* Crazy Men (Hilger 1952:118). As discussed in chapter 3, the stem for 'crazy' (*hohookee*) is a general descriptor of behavior that is foolish, immature, or without proper knowledge. Mooney (1896:988) states that the Crazy Men did not go to war; they served only religious functions. The lodge and the ceremony were similar in form to the Clubboard and Spear rituals. One member of the age set pledged out of pity for the life movement of a family member or the tribe, and then other age-set members had to follow. Ceremonial grandfathers and elder brothers were also called upon to assist. Again, the elder brothers were drawn from the Old Men's society, and the grandfathers had to be very old men, likely from the Seven Old Men, who had passed through all the lodges. As in other lodge ceremonies, three days of preparation were followed by three days of dancing with similar exchanges throughout.

In the Crazy Lodge there was only one dancer of highest degree, called *nookohookee* 'white crazy man'. His quiet and still leadership behavior exaggerated that of the lead Spear man: "As the dancers move about the camp-circle, he always goes last, being markedly slow in his actions in contrast with the lively and untiring movements of all his companions" (Kroeber 1904:189). In this grade, leadership required yet slower movement and stronger duty to follow others. Whereas the white crazy man wore an all-white cape and was painted white entirely, the other dancers wore white and red capes. In this dance the men carried small bows with specially prepared arrows, which they shot backward in a contrary way.

On the evening of the first day of the ceremony, the Crazy Men danced before their grandfathers, but then they performed a crazy ritual act. With bare feet they entered a prepared fire, "stamping or dancing on it until they have trampled it out" (Kroeber 1904:189). The dancers thus mimicked the behavior of the moth *hohookehe'* 'little crazy', which often flies into fire or light. Following the fire dance, the men spoke and acted contrarily for the remainder of the three-day ceremony (1904:190).

Throughout this time, the men wore a medicinal root attached to their owl-feather headdresses and capes. Kroeber (1904:190) identifies the root as tcectäätcei (*ceceecei*). Any living thing touched by the root or by a dancer's cape was paralyzed. Even passing the cape over an animal's track would immobilize it. According to Kroeber, the same root with this power protected the men themselves from its paralyzing effects. Each lodge in the *beyoowu'u*, along with the old women's quill ceremony, used different roots from a set of seven sacred Arapaho medicines. The crazy root was used only in the Crazy Lodge and the Offerings Lodge. In the arrangement of medicines for the Offerings Lodge preparations, the crazy root was also placed in the center, as the "heart" (Dorsey 1903:64–65). According to Dorsey the crazy root was really a mixture of medicines and signified "law and order" as well as "everything reversed" (1903:66). The connection is that by the time men had reached age, they had acquired their medicine power and could be initiated to using *beetee* power to control others' behavior. The use and symbolism of the crazy root embodied the appropriation of medicine power for maintaining "law and order," that is, doing things in a good/correct way. In other words, the Crazy Men had control over life movement itself, a power that culminated in old age.

While wearing their regalia and root, the Crazy Men acted as "contraries," saying the opposite of what they meant and doing the opposite of what they were asked. For instance, "When one of the dancers is carrying a comparatively heavy load, such as a dog, he acts as if it weighed almost nothing" (Kroeber 1904:192). There are two symbolic aspects of the crazy practice. One is that the men at this stage in life have become immune to harsh conditions, that is, unaffected by or "closed" to the external world. The second is that the men have by this time acquired medicine power to immobilize, that is, suspend the life movement of others.

Kroeber adds that the Crazy dancers also put a root, haakahaa, in their ears that made them deaf and thus "crazy" (1904:192). As discussed in chapter 3, the practice of craziness implies "not listening" or having one's senses blocked up so that one cannot hear what others advise and cannot sense what is going on in the environment. Adding to their closed senses, the men also danced with their hands over their eyes. The Crazy Men enacted blindness as well as deafness, then, both of which contribute to crazy behavior, or not being able to see or hear dangerous situations approaching.

The owl-feather circlets they wore were also believed to make them act foolish. The color white, dominant in the Crazy Lodge, is associated with the owl and winter. The Crazy Men annoyed everyone in camp with their foolish behavior, except their grandfathers, grandmothers, and others who perhaps had more powerful medicine (Kroeber 1904:192). When it came to old people, the prescription of respect superseded even the foolish behavior of the Crazies. Ritualized craziness thus allowed a temporary and limited suspension of respect. It is interesting to note that the crazy behavior was confined to the space outside the tents and tipis. When eating or entering a tent, the Crazy Men removed the owl circlets. In doing so, they could not harass people while they were in their tipis, perhaps because of respect for children or other vulnerable persons inside. The symbolic content of the regalia and articles used, according to accounts compiled by Kroeber, connoted abundance and long life, or life movement in general.

In the story called "Lime-Crazy" (Dorsey and Kroeber 1903:23–30), recounting the origin of the lodge, a man is banished from the tribe for foolish laziness and spending too much time with women. Thus, he acts immaturely by violating the value of being useful through doing and by crossing the boundaries of gender segregation that accompany adulthood. As a result of complying with the people's wishes to banish the man, his brother, the Chief, becomes increasingly poor and thus pitiful. To relieve his difficulty, while on a buffalo hunt the Chief leaves his younger brother, instructing him to walk in circles around a buffalo carcass to drive off the flies. When the Chief does not return, the younger brother continues to walk around the meat. After three or four years, the people shun the Chief and his wife for having abandoned Lime-Crazy. The Chief then goes out to look for his brother and finds him in a pit formed by years of walking in circles. Lime-Crazy then returns to the people with the knowledge of the lodge and the power to immobilize and remobilize others through use of the crazy root.

As in other stories, a person acquires knowledge after being estranged from the camp circle and enduring a difficult, pitiful ordeal. In all such stories, the individual must return to the camp circle and give back the knowledge to the people so that it can be channeled into blessings for collective life movement. In that way the power of craziness is appropriated within the ceremonial lodge and the camp circle, where it can be kept within the right age groups and ritual boundaries.

Consistent with other American Indian cultural contexts, craziness or contrariness is not intrinsically evil or threatening to the order; rather, within boundaries, it provides a source of energy for life movement itself. The Crazy Lodge circumscribed "craziness" in a ritual context and thus channeled the power into the desire for abundance and life. It also brought together in the age grade three key dimensions: craziness, maturity, and medicine. It is about at the age of Crazy Men that elders and the tribe could recognize a person as an adult in Arapaho terms. Ironically, just as men were reaching full adulthood, they passed through the Crazy Lodge.

As suggested by the mythical character Lime-Crazy, medicine power is acquired through fasting or apprenticeship at or by this time in the life cycle. Hilger's informants agree that very young men did not fast for personal medicine: "There was no such thing as young men fasting. Men at 30 went out on hills or mountains to fast" (Hilger 1952:128). Kroeber corroborates: "The custom of more easterly tribes, for young boys to go out soon after the age of puberty, and fast in a given way for a certain number of days, is not known by the Arapaho. The men who go out to obtain supernatural power are usually fully adult, and sometimes of middle age" (1907:418). It is clear, then, that by the time men moved from the Spear to the Crazy Lodge they had been allowed access to medicine in one form or another. Furthermore, the acquisition of medicine as one moved through the life cycle was associated with increasing exposure to heat, as in the sweat lodge set up for a person who was fasting and the heat of the fire into which the Crazy dancers danced. Recall the association with heat in the Arapaho life-cyclical model that required the separation of children and medicine.

The use of the crazy root ritually expressed the acquisition of power to immobilize others through the use of medicine, thus anticipating the power older men exerted for social control. As age sets moved from the junior lodges into the Crazy Lodge, they progressed from the use of direct physical force to the use of indirect medicine power to control the movement of others. Power was a matter of paralyzing other people and animals by using roots and other medicines along with the knowledge to cause others to become sick. As in the Crazy Lodge dance context, when Arapahos did have medicines of that sort, it was necessary to be careful not to cause arguments or act improperly toward people who had such power, for they could cause illness or even death.

The association of owl feathers with the ability to paralyze is related to the idea mentioned above that dead people turned into owls. Objects shot into people were called ghost/skeleton arrows (*3iikono3ii*), and illness was thought to be the result of arrows or other objects shot by ghosts into people (Kroeber 1907:437). The Crazy dancers in this way personified ghostlike behavior. Their bows and arrows paralleled those that ghosts use. The white paint of the highest-degree dancer suggests a ghostlike appearance. In the story describing the origin of the Crazy Lodge, the younger brother "dies" in a sense, for the tribe believes him to be dead. Then, because his people and his brother wronged him, he returns to use his power over others.

The Crazy Lodge, then, was a rite of passage in Van Gennep's terms, as a reversal and a reincorporation back into the total life movement system. In previous age grades, young men were oriented outside the camp circle to form peer groups for horse care, war parties, police duties, and hunting. The strong warrior message of the Clubboard Lodge and the Spear Lodge is replaced by the use of "medicine" in the Crazy Lodge. The crazy behavior of the lodge was an inversion of maturity and a symbolic death in order to mark the transition to adulthood. In a sense, the ritually bounded expression of craziness aimed at a culturally constituted catharsis to preempt or at least discard ahead of time subsequent crazy behavior by adult men outside the ritual context. In the Arapaho theory of practice, that is homologous to the ritual expression of suffering as sacrifice in order to preempt future suffering. There is thus "reversed" rather than "sympathetic" logic at work in the Crazy Lodge and elsewhere in Arapaho ritual. Fasting averts hunger, sacrifice brings abundance, alienation brings knowledge to the tribe, enduring an illness makes it possible to cure that illness oneself, opening effects closure, and craziness effects maturity.

In the ear piercing ceremony discussed in chapter 5, the expression of pain by the child was good, for it would avert future pain. Among the old medicine men, swallowing objects that they removed from others made it possible for them to cure illness. For the Crazy Men, their inappropriate behavior instilled future appropriate knowledge as they took on more and more ritual and social responsibilities. They had to become like the white crazy dancer of highest rank (Kroeber 1904:189). As in the Spear, Dog, and women's Buffalo Lodges, the leader's actions were opposite to those of the lower-ranked dancers. Leadership required immobility, not moving ahead of all others. In the Clubboard Lodge, the leaders charged ahead of everyone else, activating the motion of youth. In the Spear and Crazy Lodges, the leader moved slower than the others.

The Dog Lodge

The Dog Lodge (*he3owo 'oowu'* [*he3ow(o)*- 'dog'/ -*'oowu'* 'lodge']) was a grade for men about fifty years old or older (Kroeber 1904:196). As with the other intermediate lodges, a man made a vow to participate in the lodge in order to avert his own or a family member's misfortune. Following the logic of the lodges, only the oldest men could serve as grandfathers and elder brothers. As in other lodges, three days of preparation preceded the dance itself.

The "shaggy dog" of highest rank moved even slower than the leaders of previous lodges. As Kroeber states, "This dancer must have some one to drive him, before he will move. He must be struck like a dog. He does not even eat of his own accord" (1904:197). From the Spear Lodge on, there was an increasing loss of mobility as an age set moved through the ritual sequence. Men were thus moved more and more by others rather than by their own will or motives.

The highest-ranking dancer was called tciiyanehi *(ceiyooneihii)* in Arapaho (Kroeber 1904:201). There were four dancers in each of the second and third degrees. The remainder of the dancers made up the rank and file. Second- and third-degree dancers wore scarves called 'ropes' *(seenook)* or tayaantceiyan *(toyooceiyoo)*. In modern orthography, the name of the first-rank dancer and the scarf share the *ceiyoo-* stem, referring to a 'leash or reins'. A modern association with 'ropes' is the term *toyooceiyoo* (Salzmann 1983:200), which also means 'rein'. The scarves were the reins to leash a Dog:

> In battle the men wearing them fasten the ends to the ground with an arrow or a stick. When they are thus fastened, they do not flee, however great the danger, until a companion releases them and orders them away. The shaggy dog follows a similar practice. He remains in his place, even at imminent risk of death, until he is driven away. [Kroeber 1904:197]

As in the other lodges, the preparation of the dancers' paraphernalia by the grandfathers was itself a carefully bounded practice. Unlike the practice in previous lodges, though, the Dog Lodge structure was taken down after the regalia was made:

> The dancing in this ceremony differs somewhat from that in the preceding lodges. When the participants have received their regalia, the lodge is taken down. They dance for four nights after this, in each case for the entire night. These four nights do not follow in succession, but occur at intervals as there is occasion. The dancers go to some tent in the camp-circle, and, forming a ring in front of the tent, whistling, and shaking their rattles, they dance. . . . In dancing, the feet are barely raised from the ground. The four men wearing scarfs have the ends of these regalia held up by other men, so that they do not drag on the ground. [Kroeber 1904:198]

The owner of the tipi then gave the company gifts and food that they carried back to the tent of one of their own society.

The solicitation of gifts from tipis was part of the younger intermediate lodges, as well; a difference here, as Kroeber recognizes, was that the Dogs did not do this on successive nights and did not dance in the lodge. Also, the Dogs did not ask for gifts from their grandfathers. In the morning following each dance, the Dogs feasted and distributed gifts. Then their grandfathers painted them.

The lodge originated in mythical time when a man pitied a poor, starving dog by giving him a root (Dorsey 1903:67). The dog ate it and then became strong again. To show his gratitude, the dog gave the man the paint and directions for the structure of the Dog Lodge. Along with dog root, the ceremony employed main root. Dorsey states that dog root signifies "Bear's Medicine," along with "purity, protection, and expectation," whereas main root means "peace, comfort, [and] quietude" (1903:66). The same two medicines, which were also used in the Old Men's Lodge and the women's quillwork ritual, generated ritual expressions of personhood synthesizing the protective function of former grades and the quiet life of old age. As mentioned earlier, each lodge carried on elements from the past, discarded something, and introduced new things for the stages to come.

There are a number of symbolic dimensions of life movement unique to the Dog Lodge. First, taking down the Dog Lodge during the progression of the ritual itself symbolized the movement of men out of the public lodges into a less public and more enclosed domain of sacred knowledge. In the Old Men's society to follow, there was no open lodge. For another thing, mobility decreases even more. Not only the highest-ranking dancer, but all the dancers, had to be "moved" by others. Their dancing itself, with feet close to the ground, also expressed less mobility and activity than did that of the younger lodges.

As Kroeber observes, there were no weapons utilized in the Dog Dance. The Dogs were, according to Mooney, leaders in battle, but they were not warriors themselves:

> When forming for the attack, they dismounted, and, driving their lances into the ground, tied themselves to them by means of straps, thus anchoring themselves in front of the battle. Here they remained until, if the battle seemed lost, they themselves gave the order to retreat. Even then they waited until some of their own society released them by pulling the lances out of the ground and whipping them away from the place with a peculiar quirt carried only by private members of this division. No one was allowed to retreat without their permission, on penalty of disgrace, nor were they themselves allowed

to retire until thus released. . . . When pursued on the retreat, they must give up their horses to the women, if necessary, and either find other horses or turn and face the enemy alone on foot. [1896:988–89]

MaryAnne Whiteman told me that the Dogs were also the last to go when the camp moved. They were always the last to break or make camp and always traveled in the rear. Anticipated by the movement of individual leaders in the younger lodges, the Dog Lodge itself became the leader group (i.e., the chiefs) of the camp and the tribe. In turn, their slowness anticipated the quiet and stillness of old age.

Another key difference from earlier lodges was the longer duration of the dancing and the painting. Each Dog, according to Kroeber, was painted each morning by his grandfather for forty or up to ninety days (1904:199). The men of the younger lodges were painted only for the three-to-four-day ceremony itself. Also, each time he was painted, the Dog had to give a present to the grandfather. The Dog's exchange status was less symmetrical and reciprocal than in junior lodges. As leaders, the Dogs had entered the stage of "giving it back," that is, a greater obligation to redistribute knowledge and wealth. The association of the person and paint became longer, anticipating the old men's groups, in which members were painted each and every day.

As an age set moved into the fourth stage of life, old age, its members became more and more closely associated with wearing paint and painting others. Red paint was tied to humanness and Arapaho cultural identity. As people matured they became more and more "human," thus more and more Arapaho. Dogs carried the symbolic content itself out of the dismantled lodge into the camp circle. The Dog dancer's wife was also painted each day by the grandfather's wife (Kroeber 1904:199–200), thus beginning the more complete identification of husband and wife in the age-grade status reached in elderhood. By this stage of life, gender distinctions began to dissolve as the shared participation of the immediate family in age-grade status became more integrated into the ritual process. Throughout the sequence, a woman identified herself with the grade her husband had last achieved.

As one became older, one's personal mobility decreased along with the decrease in public expression through ritual and political life. According to Kroeber, the chiefs of the various bands were selected from the Dog Lodge:

The Arapaho had four chiefs, as against five of the Cheyennes. They also had no official principal chief, while the Cheyennes did have one. When one of the four head chiefs died, another was chosen from among the dog-company,—men about fifty years old, who have performed the fourth of the tribal series of six ceremonials. [1902:8–9]

Clearly, then, chiefship was a function of age-grade status as well as war experiences and personal qualities. Mooney's statements about the age grades place a unique emphasis on the functions of political leadership and warrior societies. As in other contexts, political leadership was not inherited along lines of descent but rather was dependent on the age-grade system and the elders' control over the movement of age sets and individuals through it.

Chiefs, as in other Plains political systems, had to be moved by others but were expected to be unmoving in the face of personal threats, as seen in the symbolic behavior expressed in the Dog Lodge. That connection also supports Fowler's thesis that political leadership roles were confined to men in the third stage of life, or the "younger generation," a pattern that carried over into the reservation period. As Fowler relates, Arapaho leaders traditionally did only what others told them to do, as in the Dog Lodge, where others led them around. Again, an interesting reversal operates here. To lead is to be led by others. To lead is to follow the camp, not ride out ahead.

7
Old Age and the End of Life

The Old Men's Lodge

The next lodge in the sequence, referred to here as "Old Men," was for men at least in their sixties. Among all age groupings, the least evidence is available for the Old Men. Mooney gives the term "Nûnaha'wŭ" for this grade and states that it had no dance (1896:989). Both Kroeber and the Dorsey and Warden manuscripts offer the name as hinanaha^{n}wu (*hinono'oowu'*), which is difficult to translate. Kroeber suggests, "It is not improbable that the word contains the root of the word for 'man' (hinen) [*hinen*] or 'Arapaho' (hinanaei) [*hinono'ei*]" (1904:154 n). The Dorsey and Warden manuscripts (1905:Box 2, Folder 5:3) also trace a connection to *hinono'ei* but through a shared root referring to 'red granite' or 'red paint', perhaps incorporating the stem *hinow* 'red paint'. Putting the two together, Warden offers that 'Arapaho' as hinanaha (*hinono'o*) meant 'red paint being' or 'man'. Jessie Rowlodge, a Southern Arapaho, gives the literal translation 'painted sky' for *hinono'ei*, interpreting it as a compound of *-ono'-* 'sky' and *-o'ei-* 'paint' (Michelson 1910). The connection of age to paint thus applies to the Old Men, in that becoming older increasingly identified persons with red paint, and thus with Arapahoness. In this lodge men were painted red only, over the entire body, and for a longer duration than in any previous grade (Kroeber 1904:206). In earlier lodges the men were painted only temporarily or partially red; sometimes red was combined with black or white.

Contradicting Mooney, Kroeber states that the Old Men's society did have a lodge, in which there were four nights of singing but no drum. The Old Men and their only senior group, the Seven Old Men, used only rattles for their songs. In contrast to the practices of the younger men's lodges, the dancers were not ranked and did not have elaborate regalia:

> They are naked except for a buffalo-robe painted red. The fourth night they sing until twilight. Then, taking their robes and squatting low,

they form a circle and hop about, imitating prairie chickens, and calling as the prairie chickens do. . . . While they dance they sing a song that has reference to prairie chickens. When the sun rises, they leave the lodge in all directions and shake their blankets, just as birds stretch and shake their wings in the morning. [Kroeber 1904:206-207]

Young people were not allowed near the lodge. Inside, the Seven Old Men questioned the Old Men about their knowledge. As in all the other lodges, the Old Men were given häçawaanaxu (he3owoonoxu' 'dog root') to promote endurance, but in this case it was to facilitate learning rather than war exploits, physical movement, or the other duties of the junior grades. Main root, which effects quietness, was also used for this lodge. For men and women in this stage of life, quietness combined with endurance shaped their ways of acting and being persons.

There remained in this lodge a brief public expression through dancing. The Old Men's ceremony may be the dance referred to by Gunn Griswold and Sherman Sage as the Sage Chicken Dance held regularly at the same campsite near the east gate to North Park on the Big Thompson River (Colorado):

Apparently the sage chicken dance was a regular festival of the Arapahos, always held in the same place. It was part of a ceremony during which for three days no one was to speak a cross word,— "Everybody had a good time." Then there was a fast during the day, a big sage chicken dinner at night, and afterward this particular dance. [Toll 1962:12-13]

Two elements are consistent: dancing like sage chickens on the night of the fourth day and the quietness that had to reign during the dance.

Though they retained a dance form consistent with earlier grades, the men making the transition to the Old Men's group began to withdraw into the inner, quiet, and still world of old age. In social relations, others began to maintain respectful distance in their company. As one entered elderhood, public expressions of status and identity declined. The dance of these men was no longer as public persons, speaking and acting openly in camp social space. Also, the use of red paint exclusively is associated with decreasing mobility, since variations of both defined rank in junior grades. In addition, men entering or already in the fourth stage of life were not ranked; they were equal among themselves. Age equalized persons and dissolved such distinctions. Whereas younger men were ranked and often wore signs of differences of rank, as in war exploits, older persons discarded such things as those. Appropriately, the Old Men were also naked in the lodge except for robes to keep them warm.

The Seven Old Men

Within the model of the four hills of life, eldership was the final stage. The word for elder in Arapaho is *beesnenitee*, which literally means 'big person', recognizing achieved maturity. Eldership is often spoken of as "having made it" or "reached it," meaning that the old person has become a complete person. By contrast, the term for old man in particular is *beh'iihehi'* and for old woman, *betebih'ehihi'*. Each word appears to end with a diminutive suffix, *-hehi'* or *-hihi'*, suggesting 'little'. This same idea is conspicuous in Arapaho kinship terminology, in which any old person is referred to as grandfather (*nebesiibehe'* 'my grandfather') or grandmother (*nei'eibehe'* 'my grandmother'), also suffixed with the diminutive. The reference to smallness in these terms perhaps related to the withdrawal of the public self into a smaller but centered space and the association of elderhood with a return to closeness with children. To repeat, grandparent-grandchild relationships were and are especially close, closer perhaps than those maintained by parents.

The retraction into a small space combined with greater power and knowledge is evident in the highest level men could attain, called *ciinecei beh'iihoho'* 'Water-Sprinkling Old Men' referred to here as the Seven Old Men. The first term, *ciinecei*, refers to an act of sprinkling water on hot stones in the sweat lodge, as in the command *ceeceneceikuuti* 'sprinkle it!' (Salzmann 1983:192). The second term is simply 'old men', but again it contains the plural diminutive suffix *-hoho'* 'little'.

Kroeber states:

These seven old men embodied everything that was most sacred in Arapaho life. They directed all the lodges. The actual part they played in these consisted chiefly of directing the grandfathers, often only by gestures. The grandfathers, in turn, instructed the dancers. This oldest society is therefore said to contain all the others. Every dance, every song, and every action of the lodges was performed at the direction of these old men. [1904:207–8]

Because this age group was the most sacred and the least public, less is known about it. The ceremony the Seven Old Men performed was called chĭnachichi'bät by Mooney (1896:989–90), rendered *ciineceiciibeet* 'Sprinkling Sweat Lodge' in contemporary orthography. Only seven men belonged to the society at any one time, so it was not strictly an age grade into which an age set entered together. There is no existing evidence for how the men were replaced, though the logic of the age structure would hold that upon the death of one member, the other six made the selection, for they would be the only human persons eligible to do so.

Each of the Seven Old Men owned one of the sacred bundles made of buffalo skin and containing a rawhide rattle, a buffalo tail, paint, and other objects, all of which were used in the sweat lodge: "A Sweat lodge is located in the center of the camp circle, to which these Water Pouring men take their sacred bags, sacred stones, bear claws, incense weeds, paints, and buffalo tails to sweat" (Dorsey and Warden 1905:Box 2, Folder 7 1/2). Unlike the practice in the junior lodges, the objects for the Seven Old Men were not remade upon each transfer. Rather, the rattles were handed down generation after generation. The sacred bags themselves were not, as Kroeber explains, personal property or connected to an individual's personal medicine bag containing knowledge and objects acquired in a fast or by purchase. It was customary to bury some personal ceremonial objects with the deceased and to dispose of "powerful" medicine in the hills if it had not been passed on in the correct way. However, the sacred bags of the Seven Old Men were returned, upon the death of one of the men, to the remaining old men in the group.

The Seven Old Men did not dance but performed a four-day ceremony inside a sweat lodge at the center of the camp circle. Entirely within this centered, enclosed space they fasted, sang songs, and remained naked. The painting was purer and more enduring than in any other group: "They paint only in red. Black is said to belong to all the preceding lodges, but not to this. Even after having performed this ceremony they must paint with red daily" (Kroeber 1904:208). As one moved through life and the age grades, one became increasingly associated with redness. In the Old Men's Lodge, men kept being painted red longer than in earlier lodges. Further, red paint became the exclusive color of old age.

> Red also sometimes implies age. The association of ideas in this case is through the use of paint itself. Red is the paint *par excellence*; and it is the old people, who most paint themselves for religious motives, who direct the painting of the young in ceremonies and its use on objects. Then, too, old people, leading a simpler life, discard the other colors of youth, and paint themselves in red. [Kroeber 1907:417–18]

Thus, what began in the Dog Lodge, where older men are painted red for increasingly longer periods of time, continued until they received paint every day if and when they became one of the Seven Old Men.

To reiterate, red paint is associated with being a true person, an Indian (*3owo3nenitee*), and an Arapaho (*hinono'ei*), as in the origin myth in which Indian people were given red paint: "Then the man said to the Indian, "Here is this paint. It is red paint. You shall have it always and use it always" (Dorsey and Kroeber 1903:6). White people (*nih'oo3ou'u*) were given not red paint but other things to identify them. Red paint is also associated with cleanliness, prayers, and the wish to live a long life (Dorsey 1903:113).

The exclusion of black paint in old age dissolved for the old men association with victory, happiness, and overcoming suffering—all represented by the color black (Dorsey 1903:113). As male age sets moved through the graded sequence, youthful motion followed a trajectory outside the camp circle, as in war and hunting. The intermediate age grades involved a transition or reincorporation back into the internal circle. Those men brought back objects and power acquired in war, hunting, and fasting to be appropriated as blessings by the camp circle. Black is also the color relevant to relations, practices, and personhood outside the camp circle, whereas red is associated with things inside any boundary, such as blood, flesh, the camp circle, and the tribe. In the cosmos, red is associated with the earth, an island turtle, surrounded by the black-blue water. It is also the color on the inside of the Arapaho sacred wheel, which has black painted on the outside edge. Redness is thus connected to old age as a return to the inside of the camp circle, the center, and the essence of humanness and personhood. The variegated colors and thus personal distinctions of youthful life movement are replaced by the pure uniform red paint. Within social space, red is related to warmth in the center of the camp circle, where the Seven Old Men's sweat lodge was located (Mooney 1896:989).

Along with a move to pure redness, the Seven Old Men also moved toward dryness and increased exposure to heat. Dorsey and Warden state that "when men become water-pouring people, it signifies that they ceased to perspire, dried up; gone back to the origin of flesh" (1905:Box 2, Folder 5:4). One of the functions of painting, relevant to the Seven Old Men who were painted each day, was to seal up the body to prevent loss of moisture, as in situations of fasting. Whereas infancy involves bathing in cold water and removal from heat, old age requires heat and steam. Too much exposure to heat and steam in youth can "dry a person up" and thus hasten the movement toward the end of life. Therefore, "children were never subjected to sweat baths of any kind" (Hilger 1952:148). Heat and steam from the sweat lodge could be life giving, reviving in function, but only in ritually enclosed space and time. In myth, for example, the sweat lodge is used to bring the dead back to life, as in the story of River-Woman's return to life through sweating (Dorsey and Kroeber 1903:10).

According to Sherman Sage, sweat lodges in general were specific to times in the seasonal cycle:

> The people take sweat baths in sweat lodges but only after the sacred pipe has been sweat. When the buds on the trees begin to open, the sacred pipe is taken into the sweat lodge. Here the medicine men sweat and say prayers so that the people will live long and have much to eat. In the fall the sacred pipe is again sweated first, and then the rest of the people take their sweat. [in Hilger 1952:148]

Significantly, Sage holds that all the sweat lodges were under the authority of the Seven Old Men, or medicine men, as the translation refers to them. According to Warden on each occasion "they erect sweat tents four times, either at one place or different camp circles" (Dorsey and Warden 1905:Box 2, Folder 7 1/2). The sacred Flat Pipe was sweat twice each year in order to keep it alive as a person. Similarly, other sacred objects were commonly sweat by the old men in order to enliven them for ceremonial uses. It is interesting, too, that the lodges were held at the changes between summer and winter, another alternation in Arapaho time. Spring was a time of regeneration following the old age of winter. Fall was also a time of regeneration, the shedding of leaves and dying vegetation. The seasonal cycle moved from the green, wet spring to the dry fall, approaching the end season of winter.

Similarly, as one moved through the life trajectory, one's mobility and public expressiveness decreased. For the Seven Old Men, quietness and stillness reached the profoundest expression. At one level, their accumulated sacred knowledge required silence to ensure the life movement of the people: "They are not free with what they know about life, because they want to keep their steps from slipping, that is, to keep the natural laws given for the lodge" (Dorsey and Warden 1905:Box 2, Folder 7 1/2). One of Hilger's Southern informants adds that during the ceremony of the Seven Old Men, the participants had to sit absolutely still: "In the Sweat Lodge a man was required to fast for 3 days sitting perfectly still without moving in the slightest. In order to be able to do this, props are placed under his armpits" (1952:120). This extreme stillness is the end of a slowing path begun in early lodges for the highest-ranking member and gradually encompassing more and more members of successive grades. The immobility confined to certain ranks and times among the Spears, the Crazy

Men, the Dogs, and the Old Men culminates in the Seven Old Men. Concomitantly, as a way of sustaining the endurance of movement, all the preceding lodges used dog root, which was not used by the Seven Old Men (Dorsey 1903:66–68). A medicine called "strong root" and representing "holy sacred, good medicine" was used exclusively by the Seven Old Men. The medicine combined with the sweat and the red paint made their way of speaking soft and quiet: "A priest after this sweat has sweet words; his words are soft and his ways peaceable, and his thoughts gentle. He is painted in red all the time" (Dorsey and Warden 1905:Box 2, Folder 7 1/2). Elders were gradually withdrawn from the political, public sphere into the esoteric ritual sphere of the most sacred knowledge of the tribe, that is to a 'quiet life' (*teiitoniine'etiit*) separate from the noise and talk of public life.

The extreme respect required toward the Seven Old Men required distance, care, and quietness from others. Though their ceremony was in the center of the camp circle, others had to be circumspect: "The people look at them from the distance when they go out of the sweat tent" (Dorsey and Warden 1905:Box 2, Folder 7 1/2). The respect associated with the performance of the lodge is also carried over into everyday life: "His [one of the Seven Old Men's] tent is reverenced by everybody. Children are not allowed to play disorderly near his tent, but he loves them" (Box 2, Folder 7 1/2). In other words, no youthful, crazy behavior or speech was allowed near them. In general, one had to be quiet around old people and maintain "distance" from them, though their hearts were always closest to the people.

During the Sweat Lodge ceremony, food was the only object of exchange: "When these old men sweat there is an immense supply of food provided, of the nature of berry puddings of all kinds, meat of every description. The people who are related to the old men taking the sweat take food to the Sweat lodge. There is a long procession of women carrying food from all parts of the camp circle" (Dorsey and Warden 1905:Box 2, Folder 7 1/2). The Seven Old Men and their families thus ceased exchanging material forms of value, for they gave only sacred knowledge and power for life movement. As in all ritual contexts, out of respect for old men, food was offered by all relatives. Even though each of the Seven Old Men required the distance of respect, "Anybody can invite him to a meal, for his well wishes in a family" (Box 2, Folder 7 1/2). The distance of respect was mediated by food.

Ironically, though living the quiet life, the Seven Old Men represented the "consensus" of the people, as Fowler (1982) indicated, and extended their presence to political decision making:

When important tribal matters were under consideration, a council was convened consisting of the four chiefs, and all the members of the Sweat Lodge [Seven Old Men] and of the Nănăhăxwū [Old Men], therefore, of all the old men of the tribe that were of any account, since they were all members of these two societies, but of only the headmen of the other men's societies. [Hilger 1952:189]

Thus, the Seven Old Men did sit in council with the Old Men, the four chiefs of the four bands, and all the leaders of the other lodges to consider all serious issues facing the tribe. Any important decision for the tribe or for an individual required talking to the old people first and discovering the consensus of all the other age-grades' leaders.

Old age brought great influence over life movement and knowledge in all areas of social life. Long life showed that a person had done things in a good/correct way and lived the good life, despite making all the necessary sacrifices for others. Old people were obligated in turn, to "give back" that power of long life to the younger generations in appropriate ways. Inappropriate crazy behavior could shorten one's life or the life of a family member. In other words, proper knowledge made proper action possible. Proper action ensured long life. If one had lived a long life, then one had proper knowledge and the power to go with it to extend life for others. When elders passed on some knowledge or an object to younger persons, the capacity to promote long life for the recipient was carried with it.

Death and Funerals

In comparison to other life transition rituals, Arapaho prereservation funerary practices were less elaborate and confined to the immediate family. Upon death, one returned to the space of the tipi and close kin. There is more disagreement and inconsistency in the evidence describing Arapaho ideas about death than in evidence about any other area. It was difficult for Arapaho people to talk about death, since such discussion could bring it about, just as talking about birth can cause pregnancy. Ways of speaking in Arapaho tacitly proscribe reference to the ill health or injury of another person. This is not a fearful superstition as Euro-American ways of knowing often translate it, but rather an affirmation of life-giving thoughts, speech, and practices in all social relations. Proscriptions in "Other" cultures are often too hastily equated by Euro-Americans with social restraint, whereas investigation might reveal a positive basis.

It was believed that a person had a premonition four days before death, thus allowing a phase of preparation as in other life transitions. Upon passing, the deceased was dressed in his or her best clothes; the remaining property was left to be taken by close kin, especially brothers and sisters. Personal cherished belongings were buried with the person (Hilger 1952:162–64). Sometimes food was taken to the grave for several days after burial, based on the belief that the person remained for four days. The deceased person's personal medicine was taken elsewhere and buried by a medicine man, if the knowledge associated with it had not been passed on. As in other Plains tribes, a favorite horse might be shot and left with the grave. Stones were often placed on the grave as protection against scavengers and as a traditional marker similar in function to the *3i'eyoo,* a piled stone monument to mark places of battles, fasting, or other hardships.

Death activated relations among kin, as mourners' actions sought to ensure movement to the life above, so that the deceased's spirit would not wander about indefinitely as a ghost. The spirit of the person was thought to remain nearby for four days following death. To ensure travel to the above, certain practices had to be followed. As at birth, the deceased person's face and hair were painted red, so that he or she would be recognized as an Indian in the place above. Red paint was also applied to mourners after one year, to lift the mourning restrictions.

According to Mooney, afterlife was thought to be located somewhere in the west across a body of water (cited in Hilger 1952:160). It was referred to as *hiyei'in* 'our home' or the 'above' (*hihcebe'*). To give direction and prevent the spirit's return, the deceased was removed from the tipi through an opening in the west, not through the east door (1952:162). West is associated with the setting sun, the end of life, and other endings in time. Life follows not only the four-hills shape of motion but also a linear path from east to west on the "sun road," which defines life as "straight," not wayward. It was considered necessary to bury the body as soon as possible, generally on the day of death before sunset.

After death, both in the prereservation and the early reservation contexts, the place of death was "left behind." In early reservation life, some families even abandoned their cabins or houses. Another common practice was to set up a tipi nearby for the dying person. Upon death it could then be abandoned. Kroeber states that "clothing, beds, and other articles that were where he died, are burned, in order that his shadow (spirit) will not come back" (cited in Hilger 1952:167). In parallel with birth customs, those who had been in contact with the deceased had to be cleansed and purified. Those who returned to the person's house to live often had an older man smudge it with cedar incense to remove any lingering spirits (165–66). Smudging is still practiced today to purge any lingering spirits before moving into a new house. As older people warn today, anything associated with burial or death must be "left alone" and discarded. Hilger suggests, "Anyone disturbing burials might expect to be paralyzed, afflicted with tuberculosis, or with some other ailment." Families did return, if camp movements allowed, to burial sites: "If we didn't live at the place of burial, we went back there periodically to see our dead and to fix up the place. We went to see if they were all right. If the stones had been disturbed, we piled them up again. We would go a long way sometimes to see our graves" (Hilger 1952:163). Older people living today recall that their parents and grandparents sometimes traveled great distances to fix up graves. The present day Memorial Day activities, when families and organizations clean up and decorate graves at various cemeteries, are reminiscent of such practices.

Following the death of a family member in the prereservation period, close women relatives cut their hair and gashed their legs (Michelson 1933:604). The family returned to the grave for several days after the burial to mourn. During the burial process, an old man would speak to the family to give them encouragement and direction. As examined fully in chapter 4, old people are responsible through their lectures, prayers, and words for removing life-negating feelings and thoughts in others. For one year after the death, mourners wore old clothes, appeared unkempt, and could not participate in social events, such as dances or feasts. In some respects they became nonpersons. Mourning was thus a way to gain the pity of other-than-human persons in order to effect the movement of the deceased to the above and overcome the difficulty of loss.

Family members were required to make sacrifices and offerings to ensure the deceased's movement to the above. A person who died a "bad death"—for example, one who died alone without ties—was thought to remain on earth roaming about in a crazy way. Within the entire life trajectory, death was a transition from within to outside the camp circle and a movement to the above so that the spirit of the person would not remain on earth. Doing things in a good/correct way ensured the successful transition and movement of the person above. That is, the mourning sacrifices and restrictions of family members, like other actions associated with death, effected life movement.

In some ways, the practices surrounding death and birth were similar. Both involved finding a place in a new home. Very broadly, in both death and birth, immediate kin formed the core of actors within the tipi, the space of the family. Likewise, at each event associated elements had to be purified, destroyed, or discarded as soon as possible, whereas others were carefully bounded or bundled. In each case the person's face was painted red so that he or she would be recognized as *3owo3nenitee* 'an Indian' and *hinono'ei* 'an Arapaho'. Women were the principal actors in kin-oriented birth, childhood ceremonies, and funerals. Both historically and in the contemporary context, mourning and the care of graves and cemeteries are primarily women's roles.

However, whereas both birth and death required proper enclosure, death called forth a need for "discarding," represented by placement outside the camp circle or behind the moving camp. As in all ritual contexts, the Arapaho emphasis was on appropriate practice rather than speculation about the afterlife or otherworldly concerns in general. Nonetheless, the stone markers were places to which families occasionally returned to maintain the graves and to continue a relationship on the land with events experienced and overcome. Funerary practices, like all other ceremonies, involved the proper movement and boundaries for life.

8
Women and Life Movement

Ritual Agency

Within the ceremonial complex of the *beyoowu'u*, women's roles were neither secondary nor merely complementary to those of men. For one thing, the involvement of men through vows to participate in the age-grade lodges was not just a matter of individual participation. When an individual pledged to make a sacrifice in any context, the burden of preparation over a considerable length of time was a matter for family corporate action, within which women were the central actors. Male participation was possible only through the efforts of women in the camps, which are mentioned throughout the literature, though rarely described in full. Women produced the food and some other items of exchange for grandsons and grandfathers alike. In some instances women were visible in the ceremonies themselves. Within the age-grade ceremonies and the Offerings Lodge, the wife of the highest-ranking "first pledger" of the lodge participated directly in the ritual preparation and the performance. As described in chapter 6, the shared age-grade identity of husband and wife in ritual participation increased with rank and with advancement through the sequence of lodges, such that by the time elderhood was reached, there were fewer distinctions of gender than in younger age grades.

Women formed the core of the tipi and the camp, whereas men were pushed to the public spaces outside. In some ways the enduring bonds among women were superior to those among men that had to be constituted through public rituals. Quoting the Southern Arapaho scholar Cleaver Warden, Michelson writes, "Arapahos prefer daughters to sons because the former stick to their parents better" (1910). Relations among sisters and between generations of women maintained the continuity of the family and the camp and the solidarity of the tribe. Though much more has been written about the unifying function of the men's age structure in ceremonial and political authority, the social glue of Arapaho society was constituted at least as much by the enduring intrafamilial and interfamilial relations generated by and through women.

Outside of the age-grade sequence, the Buffalo Lodge, and the quill society, women were the central agents for life movement in childhood life transitions and in funerary practices. They were the primary agents for generating life movement, such as through the power to give birth, the shedding of blood, enlivening tipis, cradle making, keeping children's navel bags, counting the winters of life, flesh sacrifices, and many daily practices. Throughout life, women produced objects of exchange, vowed to fast, and made sacrifices to promote the life movement of kin. For instance, women often sacrificed through a vow to offer a part of a finger to help a sick family member recover from illness or a brother return from war (Dorsey 1903:186–87; Michelson 1933:608; Hilger 1952:167). A Southern Arapaho woman described her sacrifice:

> After my sister had been married several years and had had several children, she became sickly. Realizing the responsibility I was facing in the custody of her children in the event of her death which seemed evident by the failure of two of the best Arapaho doctors after periodical gifts for their services, I unhesitatingly made a vow to sacrifice my left little finger, so that my sister's life might be spared, so that her small children, who were a pitiful sight to me as they were about their helpless mother, might again enjoy happiness with their mother, and so the rest of us would be relieved from the impending sorrow, especially my father and mother who thought so much more of this daughter, as she was always somewhat frail. The next morning an Arapaho woman was called to remove my finger in the usual way. She told me that since I was slender this wound would heal rapidly, which it did. My sister commenced to get better, improving very quickly. [Michelson 1933:609]

Such sacrifices were made freely, motivated out of pity or concern for not only the afflicted person but all the relatives affected. Recall also that women took on the greater burden of mourning.

Women's life movement was closer to their kin and the domestic space of the tipi, but attributing less power and historical significance to that domain betrays a Euro-American spatial orientation that distinguishes a weak domestic from a strong political, public sphere. The so-called domestic sphere was no less powerful in Arapaho life movement simply because it was smaller than the public sphere, where men were more visible. Tipi life was not merely practical, domestic, and profane activity. None of those distinctions are applicable to the

Arapaho context.

Women's roles in life movement centered on two different, though complementary, trajectories of space and time. Whereas male ritual participation generated extensive constructed kin relations, as among age peers and ceremonial grandfathers, women's roles concentrated on maintaining kin relations created by birth, marriage, and sibling ties. The bonds maintained close to the space of the tipi were no less instrumental for life movement than those in the ceremonial life of the camp circle and beyond. In another respect, as evident in myth, women mediated great distances with other-than-human persons through marriage, art, and sacrifice. The power of women to reproduce close kinship bonds is transposed in myth to relations with other-than-human persons. In short, women's roles drew distant sources of life movement close to the center and then dispersed them outward from the heart of social life, the tipi. For this power, knowledge passed among women across generations.

The Women's Buffalo Lodge

Women were identified with and participated in the lodges of their husbands. There was one lodge, however, that women could pledge; it was called *benouhto'oowu'*, a word for which there is no translation. Kroeber (1904:210) offers "buffalo-dance" as the name of the lodge, based on the centrality of buffalo in the performance. The ritual was first practiced by the buffalo, then given to the Arapaho people (1904:211). Elements of the lodge parallel the men's intermediate lodges as well as the Offerings Lodge itself. According to Kroeber, "In the estimation of the Arapaho, the women's dance is more sacred than the dances of the younger men, ranking in this regard at least as high as the dog-dance" (1904:225). The medicines for the Buffalo Lodge are the same three (sage, cockleburs, and dog root) used in the Clubboard and Spear Lodges (Dorsey 1903:67–68). Like men, women moving from the second to the third stage of life gained access to medicines. In contrast to the ethnographic evidence for the men's societies, the Buffalo Lodge is mentioned nowhere as a society or an age set of women performing political or ritual functions outside the ceremony itself. Like the Offerings Lodge, the Buffalo Lodge did not create or reproduce age sets.

Women were ranked in the Buffalo Lodge dance as intermediate men were in their lodges. The pledger of the lodge was the highest-rank dancer, called 'white woman' (*nookuhisei*). Second in rank was the 'owner-of-the-poles' (*hiitokooxu'init*), representing an old buffalo bull. Third-degree dancers were called 'red stand' (*bee'kuu*), and fourth-degree dancers 'white stand' (*nonooko'kuu*). Two little girls acted as 'calves'. The unranked women dancers impersonated bulls, if painted white, or cows, if yellow (Kroeber 1904:211), mirroring the white for female, yellow for male duality of the Clubboard Lodge.

Women were directed by grandmothers, corresponding to the men's grandfathers, but they apparently had no counterpart to elder brothers. The grandmothers were directed by the old men in making the dancers' regalia and painting their granddaughters for specific ranks. As in the men's lodges and the Offerings Lodge, three days of preparation preceded the actual dancing. Unlike the procedure for the men's lodges, though, preparations were made in the dance lodge itself. The lodge structure was similar in a few respects to the Offerings Lodge and the Old Men's Lodge but quiet different from the other men's lodges. It appears to have been an elongated tipilike structure: "This lodge is built something like this way: There are seven tipi poles tied all together, which makes it a centre-pole. The digging stick is placed horizontal to the pole, and there are seven bunches of poles, formed in a bunch which rest against the digging stick, making the lodge appear like an ordinary tipi" (Dorsey and Warden 1905:Box 2, Folder 11). It is significant that the Buffalo Lodge should be a large tipi structure, for tipis were owned by women and identified with their power for life movement. The sides were covered with three or four tipi covers. As in the Offerings Lodge, one pole in the southwest and one in the northeast were painted black. Two poles, one in the southeast and one in the northwest, were painted red. The use of a digging stick for the crossbar recalls the Star Husband myth, in which at one point the woman used her digging stick to attach a rope over the hole in the sky and thus tried to escape to the human world below. As a result of her death and the survival of her son, all knowledge and sources of life movement were brought to the people. Basically, the Buffalo Lodge revolved around the role of women as mediators in the appropriation of knowledge and life from animals and other-than-human persons.

In a similar story recounting the origin of the Buffalo Lodge, a buffalo, who appears as a man, lures a woman away from her camp circle and her human husband. She marries the buffalo but eventually escapes underground with the assistance of Gopher and her human husband. This story is like the one of the woman who married Moon in that both women marry other-than-human husbands and escape from their camps through a hole in the ground. In each story, the strong ties of a woman to her family and people draw her back home, along with the knowledge she acquired. Upon returning, Buffalo Woman brings back "knowledge" described as "the foundation upon which we must live" and "knowledge of the laws of nature" (Dorsey and Kroeber 1903:48). Before this time, the people were without knowledge and lacked "sympathy one toward another" (i.e., pity). The woman brings back buffalo fat (an embodiment of the knowledge she brings) to the old people and thus makes it possible for them to "paint" others. For body paint, tallow (*niinen*) is mixed with earth, berries, or other natural substances. The myth illustrates that buffalo and earth are the sources of humanness.

In two other versions offered by Dorsey and Kroeber (1903:42–48), a man receives the knowledge from the White Buffalo Cow, who appears to him out of pity in a vision. That variation is more consistent with the same story found in other Plains contexts, which is a transformation of the first version, though it inverts the gender relationship. Whether Buffalo Cow or a human woman mediates, a feminine appropriation of the knowledge-power from the buffalo occurs. In the beginning, buffalo pitied humans and therefore made the humans' "burden lighter," that is, provided them with a bountiful source of food and other necessities for life movement, such as hides, sinew, tallow, blood, and other items too numerous to list. As a result of mythico-ritual practices, life movement is henceforth dependent on the sacrifices or offerings that buffalo make to humans. The knowledge of right and wrong, the age structure itself, and the origin of pity all came through the origin of the Buffalo Lodge. As in the Arapaho horse-buffalo economy, women mediate in the relationship between buffalo and humans, as the transformers of raw hides into usable skins, raw meat into storable foods, and raw materials into cultural forms.

As in other myths that explain the origin of ceremonial lodges, an individual is isolated from the camp circle and then returns with knowledge to the center of the tribe, the old people. Recognizing the need for "giving back," one should not hoard knowledge gained but should be generous by distributing it to the tribe. It is interesting that in all such stories, a younger-generation adult leaves the camp circle and returns with knowledge that he or she then gives to the old people. The Buffalo Lodge renews the appropriation of knowledge from outside the camp circle by an individual isolated from the camp. Whereas men are estranged in myth from the camp circle by banishment or fasting, women are distanced by marriages with other-than-human persons. Both men and women incorporate the knowledge gained into the age structure and place it in the center, where only elders have control over it.

The shape and tempo of motion were distinctive dimensions in the Buffalo Lodge as in the men's lodges;

White Buffalo Woman [the highest-rank dancer] has a bed in the west of the lodge, and the cows and calves by her side. These people cannot move or even go out for water, unless the relatives and friends provide the means to give relief from time to time. These things which are given as payment to the grandfathers and mothers are arrows, bags, parfleches, ponies, meat, moccasins and other useful articles. [Dorsey and Warden 1905:Box 2, Folder 11]

The fact that White Buffalo Woman and her calves (two young girls) could not move unless others "released them" echos the stillness of the White Crazy Man, the lead Dog dancer, and even the Spear men staked to the earth. In the case of the Buffalo Lodge, gifts from dancers' families to the grandmothers and grandfathers "move" the lead dancer. As in all contexts, exchange generates activity and movement. Unlike the highest-ranked male dancers, though, White Buffalo Woman fasted during the four days of the ceremony. Like the White Crazy Man, the highest-rank dancer in the women's Buffalo Lodge was painted white. The belts worn by all ranks in the Buffalo Lodge were similar to those of the men's Spear society.

Throughout the ceremony the lower-ranked dancers imitated various movements of buffalo, such as running out to a stream to drink water, raising dust like a buffalo herd, and resting and sitting like buffalo (Kroeber 1904:211–12). At one point two men assigned as "hunters" chased the "herd," counting coup on some and shooting one woman with a blunt arrow. Then, pretending to butcher her, they removed a piece of fat (*niinen*) concealed under the woman's robe. They offered it to the old man supervising the lodge, thus reenacting the original gift of tallow to the old people. The core message is that individually acquired knowledge should be appropriated within the age structure for the benefit of the whole tribe.

The Buffalo Lodge expresses the location of women in the mediation between humans and buffalo. Buffalo, as persons in myth, are the source of human laws and sympathies (e.g., respect and pity), as embodied in the tallow. It is thus through buffalo that women are oriented to the space beyond the camp circle. Moreover, it is only through appropriate practices that the relationship between buffalo and humans is sustained. Knowledge bridges distances between human and other-than-human persons. But in that process, exchange and proper relations of pity, respect, and quietness are required in order to appropriate the knowledge and power to effect life movement.

Women's Quillwork

Paralleling the Seven Old Men's authority over painting, the ritual control over quillwork rested in the Seven Old Women (Kroeber 1902:28–30). Each of the seven women owned one of seven sacred bags containing the materials and tools for doing quillwork. Several forms of quill decorating were under the authority of the Seven Old Women, including the decorating of tipi ornaments, tipi liners, buffalo robes, pillows, leanbacks, and cradles.

Transferring a bag from one woman to another required an elaborate ceremony, described in a narrative from a Southern Arapaho woman who asked to receive the bag "in the straight way" (Kroeber 1902:30–33). First the recipient had to gather and supply goods, such as food, clothing, and horses. All of the Seven Old Women were present with her in the tipi where the ceremony was held. They purified their bags with medicine and incense and then opened them. After that, they painted the petitioner's face with five red spots, representing the four directions and the center. One old woman blessed and presented each food in turn to the four directions and the center, and then all ate. Each motion and blessing required starting first in the southeast, then moving to the southwest, the northwest, and the northeast, returning lastly to the center. After medicines were prepared and incense burned, the old women painted themselves red, along with their bags and the objects that had been removed for the ceremony. They then closed the bags and left the tipi, except for Backward, the member of the Seven Old Women passing the bag to the younger woman. Backward remained to purify the petitioner's body, dress, and cloth goods with medicine. All the goods were given away except two pieces, which the petitioner kept on her stomach throughout her fast. After receiving instruction from Backward, she was left alone: "I fasted and cried for four days; on the fourth, food was prepared, and the old women came again. After they had eaten, I received the bag, with instructions how to use it. Backward made a motion four times to give it to me; then, at a fifth motion with it from her heart, she gave it to me" (33). A few days later, she supervised another woman, who vowed to make a robe.

The Arapaho women's quill society shared many features with the Cheyenne ceremony described by Grinnell (1923,1:159–69). The significant difference is the greater, though still secondary, involvement of men in the Cheyenne quillworking. Arapaho quillwork involved women exclusively, though men could be recipients of the objects made. Grinnell also makes no mention of seven sacred bundle owners in the Cheyenne case, although senior women were the directors of the ceremony.

Younger women made vows to produce quillwork objects inspired by pity and respect for close kin. In the Arapaho practice, one of the Seven Old Women offered the pledger ritual instruction in the designs, techniques, symbolism, and meanings for applying dyed porcupine quills to tipi ornaments, buffalo robes, tipi liners, and cradles. In both the Arapaho and the Cheyenne cultures, quillwork was based on knowledge acquired in mythical time from Whirlwind Woman and was directly related to the most sacred designs for generating tribal well-being, health, and prosperity.

Quillworking generated and reflected women's life movement, much as feats beyond the camp were a measure of men's life movement. Warden describes the career of a quillworker named Fire-Wood:

> An old woman of the northern Arapaho, Wyoming, began to quill cradles, tipis, robes, and various other articles when she was fifteen years old. She was induced to work and honor her kin by her parents, through home surroundings. All the old women began to observe her skill and good memory and invited her to notable gatherings of old women. After she was married her occupation continued until she reached the mark of sixty assorted baby cradles, fourteen buffalo robes, five ornamental tipis, ten calf robes and one buffalo leanback. Ten years ago [c. 1890], when Bird-Woman, mother of Fire-Wood died, her tipi bag lay idle for two years, when the latter took possession of the bag by payment of articles to the older women. Fire-Wood was instructed in the manner of handling of the contents of the bag and also in the method of consecration upon them. [Dorsey and Warden 1905:Box 2, Folder 1:8]

Women quillworkers kept a lifetime record, by notches on their hide scrapers, of the number and kind of objects they made. Counts were also kept for other women's activities, such as the scraping of hides. As part of the same process, women marked their hide scrapers or sticks to count the number of years their children had lived. The counting of art objects made was parallel to the men's war stories and counting of battles, coups, and other achievements.

There is also some suggestion that there were various degrees of quillwork during the long apprenticeship, which lasted in Fire-Wood's case for almost her entire adult life, from the time she reached the second hill of life by becoming "useful" until the approach of old age in the fourth hill. Though many women produced quillwork, the women who ascended to the quill society were selected by the Seven Old Women themselves. Only young women and girls who showed a disposition for learning quillwork became apprentices. The old women selected Fire-Wood, for example, for her personal qualities and learning abilities. As in the men's lodges and other ritual contexts, women like Fire-Wood had to cook for and make payments to their teachers. Knowledge was thus exchanged for goods, not as a "purchase" but in order to sustain the relationship between an older person and a younger apprentice.

All objects requiring a vow were under the control of the Seven Old Women in the quill society. A woman could vow to make such an object as an offering, as pledges were made for other sacrifices, for example, a person's vow to sponsor an age-grade ceremony, to participate in the Offerings Lodge, to fast, to cover the Pipe, to participate in the women's Buffalo Lodge, to cut off a finger, to offer pieces of flesh, or to make some other sacrifice to avert misfortune for one's kin and the tribe. Quill production was a sacrifice in that it required the expense of gifts and food and personal risk from the exposure to powerful objects (i.e., quills) and forces (Dorsey and Warden 1905:Box 2, Folder 1:15). As in other ritualized artistic production, objects made in the quill ceremony were not for personal possession or use but were gifts to the individual relatives with whom one stood in a respect relationship or for whom one felt pity. The recipient was expected to reciprocate: "When a man receives such a present from his mother-in-law or from a relative he enters into a tipi where old women are gathered in consecrating the robe, etc., he makes an apology to all for inferior qualities and so gives a horse to show that he is a man" (Folder 1:8). Generally, gifts produced through the quillwork ceremony moved through respect relationships across gender, such as from mother-in-law to son-in-law or from sister to brother. In the tempo of exchange, a man could not wait too long before reciprocating and had to take his return gift to a woman's social space.

Recall that a child's father's sister (*nehei* 'my aunt') generally made a cradle as an extension of the brother-sister respect relationship requiring formal exchange. Sisters also usually made buffalo robes for their brothers, and mothers-in-law for their sons-in-law. Tipi ornaments and furnishings were often made by a bride's mother as part of the reciprocal exchange between the husband's family and the wife's family. The gift of tipi ornaments and furnishings had to be reciprocated by the young husband's service to his parents-in-law, especially his mother-in-law. Motivated by respect, women produced and gave quillwork objects to narrow the distance of cross-gender respect relationships and to equalize the roles of women and men overall. All ritualized artistic production also occurred within the age hierarchy of each gender.

Significant to all the objects women made through the quillwork society is their association with containment or "covering." In general, the women produced items and designs (e.g., *hiiteeni*) that enclosed space yet generated life movement. The cradle, like the social skin of the body, encased and protected the infant; a quilled buffalo robe contained the warmth of the body; and the tipi liner and tipi ornaments enclosed the domestic space associated with women. Even outside of the ritualized art forms, women's designs in paint on rawhide or beadwork on tanned hide constructed boundaries around the total design. Similarly, White Buffalo Woman brought back the tallow for paint that covered and protected the bodies of dancers in all the lodges. Women also made the navel bags that encased the source of life movement, as well as rawhide bags, trunks, and parfleches for storing food.

As a rule, buffalo robes retained the fur on one side and were tanned on the other. Painted robes were worn by women and quilled robes by men (Dorsey and Warden 1905:Box 2, Folder 1:27). Different quilled robes were ranked, depending on the number of horizontal lines and colors used. A distinctively Arapaho quillwork pattern used red, yellow, black, and white quills to replicate the four-hills design and thus promote life movement: "The line represents a buffalo-path. The four colors—the conventional red, yellow, black, and white—represent the four lives (generations or periods) since the beginning of the world" (Kroeber 1904:65). The same pattern was used to make the circular quilled tipi ornaments: "One meets in the course of this circumference the same succession of colors, and the same relative amount or proportional width of each, as on this straight line on the buffalo-robe" (65). As shown in chapter 4, the pattern consists of (1) a medium-length red section, (2) a black vertical narrow line, (3) a narrow white space, (4) another black line, (5) a long yellow section, (6) a black line, (7) a narrow white space, and (8) a black line; then the pattern begins again. Both line and circular patterns represented the passage of time, as in the four generations of the age of the earth. Ritualized quillwork was thus intended to generate life movement through the homologous representation of space and time. And it was women who produced these sacred patterns necessary for boundaries and life movement.

The quillwork ritual paralleled those surrounding the preparation of regalia for all ceremonies. Preparation took place in the enclosed space of a tipi. Root medicines were used to purify the ritual actors. Food and gifts were provided to the old woman directing the ceremony. The preparation and the ongoing prayers required main root for incense and dog root for spittle, both of which were also used in the Dog and Old Men's Lodges (Dorsey 1903:66). After completion of the object (e.g., a cradle, a robe, or an ornament) it was passed over burning cedar, or smudged. The pledger then related the nature of her vow (1903:74–75).

When a woman made a mistake, she had to be purified, lest the porcupine quills move like arrows and shoot into her body. In myth, the culture hero Found-in-Grass entrusted to the trickster *Nih'oo3oo* a powerful bladder bag containing quills that when opened became a party of warriors (Dorsey and Kroeber 1903:375-78). When attacking a village on his fourth raid (signifying excessive use of power), *Nih'oo3oo* failed to open the bag and therefore was killed by the enemy. One of the enemy then opened the bag, and the warriors destroyed the entire village and returned victorious to the camp of Found-in-Grass. As in other similar stories, *Nih'oo3oo* was resurrected in the end after his foolish death. The association of quills with warriors connected the women's quillwork with the Arapaho concern for doing things correctly within limits through careful instruction so as to avoid injury. It also linked women's quillwork achievements with the bravery of warriors. When women did quillwork within the tipi, they were challenged by a powerful threat, the quills as arrows and warriors. They were not merely taking ritual precautions: it is well known that porcupine quills that penetrate the skin can in fact travel through the body and even attack vital organs.

Arapaho quillwork thus followed a ritually circumscribed order. It shaped the space and time for affecting the life movement of self, others, and the tribe. As Kroeber states, "it should be borne in mind that the making of what have been called tribal ornaments is regularly accompanied by religious ceremonies: that some styles of patterns found on tent-ornaments and parfleches are very old and sacred because originating from mythic beings" (1902:150). Among Plains cultures, the Arapahos are unique in the emphasis they place on the religious content and ritual boundaries of artistic production. Ceremonial objects, Kroeber observes, were subject to less variation than other art forms:

> Of common objects, the writer does not remember to have seen two that were exactly identical, or intended to be identical. Two classes of articles, however, do not fall under this rule. These are, first, certain ceremonial objects, which naturally are made alike, as far as is possible, for ceremony is the abdication of personal choice and freedom; secondly, objects which are decorated with a more or less fixed tribal decoration. These objects are tents, robes, bedding, and cradles. [1902:147]

The latter "tribal" productions, to use Kroeber's term, were those within the ritual authority of the Seven Old Women.

Quillwork was an expression and a reproduction of controlled movements and designs created in myth. In particular, quillwork originated with Whirlwind Woman (*Neyoooxetusei*), who also spread the earth out to its present boundaries by spiraling outward from center to periphery in the same motion as that used to make round quill pendants. Women's quillwork knowledge, like that for the men's lodges, centered on the reproduction of objects, using the appropriate designs and techniques. As in other types of ritual practice for replicating design and form, meaning centered in doing things appropriately and without error in a good/correct way. If errors were made, there had to be purification and an appeal to the pity of other-than-human persons. Prayers in ritual contexts were often for the knowledge to do things right, exactly as they had been done before in the same context. Women served as the source of knowledge for paint in myth and for the symbolic generation of life movement through quillwork designs. Both of those interconnected the life paths of persons with the generativity of powerful forms, including *hiiteeni* itself. The relationship of Whirlwind Woman to the Four Old Men is a contrast and a complement of two types of motion for generating life. Whereas Whirlwind Woman spiraled life outward from the center to the edge of the world, the Four Old Men sent life-giving breath from the boundary to the center. In a profound way, this complementarity is that between the adult roles of women and men, respectively, discussed in chapter 4.

In general, women's life movement was an expression of their mediating role in transforming skins, flesh, and other raw materials into forms that could generate life movement for others and contain it within boundaries of the body and the tipi. As such, in myth and ritual, women mediated distances between spatial domains, between the above and the earth's surface, between buffalo and human, and between the periphery and the center, as in the drawing of power for life movement to and out of the tipi itself.

9
A Total View of Life Movement

The foregoing description and analysis has presented Arapaho life movement along the trajectory from birth to death. The shape, quality, and phasing of life were constituted through ritual practices that activated social relations and interconnected meanings on different levels. Though there were myriad strands of life movement, it is now possible to summarize and integrate the most salient dimensions. Specifically, it is possible to offer a total view of life movement with respect to social functions, space, types of motion, color, modes of expression, and kinds of medicine power.

First of all, each of the various rituals served to define social functions for groups and individuals by connecting them to dimensions of personhood, shaped through modes of practice, speaking, and relating to others. In the first stage of life, parents, grandparents, and other kin cooperated to promote a child's life movement. Later childhood rituals marked the acquisition of the abilities associated with becoming a person and eventually a "useful" adult serving others.

Each age-grade ceremony expressed and activated particular social and political functions served by men's age sets. Those are summarized in Table 9.1. The changing of functions with movement through the grades was synchronized with shifts in types of power and rank. Kit Foxes and Stars correlated with young male activity outside the camp and service to the senior grades. The Clubboard and Spear Lodges stressed endurance, quick reactions, and the use of physical force against both enemies and those in the camp circle who overstepped boundaries. Those grades marked the transition from age peer equality, in the unincorporated youthful grades, to formally recognized rank within the age set. Women dancers in the Buffalo Lodge were also introduced to rank. Overall, movement into the third stage of life was marked by rank according to personal achievement, measured primarily by one's willingness to make a sacrifice for the life movement of others, whether in ceremony, war, or hunting. The ranking of dancers in each lodge, including the Buffalo Lodge, was also a microcosm of the wider age hierarchy. Each intermediate lodge (i.e.,

185

Clubboard, Spear, Crazy, and Dog) transposed into itself some of the dimensions of age ranking from the total system. For example, leaders in the lodge were slow to move, thus paralleling the general immobility of senior grades.

Table 9.1
Social and Political Functions of Men's Age Sets

AGE GRADE	FUNCTION
Kit Foxes and Stars	Servants for other lodges
Clubboards and Spears	Appropriation of value from outside camp circle and police force for controlling camp movements, use of physical force
Crazy Men	Ritual agency and use of medicine to control others
Dogs	Chiefship, as following others
Old Men	Learning sacred knowledge
Seven Old Men	Painting, guiding all other lodges

Upon entering the Crazy Lodge, men began to serve in leadership roles through medicine power and ceremonial authority to exert control over the life movement others. As another aspect of the transition, Crazy Men entered into the age of "giving it back," not only in the transmission of knowledge but also as ritual agents, since they served as grandfathers for the Clubboard Men. For those roles, they had the medicine power to promote life or neutralize it, illustrated in the use of the crazy root. The Crazy Lodge in general marked the acquisition of medicine to mobilize or immobilize others; that function replaced the warrior action and physical force of the preceding grades. Internal ranking continued into the Crazy and Dog Lodges but dissolved in the most senior groups, where symbolic expressions of rank were discarded.

In the Dog Lodge men became eligible for political and military leadership, expressed as slowed movement and leading by following others. Such leadership, as effected in the Crazy Lodge, was removed at this stage from direct participation in war. Though the Dogs were not directly involved, their political and military leadership checked the movement and rank functions of the younger warrior grades. In contrast to other tribes that did not maintain such a balance, the Arapaho age-grade system strictly defined and circumscribed young men's movement and activity.

In the Old Men's Lodge, men began to acquire the most sacred knowledge and take on increasing responsibilities for directing rituals in the *beyoowu'u*. At this life stage, internal age-grade ranking also was replaced by equality within the age group and ultimate authority over others. The Seven Old Men marked the culmination of all rituals and the accumulation of all sacred knowledge; the seven men exercised direction over the functions of all grades and stages. Their authority withdrew from public expression of rank or achievement into still and quiet forms engendered through respect and medicine power (*beetee*) instead of physical movement and force. Though their physical personhood retracted from public space, their influence was present in all social spaces and times. With age came the ability to see farther and deeper in space and time. Because of that, their quiet, guiding presence was required for all the lodges and life transition rituals.

Personhood, functions, and rank were further related to spatial placement and types of motion, inculcated through and expressed in life transition rituals and in the lodges themselves. Types of movement in space defined the personal qualities associated with each life stage. In infancy, the cradle tightly bundled the child. Once out of the cradle, children were allowed to move a little more, and their feats of self-movement and self-expression were honored. During late childhood, the family and the elders recognized the gradual movement of children outside the tipi and beyond, such as their first walk. In later childhood, at the transition from the first to the second stage of life, children became more associated with useful activity outside the space of the tipi. At the same time they increasingly learned to be still, immobile, and quiet around elders, becoming ready for the path to learning, which in later stages increasingly depended on listening to senior persons speak, pray, lecture, and tell stories. Girls took on the chores of domestic life (e.g., hauling water and wood), whereas boys were placed in practices outside the camp circle such as hunting and warfare. These functions followed the segregation of female and male space that marked the transition to the second stage of life. During the second stage, strong matricentric kinship bonds kept young women within tipi space close to the core of camp life; young men were pushed outward to form peer groups engaged in hunting, games, and horse care.

Those groups formed the age sets for eventual entry into the grades. Kit Foxes and Stars were placed outside the camp circle and allowed relatively unbounded activity, though even in that the heightened, directed movement of subsequent stages was anticipated. As servants for the other lodges, they brought the roles of the age of doing into ritual contexts as fetchers and messengers. The second stage of life began in more unrestrained motion for young men, introducing ritually bounded movement as age sets progressed from the two most junior grades into the intermediate lodges. Life movement for men in the second stage of life moved to the space beyond the camp and was followed by ritual and social reincorporation, beginning in the Clubboard Lodge.

In roughly the middle to late teens, young women began to participate in the Buffalo Lodge and later in the quillwork society. Though they remained within smaller spaces of activity, they increasingly generated value that radiated outward through exchange with kin and camp. Upon marriage they began to activate their reproductive roles and their function of transforming raw materials into life sources, both of which are primary, original powers in Arapaho mythological time. Through those practices, their personhood and roles extended far beyond the boundaries of what might appear to be "restricted" feminine space. For both genders and all adult stages, one's personhood was not bounded by one's body or physical space but extended widely through relations in space and time. Therefore, what women reproduced, produced, sacrificed, or transformed within local space radiated outward with a power no less extensive than that of the visibly larger and more public male actions.

In the Clubboard and Spear grades, the symbolic emphasis for men was on quick, sudden, yet coordinated movement directed outward beyond boundaries or inward to define them. Such movements were required for warrior, hunting, and police functions. For instance, the race competition between the two sides of the lodge, the short and the stout men, symbolized and encouraged fast movement toward and returning from the periphery, illustrating the principal path of activity for men at this stage in life. The intermediate lodges also focused on endurance, as in the Clubboard Lodge, when the men chewed dog root to help them sustain movement without tiring. All of these types of motion were needed so that young men could react quickly and endure as long as needed to deal with enemy threats, hunting game, and the orders of senior-grade men.

Staking dancers to the ground in junior lodges also symbolized controlled motion and anticipated the transition to the third stage of life, that is, leadership as motion controlled by age peers, older men, and the tribe. Accordingly, the first two lodges synthesized two opposite types of movement: fast and slow. The highest-rank Spear's actions epitomized the ideal, for he was slow to anger, but when provoked he reacted quickly, like the thunder of Thunderbird, who was associated with the lodge.

For both the Buffalo and the Crazy Lodges, transition to the third stage of life (i.e., "adulthood") coincided with full reincorporation inside the camp circle. The Buffalo Lodge valued and appropriated within the camp circle women's power to transform raw materials into cultural forms. The Crazy Lodge marked full passage into Arapaho adulthood for men through liminal, contrary behavior and the corresponding use of medicine power. Craziness as undirected movement was unleashed at this point in life movement, so that it could be fully appropriated in the age hierarchy, lodge, and camp circle, as in Lime-Crazy's return with knowledge and power.

The contrariness and unleashed motions of the Crazy Lodge were followed by the most controlled movement of all. The Dog Lodge centered on the characteristics of personhood required for leadership, primarily following and giving all that one owns to other people. By the close of the third stage of life, leadership became decreasingly tied to self-movement and individual property. Self-movement gave way to the consensual will of the senior grades or the tribe. Personal ownership was superseded by giving back, motivated by stronger obligations of pity, respect, and generosity. Chiefs and other men of this stage had to show the willingness to give anything another person needed, deserved, or requested. More than any other lodge, the dancers were moved only by the actions of others. In contrast to the Euro-American placement of leaders "out front," Dogs were the last to move in battle or when moving camp. Dogs also carried no weapons, since they no longer reacted strongly to threats. The dismantling of the lodge in the Dog ceremony symbolized the eventual transition of the men to a less public and less visible space in the fourth stage of life.

The Old Men's Lodge completed the transition between the third and fourth stages of life. In social space, men became enclosed within a smaller lodge, removed from the public space of the camp and the ceremonial lodges. Nonetheless, they continued to perform a dance, though abbreviated, thus retaining a link to the preceding grades. This lodge likewise restricted transmission of the most sacred knowledge to narrowly bounded ceremonial space outside of public view. Accordingly, the Old Men's Lodge was marked by increasing immobility while activating greater power to control the mobility of others.

Life movement culminated in the Seven Old Men, who were positioned in the sweat lodge at the very center of the camp circle and at the heart of the people, yet distant from others through the most profound respect. They were the least moved by external conditions, as expressed in their stillness within the lodge. Inversely, they had the greatest power to immobilize others and direct movements in all contexts. Whereas the Dogs led by following, the Seven Old Men directed all life movement by sitting still, which allowed them to watch, listen, and be open to all that happened in camp life and the natural environment. Through the knowledge they thus gained, their roles extended beyond ceremonial authority to pervade all economic, political, and cultural life.

The spatial dimensions of life movement for men are summarized in figure 9.1. Overall, the increasing movement of youth was followed in the second half of life by decreasing movement, a transition marked by the Crazy Lodge. In spatial terms, infantile containment was followed by movement outside the tipi and the eventual placement of young men on the periphery, in time followed by gradual reincorporation into the camp circle and eventual recontainment in the sacred center. For men, then, physical life movement followed a loop outward and then back again to the center of the camp circle.

With respect to the dimensions of mobility and containment, the elder stage and infancy were close because of the placement of both in the center, the elders in the sweat lodge and the infant in the tipi or the cradle. The difference is that aging brought personhood ever closer to medicine power (*beetee*) through ever more direct relations with other-than-human beings above and on earth. As physical mobility and public presence decreased, old age brought increasing power to generate or immobilize others' life movement.

Life movement was also accompanied by changes in ways of speaking and expressing knowledge. The first stage of life was associated with acquisition and social recognition of communicative abilities, including listening and speaking. Childhood rituals aimed to promote long life and to encourage and recognize abilities associated with personhood, such as hearing, speaking, thinking, walking, chewing, and being useful. Some childhood ceremonies, such as ear piercing and recognition feasts, were ways for families to show respect and acknowledge the child's acquisition of the abilities to interact and move about, in preparation for the second stage of life.

At the second stage of life, young men and women, in different ways, began to express themselves publicly through the lodges, artwork, bodily adornment, and achievements. Through those expressions, the visibility and presence of one's person became "bigger." One's sense of doing moved more and more toward "giving it back" and becoming a big person. With family cooperation, one's achievements became visible through exchanges, victories, counted feats, and honors both within and outside the *beyoowu'u*.

In the third stage, men and women took on the role of directing others' actions with their words through instruction in ritual production, storytelling, naming, lectures, public speeches, and other modes of expression necessary to keep life straight and moving. By the time they reached the Dog Lodge and the stage of leadership, as Fowler's study shows (1982:3), men became the voice of consensus, of saying what the tribe or the elders told them to say. In old age, one expressed oneself quietly, or with sweet words.

Throughout the age grades and life movement in general, requests and expressions had to be mediated through age-structured relations. All ritual practices and any public expression had to be attended, guided, and witnessed by elders. Young men had to request assistance from elder brothers and grandfathers, who in turn made requests to the oldest men, who mediated with other-than-human persons above or on earth. The same pattern carried over into everyday interaction, whereby young people had to defer to older speakers. Age brought increasing quietness as well as distance and respect from others. By contrast, with one's age peers and some kin, one could be equal and thus even crazy in speech. Within age sets, for example, competitive racing and storytelling were emphasized.

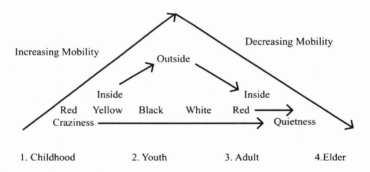

Figure 9.1. Araphao life movement.

In complex ways, the four-color symbolism also interconnected with other dimensions shaping life movement. At birth, an infant's face was painted red, symbolizing personhood as *3owo3nenitee* and placement inside the tipi. The cradle was decorated with the four-color designs of women's quillwork, expressing the desire for long life, or *hiiteeni*. Among the age grades, the Stars and the Kit Foxes lacked definite colors for their paint. Black was used more in the Clubboard and Spear Lodges, since it was associated with war and other activities outside the camp circle. White was the principal color of both the Crazy Lodge and the women's Buffalo Lodge. In both instances, white was related to the appropriation of a source of knowledge and power from outside the camp circle—in the former, medicine, and in the latter, tallow for and representing paint for all the lodges. When it is placed next to yellow, for maleness, white represents female elements, a pattern shared by the lower-ranked dances of the Buffalo and Clubboard Lodges. In the Crazy and Dog Lodges, participants' wives were also painted and thus were more closely linked if not merged with their husbands' rank and age status (Kroeber 1904:200). From the Dog Lodge on, men's bodies became increasingly associated with red paint. Through the age-grade sequence, male age sets moved from lack of color to a balance of red and black, to white, and then to red exclusively.

The color progression is thus more complex than the quarternary model outlined in chapter 2, in which yellow is the color of childhood, red of youth, black of adulthood, and white of old age. Colors had meanings relative to context rather than to fixed categories, for the two systems were interlinked in intricate ways (see table 9.2). To some extent all colors were present in each stage of life for both genders. In different ritual contexts and stages, one or two colors were prominent. In the age-grade system, the colors were more strongly associated with the social spaces in which groups were placed rather than with positions in the four-hills model. The lack of paint in the youngest grades was related to their separation beyond the camp circle. Clubboard and Spear men, in the first lodges, were most strongly associated with the duality of red and black, for space inside and outside the camp circle, respectively. Crazy Men and Buffalo women were white, because they were between outer and inner space and were associated with medicine power and knowledge from other-than-human persons. Dogs, Old Men, and the Seven Old Men were identified with red exclusively, because they were situated entirely inside the camp and at the very center of Arapahoness. Figure 9.2 offers a synoptic view of the correlates of mobility with modes of personhood, and spatial placement along the trajectory of life movement.

Related to their respective ways of moving and knowing, each women's ceremony and age-grade lodge also was associated with specific medicines from the set of seven sacred Arapaho medicines (Dorsey 1903:66-68). All seven medicines were used in the Offerings Lodge, but only combinations of a few belonged in each lodge and the women's quillwork ceremony. Children, of course, were excluded from all medicines, as were apparently the Stars, Kit Foxes, and young women in the second stage of life. Only upon the culmination

Table 9.2

The Interrelationship of Color with Motion and Spatial Domains within the Age-Grade Progression

AGE GRADE	SPATIAL POSITION	MOTION FORM	COLOR
Kit Foxes and Stars	From inside tipi or camp to outside	Unbounded	Colorless
Clubboard and Spear	On the camp boundaries directed outside for war, inside for police function	Bounded quick, sudden movement	Red and Black
Crazy Men	From outside camp circle to inside	Medicine force and crazy movement	White
Dogs	Inside and behind camp	Slow movement	Red
Old Men	From outside public world to hidden sacred domain	Decreasing movement	Red
Seven Old Men	Inside sweat lodge	Quietness and immobility	Red

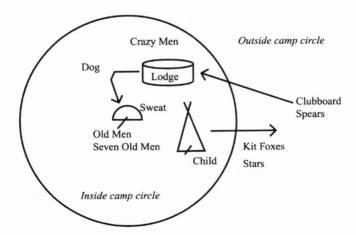

Figure 9.2. The placement and movement of men's age grades.

of the second stage and entry into the lodges were young men and women introduced to these most sacred medicines. Along with dog root for strength and endurance, the less powerful medicines sweet grass, sage, and cockleburs were used in the Clubboard and Spear Lodges and the women's Buffalo Lodge. Outside the Offerings Lodge, crazy root was used only in the Crazy Lodge, which also employed dog root, sage, and sweet grass. Dog root and main root were the only medicines of the Dog, Old Men's, and Old Women's quillwork ritual, since in those practices endurance was combined with quietude. Only the Seven Old Men, who, because they had reached the quiet life, no longer used dog root, used a medicine called strong root to make their words and ways sweet. In all, medicines and combinations of them were correlated with the progression of social roles and types of motion through the lodges and life in total.

The changing access to medicine power was also associated with changing relations to heat. After and even before birth, children were kept away from heat, because it was powerful (*beetee*). Heat was opposed to life movement in the earliest stages, whereas cold water was conducive to it. Indeed, fire and other forms of heat were medicine power that required care and respect. Traditionally, there were proscriptions about handling fire and ash that people learned as they moved into adulthood (Michelson 1910). Only adults were allowed to tend fires. By the third stage of life, men could be exposed to heat. Conforming to this association, Crazy Men were able to endure dancing into the heat of the fire during the lodge. In the two most senior lodges, men became most strongly associated with heat, the medicine power to enliven what has less life. Contrasting with the enclosure of the infant's body in the cradle, old men were naked and exposed to heat and steam in the sweat lodge.

As suggested above, life movement also generated separate though in many ways convergent paths for women and men. Women's personhood and associated social functions were less precisely phased through age grading but nonetheless evolved with life movement along paths parallel to those of men. Throughout a woman's life, her roles, as expressed in ritual, stressed childbearing and child rearing, life transitions within kinship relations, the transformation of raw materials into cultural forms, the provision of items for exchange, and cooperative work for the men's age grades and other lodges. During childhood there were no significant gender distinctions in ritual practice, adornment, and functions. Young women began the second stage of life at ages comparable to those of Kit Foxes and Stars, close to maternal kin, where they did tasks around the tipi, save for trips to the river for bathing and water carrying. Older women in the camps cautiously sequestered young unmarried women from young men. As they married and owned their own tipis, women took on more and more roles serving the life movement of others related by kinship or interfamilial exchange. For example, it is clear that women in the parental and grandparental generations were the primary agents for organizing and bringing about childhood rituals.

Entry for young women into the Buffalo Lodge compares to the transition for men in the Clubboard, Spear, and Crazy Lodges, all of which had similar elements and used the same medicines. All four lodges stressed the role of women and men in appropriating or transforming sources of life movement from beyond the camp circle and thus achieving public recognition and rank. Though the genders were segregated in the second stage of life, movement toward the third stage marked increasingly shared dimensions of life movement. As Kroeber (1904:225) recognized, the Buffalo Lodge included many elements that were almost identical to features of the Clubboard, Spear, Crazy, Dog, and Offerings Lodges. As in the men's lodges, women were ranked in the Buffalo Lodge. The highest-ranking woman, White Buffalo Woman was slow to move, as were the leaders of the men's lodges, especially the lead Dog. The drama of the lodge reenacted the mythical event in which White Buffalo Woman is immobilized and then pierced by a young hunter, who returns to the camp circle bringing the tallow used in ceremonial painting and that embodied the knowledge of the old people to direct all the lodges.

Through women's sacrifices, vows, exchange, art, and public participation in the lodges, their personhood and social functions expanded outward beyond the sphere of tipi life as they moved through the third stage of life. In that stage women also became identified more fully with their husbands' rank and age status, as reflected in the fact that wives were painted with their husbands in both the Dog and the Crazy Lodges (Kroeber 1904:200).

Women's quillwork coincided in life stage to the Dog Lodge, the Old Men, and the Seven Old Men. The ceremony itself used the same medicines as the Dog and Old Men's Lodges. Entry to quillwork marked the initiation of women to the radiance of life-giving objects from out of their own tipis into kin relations and interfamilial ties. Quillwork was the culmination of women's achievements and rank tied to counts of hides, cradles, tipis, and other objects produced. Those products indeed transcended use-value, for they inscribed sacred forms, required ritual preparation, and involved labor beyond any other products of Arapaho culture. Ceremonies for women thus emphasized artistic production as a life-giving practice, such as in the tallow for the Buffalo Lodge and the powerful expressions of Arapaho culture through quillwork designs. Through quillwork women's lives in the space of the tipi found paths for the public expression of their achievements in items visible in everyday life, such as cradles, tipis, and robes given to and used by kin. While sitting quietly, women created objects seemingly static but containing power and meaning accessible to Arapaho sight in the lived world. Women's personhood expanded in social space through those objects.

It is interesting that the things made were all associated with containment and boundaries but in a way different from the Euro-American propensity to define boundaries as confining. As they constructed navel bags, tipis, cradles, buffalo robes, and other things, women produced coverings for the life movement of other persons sheltered in them. Whereas men's roles centered on maintaining the boundaries of the camp circle and the lodges, women's practices defined the boundaries of the tipi and the family. For women's roles, bounded or bundled forms were crucial to generating and reproducing life movement.

In old age, women who owned the quill bundles moved into roles comparable to that of the Seven Old Men. Along with rank, gender was somewhat neutralized as both grandmothers and grandfathers drew similar levels of respect and deference. Older women not only had elder status toward younger women but could control the behavior and life movement of younger men. A young man became a servant to his mother-in-law upon marriage and was always under the control of his grandmothers. Fowler (1982:271–72) distinguishes the power of women as family-oriented from men's roles as extending beyond kin, but in the Arapaho context that Euro-American-based domestic-public or informal-formal distinction breaks down. Furthermore, as rank dissolved, so did the distances between male and female spaces as avoidance restrictions and social distances relaxed. The separation of feminine and masculine spaces for life movement, then, was not disempowerment of the former and appropriation of all power by the latter.

Throughout life movement, women physically remained in the center of camp and kindred while men moved outward in youth and activity beyond the camp. However, women were linked to the lives of male kin. Throughout life, women vowed and made gifts to their brothers out of respect. Following marriage, they were linked to the age-grade activities of their husbands. But women were not dependent on men for their own life movement. On the contrary, their roles were more significant in the life movement of men, both within the lodges and elsewhere. As for all Arapaho practice, life movement was effected through relations with others. The value of life was measured by how much one gave, not how much one received. On those grounds, what women and men gave, sacrificed, and produced from their life movement were commensurable and interdependent.

Taking all of those elements together, it is possible to offer a synthesis of the four-hills model with men's and women's life rituals (see table 9.3).

Table 9.3
The Four Hills and Men's and Women's Rituals

	MEN	WOMEN
FIRST HILL	Childhood rituals Kit Foxes and Stars	Childhood rituals
SECOND HILL	Clubboard and Spear	Buffalo Lodge
THIRD HILL	Crazy Men Dogs	Quillwork
FOURTH HILL	Old Men Seven Old Men	Seven Old Women

For both genders and all ages, the ceremonies were not clear and distinct in elements and meanings. Ritualized life movement combined both continuities and transitions. Each ceremony expressed values, relations, and types of activities appropriate to its particular stage, but also repeated some others from previous stages and included others that were transitional or (yet more) that anticipated subsequent stages. Kit Foxes and Stars marked the separation anticipating the second stage of life. The Crazy Lodge was obviously liminal in its contrariness and marked the transition to what is in Arapaho comparable to true adulthood. The women's Buffalo Lodge merged elements of the second and third stages, and specifically aspects of the Clubboard, Spear, and Crazy Lodges. The Old Men's Lodge marked the transition to the fourth hill of life, as did the ongoing apprenticeship in women's quillwork.

All in all, Arapaho life movement was a temporal system constituted through appropriate practices that phased and interconnected various dimensions of rank, personhood, space, tempo, function, and meaning. For both men and women, life movement occurred through practices monitored and governed within an age hierarchy that itself was continually reproduced by those same practices. Elders observed the life movement of younger people and shaped the direction and tempo of their lives accordingly. As one moved through life, the power to effect the life movement of others increased as personal mobility decreased.

Arapaho life movement involved the two complementary though paradoxical forces of giving and receiving life movement. Out of respect and pity for others, one was motivated to sacrifice a part of one's own life for them. Achievement, rank, and acquisition of knowledge required exchange and sacrifice that put individuals' lives at risk or in difficulty for the benefit of others' life movement. Advancing through life required increasingly giving one's own life for others. As one's own power for life movement was given away and therefore diminished, the next generations received momentum and direction. In other words, it is selfish to keep all of one's life and knowledge to oneself for self-motivated longevity and health. Living a long life is evidence that one has endured and overcome the greatest sacrifices and hardships. For those who endure, knowledge follows.

10
Changes in Age Structure and Life Movement

The Decline of the Age-Grade System

Beginning with the most disruptive, direct contact with Euro-American society, Northern Arapaho life movement and age structure changed significantly. Most important, the men's age-grade lodges and the women's ceremonies began dissolving even before the reservation period. The junior and intermediate lodges were last performed in the first two decades of the twentieth century, except for the Clubboard Lodge last held in 1931 at Wind River (Hilger 1952:122). The activities of the two senior men's age groups and the Buffalo Lodge had already ceased when the Northern Arapahos came to Wind River in 1878. Roughly speaking, the age-grade societies disintegrated from the oldest to the youngest.

There were a number of factors that worked against continuation of the lodges. In a broad though immediate sense, physical survival was most critical in the pre- to early reservation period. From the onset of Euro-American conquest of Colorado in the 1850s into the reservation period and up to the early 1920s, the Northern Arapaho population declined because of disease and deprivation (Fowler 1982:90). As in most other Plains tribes, smallpox, tuberculosis, measles, cholera, and other epidemic diseases contributed to population decline from the mid-nineteenth to the early twentieth century. Arapaho census records from 1885 to 1922 indicate that the proportion of men in the population especially older men, was relatively low by the early reservation period (Census of Arapahoe Indians 1885–1922).

Thus, many old people, including most of the Seven Old Men and the women's quill bundle owners, died before they could pass on their knowledge. The Seven Old Men last held ceremonies among the Southern Arapahos in 1874 (Hilger 1952:120), and the last keeper of one of the bundles in Wyoming died in 1894 (Fowler 1982:119). Elders today recall women who owned the sacred bundles for quillwork but did not transfer "ownership" and the requisite knowledge. There have been no detailed studies of the impact of disease on the social structure and culture of North American indigenous peoples, but it is clear in the Arapaho case, both Northern and Southern, that the decline of the age-grade societies and the women's ceremonies—which militates against maintaining traditional forms of succession—coincided with the decline in population.

Related to the loss of men and women with ceremonial knowledge was the abrupt change that the economy experienced before and during the early reservation period. The period of the 1880s and 1890s was especially difficult as game became sparse and rations from the Indian Agency were reduced. During the same period, farming and gardening were only beginning to contribute to subsistence for families fortunate enough to have been allotted arable lands. Acquiring the necessary natural materials and meeting exchange obligations for ceremonies became increasingly difficult as subsistence itself became precarious and access to exchange value limited. External sources for value through trade or war raids were no longer readily accessible within the confined space of the reservation.

At the political level, during the early 1900s federal law repressed traditional ceremonies. At Wind River, the Sun Dance was officially prohibited from 1904 until 1935 (Hilger 1952:153), but there was only a ten-year period at Wind River (1913 to 1923) when it was not held, even in secret (Fowler 1982:154–55). As an adaptation, the Northern Arapaho people concealed and masked traditional practices, while inventing new forms and appropriating ceremonies from other tribes and Euro-American society. By doing so, they brought new traditions into the connectivity of practices and meanings for life movement.

By 1900 the military, hunting, and movement-directing functions of the junior and intermediate grades were also no longer as relevant to life movement. Thus, political leadership, as Fowler demonstrates, became more a matter of intermediation with Euro-Americans than of ordering camp and tribal movements. The police function was taken over by the agency, though Arapaho and Shoshone men were hired to serve as officers. With the transformation of social space in the reservation context, the association of age groups with different social spaces also began to weaken. What evolved from the early reservation period up to the contemporary context was a pattern of family-oriented places and age-segregated spaces associated with Euro-American specialized functions, such as schools, colleges, senior citizens' centers, and nursing homes. New social forms have operated to segregate Arapaho people by age, family, and occupation.

Northern Arapahos did reinvent age structure for both emerging and surviving functions in reservation society. As Fowler discovered, new positions were created, and some prereservation roles took on greater authority. For instance, by the 1950s the Northern Arapahos instituted the "four old men," mirroring the Four Old Men in the four directions (Fowler 1982:215). Those positions replaced the Seven Old Men as ritual leaders for the remaining core ceremonies surrounding the Sacred Pipe, including the Offerings Lodge. Initially, the roles of the four old men were more specialized, less extensive, and less powerful than the pervasive influence of the Seven Old Men. Since the 1970s, though, the authority of the four old men has expanded beyond the Offerings Lodge and other ceremonies centering on the Flat Pipe. Today, they have become not only spokesmen about repatriation, sacred sites, land use, and education, but also intermediaries with government agencies. Many Arapaho people still follow the "tradition" of requesting permission from the four old men to schedule ceremonies or try "anything new" in ritual practice or political matters. They are also called upon first for prayers or other services in various social and ceremonial contexts, such as powwows, sweats, blessings, naming, memorials, church services, and funerals.

Their authority still centers on the organization of the Offerings Lodge, or Sun Dance, the only remaining ceremony of the *beyoowu'u* system. Since the 1960s the Sun Dance has emerged as the central element of a nativistic return to "traditionalism" paralleled among other American Indian groups. As a result, it has become a focus for life movement, drawing wider and younger participation. At one time only about ten to twenty men vowed during a year, but in recent times the number of dancers has grown to more than one hundred in some years. The growth has occurred largely because the tribe itself is now about five times as large as it was in 1885; increasing numbers of Southern Arapaho and Gros Ventre men and women participate as well. The number of times men vow for the Sun Dance has also increased from a limit of four in the past to seven, now the obligatory number of times to vow in one's lifetime. Thus, the Offerings Lodge has come to define the trajectory of life movement for many men and even women. Age status and roles in the lodge are now a reflection of this measure of experience in the lodge. Men who have been in the lodge several times can be painters, assisting the grandfathers. Upon completion of more vows, one can be a grandfather. The nature of vows to affect the life movement of others still remains very much the same. Status and respect relations generated through the lodge do carry over into everyday life, although such status is generally unrelated to social functions, in contrast with the former age-grade system.

Today, women are at the center of family preparations and can also vow to fast in the Sun Dance lodge. In the past women relatives of men in the lodge would often vow to fast for from one to four days, sitting on one side of the lodge separate from men. Teenage or adult women can now vow to fast and remain in the lodge each night. The men take positions around the periphery of the lodge, and the women sleep in the center, close to the center pole; they move to just outside the lodge during the day. In other areas, women's roles in ceremony, prayer, and political authority have become more public and visible, even since I went to Wind River in 1988.

With the widening participation in the Offerings Lodge, the growth of the Arapaho population, the revitalization of traditionalism, and the extinction of other ceremonies, there is now a greater demand for the services of older men and women with ritual authority and knowledge to perform various roles, while the proportion of such people in the population is getting smaller all the time. To meet that demand, ceremonial authority has been extended to increasingly younger men and women. One common observation about the Offerings Lodge today, for example, is that grandfathers and pledgers are becoming younger each year. A similar pattern emerged in political authority in the 1980s, when young men in their twenties or thirties began to serve on the council.

The reinvention of age structure has generated a contradiction that is still pervasive in what Arapaho people observe and talk about. To adapt and revitalize traditions, the tribe has allowed younger people more frequent participation and greater access to knowledge and types of authority once reserved for older age groups. The widening disjuncture between senior and junior generations has created the need to open up knowledge and ritual authority in order to keep younger people connected to the remaining Arapaho traditions. Concurrently, adaptation and collectivization of ceremonies has proposed competing definitions for doing things in a good/correct way that are divided at times along generational lines.

There is a wider disjuncture between generations than perhaps at any other time in Arapaho history. As of 1994 there are few if any fluent speakers of the Arapaho language under the age of forty-five. Thus, the language of elders is distant from that of the younger generations. Alongside this, high-school and college-age Arapahos often define their peer group identity through the mass popular culture of modern music, television, movies, and sports more than through the traditions of their grandparents. For some of them, their grandparents' language, culture, and lived history are more distant from their experience than the Euro-American popular culture that is almost universal in their social space and time. The surviving or invented practices for life movement discussed in chapter 9 now occupy small spaces and times in the lived world. Similarly, some younger people conflate the traditional restrictions on knowledge and ritual practice with the authoritarian knowledge experienced through Euro-American social institutions. In short, young people see the authority and knowledge of elders as similar to the control they experience in Euro-American formal institutions. Following popular culture, some resist or rebel against both cultures. Many young people I talked to repeated this concern: "I don't feel like I am part of either world. At home they tell me I am not a real Indian because I don't speak the language or know any traditions. In the white world they always look down on me."

Elders and others are very much concerned about losing the young people, but they also express apprehension about the trend toward younger participation, saying that it leads to more mistakes and excesses in ritual preparation and performance, thus proliferating potentially life-negating effects. As in other American Indian communities, the contradiction between traditional parameters on ritual performance and the need for continuity through innovation is ever present. For those involved in ritual practice, that contradiction requires a balancing act that always feels necessary but often risky or precarious. Such tension can generate interpersonal or intergroup conflict. One side defends practices needed on the basis of expediency, while another presses for the old ways of doing things.

Within the parameters of Arapaho knowledge, too, rituals or components of ceremonies once lost cannot easily be revived. Thus, there is often less resistance to inventing new than to reviving older practices. Precluding revitalization of the age grades and the women's ceremonies is the Arapaho concern with doing things in a good/correct way. In Arapaho conceptions of traditional knowledge, it is considered dangerous to try to revive extinct ceremonies or any components of them without appropriate knowledge in the possession of living persons. The cessation of ceremonies therefore often occurred as the knowledge for their preparation and performance was no longer passed on. As time passes from the last performance, the possibility of revival becomes riskier and less likely. Elders often discuss what practices or elements are soon to pass, because persons with ritual knowledge are growing older without passing it on.

The association between doing things in a good/correct way in ceremonies and the health, long life, and population growth of the tribe (discussed in chapter 11) must have been a concern in the early reservation period when most of those blessings were no longer evident. The possibility for questioning whether the ceremonies were working was present in the realities that lives were cut shorter, the buffalo were disappearing, and, as realized by the Arapaho chief Medicine Man, whites were somehow able to reproduce in great numbers. There are stories told today of elders in the past who chose not to pass on knowledge that they possessed because they saw younger people as too irresponsible or too "crazy" in comparison to the age-structured roles into which they were socialized.

Most of these issues are set aside in Fowler's portrayal of elders in the early reservation period: "Some aspects of the tribal rituals were altered or reinterpreted to accommodate the abilities of the men available to direct them. The elders emphasized flexibility in revising specific procedures and criteria for ritual leadership in order to perpetuate native religion in general" (1982:120). During the reservation period, concepts of elderhood and age status have changed and become ambiguous at times. The definition of elders itself had changed by the early reservation period, from the Seven Old Men and the Seven Old Women to a more diffuse group of somewhat younger ceremonial leaders. In the prereservation context, ceremonial leadership was reserved for the oldest men, in their eighties. Today, the criteria for elder status are not clear. Even the use of the English term *elder*, based in pan-Indian knowledge, is problematic to some older Arapaho people who did not grow up using it. Several elders commented to me that they had never heard the term elder until quite recently. In their experience older people were referred to by grandparental terms or "Old Man or Old Lady so and so." At one time a man had to vow the Sun Dance four times to become a grandfather, but now anyone who has vowed once can play that role (Fowler 1982:286). In contrast with Fowler's emphasis on the symbolic continuity of age-graded relations, there is no clear social structural continuity of "age" from the pre- to the early reservation context, although meanings survive in and through Arapaho practice.

Revitalization and Invention

Other factors contributing to changes in life movement and age structure were the various strands of innovation, re-invention, and revitalization of religious practices. In the generation after the age-grade ceremonies and women's societies had begun dissolving (that is, just after the early reservation period), new religious forms emerged, such as the Ghost Dance, the Peyote religion, the Crow Dance, and indigenous Christianity; they were appropriated to various degrees into Arapaho practices and meanings for life movement. Among Plains peoples, both the Northern and Southern Arapahos were at the center of most of those emerging traditions. Ironically, though they have long been characterized as one of the most religiously conservative Plains peoples for their fastidious adherence to traditional practices, the Northern Arapahos were among the most active participants in the religious revitalization and innovation of the 1890s and early 1900s. Subsistence was then more than precarious, disease an ever-present threat, and permanent Arapaho settlement at Wind River still uncertain. To adapt to the decline of traditional ritual forms and harsh reservation conditions, sectors of the Northern Arapaho tribe were early, active participants in the Ghost Dance and the Peyote church. The newer religious traditions adopted collective or individualized dimensions of life movement as discussed in the preceding chapters, however, without functioning to constitute age or gender distinctions. Rather than age- or gender- specific ritual practices, the tendency that emerged then and continues to the present is toward more communal, collective ritual practices, on one hand, and family-based or individualized forms, on the other.

To reiterate, the disease and deprivation caused by the Euro-American conquest of Arapaho territory opened the door to doubts about the efficacy of the ritual system in sustaining life movement, including health and abundance. As Mooney documents, like other tribes, some Arapahos perceived the harsh reservation conditions and the cultural collapse as portending the end of the world: "Another idea here presented, namely, that the earth becomes old and decrepit, and requires that its youth be renewed at the end of certain great cycles, is common to a number of tribes . . . As an Arapaho who spoke English expressed it, 'This earth too old, grass too old, trees too old, our lives too old. Then all be new again'" (1896:785). For some Arapaho people, conditions signaled the realization of the prophecy of the end of the fourth generation, meaning that the life movement of the earth was coming to its close and renewal was imminent. The Northern Arapahos, like some other tribes, appropriated the disruptive changes of the early reservation period as mythical life movement at a cosmological level of the four-hills model.

The place and extent of new ritual forms among other surviving traditions are difficult to establish from the literature. The historical pattern has been read in two different ways. On one side, Kroeber states that the new forms competed with older traditions. He concludes that the residues of the Ghost Dance and the emerging Peyote religion were, at the time of his observations, replacing traditional age-grade ceremonies among the younger generations: "Several modern ceremonies, belonging to at least two different cults, have obtained a foothold with the Arapaho; and among the people at large, especially among the younger members of the tribe, these now occupy a much larger part in their life than the virtually extinct ceremonies of the bäyaa^{n}wu [*beyoowu'u*] or the sun-dance" (1907:319).

Statements from elders at the time seem to assert, however, that the ceremonies surrounding the Pipe, including the Offerings Lodge, continued to be considered first and foremost among religious practices. Upon this, Fowler offers a second perspective by attributing the loss of traditions to other factors and defining innovations as "replacements" that either reinforced age distinctions or at least did not compete with or affect sacred traditions. As one Arapaho told Fowler, "They said that Sage had that vision that the Ghost Dance was coming and that peyote was coming. And so did Yellow Calf. And they told their people. . .that the pipe was here long before those others were" (1982:122). Fowler thus implicitly counters Kroeber and others (e.g., Elkin 1940; Gross 1949) who emphasize more recent discontinuities, with her contention that the Arapaho people continued to hold core ceremonies above the new ones and that elders continued to exert sufficient control over the entire ritual domain or "native religion" in general (Fowler 1982:122-24).

During the early reservation period, Arapaho leaders did employ a pluralistic strategy of compartmentalization by which old and new traditions were placed in their own definite times and spaces. Following the pattern chartered in myth, the aim was to appropriate the new traditions, along with selected Christian forms (discussed in the next section), within a distinctly Arapaho sense of doing things in a good/correct way for knowledge and life movement. Within the age structure, the oldest generation at the turn of the century tolerated the new forms, such as the Ghost Dance or the Peyote practices, but did not necessarily participate in or exert their authority within them.

As I have stated, one combined influence of new traditions and ways of maintaining old ones has been the centralization and collectivization of religious and secular practices. Whereas the former lodges constituted age groups and gender distinctions, the new forms were open to participants from various age groups and both genders. The new forms also did not seem to generate as extensive and enduring interfamilial and intergenerational relations of exchange. At the interfamilial level, bonds across family boundaries are no longer as essential to problem solving and ritual life movement as they were in the early reservation or prereservation context, because centralized tribal government and Euro-American formal institutions have taken over many social functions. Despite Fowler's attribution of age structure to tribal continuity, though, social life and cultural continuity have become, at another level, as much a matter of family and other local, less centralized practices as of age structure.

Likewise, in the new religious forms, such as the Ghost Dance, the Peyote religion, and Christianity, less mediation with the other-than-human realm was required. Collectivization evolved concomitantly with a tendency to remove intervening human and other-than-human persons in religious practice. There has been a shift toward indigenous monotheism, toward relations between an individual and the creator, "the Great Spirit," or God. Other other-than-human persons ceased to be as frequently connected to prayer and practice. As a result of centralization and the tendency toward a new traditional monotheism, the pattern of interrelated exchanges in the age hierarchy extending into the other-than-human realm became attenuated.

At the same time, older and revitalized traditions have become open to wider participation with fewer demands for preparation. For instance, the contemporary "paint ceremony" of the Northern Arapahos, an extension of traditional painting, was influenced by the Ghost Dance and accompanying ceremonies. In the prereservation context, painting with red paint was common in many contexts; it was done to lift mourning restrictions and to promote general health, and it was a part of rituals for the older age grades. Since 1903 a collective paint ceremony has become institutionalized at Wind River. Immediately following a funeral, all tribal members who wish to be purified can come forth to a circle where appointed painters will apply red paint to both cheeks and the forehead. Features of this type of paint ceremony are almost identical to those described by Mooney (1896:779) for the Ghost Dance, including the laying on of hands, the circular configuration of the recipients, and the open collective participation. Another type of paint ceremony is organized by the four old men when a disaster has happened in the community. For example, one was held in 1988 when a number of younger people took their own lives in a short span of time. All young people are brought by their families or bussed by the schools, and all tribal members who wish to participate come to one of the community centers, where they are smudged and then painted.

At the opposite pole to collectivization and centralization, other new ritual forms for life movement have followed a pattern of ownership and inheritance through descent within families. Prior to and into the reservation period, there were many smaller traditions, such as medicines, traditional roles, and ceremonies passed on within families. That pattern has been extended since the early reservation period into other forms of ritual agency. One example is the Crow Dance (*houunohowoot*), which was originally performed as a prelude to the Ghost Dance but survives to the present as part of the annual Christmas week dances. According to Mooney (1896:901, 921–22), the Southern Arapahos and the Cheyennes developed the Crow Dance from the Omaha Dance of northern Plains tribes, combined it with the Ghost Dance, and then passed it on to the Northern Arapahos. Kroeber (1907:367–68) adds that the Crow Dance originated among the Pawnees and the Osages, then passed to the Omahas, the Lakotas, and finally the Southern Arapahos and the Cheyennes. The Crow Dance is now part of a pattern of inheritance of ritual knowledge through descent within family boundaries. Today, people talk about the Crow Dance as "owned" by families, one in Ethete and one in Lower Arapaho.

Rather than through age-set succession and knowledge exchanges across lines of kin groups, more and more ceremonial authority has shifted to inheritance within families. There are still some channels of knowledge transmission and inheritance of ritual authority that transcend kinship, such as from Sun Dance grandfather to grandson or from traditional teacher to apprentice, but more and more "knowledge" is passed on within families or in particular relations between senior and junior.

Within the same shift, life transition rituals are now initiated and practiced more within the extended family than within age-hierarchical relations or even tribal contexts. Families sponsor naming, ear piercing, funerals, memorial feasts, powwow honor songs, birthdays, graduation celebrations, and other modern life transitions. Some of those have become part of family tradition as distinguished from tribal tradition. In other words, marking individuals' life transitions and achievements has in some practices become more an expression of extended family identity and status in the community than a matter of generating ties that cut across kinship boundaries. Arapaho ceremonies are often directed toward "life movement" in a very general sense, but there has evolved a contradiction between the tendency for collectivization and the pattern of family "ownership" or control of particular ceremonies, leadership positions, and social events.

The family, which has been more durable than age structure in reservation history, has become the center for shaping or reshaping the life movement of individuals. Even though families face many internal problems, most life difficulties that arise are still redressed through collective action within the family. And at the center of that action, there is typically a core of women: sisters, mothers, and grandmothers. It is essential, then, not to define family-centered traditions and empowerment as dysfunctional and divisive.

Different generations also define tradition within different frames of reference. In the contemporary context, it is indeed remarkable that elders tolerate much of the new culture introduced by younger generations, while observing, often quite critically, that it is displacing genuine Arapaho traditions. For example, elders recognize that distinctly Arapaho ceremonial and dance songs are heard less and less, even though pan-Indian powwow music, consisting mainly of "northern" and Lakota songs, is popular among younger people.

Even in the present, older people tolerate innovation and experimentation among younger generations, for in Arapaho conceptions of life movement, such behavior is allowed and even expected in the earlier stages of life. In the context of the life cycle, one can experiment with alternative religions and traditions in youth and return to the core religion in old age. As long as one's life trajectory ends in the right place, close to the central sacred traditions surrounding it, experiments in youth are tolerable.

As in the traditional pattern, cultural innovations are commonly attributed to the visions or dreams of individuals who then give the knowledge to the tribe. Cleaver Warden records Yellow Calf's vision validating the introduction of the Crow Dance in 1904 (Dorsey and Warden 1905, cited in Fowler 1982:123). That story, confirmed by Upper Arapahos, is not shared by all families who participate in the Crow Dance. Between families and districts there are now competing claims to origins and therefore ownership of traditions, both religious and secular.

Participation in various traditions also varies with families. The Native American Church creates bonds between families and between tribes, but within the Northern Arapaho tribe it is strong in some families and not in others. Among some families, membership in the Native American Church has become a basis for political organization and a marker of one's "traditionalism," although that ideology meets with opposition from other families. What some families embrace as part of family tradition extending back to a founding ancestor others may resist based on the proscription of their own ancestor or living elder. Some families, following the mandate of living elders or ancestors, prohibit family members from participating in various religious forms.

Like the Crow Dance, Peyote meetings are adapted to Euro-American space and time. Meetings are now held on weekends, generally Saturday night, allowing members with jobs to travel, at times great distances, without disrupting their work schedule. Within changing social space and time, the Peyote meeting adapted the tipi as a ritual enclosure, protected from the repressive eye of Euro-American society and less demanding to construct than ceremonial lodges. As already mentioned, Peyote meetings have been appropriated within Arapaho ways, such as in pledging, sponsoring, and life movement.

However, some who are involved in Peyote religion have redefined it as "tradition" in order to maintain that appropriation. There are adherents who profess that Peyote was the original and everlasting religion of the Indian people. Some revisionist mythologies hold that it was the Peyote button—rather than a root—that was found in the beginning and brought all knowledge and cultural identity to the people. Others support this specific version with general comments about the antiquity that, "Arapahos have always had Peyote." The tendency to place recent pan-Indian innovations in the traditional "past" is common among younger generations today.

Other families have placed Peyote among the traditions for effecting life movement. Peyote religion has become a way for people to overcome life difficulties, such as dependency on alcohol or drugs, grief over the loss of a family member, or some other disruption in life. A person and his or her family can pledge and sponsor a single meeting or a series of meetings to memorialize or honor a family member. In meetings, individuals can vow to change their lives in some way, from a difficult path to one tied to relations with others. Through such meetings it is possible for individuals and families to create bonds of support across family, community, and even tribal boundaries.

Compartmentalization has given way to localization and competing definitions of "tradition." What that pattern suggests is the weaker tendency among younger people today to maintain boundaries between traditions, thus merging and enacting the Peyote church, Christian influences, and other pan-Indian elements as "tradition." The younger generations thus do not consider the historical ordering of culture elements relevant to their definition of "tradition." From older people's perspectives, the younger people are "mixing things up" by conflating "Arapaho" and "Indian" culture. To an increasing extent, such disagreement contributes to differences between generations in defining tradition.

When I taught Arapaho history courses at the local community college, I found younger Arapaho people more likely to uphold presentism in the definition of tradition. They often concluded that tradition should be defined by consensus, that is, "what most people agree is tradition." They were not willing to accept Hobsbawm's remark on "invented traditions": "Traditions which appear to be old are often quite recent in origin and sometimes invented" (1983:1). To acknowledge that present "traditions" are recent or invented is at odds with their acceptance of claims to antiquity. Older people are more open to such discourse and more likely to offer oral historical accounts for origins and changes in "traditions."

To summarize, the newer traditions have been situated within families and generational domains, whereas older revitalized traditions have tended toward centralization and collectivization. In neither pattern do practices generate clear age distinctions and enduring interfamilial bonds. As a difference from the pattern of the dispersion of core traditions in other reservation communities, however, the Northern Arapahos have centralized the Sun Dance and other core traditions. While other tribes have experienced a trend toward multiple centers of ritual authority and performance of core traditions, Arapaho ritual leaders have maintained a single center.

The Influence of the Missions on Life Transitions

One seeming contradiction that is yet to be thoroughly addressed is the extensive involvement of Northern Arapaho people in Christianity (see Elkin 1940; Starkloff 1974). While constituting tribal solidarity and consensus around remaining core traditions, as Fowler documents, Northern Arapaho people and leaders actively participated in the ritual practices and schools at St. Stephen's Catholic and St. Michael's Episcopal missions. By interconnecting Christianity with Arapaho practice, the tribe averted, at least during the early reservation era, the factionalism common in some other missionized communities between assimilated and traditional groups. Throughout this time, Arapahos who found a place for Christianity among their other traditions were not troubled by the all-embracing contradiction that Deloria generalizes between the American Indian and Christian religions (1994). When areas of contradiction did arise, an indigenous solution was invoked or invented. It is perhaps only in more recent decades and in less overt ways that religious contradictions have amplified stresses.

Among cultural and political leaders of the 1880s to the 1920s, Black Coal and later Lone Bear promoted Arapaho acceptance of St. Stephen's Mission in the lower district; Yellow Calf became the focal leader in the emergence of St. Michael's in the upper district. In one way those leaders saw literacy as a source of Euro-American knowledge to be appropriated in and through schooling and recognized, at the same time, the dangers for their children through removal to national boarding schools, such as Carlisle. In another sense, early "converts" interpreted Christian doctrine as support for Arapaho religion. "The Arapahoes reportedly were interested in Christian teachings, although it appears that to a considerable extent Christianity was understood and reinterpreted according to Arapahoe concepts of the supernatural" (Fowler 1982:125–26). More significantly, Christian practices as opposed to teachings or concepts, were appropriated in Arapaho terms for local purposes.

Although the Northern Arapahos appropriated forms consistent with tradition and adapted those relevant to conditions of reservation life, both

Christian practices and boarding-school influences began a process of reshaping the life trajectory that has endured throughout the reservation period. In another way, Christian practices offered spaces and times for perpetuating some traditions and inventing others that are at the center of collective and family practices today. Overall, although the underlying aim of conversion and assimilationist programs was to redefine personhood and the life trajectory, Arapaho people selected and appropriated the introduced forms for their own sense of life movement.

In one striking illustration, in order to adapt to the corporal punishment and authoritarianism of mission boarding schools during the early reservation period, Arapahos invented hair-cutting and mock whipping ceremonies that were analogous to ear piercing and therefore interlinked traditional ritual practice. Hilger's informant states:

> Our people had a boy's hair cut before he went to a White School. They wanted him to have his hair cut by his own people; they were to be the ones to do it for the first time, not the Whites. At any tribal gathering pretenses might be made at cutting the boy's braids, and presents were given by the parents. Sometimes a braid was actually cut, but only one braid. . . .Children's hair was never cut. The old people thought it was something awful to have a child's hair cut. Adults cut the haid (sic) when someone died. . . .A child's hair was never cut in old times. [1952:43]

Old people today recount how they were mortified, enraged, or saddened by having their hair cut at school. Some recall haircuts before they went to school, usually by an old man or a medicine man. The braids were either kept by the child's mother or were given to a medicine man to keep until the child became an adult. That practice follows the logic that hair as part of the body and life movement must be kept very close. Similarly, hair and other things shed from the body were never to be left about where malevolent other-than-human persons could use them for their harmful powers.

Similarly, whipping was appropriated in a childhood ceremony to prepare children for the schools:

> Since we knew our children would be whipped by the Whites, parents took their children to a dance or a large gathering of the people before sending them away to school. They gave away presents to anyone that was there. Then they made pretentions at switching the child with a

little stick. After that they would say, "All right, my child! You can go
to school now and be whipped." [Hilger 1952:81]

To redress Euro-American-imposed institutional efforts to totally transform the
person, Arapaho people adapted the ritual form from ear piercing to prepare
children for the shock.

John Roberts recognized that two-thirds of the first class at the Government
School at Fort Washakie died from the shock: "The heavy death rate of the
pupils is undoubtedly due to the effect of civilization upon them. In school they
have good care, wholesome food well cooked. They have plenty of fresh air,
outdoor exercise and play. Yet, under these conditions, they droop and die,
while their brothers and sisters, in camp, live and thrive" (Quoted in Crofts
1997:63). Whether the Arapaho strategy to overcome the shock effect was
efficacious or not would be impossible to measure. However, it is clear that
families sustained ongoing relations with the children they sent to the school by
visiting them regularly and taking advantage of the mission policy that allowed
students to return home for the weekend or at least on Sunday. In addition,
throughout early mission history, many people congregated at the mission
grounds on Sundays and holidays for feasts, visiting, dancing, and other old and
new community activities.

During the height of the mission era (1900 to the 1950s), both missions
attempted to introduce Christian rites of transition. Arapaho followers selected
and appropriated some, while silently rejecting others. Christening, for example,
became almost universal for Northern Arapaho families, as it still is. At St.
Stephen's, the traditional naming ceremony often accompanied christening
(Starkloff 1974:76). After receiving a Christian name, the child also received his
or her Arapaho name from a grandparent or other elder in attendance. All
aspects of Christian ritual were regarded as "sacred" and powerful, as in the
Arapaho term for baptism: *beteentouse 'eiht* 'sacred head bath'. Although Euro-
American missionaries saw this as conversion, assimilation, or syncretism,
Arapahos generally kept each "road" compartmentalized. One family or
individual could follow the Arapaho road, the Christian road, and the Peyote
road at the same time. The practices were placed side by side but not syncretized
with Christian meanings, as missionaries often desired. Throughout the early
reservation history, Arapaho people accepted Christian practices but sought little
engagement with doctrine or theology.

Other introduced life transition rituals have been elaborated within contexts
for which Arapaho people now claim ownership. According to oral historical
accounts that I collected, funerals remained small family practices into the

1930s. Early on, missionaries defined Arapaho funeral practices as inadequate, in need of elaboration, and thus proceeded to stress the importance of proper funerals. The increased emphasis on funerals probably began during World War II, when returning Arapaho casualties received military funerals. In the 1940s the women's memorial clubs (i.e., St. Anne's Rosary Sodality and the Yellow Calf Memorial Club) organized to take care of cemeteries and assist the missions in preparing funerals (Fowler 1982:217–21). Women were thus continuing their roles in this aspect of life movement. During the same period veterans through the American Legion posts took on expanding roles in community events, including Veterans' Day, Memorial Day, Christmas week dances, and all funerals. Beginning in the 1950s, pan-Indian traditions began to appear at Wind River, including memorial practices at social events by which families honored their members. What was once a simple and brief occasion involving only close family members became one of the most elaborate and multidimensional life transition ceremonies in Arapaho culture, often drawing participation from the entire community or tribe. A practice that the missions introduced for the purpose of assimilation, Arapaho families and emerging organizations claimed and refined for practices directed to life movement.

In the past, funeral rites themselves were less important than the year-long mourning practices of close relatives, which involved cutting one's hair, slashing the skin, appearing unkempt, not painting, and otherwise appearing as a person withdrawn from public life. Although the self-sacrificing behaviors are no longer followed, some Arapahos still observe a mourning period of one year. Some old people still follow the mourning restrictions by not attending dances or other recreational activities (e.g., bingo) for a year after the death of a close relative. The anniversary of a death is memorialized, and though it has less to do with the lifting of mourning restrictions than formerly, it coincides with the end-of-mourning Catholic Mass.

As part of the funeral anniversary ceremony, family members often sponsor a memorial feast, which also involves a giveaway and a paint ceremony. For deceased persons who were important in the tribe as ritual leaders, the anniversary, like the funeral, draws wider tribal participation. In general, memorializing by families has come to predominate over mourning restrictions as the emphasis of Arapaho funerary practices. Memorializing is an extension of the family's former ways of honoring its members and has been reinforced by the increasing solidarity of the extended family.

The typical funeral begins with a wake or a rosary the night before, then a service in the church or the community hall in the morning. The service often includes Christian elements, traditional forms, Peyote practices for followers of that tradition, and elements of popular culture associated with the deceased. The service itself is followed by a burial service at the cemetery that also combines Christian and traditional elements. Then the funeral group moves to the community hall in the afternoon for the feast, at which the Arapaho Flag Song and honor song are sung, a dinner is served to all who want to attend, and a giveaway by the deceased's family recognizes all who assisted in the services (e.g., cooks, drummers, singers, and priests) or were significant in the deceased person's life. There is also a paint ceremony in which family members and all others who wish to participate receive the red paint pattern on their faces in order to be purified. Traditionally, painting and funerals were antithetical, since mourners had to wait one year, until the mourning restrictions were lifted, before being painted. As increasing numbers of people became involved in funeral practices, painting offered a means of purifying participants for their return to normal life and thus promoting their life movement. Newer practices are adapted to a Euro-American-imposed schedule of work and school that requires quicker reengagement in social life. More moderate mourning restrictions are still followed, although painting at the funeral feast itself is almost universal today. Following painting there may be other family-honoring forms before the feast itself occurs. At this time, people are expected to leave grief behind and socialize in life-affirming ways, including visiting and eating.

Funeral practices were also adaptations to the confined space of the reservation. Traditionally, the camp moved on after death, illness, or tragedy, thus leaving behind the place and power associated with difficulty. Reservation boundaries made that process more difficult, but the missions and inventiveness offered cultural material for its resolution. Women's memorial organizations and veterans' groups expanded the prereservation emphasis on taking care of graves. Rather than maintaining distance, there is now a stronger sense of keeping deceased family members close. The idea that the person goes home to the above is paralleled by placement in family social space. Rosaries and wakes generally occur in the family's home, and many families have their own family cemeteries to return the deceased "home." Cemeteries at the missions or on allotments made it possible for families to remain near and thus care for graves continually, as an extension of former practices.

Unlike christening and funerals, some introduced Christian life transition rituals were not readily appropriated or elaborated. Though missionaries made a very concerted effort to introduce Christian weddings, for example, they did not thrive in Arapaho practice. Early mission weddings were often staged and sponsored by missionaries themselves. Even today, the Euro-American wedding, perhaps the most elaborate among non-Indian life transitions, is rare, though it is becoming more common at Wind River. Most couples still simply go to a public official for a license and the exchange of vows.

Other life transition rituals emerged at the missions, such as confirmation, although most of those remained mission-organized forms. Some of those practices established the format for ceremonies that evolved later, such as graduation. Through the schools and missions, Arapaho families also acquired the celebration of birthdays, now often institutionalized by family dinners, especially for significant years, such as sixteen or eighty. Such events bring extended-family members together and carry on the function of "counting years" and recognition feasts in former times.

As the missions have withdrawn from the educational, political, and economic functions they once served, they continue to provide services for life transitions, primarily christening and funerals. Today, some Arapahos comment that people go to the missions at the beginning and at the end of life. The influence of the missions on the life cycle has been to concentrate symbolic significance on birth and, even more so, on death. During the early mission period, priests declared that baptism was a necessary prerequisite for receiving other sacraments and a determiner of one's disposition in the afterlife. Some priests generated the fear of being denied communion, confession, or last rites later in life. But baptism was also consistent with Arapaho practices of washing and purifying the newborn infant.

The Christian emphasis on the disposition of the soul in the afterlife and associated concepts of sin and guilt have come into contradiction with Arapaho life movement, which really has no concept of judgment, let alone punishment in the afterlife. First of all, preoccupation with death and the afterlife is antithetical to the Arapaho metaphysics of morals for living and acting in a good/correct way, from which long life will follow not just for the individual self or soul, but for one's family and tribe, as well. In short, a focus on one's own afterlife is both life-negating and selfish. The imposition of "sin," then, has been continually problematic, though early on many Arapaho Catholics accepted weekly confession because it conformed to their sense of "discarding" negative elements, as in traditional life movement. Second, mistakes and errors in Arapaho practice are not defined as intrinsic to a person's "soul" or the moral weakness of an individual consciousness but rather are considered to be the result of insufficient knowledge for doing things in a good/correct way. Just as vows and offerings are for others, wrong actions do not affect only the individual but can extend to his or her family. In the event of mistakes, though, ritual sacrifice or purification can avert life-threatening consequences. One's positive and negative actions take place in and through social relations with family members, as well as with the tribe and other-than-human persons. Substantive guilt and sin accumulated in a soul=self=person are foreign to traditional Arapaho life movement. In broad contrast, traditional Arapaho life movement was this-worldly, oriented through relations with human and other-than-human persons, whereas the Christian life trajectory is oriented to the moral substance, intentionalism, and afterlife or future of individuated selves. As with the sacraments, life is also constituted as developmental, in that past events or practices have enduring effects on the later life and beyond; that is the model carried over in the modern "scheduled" life ideal discussed further in this chapter. Despite more recent Christian efforts at syncretism (see Starkloff 1971), based on attributing a universal ground to Christianity and other religions, there is a real enduring contradiction between Arapaho life movement and Christian concepts of sin and salvation. Some missionaries did try to hammer the full brunt of sin on to the Arapaho people, but it was rarely received as a fear-generating doctrine, more often as one among other confusing sides of non-Indian knowledge.

Overall, more and more responsibility for life movement has been appropriated within families. Women's roles especially have become central in preparing for and sponsoring honoring events, as well as incorporating creative new traditions. Within the family, the place of generational kinship, as Eggan (1937) defined it, has endured and even grown for organizing social relations and directing life transitions. Grandparental authority within families is still strong, and families often center on surviving grandparents. In the parental generation, sibling relations remain a cohesive force in family identity and corporate action. Children and young people also tend to form most peer group relations around collateral relatives of the same generation.

Kinship distinctions within the extended family have become even more inclusively generational in emphasis. For example, the segregation of brothers and sisters has relaxed. Sherman Sage states: "Brothers and sisters never talked to each other. However, when people were very old they did so. That was the custom for years; even way back; and even before that time it was that way. Now [1940] all young people mix together. They even take paper and write letters to each other" (in Hilger 1952:69). In kinship terminology there has been a tendency to merge father's sisters with mother's sisters, and mother's brothers with father's brothers. Similarly, the bifurcation of cross cousins and parallel cousins has dissolved. In all, kinship relations have become less restrictive with respect to collateral relations. Shared residence and participation in family life now predominate over older intragenerational distinctions.

Today, the extended family provides a broad network for mutual support, such as in child rearing, financial assistance, and community involvement. Many responsibilities are shared among adult siblings. It is still common for grandparents to raise and even "adopt" their grandchildren when the parents are deceased, unable to care for their children, or are considered too immature or "crazy" to raise children. Financial support for children's and elders' needs are also part of familial cooperation, such that resources are freely shared by those defined as relatives by residence and kinship. Family ties also provide work and assistance for secular or religious events as well as jobs, committee positions, and political leadership.

Families also exercise considerable social control. All senior kin to some extent share in disciplining, talking to, and setting straight children and young people. When an individual does not show appropriate involvement in the family, he or she can be distanced or even shunned. Occasionally, this is a basis for fission within the extended family. A person's life trajectory, then, is now played out more within family than in the tribe or through a general age structure. The sense of personhood and identity now originate in the family rather than from larger categories of Arapaho or Indian, which are now inextricably merged with the family itself.

While families have assumed more and more responsibility for life movement, other functions have been placed within Euro-American formal institutions. Birth, illness, and death take place in hospitals or nursing homes, removed from domestic and community social space. Many critical life events and transitions thus take place in specialized time-space zones outside of family spaces or even off the reservation. In response, Arapaho people have attempted, as with Christian funeral practices, to appropriate control and activate family relations around those functions and the events they generate. For example, when someone enters the hospital with an emergency or serious illness, the entire extended family travels there immediately to form a circle of support. Other disruptive life events likewise call forth family action, such as interpersonal conflict, threats to employment, or political issues. The extended family, then, has emerged as the center for addressing and solving life traumas for its members in a broad expanse of social space.

Inventiveness in Life Transition Rituals

In the Arapaho community today, cultural inventiveness has been an ongoing response to the negative effects of Euro-American efforts to transform the life trajectory. Creativity in all phases of life is instrumental for gaining control over

Euro-American-introduced structures and adapting to changing conditions of reservation life. Sometimes I left an event believing that it replicated what was familiar to everyone else, only to hear Arapaho people themselves comment that they had never seen a particular element or practice before.

High school graduations, as one case, roughly approximate the pattern of commencement elsewhere in American society but contain additional distinctly Arapaho and pan-Indian elements. Caps and gowns are replaced by "traditional" clothes, such as ribbon shirts and moccasins for boys and traditional beaded buckskin dresses for girls. The music for the procession is provided by one of the two principal men's drum groups. The Arapaho Flag Song is also played rather than the national anthem. In recent years graduation has undergone a process of elaboration similar to the one that funerals experienced in the past. There are now Arapaho forms of graduation for Head Start, kindergarten, junior high, high school, and college.

Sports events for young people, especially basketball, have also taken on much community support and many Arapaho practices. Shortly after the missions introduced basketball, it became a gathering point for Arapaho social life and ways of relating to the non-Arapaho world beyond. Personal and community oral history unfold with stories of great teams, travels, glorious wins, and individual feats. Community basketball tournaments outside the schools have also proliferated as ways to memorialize a family member or generate income for a tribal organizations. For men and women, basketball and other sports have become a basis for lifelong peer group relations and a medium to express one's abilities for future leadership or careers. The two gymnasiums at St. Stephen's and St. Michael's also became prototypes for community centers built later to replace the old dance halls.

Families often recognize important life transitions or achievements of members through honor songs and giveaways at powwows and other community gatherings. The range of honored life events is creatively expanding. Accordingly, many pan-Indian traditions of "honoring" have become part of contemporary culture. If a young woman is elected powwow queen or princess, for example, the family is obligated to sponsor an honor dance and a giveaway, usually at the next year's powwow. Other occasions for recognition include adoption, a child's first powwow dancing, college graduation, completion of a term as powwow committee chair, return from military service, recovery from illness, and moving away from or returning to the reservation. Whom to honor and when to do it are generally decisions initiated by one family member, who in turn gathers the support of other family members to show respect for the honoree.

Along with Arapaho efforts to invent forms to claim ownership of Euro-American-imposed life transitions, there has been a movement to reinvent or reinvigorate some childhood rituals. The practice of the navel bag is still followed by many families, whereby the portion of the umbilical cord that dries out after birth is kept in a beaded buckskin bag. Ear piercing has become increasingly common again in the past few years. Since the 1970s, naming ceremonies have also been revived: an older person is invited to a family's home to give a child an Indian name. In the early reservation period, the traditional naming often coincided with christening in the church.

Naming practices have changed as a result of Euro-American-imposed forms, though even those have been appropriated to some extent in Arapaho practices. During the early reservation period, beginning with the administration of Superintendent H. G. Nickerson, Arapaho names were anglicized as part of assimilation efforts (Census of Arapahoe Indians 1900). At the actual name-changing enrollment, Arapahos regarded the process indifferently and even humorously. Some people received surnames approximating the name of the head of household, such as Sage, who became Sherman Sage. Others were assigned American surnames: Caldwell, Brown, Whitman. Some were assigned famous names: Garfield, Washington, and Penn. Although the "agency names" gradually replaced Arapaho names in legal documents and records, people themselves continued to use their Arapaho names for decades. In time, a dual naming system developed. One had an "Indian name" by which one was recognized in the community and an "agency name" for one's relationship to the government and other Euro-American institutions. The Euro-American names eventually displaced traditional names in common usage, however.

Since the Bureau of Indian Affairs administered enrollment, inheritance of allotted land, health services, and so on during the early reservation period, one's agency name became indispensable for legal personhood and thus for acquiring services and resources. In the process, patrilateral inheritance of names became central to personal and family identity and continuity. Although new names have been introduced through intermarriage or through children receiving names from other tribes, at present there is a finite number of prevalent, original Northern Arapaho surnames. Since some families in the first and second generations after the names were changed ceased to have male children, their surnames no longer survive. Patrilateral naming stands in contradiction to the feminine core of many Arapaho families. Nevertheless, while men pass on the name, women still sustain family solidarity and continuity. This contradiction was at the center of the enrollment controversy discussed in chapter 12.

The practice of giving and taking Arapaho names from others continued in the reservation period, though they no longer appear in census records by the 1920s. A World War II veteran, for example, would take a new name from an older person upon returning from war, leaving his name on the floor, as embodied in a blanket, for someone else to pick up. At present, Arapaho names have become more a part of family cultural continuity, in contrast to the prereservation practice of passing on or taking up names because of their power to overcome difficulties.

Gradually, Euro-American surnames came to define extended-family boundaries and interfamilial relationships. One way of referring to person's identity is to say "So and so is a [surname]." When children meet, they commonly ask "What's your last name?," as a marker of family and place in the social world. Women who have taken their husband's surnames often refer to themselves or are defined by others by their maiden names. Surnames also serve to define relations between families as close or distant. Between some named families there is a sense of kinship based in shared ancestors, whereas between others there may be distance founded in past conflict.

Within a family, Euro-American personal names also shape life movement by maintaining continuity with parents, grandparents, and even generations long past. Arapaho patterns for keeping and passing on names have been extended to given names so that individual life movement and family continuity are intertwined. A boy named Joseph may have inherited his name from his father, an uncle, or a grandfather, who in turn may have received it from an older kinsman. A girl named Jane may have inherited her name from a line of women namesakes, living or deceased. Some names may cross over from a male to a female, such as in the shift from Paul to Pauline. There is a feeling that the names of respected and long-lived family members, both male and female, should be given to children of the family so that they can carry on those characteristics as well as "honor" and "memorialize" their namesakes.

Most families now pass on both surnames and a pool of first names, most of which originated with the first ancestors to receive Euro-American names around 1900. Those names function both to sustain family continuity and to honor forebears, living or deceased. If the name of an important ancestor has not been used, there is a sense of obligation to use that name again. Name changing was intended to assimilate by introducing Euro-American ways of defining persons, but Arapahos have appropriated the introduced forms within traditional practices and for maintaining family solidarity. Names have become part of family cultural continuity as life movement, a way of linking present members to the past.

Although this seems identical to the uses of names in the Euro-American family, the Arapaho practice performs unique enduring and newly evolving functions. The enduring function combines passing on power for life movement from ancestors with ways of memorializing them. One new function is to express and perpetuate extended family identity and solidarity within the Arapaho community. Unlike Euro-American names, save for a dwindling number of rural families, they tie Arapaho people to a past that is in and of the very land they live or walk on. Names also define contemporary social relationships an individual or family can have in the community. In almost all social encounters, names allow actors to mutually situate themselves in actual, known history and place.

As part of local lived culture, a nickname is also often used; it derives from a significant or humorous episode in a person's life. Such names are also, in one way, a marker of closeness and "joking" between friends and family members. In respect relationships one should never use such a nickname, but between those who are close it is acceptable. An out-group will use a nickname for a person—but conceal it from him or her—as a derogatory way to define that person as an outsider. In other words, nicknames serve to define in-group–out-group boundaries for persons.

Changes in naming practices have emerged in recent years. For example, some families and individuals have begun reverting to the original name of the ancestor from whom their surname derived. Thus, some people with the name Brown have changed back to Lone Bear, the name of the Lower Arapaho chief with the agency name Lon Brown from whom they descend. That makes Arapaho identity visible, because it reestablishes ties to the past obscured by Euro-American names and thus reclaims family ancestry.

Throughout the reservation period, Northern Arapaho people have adapted life transition rituals to the spatial and temporal forms imposed by Euro-American institutions. More precisely, Northern Arapaho society has attempted for many years to appropriate the emerging, imposed practices into both an indigenous theory of practice and an evolving family-based solidarity and continuity. Older traditions were placed in spaces and times allowed by Euro-American culture and performable with resources at hand. Naming became attached to christening, the Crow Dance to Christmas week, and ceremonies to weekends. New pan-Indian forms, such as Peyote and powwows, were placed in convenient times and spaces. Arapaho meanings were injected through invention into Euro-American life transition forms such as funerals, graduations, and military service. Despite efforts to synchronize tradition with Euro-American space and time, though, some dissonant points remain. Pulling very strongly in the opposite direction institutions based in or borrowed from Euro-American knowledge, structures, and political economy continually seek to gain more and more control over the definition of personhood and the shape of the life trajectory.

Social Control and Political Authority

In the past, elders wielded a great deal of social control over life movement by interpreting the appropriateness or inappropriateness of younger people's behavior: "They could interpret the cause of unfortunate events, and in this way could single out and associate the actions of disruptive individuals with supernatural retribution" (Fowler 1982:155). Elders thus controlled the life movement of younger people through the power of their knowledge. Today, family-based problem-solving strategies, formal institutional controls, and a centralized tribal administration have come to predominate over age-structured modes of social control.

Some believe, while others do not, that elders still have *beetee-* medicine power to shape people's lives. Whatever the case may be, it is clear that elders' influence is not as pervasive or efficacious as it once was. Ritual leaders can still invoke their authority to shape tribal policy or direct individuals' lives, but that is now limited in space and time. Elders are occasionally asked to "talk to" (lecture) a younger family member in need of direction. They are also often called in to serve as advisers or consultants when a new tribal initiative or program is being considered.

These public contexts aside, there are now barriers to communication between old and young. When elders do exert control, it is often through "subtle" means of expression accessible only to those who can decode them through traditional language and culture. Not only do younger people lack language fluency, but they are also often oblivious to or incapable of deciphering or even receiving the other messages conveyed by elders. Older people remark that younger people no longer listen, since the traditional ways of teaching children how to listen no longer exist. From the other side, younger people can confuse older people's efforts to correct them with "shaming" behavior; they may interpret such efforts as "putting them down." With this potential for shaming on their minds, middle-aged people fluent in the Arapaho language may hesitate to speak it in public for fear of being corrected and thus ridiculed. Conversely, elders stated to me that the younger generations do not keep them well enough informed about what is going on in the tribe and often go too fast in making decisions. In order to gain information or direction for decision making, all ages have had to become much more vocally acquisitive and assertive than former traditions would dictate. For such expressiveness, English provides both bilingual and monolingual speakers less restriction from traditional age-structured ways of speaking in a good/correct way. As a number of elders told me, you have to be more careful with what you say in Arapaho, but in English you can say anything. Although language shift has brought less restricted and less deliberate ways of speaking, it may also be a primary contributing factor to weakened tribal solidarity and increasing factionalism.

In the past old people were able to mediate most conflicts that arose in the tribe. "Elders . . . worked to mitigate dissension and social schism by preventing one band or residential community from dominating tribal leadership positions" (Fowler 1982:156). The power of elders to resolve factional disputes is much more limited today. For one thing, there is now a tendency to identify elders, like other people, with their families' or groups' interests, rather than with tribal consensus. Also, the "consensus" among older people observed by Fowler has become overwhelmed by divisions, even among some elders themselves. And when a consensus is reached, there are now fewer means at hand to enforce it.

Through Euro-American institutions or those in the tribe modeled after them, ultimate social control and conflict intervention have been appropriated largely by formal procedures based not on age but on the legal-rational authority. Police officers or social workers intervene in family or intergroup conflicts. Crimes are handled within the tribal, state, or federal court system. Victims of misuses of power from within or outside the tribe also usually have no recourse but legal action. In other contexts, schools discipline young people, social agencies address personal problems, and myriad other programs deal with other problems. Most contemporary conflicts and problems that are beyond family control are thus handled through formal institutional mechanisms. When those fail, individual, family or local group action is often the only recourse.

Tribal leadership roles have also expanded considerably since the early and prereservation period. Externally imposed and internally emerging changes in the Arapaho community have brought about new responsibilities for political leaders. In the early reservation context, the emergence of new community events generated new forms of leadership. By the 1920s Christmas dances were held each year in dance halls at each of the three districts, St. Stephen's, Mill Creek, and Bridgeport (Ethete). Each district had its own dance hall, used for meetings and the Christmas week dance, which consisted of the Crow Dance, social dances, feasts, speeches, giveaways, and games. Membership on the Dance Committee to organize Christmas week was a great honor and responsibility. Just as they selected chiefs for the council, elders appointed new members each year during a selection ceremony, in which they danced around the hall and touched each new member on the foot. The group of elders and initiates would then leave the hall, returning with the new members wearing warbonnets. There were usually four to ten members on the Dance Committee for each district. The "Dance Committee," an important organization for many years, served as a preliminary for chiefship and evolved into an integral phase of Arapaho tribal government. Ways of organizing and soliciting funds for community dances followed the model offered by the missions. For instance, the solicitation of donations from the local white towns, along with the use of bingo, raffles, and penny parties, were year-round activities for the committees.

Over time, social events and committees on this model multiplied. Concerned about potential factional divisions, Arapaho leaders and elders brought many dispersed social activities and committees under centralized tribal control. By the 1930s the district dance committees were coordinated by a single Dance Committee, which became known as the Entertainment Committee and was composed of six elected positions in the tribal government (Fowler 1982:217–19). During my stay at Wind River, the name of the committee was changed to the Tribal Committee to better represent its functions, which have expanded to encompass control of the public use of all tribal facilities, including the powwow grounds and the community centers. In the 1960s the dance halls were replaced by modern community halls, where most indoor social events and public gatherings now take place, such as funerals, winter and spring powwows, basketball tournaments, and General Council meetings.

The tribal government centralized some functions, but more committees and community groups also emerged. Veterans' groups became a central part of all Arapaho public gatherings after World War II. Beginning in the 1950s, committees organized to raise funds for powwows. Since the 1970s committees have proliferated in tribal government, the schools, and outside of formal organizations. Within the tribal government, there have been or currently are the Arapaho Ranch Board, the Arapaho Trust, the Economic Development Committee, an elders' group for repatriation and sacred sites, a higher education board, a utilities board, a language and culture commission, and various others. In the schools there are parent committees, locally elected boards, sports booster clubs, and many more. At any given time, there are incipient and informal groups and committees forming for various aims, such as law and order, tribal college planning, youth activities, and so on.

Fowler argues correctly that the emergence of committees, sodalities, veterans' groups, and other social formations for organizing community events replaced the functions of the age societies and the women's groups by allowing younger people opportunities to show their leadership potential in preparation for political roles in the third stage of life (e.g., serving on the Business Council and the Entertainment Committee) (1982:218–20). For the time, Euro-American social forms offered models for the Arapaho people to construct organizations and committees that then pursued traditional aims and new functions in ways acceptable to agents of the dominant society.

The veterans' groups have served functions parallel to the age societies of the past, but especially having to do with emerging new roles for life movement. After World War II, American Legion posts at Arapahoe and Ethete took on many roles for organizing or assisting with Christmas dances, memorials, and powwows. Even today veterans continue to tell war stories for ritual transitions and are present at almost all tribal events, including powwows, funerals, memorials, and sports events. They also became the main source of "security" personnel for tribal gatherings, thus paralleling the former Spear society. The general pattern once associated with progression from warrior to leader stages was reinvented through the connection of veterans to tribal leadership. From the 1940s until recently, military service has been an unstated requisite for election to the Business Council or selection to other positions of leadership.

By the 1930s and 1940s, the decentralized local committees and functions had been brought into the gradually centralizing tribal political system, subject to the authority of the Business Council, the elders, and the General Council. Fowler identified that pattern as continuous with the traditional age structure for maintaining tribal solidarity and consensus. Within the dialectic of reservation politics, though, the centralization process was itself an adaptation to new conditions and has been accompanied by increasing factionalism as families and districts compete for scarce resources. From the 1970s to the mid-1980s, elected tribal leaders redistributed more tribal funds, which became available from mineral leases of trust lands, to subsidize tribal committees and events. Many people recall of that period that "money was everywhere." It was a time, too, when questions multiplied about what certain tribal funds were used for and how different groups or individuals received them. With the decline of tribal income since the late 1980s, the ongoing tension has become sharper in the Arapaho political system between centralized control of resources and increasingly unmet local needs.

One of the concerns I heard repeated many times, was that money is now at the center of all tribal politics, culture, and social relations. As in many communities entering a money economy, exchanges of food and objects of value that once constituted social relations have been displaced by money exchanges, which are less conducive to activating enduring social relations and interconnecting multiple levels of meaning within the cultural system. Money is also less controllable within traditional systems of authority, for its source, uses, and relations are less visible in public space. It also tends to perseverate Euro-American claims of control over allocation of money based on suspicion of the Arapaho administration. For our purposes here, money is now involved in all Arapaho forms of authority and life movement. All social events, ceremonies, educational programs, family events, leadership roles, committees, and other dimensions of the lived world now require money.

Since the self-determination policy began in the 1970s, the trend has been to assign specific functions to an expanding number of offices, administrative positions, committees, and commissions subsumed within tribal government. Though self-determination and the Arapaho effort to "do it on their own" are served in that way, it has become increasingly difficult for the Business Council and the General Council (a meeting of adult tribal members) to scrutinize the expanding programs, let alone to bring them all into traditional forms of decision making. Today, one of the commonly expressed political concerns is that there is no coordination or even exchange of information among various offices and programs. The Northern Arapaho tribal government has taken over more services once funded by other governments and administered by federal or state agencies or jointly with the Eastern Shoshone tribe. In addition, a few former voluntaristic groups and activities have been absorbed. From the mid-1980s to the 1990s, tribal income and federal funds decreased, stimulating some decentralization, as community groups and activities once subsidized in whole or in part by the tribe have had to become independent from tribal political control. Tribal funding for powwows, special school programs, language and culture efforts, and other organizations have had to be removed from the tribal administrative budget. As a result there is a growing sense at both the tribal and the community levels that "we are going to have to do it on our own now."

Like religious participation, then, political involvement has become more of a personal choice, first and primarily activated within family relations. In terms of life movement, Arapaho people today face a choice of whether to "get involved with the tribe," that is, to become active in tribal politics at any level. Some people now have careers in "the tribe," while others pursue the "quiet life" by staying out of the public sphere, confining their lives to family, work, and local cultural traditions. Behind that decision is a strong Arapaho sense of service to the community and the tribe. Most individuals and families at some point put forth immeasurable work, time, and resources for the community or the tribe. In such cases, the sense of "giving back" transcends the desire for political advancement or economic self-interest. It is still moved by Arapaho values of showing pity for those in need and giving or receiving respect. Ideally, one should not expect a return for such service, though many people comment that the infusion of money into almost every aspect of Arapaho life now challenges that ideal. All tribal, educational, and agency positions are now full-time professions under centralized control. At one time, participation in tribal leadership was compensated only by small per diem payments, but now councilpersons are full-time, relatively well paid office holders, if often only for a short term of two years. What happens in many work careers is movement in and out of positions with shifts in funding, political control, or workplace tolerance. To work for tribally or federally funded programs can thus be precarious. With a professionalized and wage-labor economy, it is now very difficult to keep money and service to the tribe separate. On a broader scale, differential access to jobs and resources through centralized tribal government has contributed to greater social stratification among families.

Traditional life movement required the lack of attachment to political or economic self-interest as a measure of potential for leadership. Elders selected those most suitable for leadership on the basis of their personal qualities and ways of relating to others. Today, those who try to live according to the traditional values of respect, pity, and quietness face contradictions and struggles. Even when pursuing traditional values, one may still be suspected of self-interest. It is around those issues about participation in tribal political life that adult life movement now unfolds.

As Fowler (1982:3) observes, what Arapaho people, led by elders, constructed in the early reservation period was a separation and a balance of powers between ceremonial authority confined to people in the fourth stage of life and political authority assigned to those at least in the third stage (age fifty or above). Within that system, political authority was dependent on ritual authority. Elders selected members for political leadership in the Business Council and other committees that emerged. Only men and women who showed the proper maturity and "respect" were chosen for political leadership and positions of apprenticeship to learn ritual knowledge from elders. The link between socially recognized age and potential leadership abilities is still present, though it has been weakened considerably by the adoption of an electoral system and credentials criteria for employment.

The pattern by which elders framed a consensus for selecting political leaders persisted until the introduction of the so-called white man's ways (*nih'oo3ouniisinewo*), which, according to local knowledge, clearly predominated by the 1970s. By that time Euro-American electoral procedures had replaced the authority of elders for the selection of members of the Business Council, the Entertainment Committee, and various special committees. Although the Wind River tribes jointly rejected reorganization in the 1930s and the Northern Arapahos remain today without a charter and a constitution, they nonetheless eventually acquired an electoral system, along with all the problems associated with it that now plague many reservation communities.

Within the current system, a candidate who can muster three hundred votes from the approximately two thousand eligible adult voting members can be elected to the Business Council or the Tribal Committee. Though elders have ceased to have a major role in selecting political leaders and can no longer ensure consensus, they still wield some influence in shaping community and family opinion about the candidates. With an electoral system, however, special interests and factional politics have weakened the age-structured political authority. Today, access to positions of both political and ritual authority is based on the support of one's extended family and groups that accept one's platform made known through campaigning, a practice unthinkable in the former system. Overall, selection for leadership is gradually moving away from a basis in life movement according to which only those who lived up to the requirements of their age in their socially recognized life history would be selected for leadership. Many people talk about strategies for regaining the old system and discarding the "white man's ways," but there is a growing sense that the "tribe" is now a political entity beyond the control of tribal members, individually or collectively. As such, it becomes for many an entity like any other government that is distant and "difficult to move" except by strategizing for needed jobs, resources, and services. Accordingly, when a problem or a barrier to life movement occurs, individuals turn to family support for initiating action by the tribal government, schools, health care facilities, and other formal institutions.

Euro-American Education

Elders see young people today as "crazy," "moving too fast," and "growing up too fast." That is part of the general perspective that modern life is "too fast" for people to follow the right steps and procedures for doing things the right way, according to the Arapaho theory of practice. Arapaho elders echo the same concern expressed to Hilger over fifty years ago; "Children need punishment for they act 'crazy.' They have too much freedom. They won't stand being reared the way we are" (Hilger 1952:82). Some elders who experienced the age-structured order of respect in their homes and strict discipline in the mission boarding schools see contemporary young people's behavior in and out of school as "out of control." To some extent they hold parents in the younger generation responsible for that, as well as Euro-American culture. Whatever the case, they recognize, as many parents do, that they are increasingly distant from the lives of children and youths.

Euro-American society infuses an ideology that human development is best encouraged and social problems are most effectively solved through formal education. From the early reservation period to the present, formal education has always been the externally accepted solution to the "Indian problem." Deloria states, "As preaching in the Roman world was thought to be the key to one's salvation, so education, its secularized counterpart in the contemporary world, is thought to be the final answer to social ills" (1994:188). The religious sense of conversion of a soul or inner self has evolved into the broader policy of assimilation, which has in turn emerged as "educational success." Education has become the basis for resolving all psychological and social ills, for effecting self-determination, overcoming substance abuse, developing the economy, and improving health. Concerns about unemployment, crime, illness, substance abuse, and other contemporary life issues are phrased in terms of providing education. For community members, though, especially young people, there is no guarantee that education will solve the problems of everyday life, let alone offer a clearly defined trajectory for one's life as a whole.

As in many culturally distinct communities, the life trajectory called for by formal education required a break with the Northern Arapahos' local life situations. From the 1880s on, Euro-American society has sought to appropriate control of the life trajectory through formal educational institutions, generally removed from the direct control of families and intergenerational relations. Originally, boarding schools aimed to sever the link between generations, though many agents and missionaries soon realized that in doing so they actually killed many children. A latent function beneath the ideology of education is to negate or at least neutralize relations to former generations and their culture.

It is that estrangement and "break" from the ordinary flow of life and, in this case, Arapaho life movement, that education borrows from a Christian eschatology. As Deloria adds, Christianity has evolved as a "totally coherent process of repentance, conversion, redemption, salvation, confession, absolution, and eternal life . . . constructed as the Christian description of the effect of the sect's religious beliefs on the human personality" (1994:188). Thus, Christianity offers a total break in time from ignorance and sin both posited in the past. The break and transformation of Christianity has been infused into the Euro-American model life cycle in various institutions, but especially education. The emphasis on a break from the past and a promise of future redemption has been transformed into an unquestioned promise of education to deliver the individual from past poverty and ignorance and provide economic success, upward social mobility, and self-actualization. Whereas Christian "salvation" was oriented to eternal life, education is oriented to future self-development.

In the contemporary Arapaho context, as in other reservation communities, education also requires a break in social space from the family and the community. Schooling takes place in social and cognitive space and time that are segregated from the family, the community, and the tribe. Engendered at Wind River is a pattern of regular and even daily "transculturalization" (from Hallowell 1963a:505) that is familiar to other peoples subject to similar conditions. Some Arapaho college students reported to me that they have to be different persons and activate different ways of relating to others when they cross the bridge into the "white world."

By contrast to the former Arapaho ritual system, the Euro-American education system in particular does not function to create enduring social groups or true age sets. Peer group formations are informal, incidental, and at times resisted as antithetical to institutional functions or as the source of "problems." Indeed, much of the mechanism of the educational institution and Euro-American society in general resists the formation of peer groups, especially among adolescents. Furthermore, educators themselves do not form cohesive age groups but only compose aggregates of persons defined by profession. As a separate time-space zone, the school has no institutionalized function for generating groups with functions or even ties to the community. Within reservation schools the majority of non-Indian teachers and administrators have no real social connection to reservation communities outside of their jobs.

Since the beginning of the reservation period, assimilation policies attempted not only to redefine social space but also to transform life cyclical time. In terms of temporal difference, formal education manifestly and latently inscribes a Euro-American model of the life cycle with a unique tempo, staging, and aims. For one thing, modern Western development models weight childhood as the formative stage, whereas in the traditional Arapaho trajectory, learning significant knowledge was a lifelong process. Children could be lectured and told stories, but that activity was intermittent or seasonal. Today some tendencies of the prereservation Arapaho life model persist and are at odds with Euro-American formal education. Some Arapaho parents tend to "leave children alone" to their own activities, rather than to keep them under the constant physical or mental surveillance that characterizes American middle-class child-rearing.

Euro-American idealized parenting and schooling aims for success through a properly scheduled day, year, and life cycle. To bring children in line with various scheduled forms of time, Euro-American formal education requires spatial separation of children from their families, at least during school hours. Rational scheduling requires separation from social relations that potentially "disrupt" the schedule or distract the individual from a future life course. More broadly, the ideal is an unbroken, planned course from preschool to postsecondary education. Children who do not conform to the schedule of development are defined as abnormal or hindered by a disability. Since the beginning of boarding-school education at Wind River, the primary though often latent aim has been to bring Arapaho children into the Euro-American order of time at homologous levels of "rational scheduling." The school day requires careful attention to daily schedules and curriculum sequencing. Children who conform to or accelerate in the schedule are rewarded and promoted. To both past and contemporary educators, a well-scheduled day is a model for a well-scheduled life, and that in turn contributes to a well-scheduled order for social progress. The schedule as a chronotype also pervades most other Euro-American social institutions, including such forms as a regimen of health care, a timeline for grant-funded programs, and a schedule of loan payments.

In Euro-American institutions there is generally no knowledge of contemporary Arapaho life "time"; they usually impose their own order without consideration for it. For example, a college student who leaves for several days to attend a funeral or a tribal ceremony may be punished by failure in a course. A local physician may not understand why a diabetes patient attends a powwow to "feel better." In general, Arapaho people are asked to conform their life trajectories to the Euro-American model more than non-Indian institutions conform to Arapaho life "time." Reservation schools and offices have made some adjustments, but they are marginal.

Euro-American personhood as "self" is also grounded in temporal continuity rather than in the social space of relations. The "real" self remains continuous while outward, less genuine forms shift to move through situations. The life cyclical model to support this "real" self idealizes a continuous life history, which can be described by an autobiography, resumes, a dossier, school records, and even psychoanalysis. Vine Deloria in *God Is Red* (1994) contends that the Euro-American religious view orders the world through continuous linear time, that is, along the line of "history." By extension, Euro-American life-time borrows its form from "history," "evolution," or "development." At any moment in time, reflection on the past or planning for the future, the order seeks a "history" of the unbroken linear sequence. Resumes with blank time spaces are suspicious, as are moments of one's life history that are forgotten. To secure truth, authenticity, and even a healthy life, one must make sure there are no missing pieces.

The homology for constructing the Euro-American "ideal-typical" life cycle is thus an irreversible trajectory and a continuous succession of events. Carried within that homology is the conviction that what one does in earlier stages or grades will have an enduring impact on the self and its future development. That view in turn supplies the material for powerful social control of the person and his or her life course.

Returning for purposes of contrast to an earlier discussion, Arapaho life movement was traditionally generated by interpersonal exchanges and appropriate practice. Each life transition reinstantiated the age hierarchy and social relations with human and other-than-human persons in general. Likewise, the "record" was a reflection of and owned by the collective memory of elders. In the traditional age structure, one's "past" or life history was a part of collective memory: "From birth the Arapahoe is carefully observed by other Arapahoes and his behavior is constantly discussed both in his presence and absence" (Fowler 1982:257). Within that public scrutiny and memory of a person, "elders, and especially ceremonial elders or ritual authorities, are particularly involved in monitoring reputations and effecting behavioral transformations" (256). In the age-structured context, one's "past" was part of the orally transmitted and mnemonically stored knowledge. In short, one's past was inscribed in one's human relationships in the community. Through those relations, Arapaho life movement allowed room for one to reverse one's life course, to "straighten out," as through a vow or a life-changing experience. One can be "crazy" in youth but still become a responsible adult when he or she "settles down," as Arapaho people still say.

Euro-American "life history" is grounded in literate documented knowledge of the person, as in school records and credentials that give an individual an objective "past." What is framed by the "documented self" eschews or at least devalues elements central in Arapaho personhood, such as family, kinship, ceremonial participation, and service to the community or the tribe. Service to the community and the tribe, central to Arapaho personhood, could indeed be added to a resume, but it would have to be secondary to academic and work history. In the contemporary context, contradictions between literate credentials and community knowledge about a person often result in confusion and even conflict. Written records are constructed by but estranged from persons and the effects of social action.

The use of culturally defined age as described throughout this book is still an important consideration for Arapahos when decisions are made about filling jobs or electing leaders; the Euro-American emphasis on academic credentials and work experience is often at odds with such traditional concepts. The mainstream formal educational system has given room for only some traditional definitions of expertise, such as in the certification of nondegreed teachers of the Northern Arapaho language. However, those institutional changes have been special addenda to the school curricula, rather than a fully integrated system. For the most part, non-Indians in Euro-American organizations consciously or unconsciously continue to construct and objectify idealized life-cyclical models that they accept as empirical, rational, and practical but which are not synchronized with either traditional life movement or modern reservation conditions.

As Giddens argues, the association in modern organizations between the "storage and retrieval of enormous quantities of information about their subjects" and the bracketing of time-space is more than coincidental: "If the modern period is the era *par excellence* of organizations, it is by the same token an era of maximizing of information, employed in that bracketing of time and space upon which time-space distanciation takes place" (1987:149). Literate knowledge about persons allows surveillance and control over the course of their lives from a distance. And that control has been the universal theme of reservation schools since the initial efforts at sequestration in total institutional boarding schools. Power over the course or schedule of life thus derives from some knowledge that exists somewhere else, outside of copresent persons, and is imposed from the top down, but which is constructed and reproduced by local actors through their practices. That same distancing explains why Euro-American organizations do not "know" the local sociocultural context or share the same space-time, including the ways Arapaho people constitute life movement (see chapter 12).

Euro-American school-work history, constructed to define the self, also corresponds to the "market" of persons in which one must engage in "selling oneself" through Goffmanian impression management to people with whom one has no real shared history. In filling jobs, records of educational attainment, credentials, and work experience have replaced socially produced decisions based on "maturity" in the traditional Arapaho sense. At Wind River, those who have more formal education and a documented life history have access to employment and resources within Euro-American constructed criteria, but they may or may not have any real place in the community. In the Arapaho tribe, those with such "credentials" tend to be younger and better educated yet often with less involvement in what senior generations define as "tradition." In the contemporary Arapaho context, then, there are two competing ways of defining movement through the life trajectory. One is the force of Euro-American institutions with their "scheduled" life, and segregation into separate social spaces for each stage of life. The other is the centripetal force of the extended family and the enduring sense of life movement. Formal organizations, especially schools, promise resolution of that contradiction, but in the one hundred years of their operation, they have provided it to only a few individuals. Northern Arapaho people today thus often express ambivalent attitudes toward "education." It is held as the main hope for the future of the tribe in some contexts, but in others it is referred to as "taking young people away from the tribe." Young people today therefore commonly find themselves living a contradiction. If they achieve a college education, they are seen as distant from the community. If they do not, their lives are engaged in relations with their family and the Arapaho reservation community, but they move little in the Euro-American life trajectory of career and financial success.

There are Arapaho efforts to gain ownership of the educational process, though they generally become confined to small spaces and times in the schools. In the 1970s several concerned people instituted Arapaho language instruction in the schools. Given only small slots of time in the daily schedule and less-than-adequate training and resources, such programs have had minimal results. In recent years an Arapaho language immersion program in Headstart and kindergarten programs has shown promising results, but it has yet to gain a place in the entire K-12 curriculum. Also in the past few years, initial efforts have been made to establish an Arapaho tribal college on the model of similar institutions in other reservation communities, but, given the tribe's difficult economy and the state and county monopoly of the local tax base, it is difficult to muster start-up resources for such an initiative. Families, individuals, and community groups continue to engage schools and colleges in dialogue that aims toward greater Arapaho ownership of formal education, but, as in many similar contexts of minority action, only nominal, gestural, and ghettoized programs seem to follow. Rarely do such efforts gain more than a small budget, office, and slot in the schedule. Efforts toward Arapaho control of education require ongoing and extensive social action and will only succeed, perhaps, if the takeover is total.

Euro-American Life Space and Arapaho Life Movement

In Arapaho life movement, age was defined according to a distinctive tempo and rhythm and was grounded in relations in space, not an abstract totalized time. As suggested in the previous section, orders of time in both the Euro-American system and Arapaho life movement are inseparably related to ways of shaping social space. In Arapaho life movement, social space was ordered by age distinctions. Both the age-grade ceremonies held in the fall and spring and the daily activities reproduced the age structure by the orchestration of practices in social space. All age sets and groups of women had their own "places" in the tipi, the camp, and collective gatherings. Age had more to do with situating groups in social space than with measuring personhood against a yardstick of time.

This spatial order changed significantly with reservation life. As the Arapaho architect Dennis Sun Rhodes (1994) astutely observes, modern Arapaho homes are no longer oriented to the four directions, relations of respect, and age-ranked spacing. With the imposition of Euro-American forms, spaces associated with family, faction, or function have gradually displaced those orientated by age. The shared space of the tipi, the tent, or the one-room cabin has been replaced by the modern home with multiple rooms for specialized occupancy and functions. Outside the home, shared social space for the community and the tribe is now limited to specific places and times. At all levels there are fewer contexts for ordering intergenerational and interfamilial social relations based on age distinctions.

In the past, public gatherings, such as social dances, General Council meetings, and even smaller gatherings were ordered by age distinctions. Inside the tipi and other structures, the oldest persons sat on the west side. Within the camp circle, the sweat lodge of the Seven Old Men was in the center. In the old dance halls of the reservation period, too, old people sat in the front row near the heat stoves, and the women and children sat behind them. Adult and younger men stood in the back (Joe Goggles). Today, age-ordered social space is confined to the extended family and limited contexts in the public world. In the past, one would walk into a public space looking for age peers to join. Now, as people say, you walk in looking for your family or relatives. When an age-structured space is evident today, it is only in very specific contexts, such as ceremonies.

At one time the entirety of Arapaho social space and time was age structured, but today different age groups occupy discrete spaces for much of the day, following an order imposed by a Euro-American time-space zoning that segregates age groups through day care, Headstart, schools, colleges, and senior citizens' centers. Euro-American society is generally age segregated without activating vertical inter-age group relations that extend beyond family boundaries. Thus, older, fluent Arapaho speakers reflect that it is very difficult to find social situations in which they can speak the language among their age group, save for brief interaction here and there. The specialization of social space is also primarily for the activities of younger age groups, save for the senior citizens' centers that provide weekday lunches, mostly through home delivery. With dispersed family housing and loss of mobility resulting from the physical limitations of aging, there is also a tendency for older people to be isolated from each other. While younger generations go to school, work, or engage regularly in activities with people their own age, many senior citizens have little day-to-day social contact with their age mates. Social space has been reordered by an imposed Euro-American space, confined to bureaucratic offices, schools, "square" houses with separate rooms, roads for automobile travel, and other specialized spaces.

In spite of those changes, Arapaho social space has not merely been a replication of the Euro-American model. To give one example, Arapaho parents and grandparents often take their children into a wider range of social spaces than Euro-Americans do. Family ties can also move into or interrupt any formal space, something that non-Indian people often find intrusive, even chaotic. One year at St. Stephen's I taught a college credit Arapaho history course in the evenings, with students' children or other family members present or coming and going throughout the class. Similarly, it is very common for Arapaho people to enter non-Indian formal contexts accompanied by one or several family members or friends. Entering a space with no such ties, either on or off the reservation, is very uncomfortable for many Arapaho people; I grew to share the feeling, myself.

Another Arapaho adaptation to Euro-American space and time is the construction of permanent places for the performance of ceremonies and social events. Since the 1970s the Offerings Lodge has been held in the same place, at the Arapaho Sun Dance Grounds near Ethete. In the past the Sun Dance was held at a different place each year, usually near the home of the sponsor, the principal pledger of the lodge. The community halls are also utilized as fixed places for social and ceremonial functions. Annual and special events are now scheduled according to the calendar and the weekly cycle. For instance, ceremonies and powwows are generally held on weekends, usually ending on Sunday evening. Within the permanent places for tribal events, social space is now ordered more by extended family placement. Typically, a family sits together in the same relative location for General Council meetings. The Sun Dance Grounds is also organized by family camps, which are consistent from year to year. Interestingly enough, family camps are organized by the geography of reservation residence and the closeness of ties between families. Upper Arapaho families generally camp on the north side of the lodge.

Contemporary life movement is most strongly tied to spaces defined by kinship and family "place," rather than either tribal age structure or Euro-American time-space zoning. Nonetheless, Arapaho and Euro-American ways of ordering space stand in contradiction. Euro-American forms continue in many tacit ways to zone spaces by function, whether in the home, the school, or the reservation landscape. At the same time, Arapaho people continue to try to interconnect those spaces through social relations.

Summary

Despite the imposition of Euro-American life-cyclical models and changes in Arapaho age structure, there is still a "difference" of tempo, rhythm, and homology between Euro-American and Arapaho life models. Through their different order, Arapaho people define their distinct cultural identity as individuals, families, and tribe. Within the space and time still "owned" by Northern Arapaho practice, age distinctions and some life transition rituals survive. In political, ritual, and educational forums, men and women under the age of fifty are still seen as "too young," that is, too "crazy," to be taken seriously. Elders are still respected, though specific opportunities and practices for expressing that respect have become fewer. Likewise, elders' influence in political decision making has decreased in the past twenty years or so, but ceremonial authority based on age persists. Though social organization, including age structure, has changed greatly, life movement remains the guiding force for Arapaho ritual practice. Ceremonies still seek to effect life movement for the self and others.

Like other aspects of Arapaho culture and language, age structure and life movement itself have become compartmentalized and factionalized in social space-time. Traditional values, representations, and practices of life movement and age structure have been confined to specific places and times surrounded by the milieu of Euro-American, contemporary "Indian," and distinctively modern "Arapaho" elements.

Many of the Arapaho people's comments about their lives and recent history include observations about space and time. With regard to social space, there is some recognition that the seclusion of social life into private domains, primarily family homes, has made it much more difficult than in the past to maintain social ties. Elders contrast the former frequent and open visiting among people with the need-to-call-ahead, closed-door attitude of today. Elders also observe that young people are growing up "too fast," that is, doing things at a younger age today than in the past. And there are those of younger generations who, like the elders, experience Euro-American time as too fast-paced and thus hold it responsible for tensions, conflicts, and personal problems.

Others, following the Euro-American mandate, see the need for "planning" as the key to solving problems on the reservation and thus show little patience for tribal members who have a lax attitude toward "scheduled time." For Euro-Americans working in institutions on the reservation or for some Indian people, the issue of scheduling is still in the center of what they see as "solutions" to the problems faced by Arapaho people. Specifically, they hold individuals, families, and even tribal governments "accountable" for problems that betray "not following a budget, plan, or schedule." There is a self-fulfilling process by which Arapaho students and other people are defined as a "problem" because they do not conform to the Euro-American life time model. The solution to the problem becomes the ground for its definition. In Euro-American society at large, the stratified conditions for the life cycle have long been the basis not of equalizing differences but of reproducing class, ethnicity, and other social distinctions. The latent function has always been antithetical to the manifest purpose. Ignoring local conditions at Wind River, Euro-American-imposed structures to universalize a life cyclical temporalization have never succeeded in total. In short, the structures set an ideal path for life that few can follow by self-initiative alone, as the myth promises. As with all other Euro-American contradictions, an ideal form is imposed that is impossible to replicate given the conditions of the local sociocultural system, which the structures that impose that form have no time or place for.

At Wind River today the conditions are neither continuous in total with the prereservation life movement system nor a replication of the Euro-American individualistic life model. Since the beginning of the reservation period, Northern Arapaho people have continually appropriated and adapted to Euro-American imposed time and, within it, the life cycle. New and adapted traditions depart from past practices but are, in large part, efforts to retain, claim, or reclaim ownership of life movement.

11
Arapaho Knowledge

Knowledge and Practice

In Arapaho society, knowledge has never been just a body of information transmitted automatically or informally from generation to generation. Certainly much enculturation was indirect and informal, but "knowledge" here refers to that portion of what is commonly termed culture that is bounded by socially constituted channels for appropriate transmission, exchange, and practice. As already elaborated, Arapaho knowledge was an object of exchange channeled within kinship relations and an age-graded hierarchy, both of which extended into the realm of other-than-human persons. As for any type of transmission, the exchange of knowledge was structured by Arapaho space-time or, more precisely, by what is referred to here as life movement. Arapaho knowledge was also not disembodied from the lived world prior to action but was transmitted in relations between persons activated through pity, quietness, respect, and craziness. Arapaho knowledge was, in various forms, about the cosmos, metaphysics, and the natural environment, but it was inextricably in and about relations and practice, that is, appropriate ways of acting and interacting in ritual and nonritual contexts. Knowledge was also the basis for both social differentiation, as between age grades, and unification, as in the mythical co-origination of knowledge and Arapaho cultural identity. Exchanges of and for knowledge reproduced the age hierarchy and extended the ties between families, camps, and bands. At any given moment in life, senior age groups exerted power through possession of knowledge and regulated the tempo and channels of its transmission. Only in Euro-American contexts can knowledge be distanciated from concrete practices and social relationships and thus alienated as abstract or universal truth presented to an individual knower.

Within life movement, knowledge was for doing things in a good/correct way, as contained in the Arapaho verb stem *nee'eestoo-* (*nee'ees-* 'right'/*-too-* 'do'), in order to ensure long life for the tribe, the family, and the self. The verb form *nee 'ees-* can be combined with any action verb form, such as *nee 'eesinihiit* 'he/she is saying it right'. The form *nee 'eesoo'* 'it is right' follows all prayers and supplications, affirming the veracity of what is said and the propriety of what is done. Today, in reservation English, informed by pan-Indian influences, Arapaho people often say "in a good way" following any ritual action or narrative. The synthesis of "good" and "correct" thus combines the original Arapaho term with contemporary usage.

Appropriate knowledge ensures appropriate ritual practice, which in turn brings about life movement for Arapaho individuals, families, and the tribe. Conversely, only those people who exhibit appropriate relations through relevant pity, respect, quietness, and even channeled craziness are allowed access to knowledge. It is not so much that increasing knowledge brings one closer to a total view of the world, as in the universalizing aim of Euro-American knowledge, but rather that it contributes to living in a good/correct way and thus to living longer by extending blessings to others.

The ritual, pragmatic emphasis on doing things in a good/correct way within limits is distinctively strong in Arapaho knowledge. Though concern for appropriate practice is characteristic of many North American Indian cultures, Arapaho people themselves, as well as outside observers, have asserted that it is particularly strong in Arapaho ways. Many observers have commented on Arapaho ritual fastidiousness in comparison to what they have seen in other American Indian cultures (see Kroeber 1902,1904,1907; Starkloff 1974; Fowler 1982). It is the basis, for instance, of Mooney's characterization of Arapahos as "devotees and prophets" (1896:775). Accordingly, exegesis, speculation, and self-conscious reflection on religious knowledge are not typically the Arapaho way. Letting one's mind and mouth wander about religious matters is considered dangerous. One should also avoid being ostentatious or boastful about one's knowledge. For example, men who vow for the Offerings Lodge should not divulge what they learn or see in the lodge. In my experience, almost all discussion about religion is directed to issues of preparing and conducting ritual practice appropriately.

Carl Starkloff, who served as a missionary at Wind River in the 1970s and 1980s, observes that this pragmatism is exactly why Arapaho people were attracted to Catholicism: "Magicalism and moralism are both prophetically avoided in Arapaho ritual. Rites are carried out exactly, as the author was told, not out of fear of an angry God, but because things should be done 'just so' out of respect for order" (1971:334). Rather than through the Western primacy of the doctrine or the "word," priority of the "act" is where Arapaho people found a connection to the Catholic Mass and other rituals. As mentioned elsewhere, the "word" as speech itself is encompassed in the Arapaho sense of doing things in a good/correct way.

Another author writing about the missions at Wind River states that during the first half of the twentieth century, the Arapaho attraction to Catholicism was greater than to St. Michael's Episcopal Mission and other missions because "separating belief from the opportunity of worship through some rite or prayer was somewhat foreign to their way of replying" (Hasse 1965:73). Today, despite the decline in the influence of the missions, the Catholic and Episcopal clergy are still called upon more as practitioners to administer last rites, christenings, and funerals than as theologians to espouse or clarify doctrine.

People from other tribes either express great respect for the Arapaho attention to ritual or feel that Arapahos are overly fastidious or even superstitious about details. Conversely, Arapaho ways of speaking sometimes criticize or mock pan-Indian or other tribes' haphazard practices or loose discourse. Much of modern Arapaho identity thus centers on their sense of practice; other, non-Arapaho groups are often perceived as "less careful" or at least are evaluated in terms of the way they do things.

Those who have an anthropological or specifically ethnographic perspective tend to privilege the symbols and meanings behind or motivating practice. The same seems to be true of many non-Indians, who are ever ready to ask "What does that mean?" when interpreting any religion. To Euro-American hermeneutics, meaning is retrieved through interrogation, interviewing, or other modes of discourse that look beyond the surface to something deeper or higher. During my stay at Wind River, non-Indian people who came to visit or do research often expressed disappointment that the Arapaho people did not provide adequate "meaning" in answer to their questions, whereas the Arapaho people had told them a great deal, often by bringing them into their practices. According to the Arapaho perspective, meaning is constituted through practice and the relations activated through it.

That is not to say that Arapaho religion is pragmatic and concrete, for through practice it interconnects many strands of meaning and activates intricate social relations extending beyond the physical world. The concern for doing things "just so," or in a good/correct way, cannot be said to signify a more "concrete" religion, for that would reify the Euro-American distanciation of the sacred as abstract, mysterious, or transcendent. Euro-American hermeneutics of religion tend to place belief, text, doctrine, symbolism, or consciousness prior to practice and view them as motivating action. In Arapaho life movement and other homologous temporal frames, practice is prior to belief and consciousness. As elaborated in chapter 4, for example, young people learned the right way to do things before acquiring a total worldview to explain or justify their actions.

As a further qualification, Arapaho knowledge is not now nor has it ever been a "closed system"; there has always been access to new knowledge as sources of power from outside the boundaries of the society or culture. It was thus not a system for explaining the world in terms of a finite set of premises. In myth, history, and the contemporary context, knowledge acquired from beyond the boundaries of the system could be appropriated within accepted channels. In Arapaho myth and ritual, things beyond current knowledge are ever real but may have the power to do either harm or good, depending on how humans acquire them. The sense of the 'unknown' Kroeber cites as *cee'inoo'*, which he translates, for lack of an English gloss, with the German term *unergründlich* 'unfathomable' (1916–1920). Salzmann offers 'confused' as a gloss of the same stem (1983:69). Containing the same stem, the fringes on the sides of a rawhide bag Kroeber describes as meaning *niitcäantetanani* "what we do not know; that is objects out of our possession, or various things too numerous to mention" (1902:125). In Arapaho practice, the power of this mystery beyond human knowledge and social space must always be respected, for it is the source of life-negating forces; it is never rejected outright, however, for life movement can follow from the new knowledge it brings. Ultimately, it is never possible to encompass all knowledge, for the mysterious realm has "various things too numerous to mention." However, Arapaho knowledge is oriented to infinite possibilities. Life movement continually goes forward into those possibilities.

Knowledge and Mythical Time

From the very beginning of time, knowledge has been acquired from beyond boundaries. Arapaho cultural identity began and endures over the long duration of mythical time by way of knowledge activated through exchange relations with other-than-human persons. The very term for the tribe, *hinono'ei*, derives from a mythically established relation mediated by knowledge, between Arapaho people and the above. The stem *hinono'ei-* is used in a number of noun and verb forms, such as *hinono'eiteen* 'Arapaho tribe', *hinono'eiitiit* 'Arapaho language', *hinono'ei'* 'town of Arapahoe', and *hinono'eininoo* 'I am Arapaho'. Both Mooney and Trenholm translate the form *hinono'ei* as "our people" (Mooney 1896; Trenholm 1970:xvii), its sense at one level, but like many such terms, it has multiple meanings.

In my own enquiries, the most commonly suggested definition of *hinono'ei* associates it with 'digging the wrong root' (Helen Cedartree). In a narrative context, the *hinono'ei-* form is present in *he'ih'iinono'oeno'* 'they dug the wrong root'. There are many ethnopoetic associations in Arapaho, embedded deeply in myth, that may account for the connection of digging to painting and sky in the alternative meaning of the form as "painted sky," cited in chapter 4, which combines forms of *-(h)ono'* 'sky' and *(h)o'oe-* 'paint' (Michelson 1910). As will become clearer, there is a strong connection of "wrong root" to the origins of Arapaho knowledge from the sky.

The sense of "wrong rooters" (Arapahoe Stories 1979) derives from the story that is referred to in many contexts throughout this work, called "The Porcupine and the Woman Who Climbed to the Sky" (Dorsey and Kroeber 1903:321 ff.) or "Little Star" (Dorsey 1903:212 ff.). Two brothers, Sun and Moon, decide to marry earth beings. Moon goes down to earth as a porcupine and lures a human woman up to his home in the sky, where he marries her. At the same time, Moon's brother Sun marries a frog (or toad), who proves to be a "useless" wife. Because she fails a test of her humanness—she cannot chew—the frog jumps into her brother-in-law's chest and there remains for all time.

In a later episode, in one version, the human wife, not heeding the warnings of her mother-in-law and her husband, digs up the "wrong root" and then looks through a hole left in the ground (that is, the sky). Upon seeing her people's camp below, the woman plots to climb down with her son, who was born to Moon, to the earth and, in this way, return to her people. While they are trying to escape, Moon finds them suspended from a sinew rope tied to a digging stick placed crosswise over the hole. He then throws a rock down killing his wife.

The son, Little Star (*ho3o'usoo*: *ho3o'uu-* 'star'/ *-soo,* 'offspring') makes it to the earth below, is adopted by an old woman, and becomes a culture hero. Also known as Found-in-Grass (*bii'oxiyoo*) for where he was discovered, the culture hero brings the knowledge of hunting with bow and arrow to the people, leads the first war parties, learns to "listen" to elders, and serves his relatives well. In short, he brings the "ways of doing things" as responsibilities for defining male adulthood or "usefulness," as acquired in the second stage of life. Here there is a close relationship between the advent of "knowledge" and the acquisition of "adult" responsibilities or becoming "useful" as in the term *heniixonoh'oehiinit* 'he/she is useful, or an adult'.

Lévi-Strauss includes the same myth as a variation of the Star Husband complex that extends throughout North America (1968:199–273). From "above" humans acquired the power for movement of time, for change, becoming, and then life movement. Found-in-Grass is the mediation of "near and far," the offspring of a marriage between a human woman and the moon. He thus provides a kinship link between the people and all of the above (*hihcebe'*) in that he is the son of the moon and the sun his brother and the grandson of the creator, their father. As a result of that link, a timeless darkness was replaced by the alternation of day and night, the seasonal cycle, and passage from mythical time into human time. Arapaho knowledge began, then, with the origin of time. As Lévi-Strauss interprets the Star Husband myth; "before the right alternation of night and day was established, and when dense darkness still prevailed, mankind lived in confusion and without rules. A human had to go up to the sky and be changed into a moon, before absolute night could be replaced by tempered day" (1968:209). Similarly, the establishment of spatial directionality, including the connection to the above (*hihcebe'*) and the trajectory of the sun and the moon, also coincide with the origin of knowledge.

Other-than-human persons have the "power" of metamorphosis: they can appear, as in mythical times, as persons, animals, or in their "original" form. It is that transformative power that is appropriated by humans from powerful beings above through the acquisition of knowledge. For Found-in-Grass it is that power which becomes life movement for the people. As Lévi-Strauss realizes, the transformative power of the day : night : : sun : moon alternation is generated through the events of the Star Husband myth (1968:223). The transformative ability embodied in the sun and the moon is brought back to the people as a result of the woman's "digging the wrong root"; an instance of "not listening" followed by a death or sacrifice brings this power to the people. The periodicity of doing things at the right time also rests on the emergence of light from darkness and earth from water. Following Lévi-Strauss, the origin of knowledge establishes the homology of different levels of space-time, and the beginning of time sets the tempo and periodicity for the transmission of knowledge.

Knowledge had much to do with the appropriate times for holding ceremonies and the timing of practices within them. Certain forms of knowledge could be transmitted only at particular times of the day, the year, and the life cycle. At the center of all knowledge, life movement, and time are practices relating to the sacred Flat Pipe, which is necessary for the survival of the Arapaho people and the earth (Mooney 1896:959). When that knowledge and the Arapaho people cease to exist, the end of this world in this age will come. All tempo and timing of sacred actions and knowledge transmission revolved around the Pipe. Decisions to move the camp were made by the Pipe Keeper, who signaled the time and direction of camp movements by placing the Pipe outside, pointing in the direction of travel decided on by the Old Men, the chiefs, and representatives of the age societies in council (960). When traveling, the Pipe Keeper went on foot, thus regulating the pace of camp movement.

In the seasonal cycle, as well, certain ceremonies could be held only at certain times of the year coincident with observed changes in the natural environment. According to one of Hilger's informants and several Arapahos I have talked to, there was a seasonal order for the men's age-grade societies: "When dances were held, none could do so until the dance of the Spear Lodge had taken place. After they had finished, the Tomahawk Lodge was held, then the Crazy Man's. There was no set time in which lodges had to be held, but they had to follow each other in that order" (Jane Hungry Wolf, in Hilger 1952:123). Much of the knowledge and authority acquired through the age-grade sequence centered on regulating the tempo of ritual and non-ritual practices according to the periodicity of daily, seasonal, and life-cyclical time. As another example, the Offerings Lodge had to be held in the summer, that is, between "when the trees bud" and "when the leaves fall." Dorsey cites a Southern Arapaho informant: "The proper time for the beginning of the ceremony was from seven to ten days after the new moon, and hence an equal number of days after the menstrual period" (1903:22). Women in menses are prohibited from coming near the lodge and other sacred spaces, for the power of shedding blood is original and greater than many medicines.

In mythical time, people who are alone for various reasons acquire knowledge from other-than-human persons, including both animals and sacred beings. At the very beginning, the sacred Flat Pipe was a person, floating on water alone and weeping and crying: "and seeing that he was fasting for good, the Grandfather took mercy [pity] on him" (Dorsey and Kroeber 1903:1). As a result, the Pipe, referred to as "the Father," knew what to do to create land on earth. Shortly after that, women's quillwork originated with Whirlwind Woman (*neyoooxetusei*). In another story, *Nih'oo3oo* gives the Arapahos knowledge of the age-grade lodges (18). Similarly, the Arapaho people acquired the practice of flesh offerings from *hiincebiit* ('water monster', 'last-child', or 'Owner of the Waters') (143). Recall, too, that the buffalo was the source of knowledge about much material culture, such as knives, and the bow and arrow, and ceremonial knowledge, such as the paint kept by the Seven Old Men. Knowledge is thus channeled from the periphery or above to the center through individuals.

In another myth, entitled "The Origin of Culture," three men successively go off alone to fast and "think hard" (Dorsey and Kroeber 1903:7–8). The first man hears a voice telling him how to corral buffalo and horses. The second man acquires knowledge about knives, bows, and arrows. The third man learns about making fire with flint. Elsewhere in myth (17), the first murderer, Woxuhunen (*woxuuhunen* 'Bear Man'), is banished and wanders about crying and making arrows. *Nih'oo3oo* then pities him, giving him buffalo meat to take back to his starving people. The people thereby gain knowledge about eating buffalo, and the murderer is vindicated. In all these cases, knowledge acquired through fasting or other individual experiences is contained in or identified with a particular object. For example, the knowledge for the old people brought back by White Buffalo Woman is embodied in the tallow or fat used in making ritual body paint. The knowledge of hunting is likewise objectified in the bow made from a buffalo's rib.

In Arapaho mythology, the creation of the earth, the acquisition of knowledge, and the origin of religious ceremonies result from the "pitiful" actions of an individual isolated, for various reasons, from the camp. Distant marriage, banishment, and getting lost are among the various forms of isolation in cosmogonic myths, though fasting is the most common (Dorsey and Kroeber 1903:1–8). Frequently, those who bring back knowledge exhibit "crazy" behavior (*hohookee-*) by violating the limits on appropriate practice, as did Bear Man or the woman who dug the wrong root. In the mythical world a degree of craziness was necessary in order to go beyond accepted limits and to meet the ever transforming, mysterious, and powerful forces found there.

All ritual fasting for knowledge replicates the mythical process of weeping, praying, and thinking "hard" through pity in order to receive knowledge as a "gift" or "offering" from other-than-human persons above. One must experience hardship and make a sacrifice in order to compel other-than-human persons, who are "difficult to move," to show pity (*hoowounon-*) and give blessings for life movement and knowledge. For instance, the flesh that buffalo offer is a "sacrifice" to humans in much the same way that human persons "make offerings" to other-than-human persons. In other words, buffalo "pitied" humans by giving them "knowledge" and food. To reciprocate, humans must continue to make offerings and sacrifices

By contrast, it is only in the camp circle, at the center where elders are situated and where the Flat Pipe is kept, that knowledge can be constrained and channeled for the benefit of the tribe. Outside of that domain, it is difficult to keep the power of knowledge within boundaries. When knowledge is brought back to the camp circle, placed in the center and channeled by the authority of elders, it takes on a positive power to promote life movement of the tribe. Knowledge "beyond limits," outside the camp circle and external to the spatial and temporal direction of age hierarchy, is dangerous and threatening. Wandering around alone, like *Nih'oo3oo*, Whirlwind Woman, or other powerful beings, is considered dangerous and crazy behavior, susceptible to life-threatening forces.

To repeat, a core theme in myth is that knowledge must be returned to the camp circle and distributed or "given back" to the people. Specifically, it is required of individuals at the third stage or hill of life that they "give back" knowledge, like material goods. When an individual acquires knowledge outside the camp circle, he or she must return to the people and share it, by distributing it to others or by giving it to the old people. The phrase for stinginess in Arapaho is *ceniiko'ooteiht* 'he or she is stingy', which applies to keeping either material goods or knowledge for oneself. One must share whatever one has accumulated, whether it is comestible goods or other objects of value, not hoard it or keep it away from others, for that would threaten one's own and one's family's life. Individually acquired knowledge and its life-giving power or "blessings" must, like economic resources, be shared in order for all to benefit.

Knowledge from Outside: Historical Context

It was not just knowledge from above that could be appropriated. Following a similar pattern in the history of contact, Arapaho people sought to appropriate selected forms of knowledge from Euro-American society and other American Indian cultures. In a way, this practice parallels ethnography. For example, throughout history it was common for young men especially to set out and wander around in the world, returning years later with knowledge valuable to the tribe. There are adults, well known in the community today, who follow that pattern, returning periodically to visit the reservation. In the past it was also common for Arapaho men and women in general to visit other tribes or places in order to "watch on" and "learn" and then bring the information they gained back to the tribe and to the leaders, who then used it in decision making.

Some Arapaho observers were leaders themselves or were selected by the elders and chiefs to gather information. For instance, Black Coal's trip to Oklahoma after signing the 1868 Treaty at Fort Laramie (Fowler 1982:57–58) led to the Northern Arapaho decision not to relocate to the Cheyenne-Arapaho Reservation in Indian Territory. During the reservation era, Arapaho leaders often traveled to Washington, D. C. to gather knowledge. Such leaders were expected to "bring something back," not only material goods but knowledge, too. In the historical period of the reservation "chiefs council" (the 1890s through the 1920s) and the early business councils (the 1930s through the 1950s), leaders were obliged to sponsor a feast upon returning from trips with federal officials or non-Arapaho tribal leaders. After the feast, the chief or the councilperson would "tell everyone what had gone on" (MaryAnne Whiteman). As in mythico-ritual life movement, knowledge brought from outside was to be shared first with the elders, and then with the other leaders and the people. As described in chapter 4, during the third stage of life, the "age of giving it back," adults were required to share not only the economic resources at their disposal but also the knowledge they had accumulated.

To offer another example, as Mooney relates, Sherman Sage traveled in 1889 with several Shoshones from Wind River to Mason Valley, Utah, to investigate the Ghost Dance (1896:894). Again in 1891, after some growing disillusionment with the movement, Chief Black Coal sent Yellow Eagle, who had been educated in a government school, to observe the Ghost Dance again. Upon return, he confirmed Black Coal's skepticism. By this time, Black Coal had developed a close association with the Catholic mission at St. Stephen's, whereas Sharp Nose's camp to the west continued to follow the Ghost Dance at least until 1892.

There are other cases of Northern Arapahos traveling to other tribes to observe and bring back knowledge. According to Kroeber, the Crow Dance (*houunohwoot*) was acquired through a ritualized intertribal exchange: "The Sioux brought the dance to the Arapaho and other tribes. They brought it in connection with the tceäk'ça^n [*ce'eek(u)3oo*], a sacred bundle offered to friendly tribes, and which, if refused, would cause defeat in war" (1907:368). In another version, an Arapaho political and cultural leader named Yellow Calf is said to have originated the Crow Dance from a vision he had during a serious illness (Fowler 1982:123). Today, the dance is still performed and "owned" at Ethete by Yellow Calf's descendants. In oral history, elements acquired through travel and exchange with other tribes are often appropriated through visions or dreams.

As Fowler's ethnohistory of Arapaho politics documents, men and women with schooling or other experiences in the non-Indian world were, by the late 1930s, chosen to the Business Council (1982:57). Throughout the reservation period, "scholars" of other cultures and languages were also important sources of direction and leadership. A prime example was William Shakespeare, who traveled around the world, studied at universities, and attended boarding schools (see Fowler 1978). People who had wandered about in their youth and then returned in adulthood to the tribe were commonly seen as important agents for dealing with the outside world, for becoming what Fowler calls "intermediaries." It was not unusual in the past for some men of the tribe to be fluent in several Indian languages as a result of having traveled about, living in different places. As they became transculturalized, though, such persons risked being defined as marginal to the traditional center of the culture. They served a necessary role but were (and are) also suspected of mixed loyalties and of possessing potentially "dangerous" knowledge. Those who wander continually can be seen as "crazy" in a sense, as constantly looking for something without purpose and direction.

In history Arapaho epistemology has never been a "closed system." As for the individual person with closed senses, collective closure to knowledge is a form of "craziness" (*hohookee-*). Just as for persons, the group and the tribe must be cautiously "open" to new sources of knowledge from the outside. Innovations and responses to difficult times were necessary and made within Arapaho ways of knowing. Travel, observing, dreaming, and activating relations combined as modes of acquiring knowledge and practices once beyond boundaries. As mentioned in the context of the Ghost Dance, the decision to receive or reject external forms was made through the traditional leadership. Though the influx of outside elements from the non-Indian and pan-Indian world has become a very deep stream, elders still try to maintain control over the most sacred traditions. The quest for new knowledge, then, is not a monopoly of modern Western civilization. Ironically, through culture contact, the Arapaho people have had to learn more about the non-Indian world than the latter has been eager to understand about Arapahos.

The Enclosure of Knowledge

As I have suggested, some knowledge must be carefully placed, contained, and transmitted in space and time. Inappropriate use of sacred knowledge can negate life movement. In myth and ritual, the most powerful life-giving knowledge had to be contained and channeled by elders. Only they had proved by their longevity that they could care for such knowledge and its power. Within such boundaries, life movement was ensured through the proper transmission of knowledge from one generation to the next.

Sacred knowledge itself pertains to ways of enclosing and opening knowledge to others. Specifically, all objects and persons with power must be bundled, enclosed in a dwelling, or bounded in some way. As in many American Indian cultures, personal medicine, quills, paint, sacred objects, and other powerful objects must be bundled when not in use and opened only in carefully prepared and circumscribed places. Much of the preparation stage of ritual involves constructing the proper enclosure, purifying it, and connecting it to other spaces beyond, as in the appeal to the four directions. Lodges, tipis, bundles, and even the bodies of participants had to be ritually prepared for both the protection of what was inside and the exclusion of what was outside. In the age-grade trajectory and the women's quillwork society, the older the group involved and the more sacred the knowledge to be transmitted, the more extensive was the preparation of the space and the layers of enclosure, symbolically represented by coverings, bundles, or bags. The Seven Old Men's and the Seven Old Women's bundles were the ultimate and strictest enclosures of knowledge, associated with the authority of old age. So, too, all of the most sacred knowledge transmitted for the Offerings Lodge is passed on during the preparation phase in the Rabbit Lodge, not in the more publicly accessible ceremonial lodge. Among sacred objects, the Flat Pipe is the most enclosed and protected, for it is the most powerful source of knowledge, life movement, and cultural identity; yet it can be opened in ritual contexts so as to share its power for life with the people (see Carter 1938). Its bundle can be opened or moved only with the most exacting precautions and care that respect can engender.

In all contexts, enclosure serves two complementary functions: first, to care for and protect the object from external threats, and second to enclose and thus protect others from its power. Life-giving objects and persons become life-threatening when their knowledge is taken, released, or disclosed improperly, that is, acquired by those not prepared or in an unsettled, fast, or crazy state.

When one enters a ritual context, then, it is necessary to be calm and not angry or moving fast on the inside. Moreover, quietness in ritual contexts allows for other-than-human persons to hear and listen to Arapaho prayers. Sacrifices and making oneself pitiable in ritual practices aim to get other-than-human persons to "listen" to human beings. Prayers often specifically request that other-than-human persons "listen" (see Kroeber 1904:173). Like the younger person petitioning an elder for knowledge, humans must get other-than-human persons to listen and pay attention through offerings and sacrifices.

The concern for transmission of knowledge constrained by age structure and the value of quietness are often phrased in terms of keeping knowledge within Arapaho boundaries. That control is not only an effort to shield younger Arapahos from access to knowledge but also to keep the knowledge from other-than-human and non-Arapaho persons. As in the numerous *Nih'oo3oo* stories collected by Dorsey and Kroeber (1903) and Salzmann (1980), non-Arapahos and non-Indians are portrayed as acquisitive of Arapaho knowledge. Likewise, other tribes are commonly thought to have stolen songs, ritual practices, social dances, and other cultural elements from the Arapaho peoples. To that extent, older people today often represent the Arapahos as the "mother" tribe, from which all the traditions on the Plains have emanated outward.

The strategy of bounding and channeling knowledge within Arapaho space was reinforced during the early reservation period as a response to Euro-American repression of certain ceremonies, including the Sun Dance. In Mooney's fieldwork in 1892, the agent at Fort Washakie told him that the Ghost Dance was no longer performed at Wind River. Upon visiting an Arapaho logging camp in the mountains, Mooney heard the people say that they had abandoned the Ghost Dance. The first night in the camp, he heard familiar songs over the hill. His interpreter reported that indeed it was the Ghost Dance (1896:809).

My own experiences confirm Fowler's observations that the Arapaho people adopted a strategy toward Euro-Americans of "don't tell them White people about it" (Fowler 1982:244 ff.). Throughout the history of contact with non-Indians, a front stage–back stage orientation toward the white world has developed as a strategy for boundary maintenance. As Fowler records, Arapahos generally presented to whites an image of "willingness to assimilate" in political intermediation while continuing in the back stage to maintain traditional practices, although some practices were lost. That strategy was employed by other tribes as well. The point here is that it was an extension of the traditional boundaries of knowledge in ritual contexts.

At Wind River the issue of keeping certain domains of culture separate from the white world is now a shared and often controversial concern in the Arapaho tribe. Strategies for keeping some things "Arapaho" are still practiced. Ceremonies, social gatherings, and other events are talked about through informal networks of communication, never publicized in newspapers or on the radio. Similarly, researchers and visitors who come to Wind River still receive evasive responses to questions about religion, private life, and social problems. There are also strategies for handling inquiries from people who may not appear genuinely interested. After a few years at Wind River, I began doing the same things myself, without always being aware of it. One strategy is to deny that one possesses the relevant knowledge and then refer the person to someone else who does. An alternative motive behind such a response is respect for others in the community who are older or more knowledgeable about the issue in question.

With contemporary revitalization, sacredness and circumspection about knowledge have centered on the remaining traditions and recently invented forms. As Hultkrantz observed the loss of most of the ceremonies in the *beyoowu'u* complex has placed greater significance on the Sun Dance:

> There are several reasons, both religious and secular, for this secretiveness. One of these, which has increased in importance of late, has been, without doubt, the disintegration of the old, rich religion and

transference of its power to the Sun Dance, which has now become the focal point of the religious and social interests of the people, the center of tribal life and thus, the unifying symbol of the racial will to exist. [Hultkrantz 1952:26]

In the contemporary context, Arapaho religious leaders are vigilant in keeping the Sun Dance within boundaries. Efforts to protect traditions do center on that ritual, where the Arapahos, like other tribes, are careful to prevent non-Indians from using cameras, tape recorders, or videocameras. As a number of people explained, watching and especially photographing or videotaping are ways that things "can be taken away" from the Sun Dance. In contrast with the Euro-American sense that viewing is passive, Arapaho ideas about knowledge link seeing to appropriation.

In the altered space and time of the reservation period, ritual has become more and more compartmentalized, yet collectivized. The directionality and periodicity that once structured every level and dimension of the lived world no longer structure the space and time outside of specialized ritual contexts. With the influence of Euro-American culture and the tendency for Arapaho culture to be objectified in specific forms, the proper placement of boundaries is an ongoing concern.

Maintaining the boundaries of the sacred today poses contradictions for the Northern Arapaho people. On the one hand, since the 1970s the boundaries have shifted with the strong influence of pan-Indian initiatives for revived traditionalism and political self-determination. Those new voices have called for defining the spatial and temporal boundaries between sacred and profane much more clearly and distinctly than in the past. Whereas the age-graded system of life movement once operated through graduated boundaries on knowledge relative to age, there is now a stronger concern with a generic distinction between sacred and profane as the boundary between Arapaho and non-Indian traditions. Therefore, whereas the Arapaho compartmentalization has allowed Christian and other non-Indian traditions into the definition of sacred, modern, more militant voices call for exclusion. On the other hand, consensus about the boundaries has become increasingly difficult to achieve as more and more people and their traditions from divergent family, generational, and even tribal backgrounds are drawn into more collectivized ceremonies. For example, some formerly unsacred practices or new pan-Indian forms enter collective ritual space and time, where they are redefined as sacred. Especially when young people look at the two conflicting trends, that is, solidifying the boundaries and broadening participation, they are confused about what is sacred and what is not or what is real tradition and what is not. When serious questions arise, ritual leaders and elders are still called upon to clarify the boundaries, but their control over the definition of the sacred cannot always keep up with the increasing pace of new traditions and expanding participation in collective ceremonies.

Going to Extremes

The enclosure and protection of knowledge goes beyond the maintenance of physical boundaries to encompass socioculturally constituted limits on the accumulation and uses of knowledge. As elders say today, "things must be done within limits." When knowledge is overused beyond limits, employed for improper purposes, or accumulated excessively, it can become life-negating. Gaining more knowledge through ritual participation or fasting does not necessarily bring longer and easier life for self and kin. For limiting extreme uses and acquisition of knowledge, Arapaho practice has its own principle of moderation or "doctrine of the mean."

A common theme in traditional stories is that one should not "go to extremes" in using or accumulating knowledge. One story told by Paul Moss, entitled "The Eagle," relates how a young man who was going to hunt for eagles consults his grandfather (Moss 1988). Before venturing out, the boy consults his grandfather who tells him to be careful and not to hunt eagles more than four times. The first time the boy returns with an eagle, his grandfather warns him again not to go too far. The second and third times, again the old man repeats his warning, but the boy does not listen and climbs the cliff the fourth time anyway. In the end the eagles carry him off. According to the Arapaho "doctrine of the mean," when knowledge is acquired by individuals who fail to "listen to" and act within the guidance of elders, dangerous consequences follow, such as death, blindness, banishment, or metamorphosis into an animal. The principle is also temporalized, for it limits how many times in his or her lifetime an individual can use a certain power or participate in ritual.

As Martha Woodenlegs explained to me, when someone is "overdoing" anything, the statement *cebtoot* applies, meaning 'he/she is going too far' (*ceb*- 'going beyond a limit'/ *-too-* 'do'/ *-t,* third person singular actor). The term can be applied in everyday conversation to a person who "goes too far" with any type of behavior, including joking, talking, or laughing. In ritual contexts, the term relates to "going to extremes" and thus making dangerous mistakes in practice. Anything beyond the boundaries of appropriateness is linked to "crazy" behavior, a propensity of youth, not listening, and tricksterlike behavior.

In many *Nih'oo3oo* stories, for instance, the trickster acquires a particular knowledge power and overuses it, suffering unwanted transformation or even death (Dorsey and Kroeber 1903:50–121). Of course, *Nih'oo3oo* is immortal and always returns to his original form, but in the process, like other tricksters, he creates and transforms aspects of the world around him. *Nih'oo3oo* typically exhibits an impetuous desire to learn and becomes "greedy" by trying to accumulate more power and knowledge than he actually needs. In many stories he is warned not to use a power or an object as many as four times, a number that defines the limits in Arapaho ritual and myth, as in the eagle story.

One trickster story tells of how *Nih'oo3oo* acquires the power to throw his eyes up into the cottonwood trees and then retrieve them. When a man teaches him the trick, he also tells him "that this is the way you must do it, but not excessively" (Dorsey and Kroeber 1903:50–52). After learning the trick, *Nih'oo3oo* throws his eyes up into the trees and retrieves them three times. On the fourth attempt, his eyes remain stuck at the top of the cottonwood trees. In one version, after trying out the eyes of several animals, *Nih'oo3oo* finally takes the eyes of an owl, while his own eyes remain at the top of the cottonwood trees. In another variation, *Nih'oo3oo* acquires the eyes of a mole, who then becomes blind for all time. The story illustrates a common theme in Arapaho parables: excessive use of any kind of knowledge or ability is dangerous. The "fourth time" is a marker of excessive use of knowledge

The same principle is found in other cultures; an example is the Ojibwe limits on overfasting or accumulating a surplus of blessings (Hallowell 1963b:419). One of the points is that one must not acquire too much knowledge and power for oneself—only what is enough for the good of the family or tribe. One can be as selfish (*ceniiko'ooteiht*, 'he/she is stingy') with knowledge as with material goods. With both one must be generous by extending blessings and goods to others. Overparticipation in ritual activities raises suspicions of self-interest and the associated increased risk of mistakes.

Because of the Arapaho limits on knowledge, the view that individuals should not too anxiously seek to acquire knowledge for personal motives, the term *vision quest* is misapplied with reference to the Arapahos, as several people told me, since the aim, as in other ritual contexts, is to complete a vow by fasting and thus discarding the suffering at hand. Stewart recognized for the related Gros Ventres that the "quest" for individual power was less emphasized than in other Plains cultures because "power of this kind was held to shorten a person's life" (1977:320). Becoming too active in ceremonies or acquiring too much powerful knowledge—at least in the Arapaho case, and perhaps others—implies increased responsibility as a burden on oneself and one's family. Religious practice thus does not make one's own or even one's family's life easier or more sufferable. Rather, it intensifies the responsibility to share one's knowledge with the tribe, heightens the risk of making mistakes, and thus increases the possibility of life-negating forces. To become a ritual leader, then, requires great sacrifice that may shorten one's own life. That may be why older men tried to evade younger men who were seeking them as grandfathers for the lodges (Hilger 1952:121).

When an individual person acquires "medicine" (*beetee-*), there are certain prescribed and proscribed practices that extend to the daily lives of the entire family. For example, any medicine in the house requires that the place be kept clean, that no one walk in and out with anything burning in hand, and that one not come in or out through a window. It was and is especially necessary to keep medicine clean, that is, off the ground and not exposed to defiling elements:

> When a person lived in a tepee, tent, or house, and had a medicine bag, he would go into the tepee, go to the left and get the medicine bag, then go right, and on out the door to the right side of the tepee on to the back. There he would hang it on a forked pole. Then he would clean the ashes. And when you went out to pick up the medicine bag, he would keep going around the house to form a circle then you hang it back up. [Ernest SunRhodes, "Do's and Don'ts of the Arapahoe Tribe," Wyoming Indian School 1979].

It seems that whenever one was cleaning or even cooking, medicines had to be removed from the lodge and placed outside, off the ground on a tripod or forked stick. Medicine, embodied in a bundle or an object, must be "cared for" as a person.

There also were and are individual proscriptions acquired from a spirit helper in a vision. Hilger cites a vision in which a man was told by some being, "We are going to give you power to heal sick people with turtles, snakes, water-dogs, and lizards. You must not harm these animals ever, and you must keep others from harming them" (1952:128). Oftentimes, the animal appearing in a vision is the object of a taboo. Some animals are thought to have harmful medicine. Thus, no one should touch snakes, moles, or some insects. Animals underground seem to have been especially important "medicine."

In some instances, individuals offered medicine "power" were reluctant to accept it or even turned it down. On other occasions, bad medicine was accepted with harmful effects (Kroeber 1907:451). Kroeber's account offers a number of such stories: "An old woman stated that she had once been attacked and bitten by a bear. From that time on, she dreamed much of bears. In one of her dreams, a bear told her to wear bear-claws, to paint in a certain way, and to use certain plants for medicine and incense, and she would become a doctor; but she refused the supernatural gift" (1907:434). Medicine brings added responsibility and greater risk to oneself and one's family: "Sometimes the supernatural power given to a person is bad for his family. The spirit does not mention this to him; but the recipient's family dies off one by one, leaving him alone. Sometimes a man takes such power when he should refuse it on account of the effect on his relatives" (436). When other-than-human persons deceive a human person into receiving dangerous knowledge, the person can be pitied if the knowledge acquired was not the person's fault, that is, if he or she had no way of knowing. Today elders warn younger people to "stay away from things they don't know anything about," because of the same assumption that lack of knowledge for doing things in a good/correct way can be dangerous to one's family. One's life course, then, is a matter of appropriating good knowledge and staying away from knowledge that is potentially dangerous. The distinction is not always clear, thus contributing the dimension of "mystery" or "things we do not know" (*cee'inoo'*) to experience.

During a vision or as a result of some extraordinary life experience, one is "called upon" to take on a burden, which one could accept or reject. As stories illustrate, it is necessary to confer with elders and one's family in the decision to accept or reject the knowledge offered. Others decide whether one is ready. Similarly, in ceremonial contexts elders selected the successors for vacant ritual positions. They would seek out a person worthy to receive such knowledge. There is a parallel here with the traditional model of political leadership described by Fowler (1982): individuals did not actively seek positions of leadership but were chosen by those senior in the age hierarchy. One did not "run" for office but rather followed others, and one did not actively seek ritual knowledge but rather vowed to help others.

In contrast with the Western, egocentric theories (see Erikson 1963:149 ff.) of visions, fasts, or medicine bundles, the acquisition of "power" was, for Arapahos, less a matter of individualistic psychological transformation and reorganization and more a relational source of power for life movement. Fasting and visions did often give an individual a road to follow in life, but that road was part of the person's ongoing relations with other persons and thus not always without confusion and hardship. Moreover, in the Arapaho context, personal "fasts" were not adolescent rites of passage but were reserved for "adults," that is, those in or just entering the third stage of life. In broad comparison, Arapaho fasting was less individualistic than the same practice in other North American Indian contexts. Fasting, like all ritual participation, requires a "vow" to help others overcome difficulty. Acquiring medicine also did not necessarily improve one's life or bring instant life purpose, for it often required personal expense, sacrifices, and an obligation to aid others.

Furthermore, in the Arapaho context, personal medicines were subordinate to the medicines and knowledge in the lodges of *beyoowu'u*, where the traditional order required the mediation of elders or even representation from all intermediate grades in the age hierarchy. In the same way, when one had a vision or a dream, it was necessary to confer with an older person about its meaning and the subsequent actions to be taken. In the age-grade lodges, a dancer's relationship to the other-than-human persons above was mediated by a ceremonial brother from two grades higher, a ceremonial grandfather from three grades higher, and the old men of highest rank. Through such requirements age-hierarchy boundaries were placed on the acquisition and use of knowledge.

To bring the pieces together, adequate knowledge ensures doing things in a good/correct way through sacrifice, within boundaries, and by not going to extremes. From those practices, life movement follows and more knowledge is received (i.e., health and longevity). On the not-so-straight path, improper action based on inadequate knowledge can result in life-threatening circumstances. The value, effects, and limits of knowledge are not given a priori as a substance but are constituted through ongoing practice. It is thus not merely the "possession of knowledge" that promotes life movement, for only in and through exchanging and giving knowledge away does it generate life.

Throughout history, limits and channels for knowledge have adapted to meet changing life conditions, though not without some uncertainty. In the Northern Arapaho community today, elders are concerned that younger people often "overdo it" both in traditional ceremonies and in those acquired in the reservation period. As there are fewer paths for participation than in the past, younger people participate to a greater extent in those that remain, requiring leaders to expand the parameters of appropriateness. Even so, older and younger generations have a different sense of what those limits are. Elders express concern, for instance, that young people who sweat every night are harming their health. Those who take too much peyote in order to have visions are warned that they are going to extremes. Similarly, at one time a man would vow to fast in the Offerings Lodge only four times as the limit; innovation has extended it to seven times, and seven is even regarded as the required number. There is thus an ongoing tension between the new traditionalism and older limits on participation.

Contributing to this contradiction is the infusion into new traditionalism of a Euro-American orientation to knowledge and religion. Namely, young people are told by mainstream culture that knowledge is for the self = person, to be accumulated without limits and with right of access, so that all should share equally. That is not to say that many young people capitulate to this way of knowing, but only to affirm the presence at Wind River of a Euro-American mission of knowledge acquisition without limits.

At another level, Arapaho leaders have opened up remaining traditions to wider and younger participation and have had to allow innovations in order to maintain continuity. The Northern Arapaho tribe, like many others, thus faces the ongoing contradiction, present since the early reservation period, between opening up knowledge to reinvigorate and maintain tradition and staying within traditional parameters to do things within limits.

Ritual as the Exchange of Knowledge

Knowledge for doing things in a good/correct way and within limits was and is activated and circumscribed by an extensive system of exchange. In all ritual contexts, in both the historical and the contemporary context, knowledge has been transmitted from senior to junior age groups and from other-than-human to human persons. The efficacy of ritual actions to bring about long life, health, and prosperity was contingent upon the proper exchange of knowledge. Thus, prayers often request appropriate knowledge to guide ritual action, speech, and life itself. Exchange in ritual practice involves two complementary operations: knowledge and its power must be channeled and bounded, negative elements must be "discarded," that is, offered, sacrificed, or left behind. In the spatial dimension of knowledge and life movement, positive elements must be brought in from the outside and shared; negative elements are discarded or left behind or outside lived social space.

Though knowledge is exchanged as a value, it is not considered a commodity. In the extinct men's age-grade ceremonies and women's Buffalo Lodge, as well as in the extant Sun Dance Lodge, knowledge was and is transmitted through an intricate hierarchy of exchange. As elaborated in chapters 6 through 8, there are a number of general principles for the exchanges in the *beyoowu'u* and the quill society. First of all, grandfathers, grandmothers, and elders in general controlled who received what knowledge and when. It was not a free market open to any purchaser but was contingent upon senior persons' perceptions of the maturity and appropriateness of younger people's behavior. Second, exchanges of goods between grandsons and grandfathers were reciprocally balanced and protracted. Third, as already outlined, the exchange of ritual knowledge extended far beyond the relation of grandfather and grandson, for a vow activated extended-family cooperation, camp contributions, gifts to the oldest men, and relations to other-than-human persons above. Knowledge flows down the hierarchy, not just between grandfather and grandson but through all levels. Reciprocally, compensation flows up the hierarchy, such that no one should really accumulate "value," only transmit it upward and outward. The whole system of ritualized exchange activated all levels of the age hierarchy and interfamilial exchanges and extended into the other-than-human realm. Accordingly, all ritual participants are in fact intermediaries on behalf of someone else or some other group—the pledger for a relative, his or her family for their kin person, grandfathers and grandmothers for pledgers, and the oldest people for the good of all.

For acquiring knowledge about various types of "medicine," however, the exchange pattern was dyadic, less extensive in space, and shorter-lived in time, though likewise governed by limits and appropriate practices. Outside of the *beyoowu'u* system, some men and women possessed personal knowledge that allowed them to cure one or several particular illnesses. Such knowledge could be acquired through fasting or other states from an other-than-human person, and "sold" to others thenceforth (Kroeber 1907:450–54; Hilger 1952:136). As Kroeber mentions, fasting was not the only original source of power. "The appearance of the spirits takes place in waking visions as well as in dreams" (1907:450). Indeed, one could be visited by a spirit while going about daily activities or just falling asleep. The point is that knowledge was not always actively sought.

The original owner of such knowledge could pass it on through exchange. That applied to plant medicines as well. Sherman Sage related to Hilger, "One time I paid a horse for knowledge regarding some herbs" (in Hilger 1952:136). One of Hilger's Southern Arapaho consultants described the process:

> When I was about 30 years old, I took lessons from a great medicine man called Black-Man. He is dead now. I still use his medicines. He knew medicines with which to cure people. I took between 20 and 30 lessons from him. I had to learn each lesson separately, one at a time. Each was different and each had different songs. When applying the medicines today, I sing the songs and shake a rattle and follow the old man's instructions. [1952:136]

Though such exchanges, unlike the *beyoowu'u* system, did often create an ongoing teacher-apprentice relationship, they were not part of a wider system of exchange in the age hierarchy. The same dyadic relationship applied to various other forms of knowledge and roles, such as drum-group leadership, shield and arrow making, various art forms, camp crier, and some ritual leadership positions.

Knowledge and Sacrifice

As an extension of exchange, all ritual contexts involved "giving away" or a "sacrifice" to beings above in order to effect life movement and acquire knowledge. Cleaver Warden relates the mythical foundation of sacrifice and offerings:

> Remember that when the father was giving the elements to his daughters in law, this act of cleansing the spirits was spoken of, in other words flesh was commanded. Haw sa nai [*hoosonei??*], Hawsey yaa [*hoseiyoo'*], disposing of article [sic] bad for lucks or trouble.
>
> When a man sacrifices a red blanket or a moon shell, he disposes them to his Gods in place of his death or death of his relative. It is like giving the heart to god for salvation and also means the consecration of the person. When a woman disposes her fingure [sic] (one joint) she saves her relative from death. It is a payment of respect and love to the duties by grown people. If I remember well, a man who disposed of a piece of calico was in the camp circle and held a stick which had this piece of calico (like a flag) or stood there facing to the rising sun. All the young children went and touched this calico, rubbed themselves with that spirit. [Dorsey and Warden 1905:Box 2, Folder 7 1/2]

This passage is fascinating for a number of reasons. First of all, Warden identifies "flesh" (*hoseino'*) as the original sacrifice and associates it with *hoseiyoo'*, which means sacrifice or offering. Flesh itself or a symbolic equivalent in cloth or shells was commonly offered in many contexts in order to effect life movement, though acquiring knowledge was not the prime motive. In one sense, buffalo offered meat and hides as a sacrifice to humans in mythical time. In another, women and men offered sacrifices of flesh to ensure the health of family members. Further, hanging pieces of cloth for offerings represented "pieces of flesh" for the person who was the object of a vow. Hilger also associates the *hosei-* form with the hides and blankets given by Sun Dance grandsons to their grandfathers and other ritual agents: "The term, hasa'a, is thought to have originated in the custom that at the Sun Dance each dancer had lying before him, while dancing, a pile of tanned hides or robes. The hides or robes were his gifts to his sponsor, to the drummers and to others" (1952:149). The form *hosoo-* and the related *hoseii-* form are thus linked to offerings of flesh, hides, or cloth. Cloth is still used in covering the Flat Pipe (see Carter 1938) and for "prayers" hung on the rafter poles of the Sun Dance Lodge each year. Children's clothing was also hung on the lodge, on sacred trees, and at water places associated with Water Monster. Cloth also predominates in gifts to older persons for their services. The hanging of cloth, according to the reference in the Warden account, is based on identification with "flesh," such as the meat hung to dry on the racks outside the tipi or pieces of flesh sacrificed during times of grief or stress.

Semantically, the *hosei-* root connotes 'discarding,' which ties a number of terms together with *hoseiyoo'* 'offering' and *hoseino'* 'meat or flesh'. Dorsey translates *hoseino'oowu'* as 'Offerings Lodge', but it could equally be called 'sacrifice lodge' or 'throwing away lodge'. The *hosei-* form is used in a number of common expressions, such as *hoseikuuti* 'throw it away!' and *konoutoseii'*, the traditional term to refer to the town of Ethete which means 'shedding from the body away' and is somehow related to the term for Round Dance, once performed in the Ghost Dance. At one point in the Ghost Dance, women would shed their blankets and shake them in the air to drive away evil influences (Mooney 1896:921).

Kroeber also cites the concept of "offerings" in describing an event during preparation for the Sun Dance:

> On the morning of June 16, about sunrise, all the children, it was said, were brought to touch a piece of calico which had been "given away" or sacrificed (haseiyaa) [*hoseiyoo'*] to the supernatural beings (tcäyatawunenita^n, [*ceyotowunenitee*] untrue person), and was now being held out toward the east. The man who "gave away" this cloth sacrificed it on account of his wife who had been sick. After the children had all touched it, it was hung up over the door of the largest tent in the camp, which was at the southeast of the camp-circle. . . . The man "gave away" considerable property, and furnished food. Other people also contributed. The gifts were made to old men. [1907:283-84]

In general, this passage shows the connection between "sacrifice" and "giving away." After an offering is made, the object used can extend its blessings to others as can the offerant through a final giveaway. Sacrifice to an other-than-human person (*ceyotowunenitee*) is thus associated with and followed by extending the blessings to others, especially children, through touching and, finally, "giving away" food and goods to others to similarly radiate life movement outward. In time, giveaways came to follow any ritual sacrifice or period of suffering, as release from the burden carried and a way of extending blessings to the camp and the world. The giveaway also culminates a long period of collecting enough goods or money to hold the ceremony. The farther the goods extend, the better. Thus, it is especially good to give to strangers or visitors.

The discarding of material goods as offerings is thus connected with giveaways. Giving away to human beings in public contexts is referred to by a different term, *neeceenohoot*, translated as "chief gives away" (Kroeber 1907:168). Despite the distinction, though, giveaways to human persons are always done on behalf of someone else. It is interesting to note that the offering of cloth is also related to the predominance of cloth goods in "giveaways" sponsored by families to recognize an achievement of a living family member or to memorialize a deceased member. Blankets, quilts, dishcloths, towels, cloth for sewing, and floor rugs are the main objects in a modern giveaway. As in all contexts of exchange, the old people recognized to receive gifts must come first, usually in order of age. Until recently, too, cloth objects offered to the Flat Pipe were given away by the Pipe Keeper at the end of the Sun Dance or Pipe Covering ceremony. In general, "giving away" to others and making offerings to other-than-human persons are both part of the "sacrifice" for and the "discarding" of suffering.

Giveaways today occur at feasts, funerals, powwows, Peyote meetings, dances, and any social event. The purpose is to honor a family member, either as a memorial to a deceased kin person or to mark an achievement or a transition in life. In other words, giveaways are ostensibly on behalf of others, to compensate those who have helped the kinsman, family, or tribe. In the past a giveaway was more obligatory in certain prescribed situations. Today, giveaways are more voluntary, although some degree of obligation remains. Nonetheless, the aim of a giveaway is to disperse property horizontally; the giveaway is, in a way, a "sacrifice" or a discarding, much like the vow to participate in rituals.

Offerings to other-than-human persons are continuous with giveaways and gifts to old people. To illustrate, offerings were made to *hiincebiit* (Owner of Waters or Water Monster), who lived in rivers and springs, such as Manitou

Springs, Colorado (see Ruxton in Trenholm 1970:127). To ensure long life and safe passage across water or safe travel over land, offerings of cloth, hides, shells, and other goods were left hanging in trees nearby. Older Arapahos living today recall their parents or grandparents leaving offerings at springs and beside rivers.

Offerings to other-than-human persons often consisted of objects of value common in giveaway and intertribal trade, especially cloth and shells. Along with horses, both were considered objects of value for exchange outside the boundaries of the camp circle. In historical time, money has replaced shells as an offering. In fact, the Arapaho term for money, *bei'ice3eii*, combines the terms for 'shell' (*bei'i,*) and 'metal' (*-ce3ei*), thus suggesting historical continuity.

Sacrifices and offerings are also made to sacred objects, regarded as persons with spirits enlivening them. Offerings of cloth or shells are left to the sacred Flat Pipe during the Pipe Covering ceremony (see Carter 1938). In daily life, offerings of food had to be given to any ritual or medicinal object in the house or lodge. As long as such objects were fed and cared for, they continued to be life-giving and provided knowledge.

The sacrifice of flesh itself was also common in the prereservation period. As in some other Plains cultures (e.g., the Cheyenne), women commonly sacrificed the first joint of a finger to assure the health of a sick relative or so that a brother or other male relative would return from battle (Michelson 1933:609–10; Hilger 1952:141–42). Men also often vowed to have small pieces of flesh removed in order that a family member would recover from illness. It was common as part of mourning practices for women and occasionally men to sacrifice flesh, either by gashing their legs, having a specialist remove one joint of a finger, or removing a specified number of pieces of flesh from the arm. The flesh sacrifice in mourning was intended to guarantee the safe passage of the deceased to the afterlife (Hilger 1952:228).

The discarding of flesh, the shedding of blood, and the offering of goods are all also related to "fasting." The movement of flesh or material possessions out away from oneself is the other side to fasting, that is, not bringing sustenance to oneself. In the process, one may receive knowledge from other-than-human persons that can be channeled into life movement.

In terms of life movement and knowledge, offerings and sacrifices aim to avert threats to life and, in the end, allow bad forms of power and knowledge in people's minds to be left behind. Rather than attaching irreversibly to the person, as in the modern Euro-American construction of personhood, traumatic events and the knowledge associated with them are allowed by Arapaho practices to be discarded, left behind in the past. Of course, that does not mean forgetting, but rather the placement of suffering in the past or out of lived social space. To paraphrase what a number of Arapahos explained to me, "We get it all out and then leave it behind us. Then, we get on with our lives."

The power of that theory of ritual practice endures and cannot be overstated. Such discarding, though, is at odds with the mission of Euro-American knowledge to preserve all of the past and of life history, to attach all past traumas to the self. In Arapaho memory, there is reluctance to relive past traumas experienced by oneself or a group for present political or psychological purposes. One can talk about such events, memorialize the kin involved, or even feel sorrow or grief, but the bad elements of suffering itself must be left to the past.

It is interesting that the Christian concept of "forgiveness" is phrased in terms of the "throwing away" concept in Arapaho. An old translation of the Lord's Prayer into Arapaho renders 'forgive', as in "forgive us our trespasses," as *cih'oseihii* 'throw it away, set it aside' (Sifton 1908). Thus, the aim of Arapaho ritual practice is to 'leave behind', 'drive away', or 'set aside' bad things but not really to eliminate them or seek "forgiveness" from an other-than-human person. In the logic of Arapaho life movement, nothing difficult or harsh is ever negated as a reality once and for all but is "put somewhere else" at a distance. That is why it is necessary to be careful in distant places or when one is alone; such things are scattered about on the human plane of experience. Therefore, young people were instructed to leave unusual things alone when traveling about.

In all ritual practice, then, some things are thrown away while others are carefully bundled. In some lodges grandfathers passed on their regalia, whereas in others, some elements must be left behind. For instance, the bows and arrows used by the dancers in the Crazy Lodge were thrown away, though the medicine was kept (Kroeber 1904:189). It was not uncommon that things that had been in contact with medicine or had been used in ritual contexts were discarded. Incidental to the contemporary context, that raises some concerns about ritual objects, currently in museums, which were originally "discarded" by their owners. Some objects, including any powerful object for which no knowledge is available, should, in the traditional way, not be "preserved" but "thrown away."

Bundling and discarding are two complementary movements in the same process. Anything that has the power to produce long life is bundled, enclosed, and placed at the center. In birth practices, whereas the afterbirth is discarded, the navel, the center of the person, is kept and bundled. The umbilical cord produces long life, but the afterbirth does not, because of its association with blood and "sacrifice." As elaborated in chapter 5, naming practices exemplify that bidirectional process, as well. After overcoming a life-threatening situation, a name may be discarded by its owner, who then picks up another name. Another person, recognizing the power of the name to overcome misfortune, may "pick up" the discarded name. The younger person who picked up a discarded name could expect it to bring him or her up to the age of the older person. An adult would take an elder's name to ensure that he or she, too, would reach that age.

People who have been able to endure and discard life-threatening experiences receive greater knowledge and the ability to extend life-giving blessings to others. Warriors who have the power to overcome misfortune can give their power to others through ear piercing, naming, telling war stories, and other means. After a man or a woman leaves the Sun Dance Lodge on the final day, he or she shakes hands with others outside. Touching a person who has endured hardship is a blessing. It is considered good for children to take them into the lodge after the final dance, for the power of longevity and health still lingers in the lodge. Recall that in the passages quoted in this section, children also touched the cloth used as offerings. To complete the process, then, once discarding and bundling have been done, all blessings must emanate outward through touch, gifts, feasting, and even shared joy.

Knowledge, Art, and Ritual Objects

As mentioned at several points throughout this work, one focus of Arapaho knowledge is the production of ritual objects. That concern permeates all aspects of the Euro-American sense of "art," for which Arapaho has no all-inclusive term. The production and use of aesthetic forms and objects is what traditional Arapaho knowledge was for and about, from women's quillwork to body paint and regalia for the *beyoowu'u*. Art, life movement, and knowledge are thus complexly interrelated. Clark Wissler comments on a uniquely Arapaho pattern of injecting significance into practice:

> The attitude of the Arapaho toward all important matters impresses observers as even more devout than that of most Indians. They extended symbolic thinking to many everyday acts; for example, when a woman did some beadwork or painted a skin bag to beautify it, the designs she used were given names suggesting hidden meanings and

sometimes ideas of deep religious import. [Wissler 1956:93]

Kroeber (1902:150) recognized that some Arapaho art forms require ritual practice, have ancient origins with mythic beings, and can originate in dreams or visions, and other nonritualized art forms also contain sacred elements and references. See the discussion of women's quillwork in chapter 8. Even a seemingly mundane, utilitarian object such as a parfleche had mythical symbolism. The geometric and representational forms of Arapaho art were part of the literate-like "language" transmitted through the channels of age-structured learning. Through art one learned about myth, ritual, cosmology, dreams, and what Sapir calls "form-feeling," the sense of connectedness and vitality carried in forms. As such, an object's knowledge was not contained iconically in it, that is, as separate from the practice of producing and caring for it. In Arapaho practice, knowledge was, more than perhaps any other thing, a set of parameters for producing and reproducing movements, shapes, designs, rhythms, and forms. Art as practice tied the maker to the forms and invoked relations to other-than-human persons.

The production of sacred objects was always either part of a larger ritual context (e.g., the *beyoowu'u*) or was itself a ritual process (e.g., quillwork). Each preparation phase for a ritual also had an instructive function. Younger people apprenticed to ritual leaders learned the appropriate procedures, such as songs, prayers, designs, colors, and paint forms. In ceremonies, the production of paraphernalia was as important as the actual performance, if not more so. Kroeber describes two phases of ritual in the Offerings Lodge: "The division of the sun-dance agrees exactly with that existing in the age-company ceremonies, in which there is exactly a three-days' period of preparation, more or less private or secret, and a three-days' period of public spectacular performance" (1907:303). The production or reproduction of ritual objects and the transfer of knowledge for that production were usually done within the boundaries of an enclosed space. It was not so much an effort to conceal or hide knowledge from others as an effort to control the "power" that such knowledge carries. Those who are uninitiated or unprepared can potentially be harmed by access to highly sacred knowledge. Children in particular were and are always kept separate from such areas and all other things that have the power to generate or threaten life.

Along with seclusion, the actors required a quiet, undisturbed space so that other-than-human persons petitioned for guidance could "listen" to the prayers and so that the human persons preparing the objects could listen to them. As a wife of a ceremonial grandfather was about to make the digging stick for the

Offerings Lodge, she voiced the following prayer:

> Now, please, old man, be merciful to me! I am about to cut the
> digging-stick in proper length. I have laid everything aside, because I
> took pity on the Lodge-Maker, my grandchild. Although I do not know
> the method of cutting this digging-stick, may I do the act in harmony
> and sympathy with our Man-Above, in order that the great
> understanding my be easy and light for all. [Dorsey 1903:55]

The petitioner makes objects out of pity for the lodge maker, the one who first
vowed and is the principal sponsor of the lodge. The prayer focuses on several
of the core principles discussed here about receiving right knowledge for
making the digging-stick. The appeal to pity for an easy and light undertaking
through prayers to the above focused on the production, care, exchange, and
discarding of ritual objects. In the historical context, the Southern Arapaho
Offerings Lodge was performed at a time when many of the participants were
uncertain about the performance and preparation for it, since it had not been
performed for a number of years and many of the old people with the
appropriate knowledge had passed away.

Objects produced for or through ritual were also considered "gifts" from
above. In the beginning, the knowledge to make them was given to the people
by the creator or some other powerful being. While making a lance for the Spear
Lodge, the maker prayed, saying: "This lance is a gift from the father to the
people. It is not made by men themselves, but is made as the father directed that
it should be made" (Kroeber 1904:176). As in quillwork, the painting of dancers
for the lodges, and many other contexts, art was directed by older people who
were in turn guided by other-than-human persons. Through art, knowledge
flows from past into present, from above directly into human practice, and from
internal experience into objective form. Indeed, it is this connection that is
distinctly Arapaho: art is the center and the continuity, more perhaps than
symbols, myth, and ritual performance itself.

Preparation also transformed ordinary materials into sacred objects with the
power to generate life movement. In the Sun Dance described by Dorsey, the
robe for the lodge maker had to be revived: "With the ceremonial killing of the
buffalo, the life-element is transferred to the hide; this life element is renewed
or revivified as the hide is passed over the incense" (1903:71). Sacred objects
and artistic forms were enlivened or revitalized by the same methods used for
healing or purifying persons, that is, through smudging and the sweat lodge.

Objects themselves could also be sources of knowledge. Once an object was completed it could have the power to speak or create images in one's mind. In fact, the "object" could convey knowledge even before it was made. As Kroeber describes, artistic designs often came from "dreams" or visions; thus, the objects embodied the power of the vision or dream. Parallel to Speck's observations for the Naskapis, the power of a dream only becomes beneficial for the individual when the dream is represented symbolically. Similarly, Speck mentions that art objects were used to induce visions or for divination (Speck 1935:159).

There is evidence for that in the Arapaho context, as well. Cleaver Warden's notes contain several examples. One time while visiting a woman's tipi to discuss art with her, he noticed a rawhide bag coming "alive" and moving. A Southern Arapaho named Scabby Bull mentions that his shield often warned him of approaching enemies (Dorsey and Warden 1905:Box 1, Folder 2, File 2:203). As long as the object was cared for in the proper way, the spirit would stay in it and provide ongoing knowledge and life. That is not to say that such objects were iconic relics worthy of awe and worship but rather that they had life that needed to be cared for. In probably almost every Arapaho tent or cabin in the pre- and early reservation period, there were living articles that required such daily care and attention.

Apparently some objects were used for instruction, too. One story mentions a painted record of all the lodges used to instruct men in their performance: "The painted record of the lodges was kept until forty-one years ago, the narrator said in 1899. Then the old man, of the tciinetcei bähäeiha^n [the Seven Old Men], who was its keeper, lost his wife and buried it with her. When this became known there was much talk, and it was said that the tribe would decrease, as indeed they have" (Dorsey and Kroeber 1903:19 n. 2). The story relates that *Nih'oo3oo* gave the painted record of all the lodges to a man the camp had previously shunned for murder. Knowledge contained in the record was thought to ensure the abundance of buffalo and the increase of the people. Sacred objects contain knowledge that contributes to life movement but can also be threatening if proper care is not taken.

Why one of the Seven Old Men buried the record is unclear, but the incident is the earliest available reference to burying an object containing sacred knowledge with a deceased person. When a person died without passing on knowledge, objects embodying that knowledge could be buried with him or her and thus discarded. During the reservation period, written documents relating to a person's life were also buried. From various informants I have heard of more recent incidents of sacred or at least powerful objects being buried with the last keeper. Other powerful medicines had to be taken far away, perhaps into the mountains, if the knowledge had not been passed on.

In general, Arapaho ritualized art production, care, and ongoing personal relations were about and for transmitting knowledge so that people could do things in a good/correct way. Very simply, process carries knowledge as much as the product does. Ritual efficacy depends on preparation as much as on performance, and the ongoing care of objects was related to artistic practice, either as products or instruments. Knowledge thus diffused through the objects made, the persons making or caring for them, and the entire life movement of both "things" and persons.

Knowledge and Ways of Speaking

In the traditional context of knowledge, speaking was likewise channeled through all dimensions of doing things in a good/correct way. Child-rearing practices, storytelling, leadership, ritual preparations, and everyday interaction were to various degrees constrained by limits to ensure the veracity of speech. Hilger mentions the strong emphasis placed on truth telling in early childhood. For example, parents pressed children to offer proof of their actions in an effort to curb boasting:

> Children didn't boast very much. But if an Arapaho child came home and said, "I caught a fish," or "I found a turtle," the mother or father would go to see if it were true. If a boy said he caught a rabbit, the father or mother would go to look at it. If it was his first rabbit, the father would take a stick and break it—the stick represented a pony—and call some person by name to come to see the rabbit. This person might not be present, but the announcement that the parent had made would eventually travel as news to the proper person. This person would then come to the child's house to get the horse . . . . This was the first important event in the child's life of which he spoke the truth, and much was made of it. [1952:102]

In traditional child rearing, children who had reached the age for instruction were taught that lying and stealing were the worst things to do. Sherman Sage, one of Hilger's informants, said, "When I was about 10 years old, my father said, 'Don't ever steal or tell lies'" (1952:103).

In traditional stories for children, one of the moral lessons is that lying, boasting, and deceiving are dangerous to life. The recurring trickster character

Nih'oo3oo lies or deceives in almost every story in order to get food, marry a woman, steal powers from others, or win a contest. Deception is part of *Nih'oo3oo*'s morally ambivalent or crazy (*hohookee-*) power, which can be creative or destructive. It is the power to transform, to metamorphose not only himself, but also animals, humans, and other beings. On the one hand, *Nih'oo3oo* created humans; but on the other hand, he created "death" for humans (Dorsey and Kroeber 1903:13ff). He taught humans how to maintain "life" but also created death. The lesson he instilled is that what one gains by deception or lying is reciprocated by a payment of "life."

In the past, other-than-human persons and forces also maintained conditions of truth. Ritual pledges ensured felicity of speech as much as they secured commitment to a future sacrifice. One method was to smoke the pipe: "Smoking this pipe was like taking an oath" (Hilger 1952:103). A man could thereby lend illocutionary force to his statements in a public context. In the extreme, one could take an oath before the Flat Pipe to swear one's innocence against accusations:

> When there is any serious question pending before the tribe, or a case of adultery or bigamy, the accused can come forward and swear in the name of the Flat Pipe, that he is innocent: "I do solemnly swear in the name of the Flat Pipe and that he hears me, I did not do it. In the name of the Flat Pipe—and that Thunder—that He-ne-che-beet (Water Monster) that does lie along the streams, I do tell the truth. If people used any of these oaths for falsehood, something would befall them, some sort of punishment, either by sickness or accident. [Dorsey and Warden 1905:Box 2, File 2:2–3]

In a competitive storytelling game for men, Kroeber states, "a pipe passed around and smoked during the contest serves to cause the truth to be told" (1907:319). For another context, "in recounting deeds of war (as is frequently done on ceremonial or social occasions), men told the truth, because if they lied they would surely be killed by the enemy" (1902:23). Other evidence suggests that when chiefs spoke, they could take a truth medicine, which would ensure veracity by threat of illness. Just as prayers often request that actions be done in a good way, supplications and public speeches are often framed at the outset by a concern that one's words be true.

Ways of speaking were also framed by context, function, and assigned roles. Only particular persons (e.g., ritual leaders, elders, drum leaders, chiefs, medicine men, etc.) had the right to perform forms of speech that deviated from generally expected behavior. Camp announcers could travel throughout the camp speaking loudly about recent and upcoming events. Disciplinarians could speak sharply to control children at public gatherings. Crazy Men could say the opposite of what they meant within the lodge performance. Likewise, one could joke more freely with some kin than with others. Other forms of discourse could be performed only in ritual contexts. Moreover, only certain persons, ritually prepared, were allowed to "listen" to sacred knowledge, such as that conveyed in myth. In the life cycle, as well, only certain knowledge could be imparted to persons of particular ages. For example, only the oldest people had access to the most sacred oral traditions.

As traced in earlier chapters, one's ways of speaking, along with one's personhood and knowledge, changed as one moved through life. Authority over knowledge and the power of one's speech increased as one moved into the fourth stage of life, although one's own speech became less frequent and softer. In interaction, younger people had to sit quietly and listen to seniors. Interrupting or correcting older people was considered unthinkable. "Respect" (*neeteenebetiit*) required deference to the authority of seniors' statements. That pattern persists today, but in increasingly narrower contexts, as discussed in chapter 12. Within the family one must always vote with and agree with one's grandparents, lest one be shunned or lectured. In tribal meetings, ceremonial grandsons must never disagree with their ceremonial grandfathers. Furthermore, when ritual leaders make a request or a statement, all tribal members must acquiesce, especially if the leader speaks from the authority of the Flat Pipe.

As Fowler implies, elders also eschewed divisive discourse or statements that bound off one group or faction from the tribe (1982:261). As in the past, elders today try to "talk to" people who seem to be making false statements or divisive claims. When divisiveness emerges in a club, a committee, or a family, older people try to heal the conflict by talking to the people involved. In a culture dependent on the oral transmission of knowledge, the control of speech and narratives can be as efficacious as the so-called objective standards of Euro-American literate knowledge, or more so.

Knowledge for doing things in a good/correct way thus precedes and encompasses speech. In general, as with naming, vows, prayers, blessings, speeches, and other forms, language has the power to effect long life and health. Traditionally, when conducted within the appropriate channels, speech could generate life movement for the self, the family, and the tribe. Mistakes or lies could result in the opposite, that is, illness or other misfortune. In the social context, controls over ways of speaking were the ground upon which tribal solidarity and identity were sustained.

Summary

Arapaho knowledge was both bounded by and transmitted through doing things in a good/correct way (*nee'eestoo-*) in order to promote long life, health, and well-being. In practice constituted by or through exchange, art, limits, speech, or sacrifice, objects, knowledge, and life movement were thus so intertwined as to be indistinguishable. Objects gave and embodied knowledge and thus could generate life movement. Life movement brought knowledge, and knowledge was needed for generating and guiding life movement as well as for producing and caring for objects.

Knowledge, like other powerful things, had to be carefully bounded or discarded in order to promote life movement. Ritual action was thus about regulating the spatial and temporal parameters of knowledge. Only those with the right level of maturity could have access to certain knowledge. In space, the most powerful knowledge had to remain in the center with the oldest persons. Negative elements and knowledge had to be left behind in time and pushed to the periphery of space. Knowledge was also transmitted and acquired in and through a hierarchical order of exchange, involving all age groups and other-than-human persons. "Knowing" was thus inextricable from interpersonal relations; it was not an experience for an individual standing alone before the world. Within those relations, though, acquisition of knowledge and its power to generate life movement required sacrifice and offerings, that is, enduring a life-threatening situation, offering flesh or material goods, or fasting. As a result of placing oneself in a pitiable situation, one could expect that other-than-human persons would listen to one's prayers and offer life movement and knowledge that could then be extended to one's family and tribe. The process of discarding and bundling knowledge and its power was ongoing, however, because of "all of the things unknown" that practice must ever be open to. Powerful knowledge introduced into experience could thus be avoided or appropriated. In the historical context of culture contact, Arapahos attempted to situate Euro-American knowledge within proper boundaries and maintain a proper separation of elements in reservation space-time.

12
Euro-American Knowledge

The Imposition of Euro-American Knowledge

Beginning with the treaty period of the 1850s to the 1860s and enduring throughout the reservation period, Euro-American society has claimed dominance in direct and indirect ways over the construction of knowledge and thus has maintained spatial and temporal distance from local Northern Arapaho knowledge. Euro-American knowledge as power synthesizes what Giddens (1987:153) recognizes as "distanciation" and Fabian (1983:31) terms "denial of coevalness." Namely, colonizing knowledge exists and is validated somewhere else than the here and now of real social relations, yet it invalidates local knowledge as dissynchronous with its own contemporary reality. The mission of Euro-American institutions of expropriation and assimilation has been to construct a universal system of knowledge ostensibly in order to negate, encompass, and transform local systems. However, universalization has never been a completed project, because it is durably distant from social relations in local contexts, in which Euro-American knowledge operates only in specialized places and times. Throughout the history of contact and into the present, the vast majority of relations between Arapaho people and Euro-Americans have taken place in the narrow social space and time of formal situations and political economy. From early on, the Northern Arapaho, like other indigenous peoples, recognized and adapted to this by applying strategies specific to those domains of intercultural communication.

For different reasons, Arapaho local appropriation of control over knowledge has likewise never been totalized and complete, because Euro-American "knowledge" has generated enduring contradictions for the Northern Arapaho tribe that boundary maintenance strategies cannot resolve. The contradictions with and within Euro-American knowledge are real to the Arapaho lived world at all levels. They are not merely academic or abstract formulations accessible only to an outside view. They infuse what individuals talk about, think, and do. Collectively, every issue facing the tribe today involves efforts to reclaim its ownership of knowledge—ownership that has been denied the Arapahos by the invasive Euro-American bureaucracy, literacy, and formal education. Certainly disfranchisement from land, reservation economic dependency, and political dominance are all "real" conditions in reservation history, but an insidious, largely tacit epistemological colonialism has been the durable instrument for all those conditions.

Based on knowledge at a distance that creates contradictions locally, government policies have consistently and chronically generated outcomes different from the original intent and beyond the control of any political system. In short, colonization becomes a power beyond the control of the colonized *or* the colonizers. However, the contradictions simultaneously serve Euro-American interests, provide the ground for local resistance, and limit the extent to which the Arapaho people can claim ownership of knowledge and power.

While presuming to be universal and rational, Euro-American knowledge generates power beyond its own control through real, lived contradictions. One of the most powerful mechanisms of Euro-American domination has been the concealment of interests behind the veil of assumed rational, practical, or empirical truth. Thus, Euro-American knowledge claims to be rational, empirical, and progressive, but it imposes itself locally as raw self-interest, irrationality, fixed opinion, and repetition, to which local forms must continually adapt and readapt. It is not valid to term such knowledge "ideology" or "hegemony," because it is "knowledge" and power given as contradictions and inconsistency. Euro-American society has never totalized a coherent and consistent legitimating ideology for the domination of North American indigenous peoples.

As outlined in the chapter 11, Arapaho knowledge of and for life movement is and has been in ongoing contradiction with Euro-American knowledge. Within that dialectic, the former has always stood to the latter in an asymmetrical relation such that it has had to try to "know" and adapt to Euro-American knowledge more than the latter has had to know it. In short, Arapahos have had to "know" whites more than whites have had to "know" Arapahos. Within that relation, the Northern Arapaho people have attempted to appropriate and compartmentalize Euro-American knowledge, which, in opposition, has sought to universalize itself while maintaining distance. The contradiction is that Euro-American institutions based on presumed superior knowledge have sought to assimilate and integrate Arapaho people without actually knowing them. A product of this contradiction is that problems generated by Euro-American knowledge are reified as inherently "Indian" or "Arapaho," based on the assumption that confusion or contradiction within the local culture is the generative source. Therefore, specialized and sequestered Euro-American schools, agencies, offices, and programs today have little if any understanding of the real conditions of the Arapaho lived world, yet they continue to propose and activate solutions based on the supposition of superior knowledge of those conditions. Rather than making local systems rationally effective and efficient, Euro-American knowledge reproduces structures that are irrational and inefficient for the Arapaho people.

Increasingly, Arapaho society internalizes that contradiction. For example, contemporary tribal government aiming for self-determination must administrate with the instruments of the very knowledge forms that have for so long restricted self-determination. Once entangled within Euro-American knowledge, real sovereignty may be less possible today than it was in the past through Arapaho ways of knowing. All local actions and decisions become inextricably entangled in bureaucratic knowledge that emanates from documents, agencies, and persons somewhere else, such as in Washington, with no direct social presence on the Wind River Reservation. The ongoing problem for past political intermediation and true self-determination today is how to gain control of knowledge locally.

Similarly, knowledge transmitted through formal education "happens" in other places removed from the real social world experienced by Arapaho children (Noriega 1992:374). From the beginning, Christian missions promulgated a mythico-ritual order with a history and a "story" thousands of miles away. Up to the present, formal education is held up as the solution to all social problems on the reservation, despite the fact that, like other Euro-American-based organizations, it knows nothing of local realities. Concurrent with attempts to achieve political self-determination, recent efforts to reinvigorate Arapahoe language and culture have also appropriated the knowledge forms of Euro-American formal education, thus using the same tools that have been used and are now used to effect assimilation. So, ironically, the traditional culture, history, and language taught in schools are now often placed in another space and time removed from lived culture and everyday speech.

The anthropological solution to all these contradictions has always been a mission to open and broaden Euro-American knowledge of American Indian peoples. Like the other projects that have been mentioned, that effort has been unfinished. Local non-Indian people at Wind River today probably know as little—if not less—about the Arapaho people as their ancestors did a century ago. More extensive engagement in Euro-American knowledge does not necessarily produce greater intercultural awareness. What I discovered through participation in various outreach programs is that well-educated non-Indians are often as ignorant of the local context as anybody else, and at times they are more resistant because of their arrogant confidence in knowledge they have acquired hundreds or thousands of miles away in an academic or professional institution. Those who know the least often have the immediate and presumably self-evident solution to the "problems" on the reservation. The consultants who review grant proposals, evaluate local programs, or visit to offer their expertise give advice in their first sentence. Some tourists who arrive on the reservation know everything about Indians before or within minutes after their arrival. While proselytizing about the value of education, most teachers and school administrators employed in the reservation schools drive into and out of the Arapaho community each day with little or no knowledge of the tribe's history, culture, or contemporary context. The same pattern applies to bureaucrats and professionals working for federal agencies or service institutions, as well as to missionaries, itinerant researchers, and other non-Indians who come to the reservation with knowledge-power that closes their minds and eyes to immediate realities.

Several constraints follow from these contradictions. First of all, Euro-American knowledge, articulated in top-down, bureaucratic forms, can never be totalized in local systems of knowledge. State-centered knowledge and power, however totalitarian—as in early reservation wardship or total institutional structures—cannot control all spaces and times. As Deloria (1994:104–9) points out, Euro-American knowledge seeks universality through history, its durable and transposable trajectory of time, yet fails to encompass all spaces, including the local lived world.

Second, Euro-American knowledge begins with the individual oriented to a massive totality containing authority and knowledge. Idealized Western epistemology since the Enlightenment is founded on the juxtaposition of the individual in relation to the totalized market, society, nature, nation, or God. Whether as the reader of a text, the Protestant believer facing God alone, or the person confronting bureaucratic authority, the individual knower facing a given massive world stands before a monolithic "authority" or "truth" that exists "somewhere else" in distant or abstract space. Truth ostensibly purports to free the individual from the tradition, the community, and the culture but, when subjected to critique, disempowers the individual before an even more empowered law, economy, text, library, God, rule, nature, or rationality.

As one example, literate forms become documents with persevering utility and anonymous truth value. Most importantly, they formalize a relationship prior to social practice rather than liberating the individual knower. Texts created by humans are estranged from and then exercise power over them. Through a parallel contradiction, literate knowledge enlarges the cultural universe, offering seemingly infinite possibilities for intellectual inquiry, while at the same time generating alienation (Goody and Watt 1972:340). The world, society, and God become much larger than the lived world of the individual can contain. Literate knowledge proposes a dialectic estrangement between the liberation of the "individual knower" and the shackles of tradition but offers nothing in place of tradition. The individual stands alone with no time and place, no real culture.

Western society continually defends the ideology that its "knowledge" has, throughout its long-term history from classical times to the present, had a liberating effect on knowers that in turn has led to progress as the collective accumulation of "epistemological wealth." That ideology is the basis of democracy, of a liberal economy, and of all ontologies predicated on the rational individual as a "self" experiencing an "object" world, a concept that, as Mauss (1985:20–23) has traced it, is unique to the last century and a half of Western thought. Idealized philosophies and principles of law, politics, economics, education, and health care are built upon a person=self=consciousness that also "liberates" knowledge from social relations and the collective "mind," which presumably distort or resist "truth."

That most pervasive of contradictions is at odds with the traditional Arapaho pattern by which all knowledge is acquired through relations among persons and individually acquired knowledge must be, like accumulated goods, shared with others. Knowledge must be extended outward to others in order for life movement to occur. It must be exchanged within the parameters defined by respect, pity, and other interpersonal relations. Senior persons and other-than-human persons must mediate the relationship of the individual to knowledge.

Third, the Euro-American self realizes itself within an order of life cyclical time borrowed from history as progress, evolution, and development. The individual life trajectory in schools, economy, politics, and religion recapitulates the chronotype of History as an irreversible progression toward greater knowledge and expanding consciousness. To that end, the day, the life, and history must be rationally ordered and phased. As discussed in chapter 2, the locus of knowledge becomes the isolated individual moving through time rather than the individual related to others in social space. Euro-American organizations at Wind River continue to impose those assumptions about knowledge in ways, ironically, that the agents themselves cannot bring into consciousness about their own practices.

This chapter explicates several contradictions of Euro-American-imposed knowledge, along with Northern Arapaho ways of perceiving and adapting to them. First examined are Arapaho categories and meanings for defining and expressing the contradictions of non-Indian "knowledge." Second, the discussion turns to literate knowledge at the center of Euro-American knowledge and the lived contradictions it imposes. Third to be examined are some of the contradictions internalized in Arapaho politics today that have evolved from the shift from traditional modes of knowledge to what older Arapahos call "white man's ways." Fourth, the contradictions resulting from literate-based Euro-American knowledge and internalized in Arapaho politics will be illustrated through brief examination of the imposition of tribal enrollment criteria. Finally, Arapaho adaptations to imposed knowledge are revealed in the ways elements of the early Christian missions were appropriated in Arapaho terms and compartmentalized within social space-time.

Nih'oo3oo and Knowledge

Knowledge has always been at the center of the historical and contemporary definitions of identity distinctions between Arapaho and non-Indian people. The relationship and the contrast between the different ways of knowing have in turn informed Arapaho strategies in practice to maintain the boundaries between the Arapaho knowledge defined as "tradition" and the acquisitive "white world." Throughout the history of contact, Arapaho people saw Euro-American society as not only acquisitive of material wealth and land but of "knowledge" as well, thus violating the Arapaho teaching that knowledge must not be hoarded or sought too eagerly. Tourists, journalists, "wannabes," and researchers are all subject to the criticism that they try "to take something away" without giving something back to the community—especially when they do not form enduring social relations with the Arapaho communities. When knowledge is acquired about the Arapahos, it is indeed taken away as commodity-like forms severed from social relations. Euro-American knowledge seeks to appropriate all local knowledge to be placed "somewhere else" as artifacts bounded in texts, photographs, picture frames, or museum cases. As in many regions of Indian country, much discussion at Wind River today revolves around concerns with past and present non-Indian uses of Arapaho knowledge and how to assert some control over them.

Aspects of the relation between Arapaho and Euro-American orientations to knowledge can be illuminated through linguistic evidence for and mythological behavior of the trickster figure *Nih'oo3oo* originally meant 'spider' and was eventually extended to 'non-Indian person'. Beyond those glosses, it has multiple meanings interlinking myth, history, and language. One element of the term, *nih'oo-*, connotes a 'segmented body', as if something was tied around the waist or the neck. The form also occurs in the words for other insects such as *nih'ooteibeihii* 'butterfly' and *nih'ooceihii* 'grasshopper'. Those uses relate to terms for tightness (e.g., *niih'oo'* 'it is tight') and tautness (e.g., *nih'ooteeyooni'* 'it is taut') (Salzmann 1983). The terms for spiders and insects and the set of verb forms thus share the connotation of tying tightly. It is plausible, then, that at first contact the physical appearance of whites, with belts around their waists, gave the perception of a 'tied-waist being', like a spider. There is explicit reference to this sense of *Nih'oo3oo* in Dorsey and Kroeber (1903:7) as "slender or narrow-bodied."

The extension of the term *nih'oo3oo* from spider to non-Indian person also has other explanations. One association common to American Indian conceptions is that between the hairiness of spiders and the hairiness of the white men first encountered. Another one, often heard among Plains Indian cultures, is that settlers built fences as spiders weave webs (Arnold Headley). That is a possible etymology, but it is hard to imagine that Arapaho first contacts would have been with settlers building fences. First contacts were more likely with traders, explorers, and miners passing through the area.

The most pervasive connection centers on the cleverness and unpredictability of *Nih'oo3oo* as a spider and a trickster in traditional stories. The character *Nih'oo3oo*, now equated with white man, recurs throughout traditional Arapaho stories (Dorsey and Kroeber 1903:6–7; Salzmann 1980). He demonstrates "crazy" behavior (*hohookee-*) by wandering around from place to place, being overanxious for knowledge, practicing uncontrolled sexual behavior, and "going to extremes" in his use of knowledge/power. In short, *Nih'oo3oo* is "contrary" to the Arapaho concepts of desirable personhood, life movement, and knowledge. He is not "bad" in a Euro-American moral sense, however, since he can be a source of creative, life-giving power.

That power shared by the trickster and whites is an expression of craziness. Making the association explicit, one Ghost Dance song contains the line *hohookeeni3i' nih'oo3ou'u* 'whites are crazy' (Mooney 1896:972). A related belief is that white people exhibit "crazy" behavior because they do not keep their navel cords as Indians do; thus "they are always looking for something." As described in chapter 5, Arapaho infants' navel cords were (and are) placed in reptile-shaped navel bags and preserved throughout life (Kroeber 1902:54–58; Hilger 1952:24). Loss of the bag results in wandering or snooping behavior, such as getting into other people's things or even stealing, all in an effort to find the lost bag. Possession of the navel bag ensures a straight direction for life movement, as opposed to the crooked, crazy behavior of both the trickster *Nih'oo3oo* and modern day *nih'oo3ou'u*, or non-Indian people.

In a parallel way, Arapahos often perceive whites and even non-Arapaho tribes as acquisitive of Arapaho cultural knowledge. Drum groups comment today that groups from other tribes "steal Arapaho songs." There is a common belief that non-Arapahos, and non-Indians in particular, appropriate knowledge and then use it for personal profit or prestige. For every anthropologist or other researcher of the past two or three decades, there is a story of "taking" knowledge away and profiting from selling books about the Arapahos. Within the reservation community the same apprehension encompasses tribal members who use cultural knowledge for profit on or off the reservation, which is a growing concern for many tribes. Thus, the sense of appropriate uses of knowledge has extended to the issue of "commercialization," of profiting financially in the Euro-American world from knowledge taken away by anyone, Arapaho or non-Arapaho alike. What this speaks to is the Euro-American reduction of knowledge to a commodity, which, once "purchased," can be "taken away" and used for whatever purpose the owner desires without activating a relationship with the original source. In Euro-American contexts, knowledge is convertible into money, whether through careers, marketing, consulting, or outright purchase. Internalized within the Arapaho community, money has come to predominate as a medium of value for the exchange of knowledge, such as through consulting fees, payments for ceremonial services, or salaries for professional positions in tribal administration, education, and social services. Some view that trend critically, whereas others now identify it as an obligation continuous with past traditions of knowledge exchange. The exchange of money for knowledge has generated a number of contradictions that confuse the boundaries of what is acceptable. As in so many reservation communities, money and culture stand opposed. Historically, the Northern Arapaho people adopted a strategy of increased caution and secrecy about their cultural knowledge in response both to efforts by agents and missionaries to prohibit traditional ceremonies and to the more recent trends toward commercialization. From the beginning, whites wanted to eliminate and collect culture at the same time.

For the Northern Arapahos, the mechanisms of bounding knowledge based on age distinctions have been extended to non-Arapaho knowledge and also have been determined by the concern about commercialization. As discussed in chapter 11, Arapaho sacred knowledge was kept hidden from Euro-American perception during the period of government and mission suppression, much as the knowledge of initiated groups is kept securely bounded off from immature and uninitiated persons. For example, at the Arapaho Offerings Lodge today, all recording devices and cameras are prohibited and all things associated with the lodge must be "left behind" and discarded when the ceremony is over. Photographs, sketches, videotapes, and the like are thought to "take something away" that should be left there. Moreover, sacred ceremonies and even social events are still not widely publicized, since doing so would carry a sense of commercialization.

On the outside, Euro-American researchers, voyeurs, and spectators continue to arrive at the reservation with the assumption that all knowledge is available to them; when they are faced with Arapaho formal or informal barriers, they react as if their "rights" have been violated. A central contradiction is that Euro-American epistemology idealizes free access to all knowledge as a "natural right" yet restricts access to serve interests of power, wealth, or status. To some extent that hypocrisy has been internalized as a concern in Arapaho society, at times making it difficult to distinguish self-interests from traditional forms of knowledge control. Thus, an individual withholding knowledge within traditional limits can be accused by others of holding it back for self-interests. People involved in language and culture programs tied to external sources of support can also be accused of exploiting tradition for profit. One view merges the Euro-American ideal of democratization with traditional values, maintaining that all traditional knowledge should be shared freely by Arapaho people. Conversely, people motivated by self-interest can present their efforts as being based in traditional limits on knowledge exchange. Yet another view that has emerged in recent years speaks from the pan-Indian context of tribal sovereignty and self-determination to protect "intellectual property rights." Deriving from education in American Indian policy and current human rights issues, that view also ties in with the Arapaho sense that knowledge relating to culture, language, history, and the arts should be kept within the tribe, or that "we should do it on our own." In general, the knowledge controversy is about boundaries that are no longer as clear as they once were, whether traditional, for material gain, for power, or to protect what are now called "intellectual property rights." Defining which of those motives is involved in any particular situation is not altogether salient. The contradiction between knowledge as private property and Arapaho traditions of knowledge through traditional channels has led to many arguments and even conflicts at Wind River. Those who try to keep knowledge for themselves or attach their names to it in Euro-American individualistic ways can be subject to criticism.

Other contradictions abound in identity relations defined by knowledge. Euro-American knowledge is proposed as rational, linear, democratized, and well scheduled, but Arapaho experience perceives the non-Indian world as crazy, crooked, restricted, and unpredictable. While the former has the manifest intent to universalize itself and thus integrate all people, its latent function has been to maintain separation and distance over the long term of contact history. Within Euro-American knowledge the driving contradiction has been between democratic ideals and the realities of controlled access for self-interests. Within Arapaho society today, the distinction is unclear and problematic between knowledge that should be freely shared and knowledge that should be controlled within traditional limits. Accordingly, the boundaries between Arapaho and Euro-American knowledge and associated practices are no longer clear and distinct.

Literate Knowledge

All of the contradictions in relations between Arapaho and non-Indian society are evident in the imposed literate forms of knowledge and the practices that surround them. From the Euro-American perspective, the absence of American Indian literacy has served as the basis for a perpetual distance between the cultures. As Goody and others recognize, the "us versus them" dichotomies that have abounded in anthropological and sociological discourse since the nineteenth century can be reduced to an epistemological difference, phrased as "literate versus oral knowledge." In the case of Northern Arapaho society, "literate versus nonliterate" as a basis for "Euro-American versus Arapaho" has been irrelevant for a century. What all such oppositions conceal is the multiple contradictions that have endured from the first moment of contact to the present. The boundaries are no longer clear and distinct, but the contradictions that literate knowledge reproduces persist.

There is still a stereotype from a Euro-American perspective that identifies American Indian peoples as nonliterate, or at least as unsophisticated in the use of literate knowledge, yet possessing oral knowledge infused with truth of another sort. That is, the image of nonliteracy informs both noble and ignoble stereotypes. Educators still presume that a lack of literacy is the barrier to social and personal "progress." Researchers still arrive looking for "oral" knowledge as primary. For a very long time, perhaps longer than for some families descended from European immigrants, the Arapaho people have been literate and have realized that literacy is necessary for the continuity of the tribe and life movement of individuals. After more than a century of Arapaho engagement in literacy and formal education, the dichotomy of literate versus nonliterate no longer applies.

The mission of universal literacy in the nineteenth century was to integrate, individuate, and equalize individuals and cultures. That was evident in the arguments for the prohibition of native language instruction in government-sponsored Indian schools in the 1880s and the 1890s, including St. Stephen's and St. Michael's at Wind River. The boarding schools were founded on the capacity of English fluency and literacy to transform Indian peoples into individual knowers and thus "citizens" (see Atkins 1887). Since the beginning of the liberal philosophy of the eighteenth century, literacy through formal education has been defined in Euro-American political culture as the medium for the individuation of the self in the life trajectory and, transposed to history, as the vehicle of "progress." Held self-evident in liberal education has been the power of literacy to dissolve the ignorance of the disfranchised and thus empower them—with the requirement that they be separated from traditional modes of knowledge. Therefore, nascent in the "liberating mission" has been the presumption that traditional knowledge forms are barriers to freedom, upward social mobility, and personal progress. In reality, the power of literacy to "liberate" the world has always been overstated, even to messianic proportions. For the Arapaho people and most other indigenous peoples, literacy has never achieved its promised goals, because of the persevering contradictions latent in literate knowledge and its associated practices, which Euro-American knowledge itself cannot recognize reflexively.

A basic contradiction is that what was liberating at home provided a means of colonization elsewhere. The Euro-American appropriation and accumulation of almost all forms of value (e.g., land, resources, and money) were and are enacted and sustained through literate forms. Rather than offering self-realization and collective liberation, then, literate forms have, for a long time, been perceived by American Indian peoples as obfuscation and deception concealing economic and political exploitation. Indigenous North American peoples quickly became aware that written forms of knowledge are the principal medium of Euro-American power, justifying slavery, conquest, relocation, allotment, assimilation, and termination. Accordingly, most of North America was conquered by paper rather than physical force, which itself was often justified by written mandate. The Mdewakanton Dakota chief Little Crow responded to the use of deceptive treaty strategies on the part of Minnesota traders and federal officials in 1858 "It appears you are getting papers all around me, so that after a while I will have nothing left" (G. C. Anderson 1986:103).

In time, rather than seeing literacy as a means of preserving and accumulating knowledge, American Indian people realized that it could be used as a way of forgetting, of putting the knowledge, encoded on papers, somewhere else out of sight and mind. Throughout history, Arapaho leaders had to remind government officials of written treaties, agreements, and other documents of the past.

The problem was not, of course, the "power" within the paper or the words, but rather the practices surrounding literate knowledge for the purpose of constituting and sustaining particular forms of relationships. Therefore, the wording is often in contradiction with the resulting relationship. For example, the use of a treaty to map spatial boundaries and set time limits for land cessions placed Euro-American society in a dominant rather than the ostensibly equal contractual position. Even though at the time the U.S. government recognized Indian sovereignty, its conditions were defined by the political, epistemological criteria of the Euro-American culture of literate knowledge.

The vast majority of social, political, and economic relations between non-Indians and Arapaho people have been defined by literate forms and the practices they require. Imposed from outside, literate knowledge has functioned as the most durable form of power for defining boundaries, entitlement, eligibility, indebtedness, and credentials, as well as many other less obvious facets of personhood, culture, and history. At Wind River, many forms of literacy practices have served the function of control, whether through the existence or absence of papers for the tribe or individual members. The history of control is a history of one type of paper or its nonexistence defining subsequent policies, actions, or even conflicts. When they arrived at Wind River in 1878, the Northern Arapaho tribe had no treaty recognizing their shared title to the reservation. The absence of such a paper defined the course of fifty years of Arapaho political action to gain that title. After the first census records of 1885, tribal rolls have been used to codify tribal identity and control access to resources. Based on those rolls, papers for the allotment of lands in severalty to individuals were distributed in the early 1900s. Following from that, the probate process and its paperwork defined inheritance or disinheritance of allotted lands central to the history of family ties to the land. From those initial literacy practices, many others emerged or proliferated.

Literacy has thus served to maintain an asymmetrical relation of dominance between the Northern Arapaho people and Euro-American society. In Northern Arapaho history and in the present, non-Indian institutions claim, through literacy and accordant practices, control of the construction, transmission, ownership, and preservation of knowledge. It is a power exercised through schools, the federal government, state agencies, universities, museums, and financial institutions.

Arapaho strategies of resistance against Euro-American power have also involved and often required literate knowledge. Rather than universalizing knowledge, literacy has been appropriated in distinct ways in each culture. Initially, the Arapaho people placed the new form of knowledge within the traditional parameters of power. The Arapaho people, like some other tribes, understood very early in the history of contact that Euro-American power was asserted in and through "paper," that is, literate knowledge, to control the practices of both Euro-American people and Indians. From some historical documents and linguistic evidence, the initial interpretation of "paper" was an extension of Arapaho *beetee* 'power'. An early Episcopal missionary recorded a story about Arapaho chief Medicine Man's understanding of the "power" of documents:

> The missionary was told the way in which the famous Medicine Man received his "diploma from the powers of the air." He heard a voice calling him from above. Stepping outside his tipi, he saw a paper floating down toward him. This paper . . . was reportedly shown to the soldiers when they attempted to make Medicine Man move his people to Indian Territory. It was so powerful that they had to grasp it firmly while it was being read. Through the magic of its words, the officers said no more to Medicine Man about moving south. [Trenholm 1970:276]

Although the missionary's account probably overstates the mystification involved, literate forms did become an extension of traditional empowered forms rendered on two-dimensional surfaces. In the Arapaho language, written forms, including paper, books, and documents, are encompassed by the form *wo3on(o)hoe-,* which can function as a root for verbal or nominal constructions (e.g., *wo3onhoenoo* 'I am writing'). A piece of paper or a book is called *wo3onohoe* or, in the plural, *wo3onhoeno'*. The root *wo3on(o)ho-* is derived originally from the art of painting designs on a two- dimensional surface, as described by Dorsey and Kroeber (1903:19 n. 2). Although Arapaho geometric art designs, as on rawhide or wood, were not "literate" forms of knowledge in Euro-American terms, Arapaho culture established that connection early on. The act of painting or the product is part of an animating and empowering process. Painted, quilled, or beaded forms had power over a person's health, mind, and perception. Cleaver Warden recounts the effects of a quilled tipi disk that he watched Fire-Wood make:

If I am not mistake she was making a day tipi which has more yellow quills. Whether by constantly eyeing the design or disc and glancing at her suddenly caused the strange vision I could not say, but even viewing other objects seemed to picture out alike;- that is there were rays of those colored discs on everything in the tipi, for the sun was shining brightly then. Since then I have had trouble with indigestion. [Dorsey and Warden 1905, "Material Culture: Tipis": 11]

In a broader sense, Arapaho adaptation to literacy was an extension of the traditional process of knowledge appropriation from outside the camp circle, as discussed in chapter 11 in the section titled "Knowledge and Mythical Time." In contract to some other Plains tribes, which resisted the mission schools, both the Southern and the Northern Arapahos were generally receptive. Through reading and translating Christian texts, Arapaho "converts" found confirmation for what they had already believed, not a new doctrine. Such texts were also appropriated within Arapaho concepts and practices, such as the Our Father, which I treat elsewhere (Anderson in press).

For Arapaho elders and leaders, it became clear that learning to "read and write" was crucial knowledge for dealing with Euro-American power. During the early reservation period (the 1880s through the 1920s), leaders encouraged the mission schools so that their children could learn to read and write and thus gain some control over the relationship to the non-Indian world. Sherman Sage recalled that by the early 1860s, Arapaho leaders in the Denver area showed a willingness to send children to school: "The settlers asked Bear Claw, the chief of the Arapahos who were camped near Denver, to send the Indian children to the whitemen's school to be educated, and the Indians did so" (Toll 1962:3). Shortly thereafter, two horse thieves were shot down in Denver. Seeing the lawlessness of a frontier town, Northern Arapaho leaders decided that Denver was not "civilized" as advertised, so they withdrew their children from school and left the area. By that point in history, then, Arapahos began to realize and adapt to the contradictions of Euro-American culture.

Their commitment to schooling continued, however. Much of their interest probably derived from the model of Chief Friday. On a Friday in 1831, Thomas Fitzpatrick discovered a boy abandoned after a battle and raised him for a time in St. Louis. The boy returned as a young man to the Arapaho tribe in Colorado (see Hafen and Ghent 1931; Trenholm 1970:117; Fowler 1982:40–41). Eventually, Friday, known as the "Arapahoe American," became a principal figure in Northern Arapaho history as a band leader and interpreter for all crucial councils, treaties, and meetings with the federal government. He was thus a prototype for a new type of leadership carried forth into the twentieth century. His ability to be schooled and then return to Arapaho ways, even becoming leader of his band, was evidence for leaders that Euro-American knowledge could be appropriated by the tribe. Though the impact of the knowledge he "brought back" is difficult to measure, it no doubt informed leaders and elders about strategies they could use in dealing with Euro-Americans, strategies even extending beyond reading, writing, and English fluency. For instance, Elkin notes that Friday "continually counseled his people not to join the other tribes, pleading that they were powerless against the unlimited resources of the invaders" (1940:229).

At the Wind River mission schools, Chiefs Black Coal, Lone Bear, and Yellow Calf carried on the strategy of appropriating literacy and fluency for use in intermediation with the non-Indian world. Black Coal and later Lone Bear visited St. Stephen's School classrooms regularly to urge children to learn to "read and write." Similarly, elders from the Ethete area recall that Yellow Calf walked up and down the rows of desks at St. Michael's Mission School encouraging students to learn to read and write (Helen Cedartree). The Arapaho strategy, based on Friday's example, was not complete willingness to be totally assimilated or converted, but an effort at that time to appropriate literate knowledge within traditional authority. As Fowler (1982:177 ff.) mentions, the Northern Arapaho elders recognized the importance of educated intermediaries by the 1920s.

As I argue in chapter 10, the attempt to appropriate literate knowledge through education has not been without contradiction. Educated Arapahos, like educated members of other tribes, were somewhat marginalized, as they sometimes are today. Such leaders as Chief Friday, Scott Dewey, Nell Scott, and William Shakespeare were all school educated and instrumental in intermediation with Euro-American society, yet they were never placed in the center of Arapaho cultural identity. Chief Friday's band, for example, was always set off somewhat from the larger, dominant bands. Though he was a leader of his band, his authority was subordinated to the traditional order. From Friday's time forward, educated Arapaho people served important social, political, and economic roles but were ever suspected of being too close to the "white world."

Transculturalized Arapaho leaders were able to traverse the distance not only between two languages and forms of knowledge but also between the associated cultural patterns of speaking. As Elkin observes, Arapahos tend to see "the White man as too outspoken and aggressive," whereas non-Indians tend to read Arapaho passivity as "readiness to fall into a submissive rôle" (1940:247). The best example of an Arapaho who could function in the Euro-American world, as Fowler recognizes, was Nell Scott, whom elders selected for the council in the traditional way in 1937 in large part because of "her forceful personality and her ability to intimidate verbally both Indians and non-Indians" (1982:183). Those with education and literate skills thus could be more aggressive and assertive in intermediation with Euro-American authorities. Yet that ability at times was incongruous with Arapaho patterns of respect and quietness. What emerged was a new but circumscribed role of educated interpreter-spokesperson that took its place alongside the traditional occupations in Arapaho society (e.g., camp announcer, scout, disciplinarian, etc.). Literate-based education and the modes of expression it inculcated were—and still are—both inside and outside the boundaries of traditional knowledge exchange.

The same ambivalence extends to literate texts themselves. Documents engendered Arapaho caution and mistrust of the federal government and white society in general as the Arapahos became aware that non-Indians justify their actions on the basis of documents but at the same time ignore them for the expediency of economic gain or political power. Ironically, despite the "critical mind" supposedly inspired by literacy among Euro-Americans, the Arapaho people are generally less blindly accepting of the knowledge contained in books, documents, and papers than are non-Indians. In the Euro-American view, though, such skepticism is often received as simply a "lack of education" or weak literacy skills. Educators, bureaucrats, and even researchers tend to accept literacy practices without question, even if they can critically read the content; they therefore fail to grasp Arapaho perspectives and uses of literate knowledge.

An indigenous critical approach to documents has shaped Arapaho history at significant junctures. For example, much of the Northern Arapaho vote against the Indian Reorganization Act (IRA) in 1934 was based on their suspicion of provisions contained in earlier treaties and agreements that had not been honored up to that point in history (Fowler 1982:173–74). Since the Northern Arapaho and Eastern Shoshone tribes voted against reorganization in the 1930s, several groups have made unsuccessful attempts to establish a constitution and by-laws. Rather than perceiving a written constitution and by-laws as a charter for effective and consistent political practices, as the enduring liberal democratic perspective would hold, some Arapaho people see such written laws as offering only loss of local control through weakened traditional forms of leadership and decision making. From the converse perspective, the IRA threatened the Bureau of Indian Affairs to some extent, so the BIA simply took control of the constitution as "text" by supplying tribes considering reorganization with a "model" constitution, based on the assumption that the tribes lacked the expertise of "literate" knowledge to construct such a document. The authority of Euro-American literate knowledge rests on its claim to universality and durability through separation from the flow of concrete practices. Rather than seeing progress and continuity through literate forms of problem-solving, Arapaho leaders feared loss and disruption, especially of traditional ways of doing things. That concern survives in the present. Throughout the 1980s and the 1990s, efforts and referenda to pass a tribal constitution and by-laws all failed to gain widespread support. In making decisions and choosing leaders today, the Arapahos are still concerned that formal education and literacy practices are necessary but not sufficient conditions. They have a place but are not the entire field for politics. A perspective I heard expressed often was that school-educated leaders have not been any more effective or less corruptible than those with strong ties to tradition.

Throughout reservation history, literacy has been appropriated for local purposes. One of those is apparent in the use of literacy for traditional and new cultural forms. For example, letters from and to Wovoka figured significantly in the Arapaho Ghost Dance (Mooney 1896:780–82; Dangberg 1957). Also, though texts were marginal to Arapaho involvement at the missions early on, they did serve as vehicles to appropriate Christianity in Arapaho terms. And personal files and family archives became central to conceptions of inheritance and family continuity. (Such documents are difficult to study, however.)

Ethnographic research also offered texts to be appropriated as tradition. Dorsey received many requests for copies of his work on the Sun Dance and by 1940 Hilger documented Arapaho use of ethnographic texts:

> On both reservations informants and interpreters were acquainted with published works on the Arapaho. The day following an argument a Southern informant said: "You're right on those navel cords and bags. Kroeber says the same as those old ladies told you yesterday. I was wrong. . . . A Northern man offered to let the writer see Carter's study on the sacred pipe since it was the best available study, and "that will save you time, for there is no need doing things over again." [1952:xiii n.2]

There was and still is a tendency for ethnographers to dismiss this literate-based knowledge, as Hilger did, when doing fieldwork, though by the time of my own experience I found it was impossible. Today, the texts about Arapahos are in no way ever detached from the lived culture. The literate and nonliterate cultures are inextricably intermingled, as are written and oral history. And that has probably been the case for some time.

Literacy has raised culture, language, and history into a critical discourse about what is or was true, genuine, or correct. The same critical discourse about all literate forms thus carries over to texts about Arapaho language and culture. Ethnographic and linguistic texts can be used to define tradition or rejected as flawed Euro-American knowledge. Efforts at language standardization through transliteration have generated criticism, as well. Texts allow culture and language to be disembodied from practices and thus discussed and contested out of context. As Goody and Watt point out, writing establishes a more abstract relationship between sign and referent, "less closely connected with particularities of person, place and time" (1972:331). The search for logos and later "structure" rests also on literate discourse, according to Goody and Watt. The birth of critical inquiry follows closely in the wake of literacy and does serve as a basis for reflection on myth and other oral traditions:

> Instead of the unobtrusive adaptation of past tradition to present needs, a great many individuals found in the written records, where much of their traditional cultural repertoire had been given permanent form, so many inconsistencies in the beliefs and categories of understanding handed down to them that they were impelled to a much more conscious, comparative and critical, attitude to the accepted world picture, and notably to the notions of God, the universe and the past. [1972:336]

But the critical attitude that literate knowledge has introduced into Northern Arapaho history is not, as Goody and Watt propose, evidence of a detached, rational orientation. The inconsistencies are generated by the real social and historical contradictions of Euro-American knowledge and practices, not just through a new cognitive orientation.

It is clear, then, that the critical orientation of Euro-American knowledge does not emanate from "texts" themselves. Rather, the mission of critique is a claim to a "ground" outside of the texts. Euro-American knowledge generates "ownership" not only of the text itself but also of the right to criticize, interpret, amend, and translate literate forms. Agreeing with Goody and Watt, though, Euro-American institutionalized literate knowledge precludes criticism of the literate system of knowledge in total and inhibits the altering of its conditions through social practices. In the metaphysics of Euro-American power, literate knowledge has reality in an abstract space-time detached from specific texts and local contexts. American Indian communities must appeal to and conform to epistemological objectives and parameters decided on by an anonymous authority thousands of miles from the communities themselves. That authority, presumed to possess a context-free rationality, ironically neutralizes the historical and social conditions of the construction of so-called empirical knowledge. In my experience at Wind River, for example, it was remarkably predictable that when we wrote grant proposals suited to the real needs of Arapaho communities, academic or bureaucratic reviewers were highly critical, whereas those reviewers with ties to reservation communities were usually encouraging and receptive.

Each culture has its own distinct way of reading and writing tied to local sociocultural realities. Thus, the Northern Arapaho people have had a unique literate culture for over one hundred years. As forms of Euro-American knowledge have entered the spaces and times of Arapaho social relations, they have been generally appropriated within distinctly Arapaho frames of reference. Because literate knowledge has been an enduring medium of domination from the outside, though, Arapaho people face contradictions in the process of appropriation—such as the contradiction between local control and the power of Euro-American literate knowledge to place validity in abstract space-time outside of local social relations. Arapaho people today read and write poetry, newspaper and magazine articles, books, letters, dissertations, and all other literate forms, but they do not encode and decode those texts the same way as Euro-Americans.

As elaborated in chapter 11, it is common in traditional Arapaho discourse to place limits on one's authority, recognize senior persons who are present, and describe the relational conditions of one's knowledge. For example, a speaker will commonly spell out exactly who taught him or her traditional "knowledge." Age, or extent of life movement, is also invoked as a ground for knowledge presented, rather than some objectivity congealed in texts, credentials, or bureaucratic offices. By contrast, Euro-Americans redress and hide power at Wind River through reference to massive objective knowledge that looms behind them, distancing the decision from real interpersonal relations and even broader sociocultural processes. Somehow individuals are not knowers as persons or subjects, for such knowledge must be eschewed as subjective. A sleight-of-hand is often invoked through literate practices by linking the individual in a particular context to tacitly or explicitly superior or universally valid totalities of Western science, bureaucracy, civilization, or history at large. Thus a challenge of the individual or the specific instance is rejected as an inadmissible, unthinkable challenge to the whole. The contradiction is that Euro-American knowledge is claimed for private ownership, as through authorship, intellectual property rights, bureaucratically closed files, credentials, and other practices that sever knowledge from social relations, yet the truth value for resolving problems resides elsewhere in a universality that claims not to be socioculturally constituted or infused with power.

In a similar way, Euro-American literacy carries a set of social strategies for speech performance and the presentation of self. As I suggested earlier, in the Arapaho leader selection process, a close connection was found between formal education and the ability to communicate assertively, as non-Indians do. Though more study is needed in the Arapaho context, literate knowledge does seem to have an effect on a person's ways of speaking. Basso (1972) recognizes for the Apaches and Scollon and Scollon (1981) for the Athabaskans that traditional ways of speaking require a relational context prior to speech, that is, a sense of what others think first. By contrast, literacy and formal education promote verbal self-display as a condition for speaking that functions to persuade the audience or the addressee. In short, like Euro-American knowledge in general, literacy encourages context-free speech that appeals to universal grounds of logic and rationality rather than to actual social relations between speaker and addressee. More precisely, literacy carries a mode of socialization and behavior guided by a patronizing high context explicitness based on the principle "ignore what the hearer knows and explicitly say it anyway" (Gee quoted in Devine 1994:236). Euro-American speakers who interact with Arapaho people in formal contexts often express knowledge confidently, talking like books or written laws and taking the role of teacher, lecturer, or tour guide. Such an attitude can be received, as it is by the Arapaho people, as "rude" because it is distancing, blunt, or condescending.

From the other side, Arapaho people working in Euro-American contexts (e.g., schools, agencies, and colleges) struggle to make non-Indians aware of their context of knowledge. One reaction to Arapaho speakers who bring local knowledge and social relations into formal contexts is that they are "losing their objectivity"; I heard that phrase and variants of it many times. To be "objective" is to be detached from cultural connections and social relations. Objectivity, rather than being measured by facts or logic, though, is equated with ways of speaking persuasively but dispassionately, explicitly but free from social context, and in terms that do not introduce any suggestion that the knowledge they convey is socioculturally constituted. Possession of literate knowledge is thus more than ownership of a socially estranged substance. It also constitutes power through rules of performance requiring no overt reference to that power.

Euro-American formal contexts construct a veil of egalitarianism and democracy that hides the real differences of power, status, and wealth. What non-Indians articulate as fair and objective, Arapahos see as assertions of superior knowledge and power.

That pattern, as well as the contradictions that produce struggles, is inculcated during childhood through formal education, as Elkin (1940:248) first recognized, in which most relationships of Arapahos with Euro-Americans are confined to the submissive-dominant, pupil-student relationship. Literate knowledge and practices in the educational sphere become identified with authority, though defined by Euro-Americans themselves as objectivity and facts. But the use of formal rules based on "objective" criteria meets with suspicion in the reservation community. Any Arapaho experience of the contradiction of Euro-American knowledge reinforces the view that formal structures are really only a front for personal decisions and political motives. In intercultural situations, I saw this happen many times. For example, when a local community college administrator justified an administrative decision in terms of a cost-benefit calculus, it was clear that the Arapaho listeners did not put the same trust in the supporting statistics. The strategy of quantification, policy statements, scientific evidence, and so forth that Euro-Americans use effectively in their own space and time does not always convince Arapaho people.

What Arapaho people often react to is the profession of detached objectivity exercised by the Euro-American bureaucrat, administrator, caseworker, and researcher. On one side, the actor claims authority from the "it's nothing personal" basis of decision making and criticism. Traditional Arapaho knowledge does not allow for the possibility of impersonal decisions, decisions that are separate from social relations. Literate knowledge allows a mode of legal-rational authority in which the actors can cease to be "persons" by objectifying their authority in literate knowledge. It is the power of that "distance" that has been the prime mover of Euro-American dominance and expansion. In my fieldwork, I witnessed the interaction of Euro-American authority with Arapaho people in which the former came through in speech with an authoritarian style supported by the silent partner of literate, objective, and universal knowledge. Interestingly enough, that is exactly what Arapahos see as a kind of "white arrogance," for they often perceive that the professed knowledge really is attaching itself to the individual.

As Tennessen realizes, "authority in language rests not so much in intrinsic properties of a particular discourse . . . but in the social conditions of its production and reproduction" (1986:34). Here the "difference" between oral and literate knowledge dissolves. Both are products of social practice, but each of a different sort. There is nothing intrinsic to the knowledge contained in the literate forms considered here that exudes authority. Rather, it is the way Euro-American actors behave toward Arapaho people based on the tacit belief in the superiority of literate knowledge. The fetishization of the power of literate texts is one major way that Euro-American speakers place authority prior to and behind their words.

The contradiction is that although literacy professes to be an estranged objective, universal code of knowing, in practice it becomes a set of social practices for power that Euro-Americans impose as the "matter-of-fact reality" of the world. As such, literate knowledge excludes Arapaho values and practices. In terms of social "knowledge," Euro-American literate conventions form a "closed system" to real social relations and cultural contexts.

From the other side, Arapaho and other American Indian peoples' efforts to gain ownership of Euro-American knowledge have met with resistance from contradictions on two levels. One is that the leviathan of Euro-American knowledge resides diffusely in structures that resist negotiation and appropriation in and through local social interaction. The other is the realization that non-Indian teachers, administrators, bureaucrats, judges, service providers, and other agents have power on the reservation based on their superior knowledge, yet they know nothing about the reservation community. Agents of the Euro-American knowledge can impose laws, codes, and policies without having to know anything about the local sociocultural context. Such relations take the form of authority over the recipient, as in seller to buyer, health care provider to patient, teacher to student, case worker to client, and so on.

Within the community, literate forms of knowledge have been appropriated for functions similar to and also distinct from those operating in the non-Indian world. Within families, documents have become part of the knowledge to be kept, controlled, and passed on as family culture and history. For the Northern Arapaho tribal government, self-determination has become more a task of administrative paperwork than of political intermediation with Euro-American authorities, which preoccupied past leaders. In acquiring needed resources from their own tribe, the Arapaho people have had to develop skills in researching and filing paperwork rather than working within the channels of traditional values for interpersonal relationships. For revitalizing native language use, formal educational programs have employed literate-based Arapaho language instruction with only nominal results. Nonetheless, learning about Arapaho language, culture, and history has become for many young people increasingly a matter of texts instead of the traditional channels.

Against all efforts toward ownership of literacy, there is strong resistance from the predominant Euro-American literacy, which is generated by much larger, more powerful means of intellectual production. In schools, the textbooks and resources for mainstream curricula come neatly packaged and readily available, whereas Arapaho culture, history, and language materials must be produced from meager resources by a handful of local scholars. The tribal government likewise lacks the advantage of the supporting institutions and literacy technologies available to most Euro-American governments, including legal offices, photocopying services, computer systems, temporary employment services, university-sponsored internships, consultants, and so on. Local schools, committees, and researchers want support for their own projects but often find they must conform to standards set at a distance, such as credentials, formal education, and accessibility to a wider audience. Arapaho literacy and the local practices surrounding it offer limited choices because they must confront the contradictions of dependency paralleling economic relations. Major projects for Arapaho literate knowledge must either appeal to or employ Euro-American institutions or professionals, or get by on few or no resources. The means of literate knowledge production are still owned by Euro-American society. Non-Indians control the production of newspapers, books, textbooks, laws, and journals; they also control research funding. Euro-American institutions enforce a dependency that is like economic dependency; they tell the Arapaho people they should join the progress that follows literacy and even express their own culture through it, but to make that possible they must consume Euro-American products, hire Euro-American experts, and conform to Euro-American standards.

At the life historical level, as well, Arapaho people expressed to me a great deal of ambivalence about literate knowledge. Arapaho life histories are full of incidents in which "paperwork" changed, disrupted, or redirected lives. Filling out the forms right, completing grant applications, getting one's name first on the waiting list, writing letters, and so on have become more essential social skills for life movement in many contexts than interacting with others in the traditional senses of personhood and age distinctions. As in some other tribes, there is discussion of reverting to traditional ways of knowing and learning, even the suggestion of eliminating all reading and writing in language education. Yet, once a people is engaged in literate knowledge, it is nearly impossible to revert entirely to an oral culture. Perhaps this is what Friday, Black Coal, Lone Bear, Yellow Calf, and other leaders saw coming long ago.

Politics and Knowledge Today

During early reservation history, the policies imposed by agents and missionaries aimed to engender individuality as the basis for advancing knowledge, along with other progressive values. That purpose was based on the assumption that tribalism stunted the development of the individual. Agent Ray reported in 1894: "Like all barbarians, they are communists, and are loath to take up individually any untried pursuit" (Report of Agent in Wyoming 1894:337). Progressive action and rational decision making were thought to require individual consciousness liberated from the communal mind. On that assumption the federal government sought to dismantle Arapaho tribalism and processes for making political decisions through consensus (Fowler 1982:96–98). Though unsuccessful overall, the agency tried to replace the Arapaho strategies for socially constructing knowledge with a Euro-American process by which elected tribal leaders could make decisions as individuals representing the tribe though not having to consider the immediate needs, interests, and opinions of other members. Against that effort, Northern Arapaho people maintained some control through an adapted consensual system of decision making for a long time; that was the thesis of Fowler's work.

The contradictions of Euro-American knowledge are operative in all phases, crises, and continuities of the contemporary Arapaho political process. The promise of democratization through literate knowledge has brought, in reality, the potential for modes of knowledge control, ways of speaking, and other political practices that are beyond the influence of traditional limits on knowledge. Since roughly the late 1970s, ways of decision making, speaking, and selecting leaders have changed considerably. Age-structured consensus in political decision making, as Fowler (1982) describes, has given way to more frequent and less manageable argumentation about knowledge accompanying intensifying competition for resources. Self-effacing practices and speech have given way to increasing political campaigning, persuasive speech, and accusations. Unsettled issues about information and verification are at the center of all political conflicts and contradictions facing the Northern Arapaho tribe today. One of the main factors for increasing suspicion, instability, and tensions, according to the way Arapaho people talk about these issues, is that "you can't find out what's going on anymore." It has become increasingly difficult for elders, tribal leaders, and community members to acquire information about budgets, decisions, resources, and hiring in tribal administration. Within that social change, some "knowledge" has become an object to control for political or economic purposes rather than to share freely. At the same time, those who are trying to maintain traditional ways have only weak influence if they do not capitulate to the practices associated with the politics of literate knowledge. Therefore, the imposition of Euro-American political processes has raised new questions for the Arapaho people in their ongoing efforts to maintain or regain control of their own local knowledge and ways of using it. People are also divided about the solutions to this problem. Some propose a more efficient Euro-American system of administration. Others argue for a return to the old ways of doing things. Yet another opinion is that it is hopeless to even try to solve the problem.

Fowler mentions that the Northern Arapahos were unique among modern American Indian tribes in that they averted divisive discourse: "One of the striking features of Arapahoe political life, compared to that on many other Plains reservations, is the absence of public accusations of graft on the part of the council leadership. During the 1965–78 era, no council member failed to be reelected or resigned because of misuse of tribal funds" (1978:275). By contrast, since the time of her study the Business Council has changed composition with each election, and council members have been removed by General Council resolution several times. Reelection to the council is by far the exception rather than the rule today. Further diverging from the situation Fowler describes, almost all public discussion and gossip today gets around to accusations of nepotism, graft, and corruption. At the center of that shift is a change in knowledge.

Mirroring Euro-American politics and as an outgrowth of factional politics, some groups controlling tribal committees, school programs, and other specialized functions have adopted Euro-American strategies of information management and control for maintaining economic and political security. More and more, the control of documents has become a primary political strategy, not only for leaders but also for committees, families, and individuals. Staying out of public view and discussion has become a political survival strategy against rumor, gossip, and accusation. Rather than democratizing access to knowledge, literate knowledge has, in the political context, become a source of value to be accumulated and "owned."

Since the beginning of self-determination initiatives in the 1970s, more and more administrative functions have been taken over by the tribes. The tribal government has become, regardless of the resistance to an IRA type government, an administrative statelike system governed by resolutions, law and order codes, federal statutes, and other documents of authority. Within the tribal political system, the Arapaho Business Council and the Joint Business Council (the Shoshone and Arapaho Business Councils meeting together on joint programs) have become more centralized in authority but less able to deal with the increasing volume of paperwork for the many programs, offices, and committees. Originally, the Chiefs' Council had the sole function of recording and administering land leases, for which the BIA maintained records. Today, there are dozens of programs, grant-funded projects, legal cases, and piles of documentation. As a result, in General Council meetings, which are held less and less frequently, only a small slice of tribal affairs can be dealt with in each day-long meeting. The days of open discussion bounded by age-structured authority are long gone.

At the same time, the amount of the 15 percent portion of trust income for tribal administration has declined in the last twenty years, thus reducing the funds available for administrative staff and technology. During the early 1990s, the tribal government reached a critical point and then began reducing support to many programs. Also straining resources, the size of the Arapaho tribe increased with population growth and a change in enrollment criteria, discussed in the next section. In response the tribal government has assumed control of many formerly joint Shoshone-Arapaho programs in an effort to secure a more equitable share of federally subsidized operating budgets. With a larger and poorer population, the Northern Arapahos have long realized that they would have to make do with less than the Eastern Shoshones, who receive an equal proportion though larger per capita share of federal funding and trust income. Moreover, inheriting programs from the BIA as often as not carried over a history of inefficiencies and practices that have been maintained primarily to protect jobs and offices. It also is not clear that such programs receive as much government financial support as they once did. During the late 1990s, to compensate for losses and inefficiency, the tribal leadership has aimed to centralize more programs and their administrative budgets within the tribal government.

The trend in recent years toward centralized tribal political administration, combined with a proliferation of committees and commissions, has made access to knowledge about tribal government increasingly difficult. Traditional ways of gathering and reviewing information have been unable to keep up. Knowledge has also become specific to "time-space zones," such that "truth" is no longer consensually constituted but is relative to or at least suspected of group or individual interests. Rather than letting the tribe know everything they are doing, some leaders, committees, and commissions have adopted the Euro-American strategy of silence and withholding knowledge from the public world. Access to knowledge has become part of Business Council authority, as well as the authority of commissions and committees created for "self-determination" of tribal functions.

During the era of self-determination, the tribal government has "learned" from the federal government, especially the BIA, about bureaucratic control of knowledge; for example, the tribal government now requires formal requests for information and documents in tribal files. Local practices have thus adopted the restrictive strategies of Euro-American bureaucracy to control access to information. Application forms, release forms, minutes of meetings, and other documentation have been used to "conceal" as much information as they "reveal" or conserve. For persons, the state of affairs has generated the public vs. private self distinction that is at the base of the Euro-American political economy of knowledge. Taken together, the extent and complexity of tribally controlled programs and finances has made day-to-day information about council activities difficult to disseminate widely, accurately, and comprehensively. And at General Council meetings, when all interested eligible tribal members meet to vote on resolutions in public meetings, rarely are more than half of the agenda items dealt with. The sheer volume of information pertaining to tribal government cannot be transmitted in the traditional public, oral channels of "knowledge" transformation. In the Old Council it was possible to keep all tribal financial records in small ledgers that council members carried with them and to meet once a week to handle all tribal business.

Nevertheless, many Arapaho people try in some contexts to apply traditional ways to the modern situation. People often work diligently, even throughout their lives, to make information available to others through public speech, informal channels, or modern media. When once-sequestered information does become available, it is shared verbally or in written form with family and community. Photocopied reports, budgets, and other sources of information are circulated within the community as a way to generate social action for change.

The effort to circulate information is met with the opposite tendency to hide it from public view. Today, some older Arapaho people complain that they cannot find out what is going on in tribal politics. From the standpoint of tribal leaders, public situations become intensely burdensome with the sense that tribal members constantly "corner" them to get information and explanations. Whereas once the council members sat in front of the tribe during General Council meetings, they now sit "with the people." From the other side, tribal leaders, workers, and organizations themselves have less control over the information that circulates about them. A comment often heard today is that "anybody can say anything now and get away with it," such as in General Council meetings. Once a public opinion is established and action toward it has begun, people often feel that they have fewer venues for refuting the opinion and averting the action. In other words, those on the inside are subject to the same sense that the social movement of knowledge is increasingly difficult to control.

The reshaping of social space has contributed greatly to the contradictions. With the adoption of Euro-American time-space zoning, decisions are now made in the specialized functional spaces of offices, council chambers, classrooms, and board rooms; and information that was once in public view is hidden away in those places. Knowledge is socially constituted in smaller, less accessible social spaces and times. At the same time, with the growth of the tribe and the expansion of tribal programs, it has become nearly impossible for any individual or group of elders to be fully informed on all that is happening on a day-to-day basis. Even though many meetings and proceedings are open to the public, no one can attend more than a few of them; time limits any one person or group from knowing all of what is going on. Because public life is now more problematic and involves a greater investment of time and effort, many people are less willing to participate, as is evident in the declining attendance at General Council meetings. The time required to know things competes with other life concerns and activities. Almost every group and organization I participated in raised the ongoing question of how to get the whole community involved. One recurring comment that adds to the issue is that organizations and community projects now compete with many other social activities, such as sports, television, or bingo. From the inside, all of those factors make individual or group efforts, even when done correctly in the traditional sense and with the interests of others in mind, more vulnerable to public suspicion and political reaction. When wider participation is not forthcoming, groups, including families, decide that they will "just have to do it on their own"; but in doing so, they are subject to criticism that they are serving their own interests and excluding others. What has emerged mimics the Euro-American contradiction between knowledge in public and private spaces, but in and of Arapaho social relations.

Because of that distance, there is a prevailing contradiction between bureaucratic de jure knowledge and de facto realities, between what organizations present about what they do and what they actually achieve. Euro-American bureaucracies sustain tacit knowledge about how much real practices should conform to what is written in the report, proposal, or regulations. In order to maintain jobs, budgets, and programs, administrators must have presentational management skills for encoding grants, reports, regulations, and other official documents with language that overstates real achievements and hides deviations. Some externally and internally based organizations at Wind River have kept themselves going that way for years, while doing next to nothing for the community. Bureaucratic survival requires, then, the employment of statistics, symbolic wording, and tempo strategies for an ongoing "public image."

For leaders in the past, the free distribution of knowledge was consistent with the redistribution of accumulated wealth. In the time of the chiefs and the early councils, one of the principal duties of leadership was to talk to the camp or the tribe regularly—even each day—about the actions, decisions, and plans of the tribal leaders. During the early council period, councilmen sponsored feasts on their allotments or in community centers to inform the people in their camp or district about important council activities, such as travel to Washington, leasing of trust land, meeting with the Shoshone council, and so on. Included were specific details about expenditures of tribal money. By sponsoring such feasts, the leaders showed two interrelated types of generosity: one with food and another with knowledge.

Although ceremonial knowledge was tightly channeled within the limits of age hierarchy, there was an obligation to share "political" knowledge freely and to "tell the truth." That sharing and exchange of knowledge made consensual decision making possible. The primary links in the network of knowledge exchange were elders and adults in the third stage of life. Age distinctions thus maintained the veracity of public knowledge. As many elders told me, today they often do not have enough information and often are called to meetings to vote on the spot without time for discussion of the matters at hand. There is a sense that political decisions are made "too fast." Before the introduction of "white man's ways" to the political process since the 1970s, decisions affecting the tribe required a protracted, deliberative discussion process centering on the elders. To that end, elders traveled around, sometimes for days, talking over issues and arriving at some consensus. As Fowler notes, decisions were commonly made by the tribe in such ways before the tribe began the "official" public procedures complying with Euro-American standards. That process required a time investment that impatient Euro-American officials saw as inefficient and out of pace with the modern tempo of life and therefore sought to dismantle.

Today, the deliberative tempo of decision making, still practiced by some, especially elders, is dissynchronous with the fast-paced tempo of "white man's ways," which demand expediency, culturally equivocated with values of efficiency, individualism, and intelligence. The greater volume and faster pace of tribal politics, some younger people contend, precludes traditional ways of making decisions. Elders, by contrast, complain that decisions are made too fast, without all the necessary information, just like every other action in the modern world. They commonly observe that in politics and ritual life, younger people want things done or decided "right away" and do not want to go through all the necessary steps of preparation and deliberation. As a result, the increased tempo and control of it are sources of divisiveness and conflict over knowledge.

Paralleling the change in the political economy, Arapaho society has become more dependent on Euro-American knowledge generated at a distance. The policy of self-determination, like several other federal policies, has with the respect to knowledge had the opposite of its intended effects. Comparable to the strategy of control through economic dependency is the administrative dependency that the federal government has produced through the proliferation of literate knowledge to define its relationship to tribes. At one time much of the knowledge introduced from outside could be channeled and regulated within the age hierarchy, but now that knowledge can no longer readily be controlled locally. To address the need to keep up with accumulating paperwork, the Northern Arapaho tribe has been forced at times to hire non-Arapaho firms or professionals, including lawyers, accountants, and grant writers. The profession of "consultant" has boomed in Indian country. Within the tribe also, more individuals have taken on roles as professional consultants, grants writers, developers, and so forth. Paradoxically, like all federal policies, self-determination has intensified dependency on external modes of administration. Literate knowledge generates a dependency on a trained literati, requiring either formal education of Arapahos themselves or reliance on external specialists.

Sustaining tribal government is now less a matter of effective verbal skills to be used in assertive communication with the federal government than it is an issue of grantsmanship, fiscal management, and bureaucratic skills to write proposals, submit reports, audit budgets, research information, and process data. Regardless of what culturally valued attributes a leader possesses, administration is now contingent upon formal education for internally employed workers or externally contracted services. Tribal government, schools, and grant-funded programs are only as good as the administration. One poor administrator, incompetent attorney, irresponsible grant writer, untrained business manager, or criminal finance officer can come and go, leaving budgetary chaos, a damaged tribal grant reputation, and even eliminated programs behind. In turn, the tribal government or organization inherits the resulting bureaucratic punishments, penalties, and accountability; they may hamper leadership for years to follow.

Political issues today are thus less legislative than bureaucratic. In the past, however inefficient at times, the BIA served most administrative functions. Throughout history it has justified its policies and continued existence through its exclusive ownership of the technical expertise to administer reservation resources and to protect Indian tribes from other bureaucracies (i.e., local and state governments). In reality, the BIA, like other agencies, has produced a surplus of knowledge and specialized functions to maintain its own existence. Accordingly, the BIA claimed sole control over the definition of tribal enrollment, the allotment of land, inheritance, and the administration of tribal resources through documents, record keeping, and bookkeeping.

Since the beginning of the reservation period, the federal government has also imposed structures of organization that rest, as Nelson and Sheley affirm, on an epistemological monopoly: "Bureaucratic consciousness is more subtle and more significant in the BIA exercise of control over Indians. Such consciousness represents a cognitive style, a manner of organizing and manipulating knowledge" (1985:187). Bureaucratic consciousness is given in formal, democratized norms prior to practice and preconfiguring the future. It attempts, though it never totally succeeds, to neutralize the particularities of the present. Further, bureaucratic consciousness is one latent medium for Euro-American distance between the Indian and non-Indian world. It requires not only a separate language code but a "bureaucratic" subcode within literate language.

But the BIA has not been the only source of a bureaucratic ethos at Wind River. School systems, the Indian Health Service, and countless social agencies have also contributed to a bureaucratic rationality. Today, the dominant society's strategy is that the "problems" on the reservation, some of which reflect bureaucratic influence, can be resolved if only things are dealt with more "efficiently" by Euro-American-modeled institutions.

In Euro-American culture, literate knowledge offers the least resistance for addressing and solving any defined "problem." The BIA and other formal institutions justify their presence in terms of "problems," but those problems do not spontaneously generate from within Arapaho society. The very institutions employed to solve "problems" in previous historical moments commonly generate and sustain enduring problems through their own practices. Even the very authority over the definition of problems and their solutions has been appropriated by Euro-American epistemology. Through ownership of "problem-solving," Euro-American-imposed institutions and their knowledge system persist. The bureaucratic ethos, epitomized by the BIA, other agencies, and the increasing bureaucratization of tribal administration "serves to compartmentalize tribal problems to the point that tribal members desire no active role in their solution" (Nelson and Sheley 1985:193). When Euro-American agencies take over a problem, they preempt collective tribal ownership of the problem and generally circumscribe practices to specialized domains, with no eye for a sociocultural totality or the local history. Similarly, when tribal governments become bureaucratized and democratized, tribal governance itself becomes estranged from tribal members.

Generally, federal and tribal programs set up an administrative hierarchical structure in which authority is in the hands of either a director who reports to the council or a board made up of community members representing the community. Rather than going out into the community to activate consensus as the old people used to do, directors and boards call for "community input" at open meetings. Thus, community members must find the time and transportation to come to the director or the board. It is almost impossible for anyone concerned with tribal issues to attend even most of these meetings. Outside of public view, programs sequestered in this way are prone to suspicion of or real factional interests. The Arapaho people feel that they have no control over committees, boards, and programs with which they have no real relationship. So many times, I heard people refer to such groups saying, "I just don't know what they're doing over there." The restricted sense of involvement thus channels efforts for empowerment by individuals and families toward those "places" where they have some claim of ownership through family or factional ties.

As a whole, the adoption of literate knowledge at the center of bureaucratization and electoral government has gradually removed authority over knowledge from social relations based on age distinctions and shifted it to expertise and credentials acquired through formal education. No longer are elders at the center of "knowledge" for collective decision making. For political action today, tribal members "talk it over" with the old people and get their support, but there is less certainty than in the past that such discussion will affect tribal government or policy. Literate knowledge has thus become a medium for the construction of social relationships prior to exchange and outside of interpersonal relationships. Documents and forms predefine authority and the conditions of social relationships outside of ongoing human action and thus outside of the Arapaho ways of doing things. For example, pity, respect, quietness, and craziness are not easily infused into relationships maintained by modes of authority expressed and exchanged as literate knowledge.

Politics, Knowledge, and Tribal Identity

Northern Arapaho tribal enrollment offers a prime example of the effects of the contradictions brought by Euro-American knowledge. Since the beginning of the reservation period, the federal government has employed documentation to define tribal membership, gradually removing it from the immediacies of life movement and age-structured control of social relations. Enrollment based on quantification of Indian or Arapaho blood degree was imposed as rational, scientific, and objective knowledge, but in time it became an anachronistic residual of Euro-American knowledge with immeasurable and powerful consequences and contradictions in Arapaho life. Documentation of identity was originally constructed to meet the need for record keeping, clarifying legal status, and formalizing inheritance through time. It was thus part of the centralization of power in the nation-state to define categories of persons and control access to resources. In the historical and contemporary context, census records have been employed by the federal government to define, objectify, and control the "boundaries" of tribal and Indian identity. Initially, the Arapahos saw the tribal rolls as innocuous listings of those who received rations at the agency, but in time the rolls have emerged as a source of conflict and argumentation about a form of Euro-American knowledge that is now internalized as a given even in tribal administration of enrollment. In the last twenty years, tribal enrollment has emerged as a stark example of self-perpetuating Euro-American literate knowledge appropriated within tribal government itself beneath the guise of "self-determination." The imposition of clear and distinct categories based in the science and bureaucracy of the late nineteenth century, rather than a way to rationally order reality and eliminate inconsistencies, has become a powerful source of present contradiction and conflict within reservation communities. The encoding of identity on paper as form of literate knowledge has thus had the opposite of its intended effect long after it ceased to be government policy.

Tribal rolls have imposed a definition that removes control over categories from real social practices based on lived kinship and age hierarchy. Once inscribed and transfixed in records, such knowledge becomes "fact" even though it may distort or exclude the real facts at the moment of documentation. Blood quantum has also filtered out of its original legal and administrative functions into Arapaho ways of defining identity in everyday social life. As a result, identity by inherited substance has come into contradiction, both for individuals and for families, with traditional life movement as the measure of Arapaho persons. In the pre- and early-reservation context, those who deviated from Arapaho values were impeded in the temporal process of life movement or even shunned and pushed out of the camp circle. Today, documented identity is objectified as an ascribed status prior to practice and life as lived, alterable only in rare cases of political or legal action.

The contradictions inherent in blood degree as a form of Euro-American literate knowledge in general have been appropriated into Arapaho experience. One problem is the historical accumulation of errors and inconsistencies in records that social practice cannot change even with a preponderance of counterevidence and complex formal action. In reservation history, for example, the indication of blood fractions did not appear on census rolls until the 1920s, more than thirty years after Arapaho census records were first kept at Wind River. Initially, the agency indicated only Indian blood degree without specific designation of Arapaho degree. Those original quanta of Indian blood eventually became the baseline for Arapaho tribal enrollment in succeeding generations.

Rather than being a measure of real blood degree—if there is such a thing—census rolls are also a measure of the original Arapaho standards of cultural identity at a moment in time. Those people who had become a part of Arapaho life movement were defined as Arapaho in local knowledge. On this basis, non-Arapahos who had married into or settled with the tribe were often registered as four-fourths, or full-blood degree. The list included some persons with white ancestry who had been adopted into the tribe. Others had parents or ancestors in the Gros Ventre, the Cheyenne, the Lakota, the Blackfoot, or the Pawnee tribe, for example.

Before the reservation period, there was no genetic barrier or endogamous boundary between the Northern Arapahos and other tribes. In fact, elders today point out that their grandparents often encouraged them to marry outside the tribe in order to avoid problems of "marrying too close" and to expand kin relations for alliances to other tribes. Marriages with allied groups such as the Lakota, the Cheyenne, the Southern Arapaho, and the Gros Ventre tribes were quite common. With other, nonallied tribes, intermarriage was less frequent. Only recently, for example, have Arapahos intermarried to any considerable extent with Eastern Shoshone tribal members. However, throughout history, captives from enemy tribes, such as the Utes and the Shoshones, were adopted into the Arapaho tribe. Further, many people found orphaned or abandoned were adopted by Arapaho families who pitied them.

As discussed throughout this book, Arapaho boundaries for personhood and identity were constructed through a temporal system of life movement shaped in practice within limits of mythico-ritual space and time. By contrast, blood degree is culturally constituted in part by a Euro-American cultural construction of the life cycle in which a defining "substance" originates at the moment of conception. This was based on Euro-American folk concepts of heredity and a pre-Mendelian theory of "blending inheritance," which reckons "fractions of blood" inherited from parents and mixed in equal proportions at conception. As Schneider's classic work (1980:23–27) recognizes, the Euro-American symbol of blood is a nexus for multiple meanings and is regarded as natural, material, and measurable. It is substance inherited half from the mother and half from the father that defines "particular heredity" and, through descent, "a relationship of identity." Blood is thus part of a Euro-American genealogical mode of temporalization for defining durable personhood, family identities, and social boundaries. The late-nineteenth-century scientific formalization of the racial category of "blood degree" was a transposition of a cultural construct from descent to racial categories, and thus from culture to nature. As a result, Arapaho enrollment became an ascribed, immutable "birthright" inherited from parents and ascendant generations.

Obviously, census records were not an objective measure of blood degree. Within the Northern Arapaho tribe, the imposition of blood degree has generated the assumption of an "objective ground" and an original time frame for Arapaho cultural identity, presumably external to the social construction of knowledge. There are thus discrepancies between blood degree and other ways of defining identity, such as through family relations, ritual practice, or residence. For the Arapaho people, it has brought cultural identity into a critical discourse.

As Goody and Watt observed, literate knowledge provokes criticism about family and cultural identity, because the categories have been severed from social practice and from personal identity that can be changed or reversed through social practices. For example, as a result of the original census criteria, there can be a discrepancy, which Arapaho people are aware of, between "real" blood degree and recorded blood degree, either way. Such historical and contemporary discrepancies generate much genealogical gossip and criticism. Once codified, the census records are difficult to correct. Of any two people, one recorded with full blood degree and the other with one-half, the latter may in "fact" have a greater real Arapaho blood degree than the former. Paradoxically, reckoning real blood degree itself appeals to the Euro-American assumption of "fact."

Blood degree is intimately tied now to ways of constructing family identity. From inside families, there is a tendency to understate or be silent about non-Arapaho and especially non-Indian ancestors. Many Arapaho families, for example, have significant Hispanic heritage, yet few identify with it. Knowing a little about genealogy, I once encouraged some Arapaho students to apply for scholarships designated for Hispanic students at the local community college, since they were eligible by "blood." My suggestion was not accepted. Conversely, families identify most strongly with the original "founding Arapaho," usually the source of the family surname, a tribal leader, or both.

From an out-group perspective, Arapaho families descended from non-Arapaho ancestors after one hundred years may still be labeled as really Gros Ventre, Sioux, Mexican, or "breeds," a term used for people of mixed Indian–non-Indian heritage. Ironically, the original ancestor referred to may at present account for one-sixteenth or less of the present family's blood degree. It is evident that in the past Arapahos who came from the non-Arapaho world could be adopted and identified as Arapaho within a generation. The difference could more easily be "forgotten" then. It is quite possible for literate knowledge overall, including enrollment censuses and probate records, to perpetuate differences and distinctions long past the time of their social relevance.

Enrollment has imposed a form of permanent knowledge in the form of a genealogical record with facts that cannot be discarded. In an oral culture, as Goody and Watt observe, "forgetting" serves a social function that literate forms preclude or at least resist: "What continues to be of social relevance is stored in the memory while the rest is usually forgotten" (1972:315). Contradictions generate critical discourse about social categories comparable to the situation described for British administrators among the Tiv of Nigeria. After forty years of literate record keeping, the Bohannons observed:

> These written pedigrees gave rise to many disagreements; the Tiv maintained that they were incorrect, while the officials regarded them as statements of fact, as records of what had actually happened, and could not agree that the unlettered indigenes could be better informed about the past than their own literate predecessors. What neither party realized was that in any society of this kind changes take place which require a constant readjustment in the genealogies if they are to continue to carry out their function as mnemonics of social relationships. [in Goody and Watt 1972:317]

Once knowledge is objectified through documentation, it is impossible to change it without violating the law or the bureaucratic rules. That immutability stands in contradiction to the Arapaho kinship system, which has been and still is flexible and adaptable enough to maintain strong ties among extended kin despite all of the Euro-American-imposed enrollment and genealogical distinctions. Kinship is subject more to residence, participation, and practices than to inherited substance. Within families, some members who are not enrolled may still be closer than others who are. Adoption, grandparent guardianship, ceremonial kinship relations, and same-sex close companion relationships allow flexible options for kinship and residence. Kinship is constructed out of decisions made by kin, shared life experiences, and ongoing cooperation in family activities.

In the past, elders, especially women, kept mental records of family genealogy in order to teach young people who they were and were not related to, mainly for purposes of defining respect relations among collateral kin and regulating marriage choices so that a marriage would not be "too close." In general, genealogy in the traditional oral context was based on elders' authority; it was not necessarily to trace descent to the past but to direct choices for marriage partners. Elders today observe that such orally transmitted and remembered knowledge is no longer as significant for respect relations and marriage choices as it once was.

Northern Arapaho blood degree became fully institutionalized in 1954 (Fowler 1982:222) in order to determine eligibility for regular per capita payments in the redistribution of 85 percent of the Arapaho half of joint tribal income from mineral and oil leases on trust lands. At that time the Arapaho and Shoshone Business Councils won a fight they had waged for over thirty years with the federal government for congressional legislation allowing regular per capita payments. Before that time tribal income was dispersed only occasionally at the discretion of the BIA and the agent or superintendent. Per capita payments created an administrative need to define tribal enrollment precisely and distinctly. To that end, the BIA used blood degree as indicated on tribal censuses. From 1957 to 1992 Arapaho tribal enrollment criteria included (1) that an individual be at least one-fourth blood degree Northern Arapaho, (2) that one's father be an enrolled tribal member, (3) that one be enrolled before the age of two, and (4) that one's parents be legally married.

The preference for paternal enrollment, combined with the imposed patronymic surname, has been interpreted in several different ways. One explanation favored by a few men I talked to is that Arapahos have always been "patriarchal." Another explanation is administrative, that is, that it is easier to determine enrollment and locate persons when children bear their fathers' surnames (MaryAnne Whiteman). Surnames were an imposition of Euro-American categories initiated by Agent Nickerson in the early 1900s. The introduction of a patronymic, patriarchal, or even patrilateral bias drawn from

Euro-American legal-rational concepts runs counter to the traditional Arapaho kinship solidarity, which focuses on women related as sisters, mothers, and daughters.

Some Arapaho women believe that the system was set up to exclude them and avert requiring Arapaho men to acknowledge paternity of children born outside of marriage. Other Arapahos say it derives from the pattern that women were more likely to have children by non-Indian men than men were to father children by non-Indian women. Following the caste logic of Euro-American interracial marriage and sexual access, it was more acceptable for Arapaho women to marry or have children by non-Indian men than vice versa. The inclusion of those children would supposedly increase enrollment significantly. Behind the policy was also a fear, shared by both Arapahos and the federal government, that men who married into the tribe would eventually gain access to property and other resources. That form of intentional exploitation was not uncommon in early reservation communities. A related contributing factor is the degree to which federal authorities influenced the definition of enrollment. Since the 1880s, federal policy often sought to restrict enrollment in order to reduce the numbers of Indians with recognized rights and entitlements. At the same time they imposed Euro-American family forms centering on monogamous, legal marriage and ties to the children resulting from it. The old definition of Arapaho enrollment thus carries a Euro-American cultural and legal bias.

The issue of enrollment has been an ongoing political and legal issue in the Northern Arapaho community, especially for women who were enrolled tribal members but had children not eligible for enrollment. As a concession, in the 1970s ineligible children of enrolled Arapaho women were granted "associate membership," with some privileges, including health care benefits, college financial aid, and other government services, but excluding per capita payments and voting rights. This established a situation in which those enrolled already were unlikely to vote in the General Council (a formal meeting of all adult tribal members and the ultimate political authority in the tribe) for changes in enrollment criteria, given that larger rolls would decrease the amount of per capita payments and bring in a new voting block for tribal elections.

In an unplanned and unanticipated action, however, the General Council of the tribe voted to amend enrollment criteria at its September 1992 meeting. According to the unwritten rules of order, as soon as the tribal enrollment officer introduced on the floor another concern related to enrollment, the criteria themselves were open to action by resolution. By vote of the majority of the enrolled members present, persons with associate status could now file to become fully enrolled, receive per capita payments, and exercise voting rights.

Since then, about a thousand new tribal members have been added to the rolls. The additions did not significantly reduce the per capita payments, which were already declining with decreasing profits from oil fields, but they did shift voting patterns somewhat so that younger persons and women gained some seats on the Business Council and on tribal committees. A few tribal members have taken unsuccessful legal action in an effort to reverse the decision.

As in other Indian communities, the imposition of a measured concept of tribal identity has provided material for social distinctions between individuals and between families. For over thirty years, the associate versus full enrollment issue divided people. What has persisted, even since the broadening of enrollment, is a situation described by M. Annette Jaimes:

> It has established a scenario in which it has been perceived as profitable for one Indian to cancel the identity of her/his neighbor as a means of receiving of her/his entitlement. Thus, a bitter divisiveness has been built into Indian communities and national policies, sufficient to preclude our achieving the internal unity necessary to offer any serious challenge to the status quo. [1992:136]

The attachment of entitlement to resources to tribal enrollment has created a system of rank whereby the degree of cultural identity carries the statement "I am more Indian or Arapaho than you" (136).

Quantified enrollment provides the material for an abstract unity comparable to race and other a priori "substantive" categories, while at the same time demarcating the lines for intratribal distinctions. The Northern Arapaho people today often comment that per capita payments and enrollment have "divided" the tribe by making enrollment a political and economic resource. In other words, it ties identity to economic benefits, thus generating a factional division between enrolled and nonenrolled Arapahos.

The "boom" in local oil production during the late 1970s and the early 1980s generated greater tribal income and larger per capita payments. In speaking of that period, people say that "there was money everywhere," based on the perception that money flowed out of the tribal office for grants, loans, and immediate needs just for the asking. Since the late 1980s, though, tribal income has decreased dramatically with the international decline of oil prices. In 1992 the Arapaho tribe began laying off tribal workers and cutting tribally funded programs. By October 1998 the per capita payments were down to $50 per month from a high in the 1980s of $300. For a family of four enrolled members that represented a decline from $1200 to $200, without even adjusting for inflation.

Through the allotment of trust land in severalty to families, the issue of the inheritance of real property based on degree of relatedness to the deceased has also generated contradictions between lived and so-called objective closeness of kinship. Inheritance laws at Wind River adopt local state statutes for determining the apportionment of estates through probate hearings, since very few Arapahos have wills. Euro-American probate procedures tend to privilege marriage and blood for legal definitions of relatedness and inheritance, whereas Arapaho families tend to define kinship by socially constructed "closeness," based on residence and shared social space. Thus, someone related closely by blood may not be related at all in the Arapaho sense of family boundaries and kinship ties through shared experiences. Traditional kinship thus often contradicts legal kinship. For example, despite an agency ban, a few men continued to have multiple wives well into the reservation period, though a legal marriage was recorded for only one of the wives. Early probate records show that traditionally adopted children were recognized, but only upon a preponderance of gathered testimony. A person distant by blood may be redefined as closer through Arapaho criteria, a factor rarely admitted into probate hearings. Thus, there are stories of strangers showing up at probate hearings to claim the share to which they are entitled and drawing glances and questions like, "Who are they?" Obviously, the contradiction between legal and lived kinship can create or sustain conflicts between related families or individuals.

That and related contradictions can also confound one's personal identity. For many young people, the sense that they are made up of fractions of identity generates questions and confusion in their efforts to find unity and consistency among diverse social worlds and self-definitions. A person can be labeled and related to differently at home than in the "white world" and differently yet among the several families in one's kindred. In a hypothetical case, an enrolled Arapaho who is one-half Arapaho, one-fourth Chicano, and one-fourth Shoshone could experience a different definition of identity in the family associated with each fraction. To some in his Arapaho family, he could be perceived as Shoshone, to his Chicano relatives an Indian, to his Shoshone kin, an Arapaho. And in the white world, he could be defined by physical appearance. The burden for constructing personal identity out of conflicting definitions is thus placed on the individual.

Enrollment endures as an imposition of "white men's ways" and embodies both the contradictions inherent in Euro-American literate knowledge and those between it and traditional Arapaho knowledge. Enrollment illustrates how literate knowledge has removed much authority from the age-structured relations, placed definitions of identity outside of life movement, contributed to contradictory ways of expressing family identity, and provided a ground for social tensions and conflicts. As with all Euro-American knowledge, the intended purpose of universalizing fixed categories and rational practices has never been realized.

The Christian Missions

Aspects of the historical and contemporary presence of Christian missions at Wind River illuminate similar and further contradictions generated by Euro-American knowledge, as well as Arapaho empowerment strategies to appropriate it as local knowledge. A source of contradiction in Euro-American belief systems is the aim to import text-embodied knowledge or doctrine by displacing, transforming, or subsuming local systems of knowledge. Very broadly, missionaries brought their knowledge to the Arapaho people based on the assumption that Christianity should universalize itself through history. In response, however, the Arapaho people compartmentalized the introduced forms, creating a unique local system of pluralism. Christian practices were appropriated in Arapaho terms and given a place among other traditions, without converting to the new faith as a total belief system.

Not only did Arapaho leaders welcome the schools, but they also encouraged participation in mission religious practices. Chief Black Coal, the principal leader of the tribe when St. Stephen's was founded in 1884, welcomed Father Jutz's presence and the prospect of a boarding school for Arapaho children:

> This was the country of my fathers, now dead and dying. We have many children. We very much want a good school house, and a good man to teach our children to read your language, that they may grow up to be intelligent men and women, like the children of the White man. And then, when Sunday comes, we would be glad of some good man to teach our children about the Great Spirit. [Wind River Rendezvous 1984(2):4].

The Arapaho people did not resist the Catholic religion; they effectively appropriated it as part of an indigenous pluralistic theory of practice. Black Coal also supported John Roberts's efforts to establish the government school at Fort

Washakie in 1884, the same year St. Stephen's was founded (Crofts 1997:90). The idea of assimilation as "conversion," a total relinquishing of a previous way of life for another, was not only not evident in Northern Arapaho adaptations to the mission presence but, equally interesting, was generally not pursued by the missionaries themselves. The former is evident in a statement by Chief Lone Bear, a lifelong Catholic and a traditional Arapaho: "I pray according to the way I was taught by the church and when I get through I pray my Indian way. Wherever I go and there is a church and time to go to that church and if I do not belong to that church, it does not make any difference. I go over there and go to that church. It is all for one God. We are all heading for the same God" (cited in Fowler 1982:136–37). The notion that all life movement leads to the same place is at the heart of Arapaho pluralism. Rather than being just a structural compartmentalization in social space, Arapaho pluralism placed multiple religions in a unique temporalization, "as all leading to the same place." That sense of time transposes to history the trajectory of life movement in which individuals can follow different paths in youth yet all end up in the center in old age.

The Southern Arapaho artist Carl Sweezy echoes the idea that "there are many roads to God," adding, "We had a good deal more understanding of the white man's religion than he had of ours" (Bass 1966:71). Arapaho pluralism in both Oklahoma and Wyoming was based on an openness to other traditions that was more enduring and pervasive than in other Plains cultures or among Euro-Americans. As articulated in chapter 11, Arapaho ways of knowing, in myth and history, allow external sources of knowledge and power to be appropriated and channeled into life movement. Recognizing that pluralism adds to one's understanding of Arapaho solidarity and consensus: they are not a consciousness shared homogeneously; rather, they allow differences and individuality "all moving in the same direction." Today that perspective is sometimes lost in modern definitions of tradition as a clearly bounded belief system that all must share.

Arapaho people were drawn in great numbers to St. Stephen's in large part because of the appropriation of practices, including the sacraments cited in chapter 10. Their interest centered not on the "word" or doctrine but on the Mass and other services. Noticing that preference, the missionaries eventually emphasized ritual over other strategies of conversion, such as the translation of texts, which was employed nominally during the first decades. Elkin observed that even the minister at St. Michael's copied the pattern of success at St. Stephen's: "He has added more ritual, instituted the confession, is seen in clerical garb, and has himself addressed as 'Father'" (1940:244).

Most early missionaries tolerated the Arapaho traditions. Unlike the early histories of some other Catholic missions among Plains tribes, the Jesuits at St. Stephen's did not usually attempt to defeat Satan or the forces of darkness by destroying Arapaho religious traditions. Only in the 1940s did St. Stephen's impose an either-or policy toward Arapaho religious practices:

> For most of its long history St. Stephen's had exercised a qualified tolerance of its parishioners taking part in Native American religious ceremonies, such as the Sun Dance and Peyote practices. This policy radically changed in the 1940's when it was felt that such a "dual practice" was impossible. Many St. Stephen's parishioners were, in effect, forced to make a choice between the practice of their Catholic ways and their Indian ways. [Wind River Rendezvous 1984(3):8].

Before and after that turnabout in mission policy, priests and brothers commonly learned the Arapaho language and attended traditional ceremonies, perhaps even performing Mass at the Sun Dance camp or saying a prayer before a traditional ceremony. During the repressive era of the 1940s, though, the priest stood at the door of the chapel each Sunday turning away men known to have participated in traditional ceremonies. For the most part, adult men who participated in the Sun Dance were singled out and denied access to the church and the sacraments, even told that they were excommunicated. In response, men excluded from the church either continued in their Catholic faith, sometimes by attending Mass in the nearby parishes, shifted their affiliation to St. Michael's, or rejected Christianity altogether, committing themselves entirely to traditionalism.

Early and later missionaries defended the Arapaho religion by finding common elements in doctrine, such as monotheism. On the basis of some identification of "Christianity" with a universal human religious experience, by the early period of reservation history, some missionaries, especially at St. Michael's, promoted syncretism. Early on, John Roberts, an Episcopal missionary who was sent to the Shoshone side of the reservation in 1883 and later established St. Michael's Mission at Ethete, proposed a historical, diffusive relationship between Arapaho beliefs and Christian doctrine. He even specified a link between the Arapaho and Welsh languages.

St. Michael's therefore followed a strategy of inventive syncretism at Wind River beginning as early as the teens, when it established a boarding school and a permanent church (Goff and Devito 1979:1–17). For example, the grounds were ordered on the model of the camp circle and defined by twelve cottonwood trees that were named by elders and paralleled the form of a ceremonial lodge.

Traditional medicine ceremonies were also held on the grounds. Many Arapaho elements were introduced into the sanctuary of Our Father's House, itself named following the Arapaho identification of the creator as *heisonoonin*. The church building was located on the circle and had an altar inside on the west end, the traditional place for sacred elements. Today, services syncretize Arapaho and Christian elements; cedar is used for incense; elders offer Arapaho prayers; a drum accompanies the serving of the Eucharist; and a round, altar kneeling station is oriented to the four directions. Since the 1960s St. Stephen's has followed St. Michael's example by adopting more traditional elements into its services and symbolism.

For missionaries, syncretism drew on the assumption that universal human experience underlay all religions. Since the 1970s Christian missionaries and theologians among the American Indian peoples have aimed for ecumenism, combining Christian and traditional religions and moving toward one American Indian Christianity. That effort was exemplified at St. Stephen's in the 1960s and 1970s by the work of Carl Starkloff, who finds a common ground for all religions in Schleiermacher's proposition that there "is a spontaneous religious sentiment in all men, especially children" (Starkloff 1971:320). Beneath and prior to differences in specific beliefs and ritual practices of local religions, there is a universal experience of sacredness. Using Deloria's phrase, missionaries see and saw this experience as a foundation for a "universal brotherhood of humankind" (1994:49) that dissolves the differences and thus conflicts among all human societies, including Indian-white relations, intertribal differences, and intratribal factionalism. Thus, while modern syncretism returns to a primordial sentiment, Arapaho pluralism is phrased in terms of life movement toward the same place.

For different lengths of time, both missions pursued syncretism, but such a synthesis of elements occurred only within the boundaries of the missions and Christian practice. Restraining the mission-initiated efforts, Arapaho people have always tried to control the syncretism process by selecting or resisting elements. Syncretism was not, however, the main factor drawing the Arapaho people to the missions. Indeed, there is an ongoing Arapaho sense that each tradition must be kept separate in space and time. Elements can be in the same context and event but not mixed in elements, practices, or meanings. Thus, whereas the missions syncretized, the Arapahos compartmentalized. More precisely, Arapaho pluralism kept Christian doctrine and its universalizing directive within a significantly controlled local knowledge system. Overall, the Northern Arapaho people appropriated Catholicism and later Episcopalian tradition as "practices" rather than as belief or doctrine; they converted

Christianity into their own set of concepts about personhood, knowledge, and life movement. Christian practices and speech forms merely proved to the Arapahos the correctness of what they had been doing all along.

Through the mission experience, Arapahos also developed or at least refined strategies for interacting with non-Indian people. The duality of culture and the practice of "Don't tell them White people about it" (Fowler 1982:244) combined to form a strategy for maintaining distance from and some empowerment over Euro-American society. Along with and serving their compartmentalization, Arapaho people maintained control of the boundary between the front and the back stage in intercultural contact. On the front stage they showed a willingness to assimilate in practice. On the back stage were humor, tragedy, tradition, and cultural invention. The distance maintained from the non-Indian world is, even today, often an expression of tolerance but not affirmation. There is "another side" to mission history that has never been and may never be written, since it was visible only in the Arapaho lived world of the back stage. In oral history, such "real history" is often the source of humorous anecdotes, of intense emotional reactions to Euro-American authority, and of alternative interpretations of "official" history. For instance, one Jesuit brother at St. Stephen's wanted to learn to speak Arapaho, so some of the schoolboys taught him a few words to use in the Mass. However, the boys had given him profane words for common conversational phrases. That was a great sport for the boys.

The place both the missionaries and the Arapahos made for Christianity and the missions has diminished in the last thirty years. The missions were once economic, educational, and social centers, but now they occupy a much more peripheral place in the communities. Their primary roles are to provide places and practices for Arapaho life transitions and ritual centers for Arapaho Christians. In some local historical perspectives, many unresolved issues revolve around past mission practices, such as the antitraditional period at St. Stephen's and the harshness of school discipline. There are some voices now holding the missions responsible for the loss of tradition and language, while others would like them to reaffirm their former commitment to helping the community. Some families have turned to other churches and missions with stronger missionary efforts on or near the reservation. Some are evangelical and antitraditional; others have developed new forms of tolerance and syncretism.

Summary

Since mythical time, knowledge has defined what is Arapaho and how something can become Arapaho. In life movement, knowledge is not just a body of information passed on but a dynamic process for activating age-structured and kin relations, shaping the direction and duration of life, and empowering the Arapaho people in their relations with the non-Arapaho world beyond the boundaries of camp or human experience. Beginning with the history of contact, the relationship between Arapaho and Euro-American peoples has concentrated at the interface of two different ways of knowing. On one side, the Arapaho people extended their traditional strategies for maintaining boundaries and appropriating powerful knowledge from beyond them. On the other, Euro-American knowledge sought to universalize itself while continually maintaining distance from local cultural knowledge. Between the two and within the latter, contradictions evolved to sustain Euro-American modes of domination. Arapaho society has faced and now confronts two kinds of contradictions, one between their own and the Euro-American knowledge system, the other perpetuated within and beneath Euro-American knowledge itself. Though it is often difficult to distinguish these, the latter have been the most durable and powerful.

One of the greatest sources of resistance to Western knowledge systems is that local systems resist total assimilation. The power of the federal bureaucracy has never been able to universalize its authority over the entirety of Arapaho space and time. The missions, likewise, have never succeeded in totalizing a religious system. Afforded distance from dominant Euro-American ways of knowing, Arapaho people have had and still have a unique critical perspective on the power behind Euro-American knowledge about which those with non-Indian perspectives normally remain oblivious. As Farriss says of the historical experiences of the Maya of the Yucatán, "It is almost invariably the case that the dominated understand the dominators better than vice versa. Their need is far greater" (1995:122).

The universalizing power of Euro-American knowledge is veiled in a supposedly objective truth. Contemporary institutions whose former incarnations eroded or diluted tradition are perceived as solutions to present problems. Thus, education is still valued, almost without question, as a solution to all problems from unemployment to drug abuse, from crime to government inefficiency. Introduced solutions often do have positive effects for the community's economic, educational, administrative, and personal needs, but they are always contingent on the vicissitudes of eventful or conjuctural history, policy reversals, budget cuts, personnel changes, and administrative restructuring. Some programs that really do work at Wind River often disappear within years or even months. Some that have never achieved their desired ends continue to survive. Institutions designed to be durable structures and provide rational consistency are, from a local perspective, often sources of abrupt and unpredictable changes. The sheer unpredictability and seeming irrationality are expressions of the contradictions that endure over time. To a great extent, the contradiction between a universalizing Euro-American knowledge at a distance and Northern Arapaho knowledge that compartmentalizes its local forms has contributed to the spatial and temporal distance between the Arapaho and the non-Indian worlds. Whether in the words of bureaucrats, missionaries, researchers, educators, or local non-Indian people, Euro-American knowledge professes to be true everywhere but disconnected from real sociocultural systems.

Along the temporal axis of progress, Euro-American knowledge has always claimed a monopoly on the ability to solve immediate problems on the reservation. Continually, though, problems assigned to the past persevere as contradictions in the present. Euro-American "truth" rests on irreversible, cumulative knowing, yet toward Arapaho people and American Indian peoples in general, there is ongoing "forgetting" about how past policies, institutions, texts, or persons continue to affect and effect the present. Problems in the past become local problems in the present for which yet other imposed forms must provide the solution. Another irony is that the knowledge behind that process is future-oriented and unaware of the contradictions it is continually constituting and leaving unresolved in the past and the present. In misunderstanding the link between present and the past in this sense, the vast majority of Euro-Americans are the people without history.

The once-and-for-all resolution of the contradictions inherent in Euro-American knowledge throughout history is beyond the reach of local strategies, for those contradictions are ever reappearing in various permutations within the lived world. Throughout contact, literacy and formal education have reappeared promising liberation and equality, but they are yet to be owned and controlled by the Arapaho people. Another limit imposed on the Arapahos is that Euro-Americans seek to know the world directly, as through empirical observation, but they always take the knowledge gathered and place it at a distance where it is inaccessible to Arapaho people. Finally, Euro-American knowledge is supposed to have the purpose of progress through history for both the individual and society; but within the lived world of the reservation, the non-Indian world appears unpredictable and without direction. Thus, Euro-American knowledge forms provide no promise of continuity and consistency.

The boundaries between Euro-American and Arapaho knowledge today are of course not as clearly demarcated or maintained as in the past. Elders today comment that things are "getting mixed up," that is, that the younger generations are no longer able to recognize differences between traditions within the Arapaho culture and between Arapaho and non-Arapaho knowledge and practice. There is also a sense that "things are moving too fast," such that many issues and problems, following the Euro-American course, pass by unresolved to become sources of resistance and conflict in social relations. Yet, the Arapaho will is still very strong to "do things in a good/correct way" for life movement. The difference is that the flow of knowledge from the outside is much greater than in the past; the life trajectory is tied to the non-Arapaho world in increasing and complex ways. Even though economic conditions have been much worse in earlier times, self-determination is moving forward, and cultural revitalization is expanding; nevertheless, the contradictions generated by Euro-American knowledge have perhaps never been more formidable and problematic. Self-determination means increasing self-domination through self-administration employing Euro-American knowledge and associated practices once used for disempowerment. Likewise, cultural revitalization requires appropriation of Euro-American and pan-Indian ways of knowing that historically have displaced Arapaho knowledge.

Overall, the "us versus them" dichotomy can no longer serve as the only basis for understanding difference and contradiction from perspectives on either side. The contradictions within Euro-American knowledge are real and powerful, not just abstract intellectual problems for critical discourse to resolve from an academic perspective. They are known immediately to the Arapaho people at Wind River and other peoples who have had to negotiate them. In my experience at Wind River, I too became aware of them, perhaps learning as much about my own as about Arapaho culture in the process. However, I also became aware of the limits of my own knowledge to grasp the experience of those contradictions and the ways Arapaho people empower themselves against them.

13
Conclusion

This book is about two forms of power that have affected Northern Arapahos over the long duration of their history. One is the continuity of Arapaho power through practices for generating life movement, acquiring knowledge, and defining personhood. The other is the power of ongoing contradictions that sustain Euro-American domination. For the former, the focus on practice has revealed that knowledge generates life movement; life movement brings increasing knowledge; and personhood, shaped through respect, pity, quietness, craziness, and other dimensions of social relations, is defined by and relative to life stage and respective knowledge. In the attempt to explicate those three dimensions, I have allowed meanings to evolve from various sources and domains of culture, rather than privileging or excluding certain connections. In order to at least represent the total system, I have interconnected the dimensions of personhood, life movement, and knowledge by following lines of evidence from language, ways of speaking, kinship, myth, space-time, art, exchange patterns, and lived history.

Following the American anthropological tradition of Boas, Sapir, and others, I have chosen a relational analysis rather than a formalistic or reductionistic one. Toward this aim, I have interrelated aspects of history, language, and culture rather than reifying them as separate phenomena requiring single, fixed vantage points for interpretation. As set forth in chapter 2, conceptualization has been grounded in the indigenous social and cultural context, as Hallowell suggests, in connectivity and temporalization constituted through the nexus of practice, as Munn offers, and with the openness to time and flux that Bourdieu, Barth, and others have endorsed. It has been possible thereby to go beyond narrow term-for-term glosses for indigenous concepts and imposed structural concepts that preclude the exploration of multiple meanings. Such analysis requires multifaceted connections to myth, language, the body, music, art, land, seasonality, history, and other domains without positing any one as a ground for all others. As interpretation proceeded, I left the concepts somewhat open-ended in order to follow the connections without restriction. Of course, that mode of cultural analysis always remains incomplete, for the total or potential connectivity operating within a sociocultural system is always beyond reach. There are always further connections to pursue, some of them outside the available evidence. Thus, this work at most succeeds only in representing totality, leaving many more relations to be articulated.

Unlike some other North American Indian cultures, Arapaho culture has rarely been overinterpreted despite a large body of existing evidence. From the 1890s to the 1940s, the Northern and the Southern Arapaho people left a generous amount of ethnographic evidence to Kroeber, Dorsey, Warden, Hilger, Mooney, Michelson, and others. Yet, anthropologists and Arapaho researchers have only begun explore those resources so that the original contributors can continue to "give something back" long after their passing.

There are a number of reasons for the relative lack of attention to Arapaho material, but two general obstacles seem to have been greatest. On the one hand, the anthropological imagination must overcome the assumption pervading the discipline that there are no future possibilities for the existing evidence and thus nothing left to study about past and present American Indian cultures, languages, and histories. On the other, Arapaho researchers must realize that the bulk of this knowledge is not spoken by anthropologists or other researchers but in words directly from the mouths of Arapahos of the past like Sherman Sage, Gunn Griswold, Cleaver Warden, Fire-Wood, John Goggles, Salt Friday, Pete Lone Bear, Yellow Calf, and many others. Dismissive assumptions about the worth of this material and continued research have long restrained the respective efforts of Arapaho and non-Indian scholarship and the development of a partnership between them.

With respect to the available evidence and the need for partnership, one limit of the present study is that it does not intend to define precisely how much or in what specific forms traditional Arapaho culture survives in the contemporary context. Such a mission betrays a Euro-American bias to define culture as substantive knowledge and continuity as readily visible in observed events or through interviews. Like contradictions of power, continuity is not immediately perceptible on the surface of cultural practices, speech, or objects. Despite all of the changes introduced during reservation history, Northern Arapaho people follow paths of life movement, knowledge, and personhood that maintain a clear difference from Euro-American society. Most profoundly, the concern for doing things in a good/correct way persists beneath the flux of all actions, relations, and events. Forms of respect, pity, quietness, and craziness have endured changes in the kinship and age structure, as well as the shift from Arapaho to English (see Anderson 1998). Formal vows, sacrifice, and exchange are still practiced in order to effect life movement. Retaining and passing on knowledge endure as core concerns in current efforts to achieve true self-government, reinvigorate Arapaho culture and language, and address other pressing issues.

I have employed a critical perspective toward understanding the durability of Euro-American power as enduring contradictions. Three objectives have guided this inquiry. First is the concern to study the "contact" between two cultures beneath the transient surface of publicly visible events and beneath the conjunctural level of episodic history. The second, related aim has been to identify some of the contradictions over what Braudel calls the *longue durée* (1972:20 ff.) in Arapaho "noneventful" history, to borrow Fogelson's concept (1989), and thus recognize the durability of Euro-American modes of power that connect the present to the past in Wind River Reservation history. Simply stated, "culture contact" involves much more than face-to-face encounters, crises, policy eras, and discourse. It takes in the long-term contradictions that endure at the generative source of power, even when policies, discourse, events, and texts on the surface change their content.

Another main interest of this book has been with the various strategies Arapaho people have employed for local control of their relation to Euro-American society. Such strategies draw from traditional and innovative sources to redress in a ongoing way the effects of contradictions overdetermined by Euro-American power. Recall that Euro-American power originates from a distance and moves from top down and from outside to inside, whereas Arapaho empowerment has been vested in local family relations, centralized tribal government, and ritual practices radiating outward. It is thus possible to resist, bound, or appropriate Euro-American forms locally but not affect the source of their power "somewhere else" and over the long term. Unlike some other American Indian tribes and organizations, the Northern Arapahos do not generally engage in national-level discourse, issues, or activism. From an outside view, the definition of political empowerment and large-scale activism would appear to be the only path for real social change, but that visibility and that scale of action are not necessarily measures of durability or potential for change. On the contrary, the Arapaho strategies, less visible, more localized, and seemingly without formal political engagement with the powers that be, are no less empowering for continuity and resistance. As Fogelson notes, there are multiple modes of power to be studied in American Indian ethnohistory: "Less apparent to the general public are the internal strengths of Indian societies as expressed through the idiom of kinship, in the abiding sense of community, in the adaptive significance of what we derogatively view as factionalism, and the political and legal effectiveness of native advocates" (1989:139). Little has been done to examine types of empowerment that operate outside the public sphere, let alone to appreciate how internal tribal politics, often viewed as dysfunctional, are an expression of empowerment against the dominant society that predates modern activism and postmodern decolonization efforts by centuries.

Just as it has not been possible within the limits of this book to describe all of the connections that relate to Arapaho culture, there are Euro-American contradictions and Arapaho forms of empowerment that have not been elaborated here either. Additional points of deep, pervasive, and durable "contact" and resistance could be revealed by further study. Similar analyses could shift the focus to the deeper contradictions and resistance in such fields as economic, political, technological, medical, linguistic, and even aesthetic relations between Arapaho society and the non-Indian world. Arapaho cultural continuity and resistance to Euro-American power meet, though not exclusively, in social relations and cultural connectivity localized in families, communities, and the tribe. Nonetheless, the focus here is not arbitrary, for it goes to the source of the durable, diffuse, and distanciated power that Euro-American practices continue to reproduce, both without reflection and, seemingly, without resolution within its own conditions and possibilities. Imposed forms of power are socially constructed in an erratic, hurried Euro-American time, thus given neither as natural and rational nor as a self-consistent "ideology." One driving contradiction is that Euro-American knowledge fails to become aware of its own contradictions. It has never even stopped to construct a coherent ideology to justify itself. A deep history of modern domination reveals that there is no universal Hegelian idealistic or Marxist materialistic dialectic resolution to those contradictions once and for all, for the nature of the power is much more diffuse and multifarious than most existing models recognize. The reason is that all global or general social theories of modern society have greatly understated the power of local and particular forms of resistance. The greatest obstacle to resolution is the contradiction that Euro-American knowledge and power seek universality but persistently fail to comprehend and totally dominate local sociocultural realities.

The contradictions of Euro-American institutions continue to sustain what Giddens (1987) calls distanciation. Euro-American society distances itself in time from Arapaho and other American Indian communities. Many Arapaho people recognize their loss of traditions but also disagree with statements or hints that present-day life at Wind River is just like the white world and no longer Arapaho. As for other reservation communities, many Arapaho people resist Euro-Americans ways of placing their culture in the past as invalidating their present existence and identity. As Fabian realized, "denial of coevalness" is the basis for Euro-American distance from Arapahos and other American Indian people and an excuse for not knowing what is below the surface. As cultural identity has been brought into the contradictions of Euro-American knowledge, the questions of what are "real" history and "genuine" tradition have taken on meanings estranged from the Arapaho theory of practice. In short, to ask such questions is somehow to break from the traditional ways of doing things. What remains "traditional" is in and of doing things in a good/correct way with the elders, knowledge, resources, and instruction one has at present, but not by measurement against an abstract standard at a distance in space or time.

When the domination of American Indian peoples does become an object of study, it is usually placed in the past and embodied in some "Other" actor, event, or group. The Euro-American sense of eventful, narrative history often offers silent insurance that the present domination will remain disconnected from the past—ironically, often by persons and institutions that claim sole ownership of "history" itself. Current policies are presented as an advance on and a corrective of a regrettable history placed in the past, about which few Euro-American actors have any real knowledge. Euro-American knowledge, including some anthropological and ethnohistorical approaches, thus silently remove all power relations with Native American peoples from the present. Instead of preserving knowledge, such a "history" of only the past can thus be a device for "disposing of the present."

As compensation for the past, Euro-American institutions have always offered knowledge for a brighter future, also disconnected from present realities. Education, federal policies, and religion have consistently been offered to American Indian peoples as compensation for past domination and exploitation. Based on the belief in education as a path to progress, reservation schools tacitly or explicitly deny and negate a connection to past boarding schools. Missionaries present themselves as more "enlightened" than their predecessors. Church policy and a liberal, social ethic are foregrounded as the separation of present missions from the past. Similarly, native language and cultural education in reservation schools is presented as an advance and as a corrective for the past loss of culture. Federal agencies and officials also silently or, in times of conflict, openly distance themselves from the oppressive policies of the past by satisfying themselves that they are not racist, assimilative, and paternalistic, but instead objective, multiculturally aware, and egalitarian. A temporalized contrast based on faith in moral progress moving toward the future thus severs present power from the "evil past." Missionaries, agents, traders, politicians, and other historical figures can be held accountable for their own crimes and sins, while the contradictions behind those acts remain active and undetected beneath the surface of a present moving forward into the future.

Strategies for effective political discourse with Euro-American officials and governments are thus not enough to sustain Arapaho tribal continuity and solidarity. At one time the abiding concern was intermediation, as Fowler's work establishes, but situating all issues now at the interface of the Arapahos versus the U.S. government would be an oversimplification. Not all forms of domination or resistance emanate from political discourse. Successes through legal and political action have not been and will not be sufficient to redress Euro-American dominance in all its forms. At Wind River there is a growing sense that the contradictions have become increasingly internalized and diffuse within reservation communities, not only in political spheres but also in daily social life. As some older people recognize with the advantage of their deeper historical perspective, the boundaries between the two worlds and between different traditions within culture are no longer as clear as they once were, whether in politics, personal relations, art, music, or religious practice. Much of that blurring of boundaries can be attributed to the immense flow of knowledge into the community from the mass media, consumerism, automobile transportation, new pan-Indian traditions, federal agencies, schools, and even computer technology. Countering all of that, Arapaho people endeavor to maintain or construct boundaries, a strategy especially evident in religious life and when traditional practices for life movement are activated to respond to individual, family, or community crises. From within, it is those practices that continue to set the Northern Arapaho tribe apart from the surrounding non-Indian world.

The social separation between Northern Arapaho society and the surrounding non-Arapaho world persists as a condition of experience. From the outside looking in, Euro-American "contact" with Northern Arapaho people has only rarely been within domains conducive to real, ongoing social relations. Today, the majority of non-Indians who enter the reservation each day do so in formal settings or through distant communication. The latent power of Euro-American culture has always been a matter of affirming social difference and exercising power from a distance without social contact, whether through federal bureaucracy, formal education, or the mass media. The Arapaho people are well aware of that gap between the two social worlds, though non-Indians generally have the privilege of knowing nothing about it or projecting the cause onto the reservation communities themselves.

Though social and cultural connectivity are still very strong at Wind River, they require ongoing strategies both for sustaining the continuity of old traditions while appropriating new ones and for adapting to contradictions from outside and within the community. Arapaho elders, ritual leaders, tribal committees, educators, parents, and scholars endeavor to maintain and reinvigorate "tradition" by struggling in the long run to claim ownership of ways of knowing and shaping life movement in order to "do it on their own." As part of that effort, Arapaho political leadership of the 1990s followed a course toward increasing self-determination by placing more and more joint (i.e., Shoshone and Arapaho), federal, and state programs under tribal administration. Frustrating both cultural and political initiatives, economic conditions at Wind River declined in the 1990s as the rest of the American economy supposedly flourished. Since the Reagan era, federal funding has been greatly reduced, and tribal income from mineral leases has plummeted as oil prices dipped to the lowest point in decades and oil companies abandoned the old, less productive fields at Wind River. Thus, efforts to do it own their own have had to rely on fewer and fewer resources since the late 1980s.

Within the tribe today there are also various and at times conflicting perspectives on knowledge, life movement, and personal relations, as well as on politics, the economy, and other contemporary issues. Those differences generate views about the future of the tribe that are similar and different from Euro-American perspectives. Past traditions and present conditions in lived experience are inextricable from shared or differing views of and actions for the future. How different cultures view the "future" is one of the least considered topics in anthropological, linguistic, and historical studies of American Indian peoples. Certainly much has been done in the past several decades to recognize, research, and discuss the history of peoples formerly regarded as ahistorical, but the future is still left as a void. On one level that reflects acceptance of the popular assumption that indigenous peoples live in a time that is repetitive, cold, or cyclical. On another, anthropology and history lack theoretical models to relate the past to the present and future without imposing Euro-American orders of time.

To develop that field of inquiry, it is necessary to understand local, indigenous ways of orienting present and past meanings and practices to the future. Arapaho life movement and knowledge have always been future-oriented by giving direction and impetus for practices moving beyond present conditions into the next moment in time. Life transitions, both within and outside the lodges, shaped and phased the movement of the individual, the family, the band, and the tribe into the future. Pity inspires vows for sacrifices that activate social relations in order to discard present or avert future difficulties. Respect activates exchanges for kin- and age-structured relations that endure forward in time. Senior people once watched younger lives unfold for signs of leadership or other skills to be channeled for service to the tribe. Dreams and visions provided ongoing information for future choices and actions. Councils met to plan camp movements on the basis of shared knowledge about the environment and seasonal changes. Families and individuals continue to prepare extensively for upcoming ceremonies, giveaways, trips, and social events. The Ghost Dance and other new religious forms aimed in part to see into and appropriate control of the future. In the traditional age structure, old people embodied and carried knowledge from the mythical past up to the present but also used it for seeing things coming or emerging on the horizon. There are many accounts of old people who prophesied or predicted the coming of non-Indians, automobiles, mixed marriages, language shift, airplanes, world wars, and "white men's ways."

At Wind River today, people imagine, think about, discuss, and act for the future in every aspect of life, yet not always in ways that replicate imported Euro-American senses of future time. When Euro-Americans see that their own progressive values and meanings are absent, there is a tendency for them to conclude that no future orientation exists. When individuals deviate from the ideal Euro-American well-scheduled life trajectory, they are likewise judged as without a future. If there is no self-orientation for prolonged education, savings accounts, capital investment, bureaucratic planning, life insurance, written proposals, finely tuned schedules, and the like, then outside perspectives are prone to identify no sense of a future that imposes present obligations and boundaries. The simple response is that different cultures have different futures. Today, Arapaho people are oriented to Euro-American roads of life as well as others that are distinctly their own. Granted, such future awareness and multiple roads to follow are not without confusing and disruptive effects on young and old people alike. In their own ways, Arapaho people are aware of the possibilities for their future, whether positive or negative. There are always personal concerns about employment, paying debts, schooling, where to live, how to negotiate relationships, ways of dealing with the non-Indian world, how to keep their children on a straight road, and what things are emerging on the horizon for the tribe. There are tribal concerns about keeping the language alive, changes in religion, maintaining family land holdings, crime and substance abuse, declining tribal resources, effective tribal leadership, and many other issues. Over the long term, there are questions about the enduring Arapaho sacred responsibilities that began in mythical time and have been met throughout a difficult history. Facing those and other challenges as individuals, families, and a tribe has generated distinctly Arapaho forms of empowerment for strength and continuity to move forward into the future. Continuity in time comes from completing vows, preparing for and participating in successful events that give something back to the community, overcoming tragedy through family and tribal relations, envisioning and then implementing something new and good for the community, carrying out sacred practices, and seeing traditions moving into the future. All along, there is ongoing social and cultural experimentation to see what will and will not work.

The Arapaho people have thus never been totally disempowered by the wave of changes instituted by the Euro-American imagined, utopian future forced on them in the name of progress, development, assimilation, and other Western versions of temporalization. For its frequency, intensity, and duration of strategies for overcoming challenges that the future brings, there has never been anything comparable to the Arapahos' response in my experience of the non-Indian world. They have continually appropriated new cultural forms, developed strategies, and overcome difficulties.

Historically, Euro-American orientations to the future have always fallen short of the consistency and continuity that they advertise. As concluded in Deloria's articulation (1994) of the long-term contradictions with and within Western religion, philosophy, and political forms, history offers no evidence to expect future resolution through universal application of Euro-American knowledge. More specifically, there is no reason to believe that anthropological, ethnohistorical, or other academic research strategies will have a significant effect on the future either (see Deloria 1991). Despite a century of scholarly efforts to narrow the chasm of misunderstanding toward American Indian peoples, that chasm still remains in the real world.

Enduring, traditional Arapaho strategies are still employed against Euro-American power, but some people argue that the old ways no longer work. Within that view there is a sense that it is no longer possible to maintain an "us versus them" boundary from inside the tribe. From an opposing direction, there is a strong push to "do it on our own" by claiming total control of all knowledge, organizations, and events at Wind River. I even heard half-joking suggestions that a border fence and a crossing gate be installed to monitor the flow of people and things on and off the reservation. Whereas in space there is a call for boundaries, in time there is concern with moderation. In politics, religious life, and everyday social relations, it seems that things are indeed "happening too fast" for traditional strategies to keep pace. Some personal, family, and community changes seem to occur precipitously without warning.

Yet at such times, the Arapaho people still respond to tragedies by activating intense family and community solidarity and by focusing on a religious center where a straight road for life movement can begin again.

Some problems, though, seem now to elude both traditional and Euro-American responses. Law enforcement, education, economic development, legal disputes, relations to the local non-Indian communities, and other issues seem ever more problematic or "out of control." As for many other tribes, the contradiction is that financial, knowledge, and other support still derives from outside sources. The funding for solving problems in Euro-American ways or even traditional responses is always impoverished relative to comparable programs in the surrounding non-Indian world. Many grant-funded programs come and go, even when they are successful, because most agencies assume that the local resource base will assume the cost of the program in time. That of course generally does not happen at Wind River or any other economically impoverished community. Internal support from tribal funds is precarious as income from mineral leases declines. When local appropriation succeeds and endures, it is generally less dependent on support from external organizations.

I have never known such cultural connectivity nor such sheer power of Euro-American contradictions as I saw during the last twelve years of my life tied to Wind River. As time passed, I more frequently forgot the boundaries that defined me as an anthropologist, set aside the singular motive to collect data, and tried, though not always successfully, to become an active participant in community life. Rather than conforming to the Euro-American stereotype of telling people "what we should do," I tried to join projects originating within the community, even on some occasions when I did not personally agree with the means or ends. Through all these activities, I became part of Arapaho successful efforts to shape the future, as well many more that failed.

In various roles as teacher, student counselor, local researcher, program planner, grants-writer, partner, and kinsman I learned immeasurably more through doing than through passive observing or narrowly structured interviews. Throughout these efforts I felt both the connectedness of everyone "moving in the same direction," realized the consequences of making many mistakes, and confronted the double-binds intrinsic to Euro-American power. At times, I learned what it was like to "give up" after experiencing the effects of choosing a bad place to stand, crazy words to say, or the wrong road to follow. In time, I also learned how to discard those errors to get up in the morning and start over again.

Prior to my experiences at Wind River, I had only abstractly known the contradictions of domination, but out there I came to struggle with them personally and profoundly. At first I accepted them as surface phenomena that my own knowledge could eventually explain or resolve, but in time came to appreciate their pervasive momentum beyond the horizon of my understanding and action. Ironically, only from a local perspective removed from mainstream American society and academic contexts, did these contradictions become at all comprehensible for their depth and durability. Euro-American knowledge at a distance offers less for inquiry into these problems, even when it claims a critical or decolonizing perspective, than Arapaho understandings enriched by a long history from which most non-Indians have been exempt.

My field experiences directed me to critical theories different from any others I had gained from my academic training. Euro-American ways of ordering the world I once accepted as given and objective gradually or suddenly revealed their mystification and contradictions. For one thing, I had been inculcated with the belief that anthropology was somehow exempt from Euro-American domination and distance, but became very aware that my position will always be one of privilege and detachment. Left aside here, then, are questions about how the present study fits into the contradictions it articulates.

My own future is now interwoven with issues facing the Arapaho people in the years to come. Much Arapaho discussion centers on the need to make culture, language, and history accessible to local readers and uses. Many times, I heard the call to produce materials for the people to use at Wind River, instead of investing my time in academic works, such as the present text. In trying to meet the demands of both, I often find myself torn between local needs and the demands of scholarship. From one Arapaho perspective, the imperative to "give something back" is at the center of my life, while from an academic perspective, such activities are considered community service or charity work compared to "serious" endeavors of research, publishing, teaching, and institutional service. For me, at Wind River these priorities traded places. Though the contradiction is difficult to elude, it is possible to make room for both and not just a syncretism that mixes the two. Dialogue, reciprocity, and cooperation between anthropology and American Indian knowledge are not only possible but inescapable today. The opposition between the researcher's knowledge at a distance and local resistance to research can give way to partnership. In all, I have known the distance, resistance, and, most of all among the Northern Arapaho people, a sharing of knowledge.

Bibliography

Alexander, Hartley Burr
1953   The World's Rim: Great Mysteries of the North American
Indians. Foreword by Clyde Kluckhohn. Lincoln: University of
Nebraska Press.

Althusser, Louis
1969   For Marx. (Trans. by Ben Brewster). New York: Pantheon.

Anderson, Gary C.
1986   Little Crow: Spokesman for the Sioux. St. Paul: Minnesota
Historical Society Press.

Anderson, Jeffrey
1998   Ethnolinguistic Dimensions of Northern Arapaho Language Shift.
Anthropological Linguistics 40:1-64.

in press   Northern Arapaho Conversion of a Christian text: The Our Father.
Ethnohistory.

Arapaho-Cheyenne Indians
1974   New York: Garland Publishing.

Atkins, J. D. C.
1887   The English Language in Indian Schools. In Americanizing the
American Indians, ed. Francis Paul Prucha, 197-206. Cambridge,
Mass.: Harvard University Press 1973.

Barth, Fredrik
1995   Other Knowledge and Other Ways of Knowing. Journal of
Anthropological Research 51:65-68.

Bass, Althea
1966   The Arapaho Way. New York: Potter.

Basso, Keith
1972   "To Give up on Words": Silence in Western Apache Culture. In
Language and Social Context, ed. Pier Paolo Giglio, 67-86. New
York: Penguin.

Bateson, Gregory
1972   Steps to an Ecology of Mind. New York: Ballantine.

Bender, John, and David Wellbury
    1991   Introduction. In Chronotypes: The Construction of Time, 1-15.
                Stanford, Calif.: Stanford University Press.

Bernardi, Bernardo
    1985   Age Class Systems: Social Institutions and Politics Based on Age.
                Cambridge, England: Cambridge University Press.

Bourdieu, Pierre
    1977   Outline of a Theory of Practice. Cambridge, England: Cambridge
                University Press.

Braudel, Fernand
    1972   History and the Social Sciences. In Economy and Society in early
                Modern Europe: Essays from the *Annales*. ed. Peter Burke, 11-42.
                London: Routledge and Kegan Paul.

Buckley, Thomas
    1982   Yurok Realities in the Nineteenth and Twentieth Centuries. Ph.D.
                Dissertation (Anthropology). University of Chicago, Chicago, Ill.

Carter, John G.
    1938   The Northern Arapaho Flat Pipe and the Ceremony of Covering
                the Pipe. Smithsonian Institution, Bureau of American Ethnology,
                Bulletin 119 (Anthropological Papers 2), 71-102. Washington.

Census of Arapahoe Indians
    1885-1922 Census of Arapaho Indians of Shoshone Agency. Shoshone
                Agency, Wyoming. Bureau of Indian Affairs.

Clark, W. P.
    1885   The Indian Sign Language, with Brief Explanatory Notes of the
                Gestures Taught Deaf-Mutes in our Institutions for Their
                Instruction, and a Description of Some of the Peculiar Laws,
                Customs, Myths, Superstitions, Ways of Living, Code of Peace,
                and War Signals of Our Aborigines. Philadelphia: L. R. Hamersly.

Cooper, John M.
    1934   The Northern Algonquian Supreme Being. Washington: Catholic
                University of America Anthropological Series 2. Washington.

Crispin, Tom
    1935   The Four Old Men. Indians at Work 2(20):12-13. Washington:
                Office of Indian Affairs.

Crofts, Beatrice
    1997   Walk Softly, This Is God's Country. Lander, Wyo.: Mortimer
                Publishing.

Culin, Stewart
1907   Games of the North American Indians. Twenty-Fourth Annual
            Report of the Bureau of American Ethnology to the Secretary of
            the Smithsonian Institution, 1902-3. Washington.
Curtis, Natalie
1934   The Indians' Book. New York: Dover.
Dangberg, Grace M.
1957   Letters to Jack Wilson, the Paiute Prophet, Written Between 1908
            and 1911. Smithsonian Institution, Bureau of American
            Ethnology, Bulletin 164 (Anthropological Papers 55), 279-96.
            Washington.
Deloria, Vine, Jr.
1985   Out of Chaos. Parabola: The Magazine of Myth and Tradition
            3:14-22.
1988   Custer Died for Your Sins. Norman: University of Oklahoma
            Press.
1991   Commentary: Research, Redskins, and Reality. American Indian
            Quarterly 15:457-68.
1994   God is Red: A Native View of Religion. Golden, Colo.: Fulcrum.
1995   Red Earth, White Lies: Native Americans and the Myth of
            Scientific Fact. New York: Scribner.
DeMallie, Raymond J.
1987   Lakota Belief and Ritual in the Nineteenth Century. In Sioux
            Indian Religion, ed. Raymond J. DeMallie and Douglas R. Parks,
            25-44. Norman: University of Oklahoma Press.
Dorsey, George A.
1903   The Arapaho Sun Dance; the Ceremony of the Offerings-Lodge.
            Field Columbian Museum Publication 75 (Anthropological Series
            4). Chicago.
Dorsey, George A., and Alfred L. Kroeber
1903   Traditions of the Arapaho. Field Columbian Museum Publication
            81 (Anthropological Series 5). Reprint, Lincoln: University of
            Nebraska Press, 1998.
Dorsey, George A., and Cleaver Warden
1905   Dorsey-Warden Collection, A-1, Boxes 1-8. Field Museum of
            Natural History, Department of Anthropology Archives. Chicago,
            Ill.

Eggan, Fred
1937   The Cheyenne and Arapaho Kinship System. In Social
            Anthropology of North American Tribes, ed. Fred Eggan, 35-95.
            Chicago: University of Chicago Press.
1966   The Cheyenne and Arapaho in the Perspective of the Plains:
            Ecology and Society. In The American Indian: Perspectives for
            the Study of Social Change, 45-77. Chicago: Aldine.

Elkin, Henry
1940   The Northern Arapaho of Wyoming. In Acculturation in Seven
            American Indian Tribes, ed. Ralph Linton,. 207-58. New York: D.
            Appleton-Century.

Erikson, Erik
1963   Childhood and Society. New York: W.W. Norton.

Fabian, Johannes
1983   Time and the Other: How Anthropology Makes Its Object. New
            York: Columbia University Press.

Farriss, Nancy
1995   Remembering the Future, Anticipating the Past: History, Time and
            Cosmology among the Maya of the Yucatán. In Time: Histories
            and Ethnologies, ed. Diane Owen Hughes and Thomas R.
            Trautman, 107-38. Ann Arbor: University of Michigan Press.

Feraca, Stephen E.
1998   Wakinyan: Lakota Religion in the Twentieth Century. Lincoln:
            University of Nebraska Press.

Fogelson, Raymond
1989   Ethnohistory of Events and Nonevents. Ethnohistory 36:133-47.

Fowler, Loretta Kay
1978   Oral Historian or Ethnologist?: The Career of Bill Shakespeare;
            Northern Arapaho, 1901-1975. In American Indian Intellectuals,
            ed. Margot Liberty, 227-40. 1976 Proceedings of the American
            Ethnological Society. St. Paul, Minn.: West Publishing.
1982   Arapahoe Politics, 1851-1878: Symbols in Crises of Authority.
            Lincoln: University of Nebraska Press.

Geertz, Clifford
1973   Person, Time, and Conduct in Bali. In The Interpretation of
            Cultures: Selected Essays, 360-411. New York: Basic Books.

Giddens, Anthony
1987   Social Theory and Modern Sociology. Stanford, Calif.: Stanford
            University Press.

Gill, Sam
1982   Native American Religions. Belmont, Calif.: Wadsworth.
Goff, Sue, and Tom Devito
1979   A Background and History of St. Michael's Mission with the
            Arapaho People. Ms.
Goody, Jack, and Ian Watt
1972   The Consequences of Literacy. In Language and Social Context, ✓
            ed. Pier Paolo Giglioli, 311-57. New York: Penguin.
Gramsci, Antonio
1988   An Antonio Gramsci Reader. New York: Schocken Books.
Greene, A. F. C.
1941   The Arapahoe Indians. Wyoming State Archives. Cheyenne.
Grinnell, George
1923   The Cheyenne Indians: Their History and Ways of Life. 2 vols.
            Reprint, New York, N.Y.: Cooper, 1962.
Gross, Feliks
1949   Nomadism of the Arapaho Indians of Wyoming and Conflict
            Between Economics and Idea System. Ethnos 14:65-88.
Hafen, LeRoy, and Ghent, W. J.
1931   Broken Hand. Denver: Old West Publishing.
Hallowell, A. Irving
1955   Cultural Factors in Spatial Orientation. In Culture and Experience,
            184-202. Philadelphia: University of Pennsylvania Press, 1971
1960   Ojibwa Ontology, Behavior, and World View. In Contributions to
            Anthropology: Selected Papers of A. Irving Hallowell, ed.
            Raymond Fogelson, 357-90. Chicago: University of Chicago
            Press, 1976.
1963a   American Indians, White and Black: The Phenomenon of
            Transculturalization. In Contributions to Anthropology: Selected
            Papers of A. Irving Hallowell, ed. Raymond Fogelson, 498-529
            Chicago: Univrsity of Chicago Press, 1976b.
1963b   Ojibwa World View and Disease. In Contributions to
            Anthropology: Selected Papers of A. Irving Hallowell, ed.
            Raymond Fogelson, 391-448. Chicago: University of Chicago
            Press, 1976.
Hasse, James W.
1965   Northern Arapaho Religious Reorganization. M.A. Thesis. St.
            Louis University, St. Louis, Ill.

Hilger, Sister M. Inez
1952   Arapaho Child Life and Its Cultural Background. Smithsonian
            Institution, Bureau of American Ethnology, Bulletin 148.
            Washington.
Hobsbawm, Eric
1983   Introduction: Inventing Traditions. In The Invention of Tradition,
            ed. Eric Hobsbawm and Terry Ranger, 1-14. Cambridge, England:
            Cambridge University Press.
Hugh-Jones, Christine
1979   From Milk River: Spatial amd Temporal Process in Northwest
            Amazonia. Cambridge, England: Cambridge University Press.
Hultkrantz, Åke
1952   Some Notes on the Arapaho Sun Dance. Ethnos 17:24-38.
            Stockholm: The Ethnological Museum of Sweden.
Hunter, Sara
1977   Northern Arapaho Grandparents: Traditional Concepts and
            Contemporary Socio-Economics. M.A. Thesis (Anthropology).
            Indiana University, Bloomington.
Jaimes, M. Annette
1992   Federal Indian Identification Policy: A Usurpation of Indigenous
            Sovereignty. In The State of Native America: Genocide,
            Colonization, and Resistance, ed. M. A. Jaimes, 123-38. Boston:
            South End Press.
Kappler, Charles J., ed.
1904   Indian Affairs: Laws and Treaties. Vol. 2. Treaties. Washington:
            Government Printing Office.
Kroeber, Alfred L.
1902, 1904, 1907 The Arapaho. Bulletin of the American Museum of Natural
            History 18(1, 2, 4). Reprint, with Foreword by Fred Eggan.
            Lincoln: University of Nebraska Press, 1983.
1916   Arapaho Dialects. University of California Publications in
            American Archaeology and Ethnology 12(3):71-138. Berkeley:
            University of California Press.
1916-20   Field Notes. National Anthropological Archives, Smithsonian
            Institution. Washington.
1939   Cultural and Natural Areas of Native North America. Publications
            in American Archaeology and Ethnology 38. Berkeley: University
            of California Press.

Leach, Edmund
1961   Rethinking Anthropology. London: Athlone.
Lévi-Strauss, Claude
1968   The Origin of Table Manners: Introduction to the Science of Mythology 3. (Trans. J. and D. Weightman). New York: Harper and Row.
Lowie, Robert H.
1916   Plains Indian Age-Societies and Comparative Summary. Anthropological Papers of the American Museum of Natural History 11(13):877-1031. New York.
Marx, Karl
1966   The German Ideology, Part I. In The Marx-Engels Reader, ed. Robert Tucker, 67-125. New York: Norton.
Mauss, Marcel
1979   Seasonal Variations of the Eskimo: A Study in Social Morphology. (Trans. by J. J. Fox). London, England: Routledge and Kegan Paul.
1985   A Category of the Human Mind: The Notion of Person, the Notion of Self. (Trans. W. D. Halls). In The Category of the Person, ed. M. Carrithers, et al., 1-25. Cambridge, England: Cambridge University Press.
McCoy Tim, with Ronald McCoy
1977   Tim McCoy Remembers the West: An Autobiography. Garden City, N.Y.: Doubleday.
Medicine, Beatrice
1987   Indian Women and the Renaissance of Traditional Religion. In Sioux Indian Religion, ed. Raymond J. DeMallie and Douglas R. Parks, 159-72. Norman: University of Oklahoma Press.
Michelson, Truman
1912   Preliminary Report on the Linguistic Classification of Algonquian Tribes. Twenty-eighth Annual Report of the Bureau of American Ethnology to the Secretary of the Smithsonian Institution for the Years 1906-7, 221-90. Washington.
1933   Narrative of an Arapaho Woman. American Anthropologist 35:596-610.
c.1910   Field Notes. Smithsonian Institution National Anthropological Archives. Washington.

c. 1910a   Notecards. Anonymous Personal Collection. Northern Arapaho. Smithsonian Institution National Anthropological Archives. Washington.

Mooney, James
1896   The Ghost-Dance Religion and Sioux Outbreak of 1890. Fourteenth Annual Report of the Bureau of Ethnology for the Years 1892-1893. Part 2, 641-1110. Washington.

Moss, Paul
1988   The Eagle (audiotape). Arapaho Language and Culture Commission. Northern Arapaho Tribe. Ethete, Wyo.

Munn, Nancy
1986   The Fame of Gawa: A Symbolic Study of Value Transformation in a Massim (Papua New Guinea) Society. Cambridge, England: Cambridge University Press.
1992   The Cultural Anthropology of Time: A Critical Essay. Annual Review of Anthropology 21:93-123.

Nelson, Robert A., and Joseph F. Sheley
1985   Bureau of Indian Affairs Influence on Indian Self-Determination. In American Indian Policy, ed. Vine Deloria, 177-196. Norman: University of Oklahoma Press.

Noriega, Jorge
1992   American Indian Education in the United States: Indoctrination for Subordination and Colonialism. In The State of Native America, ed. M.A. Jaimes, 371-402. Boston: South End Press.

O'Nell, Theresa D.
1996   Disciplined Hearts: History, Identity, and Depression in an American Indian Community. Berkeley and Los Angeles: University of California Press.

Ortiz, Alfonso
1969   The Tewa World: Space, Time, Being, and Becoming in a Pueblo Society. Chicago: University of Chicago Press.

Radcliffe-Brown, A. R.
1929   Age-Organization—Terminology. Man 29:21.

Report of Agent in Wyoming
1883   Report of Agent in Wyoming to the Commissioner of Indian Affairs. Annual Report of the Commissioner of Indian Affairs, Department of Interior. Washington.

1894   Report of Agent in Wyoming to the Commissioner of Indian Affairs. Annual Report of the Commissioner of Indian Affairs, Department of Interior. Washington.

Salzmann, Zdenek

1983   Dictionary of Contemporary Arapaho Usage. Arapaho Language and Culture Instructional Materials Series 4. Northern Arapaho Tribe, Wind River Reservation. Ethete, Wyo.

Salzmann, Zdenek, ed. and comp.

1980   Arapaho Stories—Hinono'ei Hoo3itoono. Anchorage, Alaska: University of Alaska, National Bilingual Materials Development Center.

Sapir, Edward

1949   Anthropology and Sociology. In Selected Writings of Edward Sapir: Language, Culture, and Personality, ed. David G. Mandelbaum, 332-45. Berkeley and Los Angeles: University of California Press.

Schneider, David M.

1980   American Kinship. Chicago: University of Chicago Press.

Scollon, R. and Scollon, S.

1981   Narrative, Literacy, and Face in Interethnic Communication. Norwood, N.J.: Ablex.

Scott, Hugh Lenox

1907   The Early History and the Names of the Arapaho. American Anthropologist 9:545-60.

Sifton, Rev. John B.

1908   Prayers in Arapaho. Archives of St. Stephen's Catholic Mission. St. Stephens, Wyo.

Smet, Pierre Jean de.

1863   Western Missions and Missionaries: A Series of Letters. New York: J. B. Kirker.

Speck, Frank G.

1935   Naskapi: The Savage Hunters of the Labrador Penisula. Norman: University of Oklahoma Press.

Starkloff, Carl F.

1971   American Indian Religion and Christianity: Confrontation and Dialogue. Journal of Ecumenical Studies 8:317-40.

1974   The People of the Center: American Indian Religion and Christianity. New York: Seabury Press.

Statistical List
1988   Statistical List by Age: All Members. Northern Arapaho Tribe.
            Wind River Agency.
Stewart, Frank Henderson
1977   Fundamentals of Age-Group Systems. New York: Academic
            Press.
Straus, Anne. S.
1976   Being Human in the Cheyenne Way. Ph.D. Dissertation
            (Anthropology). University of Chicago, Chicago, Ill.
Tennesson, Carol
1986   "Talk to me of Disaster": Authoritative Discourse in the Schools.
            Anthropology and Education Quarterly 17:131-44.
Toll, Oliver W.
1962   Arapaho Names and Trails: A Report of a 1914 Pack Trip. Estes
            Park, Colo.: Rocky Mountain National Park,
Trenholm, Virginia Cole
1970   The Arapahoes, Our People. Norman: University of Oklahoma
            Press.
Van Gennep, Arnold
1960   The Rites of Passage. (Trans. by M. B. Vizedom and G. L.
            Caffee). Chicago: University of Chicago Press.
Walker, James R.
1975   Oglala Metaphysics. In Teachings from the American Earth:
            Indian Religion and Philosophy, ed. D. Tedlock and B. Tedlock,
            205-218. New York: Liveright.
1980   Lakota Belief and Ritual, ed. Raymond J. DeMallie and Elaine A.
            Jahner. Lincoln: University of Nebraska Press.
Weintraub, Karl J.
1975   Autobiography and Historical Consciousness. Critical Inquiry
            1:821-48.
Whorf, Benjamin L.
1956   Language, Thought, and Reality: Selected Writings of Benjamin
            Lee Whorf. Cambridge, Mass.: MIT Press.
Wind River Rendezvous
1984   Volume 14(2 and 3). St. Stephens, Wyo.: St. Stephen's Mission.
Wissler, Clark
1956   Indians of the United States: Four Centuries of Their History and
            Culture. Garden City, N.Y.: Doubleday.

Wyoming Indian High School
 1979   Arapaho Stories, Legends, and Recollections. Ethete, Wyo.
Wyoming Indian Needs Determination Survey (W.I.N.D.S.)
 1982   Eastern Shoshone and Northern Arapaho Tribes. Fort Waskahie,
             Wyo.

Index

In *Studies in the Anthropology of North American Indians*

The Four Hills of Life: Northern Arapaho Life Movement, Knowledge, and Personhood
By Jeffrey D. Anderson

The Semantics of Time: Aspectual Categorization in Koyukon Athabaskan.
By Melissa Axelrod

Lushootseed Texts: An Introduction to Puget Salish Narrative Aesthetics
Edited by Crisca Bierwert

People of The Dalles: The Indians of Wascopam Mission
By Robert Boyd

The Lakota Ritual of the Sweat Lodge: History and Contemporary Practice
By Raymond A. Bucko

From the Sands to the Mountain: Change and Persistence in a Southern Paiute Community
By Pamela A. Bunte and Robert J. Franklin

A Grammar of Comanche
By Jean Ormsbee Charney

Northern Haida Songs
By John Enrico and Wendy Bross Stuart

Powhatan's World and Colonial Virginia: A Conflict of Cultures
By Frederic W. Gleach

The Heiltsuks: Dialogues of Culture and History on the Northwest Coast
By Michael E. Harkin

Prophecy and Power among the Dogrib Indians
By June Helm

Corbett Mack: The Life of a Northern Paiute
As told by Michael Hittman

The Canadian Sioux
By James H. Howard

The Comanches: A History, 1706-1875
By Thomas W. Kavanagh

Koasati Dictionary
By Geoffrey D. Kimball with the assistance of Bel Abbey, Martha John, and Ruth Poncho

Koasati Grammar
By Geoffrey D. Kimball with the assistance of Bel Abbey, Nora Abbey, Martha John, Ed John, and Ruth Poncho

The Salish Language Family: Reconstructing Syntax
By Paul D. Kroeber

The Medicine Men: Oglala Sioux Ceremony and Healing
By Thomas H. Lewis

A Dictionary of Creek / Muskogee
By Jack B. Martin and Margaret
McKane Mauldin

*Wolverine Myths and Visions: Dene
Traditions from Northern Alberta*
Edited by Patrick Moore and Angela
Wheelock

Ceremonies of the Pawnee
By James R. Murie, Edited by
Douglas R. Parks

*Archaeology and Ethnohistory of the
Omaha Indians: The Big Village Site*
By John M. O'Shea and John
Ludwickson

*Traditional Narratives of the
Arikara Indians* (4 vols.)
By Douglas R. Parks